EMERGENCY INTERVENTION

EMERGENCY INTERVENTION

Jane Allyn Piliavin

Department of Sociology
University of Wisconsin—Madison
Madison, Wisconsin

John F. Dovidio

Department of Psychology
Colgate University
Hamilton, New York

Samuel L. Gaertner

Department of Psychology
University of Delaware
Newark, Delaware

Russell D. Clark, III

Department of Psychology
Florida State University
Tallahassee, Florida

1981 (AP)

ACADEMIC PRESS
A Subsidiary of Harcourt Brace Jovanovich, Publishers
New York   London   Toronto   Sydney   San Francisco

ACADEMIC PRESS, INC.
111 Fifth Avenue, New York, New York 10003

United Kingdom Edition published by
ACADEMIC PRESS, INC. (LONDON) LTD.
24/28 Oval Road, London NW1 7DX

Library of Congress Cataloging in Publication Data
Main entry under title:

Emergency intervention.

   Bibliography: p.
   Includes index.
   1. Helping behavior. 2. Assistance in emergencies--
Psychological aspects. I. Piliavin, Jane A.
BF637.H4E46   361.3'23   80-68553
ISBN 0-12-556450-3

PRINTED IN THE UNITED STATES OF AMERICA

81 82 83 84   9 8 7 6 5 4 3 2 1

TO OUR MENTORS

Jane . . . . Leon Festinger, Vince Nowlis
John. . . . . Sam Gaertner, Bill Morris
Sam . . . . Bernie Seidenberg
Russ . . . . Edwin P. Willems, R. W. George

and to each other

Contents

Preface

Emergency Intervention is a book about "getting involved" in the transient problems, crises, and emergencies of others. It focuses on the *process* by which a bystander comes to offer assistance to or withhold assistance from an unknown other who is experiencing an unexpected need for help. In this book we attempt to summarize the research in this area; to present a predictive, processual model that is consistent with most of the findings; to provide for students a "case history" in model development; and to make a beginning toward suggesting public policies designed to encourage responsible intervention in others' crises.

Why have we set these specific goals for this book? We assume that systematizing a body of research and developing an integrative theoretical model are goals that need no explanation. In addition, an understanding of the cognitive and emotional processes involved in emergency intervention can contribute to an understanding of the more general processes of decision making under stress and human action systems. The desire to present some of our experiences in developing the model as a "case history" originates from the comments of many students indicating that they are intimidated by the polished final look of most social science publications. Students, upon reading these publications, often feel that they cannot aspire to the research enterprise because they do not think so clearly and logically. By devoting segments of this book to the reality of the research process, with its sometimes "one step backward, two steps forward" nature, we hope to encourage students to face the challenge. Finally, we take seriously Lewin's dictum that there is nothing so practical as a good theory. A better understanding of facilitating and inhibiting factors in helping situations can suggest social policies leading to the saving of lives, the prevention of injuries, and an improvement in the quality of life in neighborhoods and communities. The last chapter of the book includes a brief attempt in this direction.

This book is intended for our professional colleagues in psychology, sociology, social work, and most specifically social psychology. Its primary use, beyond colleagial communication, is in graduate seminars, where both the theoretical systematization itself and the process by which we refined and qualified it will prove enlightening.

Acknowledgments

We would like to acknowledge the significant contributions that so many other people have made to this book. We are especially grateful to Irving Piliavin, who was one of the originators of the Arousal: Cost–Reward model, designed the early research on which it was based, and co-authored the 1973 module. His participation in the preparation of this volume has included critical readings of the early drafts of the first five chapters, as well as both intellectual and emotional support to the first author. In addition, we acknowledge the significant contributions of Judy Rodin to the model and the early research on which it was based. We would also like to thank Barbara Spar, who performed the extensive literature search that provided the basis for the systematization presented in the 1973 module.

Thanks are due to Frances Graham and Bob Simon for both directly and indirectly lending their expertise in psychophysiology to this book, and to Bob Cialdini for his editorial assistance and constructive criticisms. This assistance has been invaluable. In addition, we would like to express our appreciation to Bruce Denner; William Howard and Bill Crano; Shalom Schwartz and Avi Gottlieb; Ervin Staub; and John Wilson for sending their data for reanalysis or clarification, and to John Darley for helpful comments on parts of the manuscript.

We are grateful as well to a large number of support personnel: Kathy

Adams, who has been efficient and resourceful in obtaining the necessary permissions; Bruce Frank, for drafting the figures and graphs; Kathy Wildes (of University of Wisconsin), Vicki Weissman, Lynn Leindecker, Steve Lesniak, Shelley Sykes, Donna Alger (of Colgate University), Elsie Conte, Judy Fingerle, Helen Smith (of University of Delaware), and the typing pool in the Institute for Research on Poverty at the University of Wisconsin for typing and retyping the drafts of the manuscript; Charlene Luchterhand for typing the bibliography under extreme time pressure; Allyn Hardych and Linda Dovidio for their assistance in proofreading; Colgate University, which provided us with unlimited computer time for text editing as well as for considerable data analysis; and Tom Brackett, Sam Orsini, and Jeannie Kellog of the Colgate Computer Center, whose generosity of time and resources allowed us to overcome many technical obstacles.

We also gratefully acknowledge the financial support we have received. Much of our own research reported in this book was supported by the National Science Foundation (Grants GS-1901, GS-27053, GS-32335 to Jane Allyn Piliavin and Irving M. Piliavin), by the Office of Naval Research, Division of Organizational Effectiveness (Contracts N00014–70–A–0113–003 and N00014–76–C–0062 to Samuel L. Gaertner), and by the University of Delaware Research Foundation (for support to Samuel L. Gaertner). We would also like to thank the University of Wisconsin Graduate School, which provided the first author with salary support during the spring semester of 1977 and the Colgate University Research Council, which provided the second author with travel and manuscript preparation funds.

Finally, we want to thank the members of our four families for putting up with our periodic marathon meetings at one another's homes. We are especially thankful for the gracious hospitality and refreshment provided by Linda and Shelley at two of these meetings. Whatever the virtues of this book, they would have been fewer without these opportunities for intense communication. These opportunities and, in fact, our total involvement in this project for the last 3 years have been hard on our families, who have been tolerant above and beyond the call of duty. Similarly, each of us would like to express our sincere appreciation for the unwavering patience and understanding demonstrated by each of the others involved in writing this book, making it an experience of fond and lasting memories.

EMERGENCY INTERVENTION

Chapter 1

Emergency Intervention, or the Nonapathetic Bystander

One spring evening, Mr. James Harris was riding in the subway in New York when he observed an attempted robbery at knifepoint. He disarmed the man and prevented the crime from being carried through to its conclusion. Scott Spink, 5 years old, threw a rope to his friend Nicholle, also 5, and pulled her to safety when she fell into a creek in which they were fishing. Rebecca Griggs and her sister Shirley Bowland let the air out of the tires of two bankrobbers' getaway car, then chased and caught one of the men and tied him up with his own belt. Late one night Don and Arlene Matzkin and Angela McGhee heard screams outside their house in Philadelphia. Don jumped from his chair and ran out, followed by the two women, finding a neighbor who had just been stabbed. Eleanor Harden, a 22-year-old clerk typist, jumped into a freezing river and pulled out a 75-year-old woman whose car had plunged into 12 feet of water. What possessed these people? Why would anyone intervene in someone else's crisis, especially if there was personal risk? Perhaps little Scott's action is understandable—Nicholle was his friend—but what of the others?

Current thinking in the area of altruism and helping behavior has been largely influenced by the early research of Latané and Darley (1970), which is reported in their excellent book, *The Unresponsive Bystander: Why Doesn't He Help?* Their research had been stimulated by the infamous

Kitty Genovese case, which occurred in 1964 in the New York City borough of Queens. As nearly everyone knows, the young woman was stabbed repeatedly within sight of 38 witnessess, none of whom took effective action to intervene. Thus, the emphasis in the area of bystander intervention has been on the determinants of nonintervention. The question of why people *do* intervene was discussed in their work and in the work of others, but the main emphasis until recently has been on factors that deter people from "getting involved."

The "social problem" approach is one of the commonest within social psychology. Thus, the approach of looking at what is positive in human social behavior has been relatively rare. In this book, we want to do just that—look at why people do intervene to help one another in emergencies and with momentary problems of lesser severity. We will examine the features of situations, personalities, and fleeting states of mind that lead to helping responses. We will examine many stages and aspects of the helping response. We will look at motivational considerations, facilitating factors, and the nature of the decision process. In the course of our explorations into these questions we will naturally also deal with factors that inhibit potential helpers. We want to emphasize, however, that we take as problematic the motivation behind intervention. A considerable portion of this volume will therefore be devoted to the examination of motives for intervention.

We have chosen the title *Emergency Intervention* for this volume for a variety of both conceptual and policy-related reasons. The word *intervention* is derived from Latin and means "coming between." To intervene, then, means to insert oneself into a situation in progress, to alter the impact of an ongoing event in someone's life, to put one's body on the line. Intervention is a word that implies taking action and also implies stepping into a moving process. Adding the word *emergency* creates a phrase that—we hope—carries even more a feeling of unpredictability, instability, uncertainty, and risk, plus a sense of urgency and time pressure.

This discussion of the meaning of the phrase with which we have titled our book is meant to emphasize a central aspect of our approach, namely a focus on *process*. We are far more interested in the process of deciding to intervene than in the outcome response to emergencies. How individuals *perceive* the situation, how they *feel* in the situation, how they judge the victim, how they assess their costs for intervention are all of at least as much interest as the outcome. We are, of course, not saying that we do not really care whether or not victims receive help. What we want to stress is that if we truly want to understand why bystanders sometimes do and sometimes do not help we must carefully attend to all of the intervening psychological processes that take place in the bystander as he or she decides what is going on and what to do.

There are at least three critical reasons for taking this approach. First, we believe that the outcome is strongly affected by the nature of the process. Second, it is becoming increasingly clear to many social scientists that there is never a beginning or an end to the things that "cause" human behavior. That is, there is an ongoing stream of physiological and psychological events onto which we superimpose whatever new stimuli we are interested in investigating or into which a natural event inserts itself. The impact of the stimulus, whether or not it is perceived and whether or not it is responded to, will be strongly influenced by what the individuals are engaged in at the time it impinges upon them. Finally, simple unidirectional causation is rare. When an entire behavioral system is considered, the same event may be viewed simultaneously as a "causal agent" and as being "caused." Furthermore, this event may concurrently influence many other events and may itself have multiple causes. For example, in the model we develop in this book, there is assumed to be an initial effect of emotional arousal from observation of an emergency and then secondary effects due to evaluations of that arousal, attempts to cope with that arousal, and thus consequent changes in the level of arousal. These changes can, in turn, affect the bystander's response to the emergency.

This emphasis on process has led us to concentrate on the determinants of intervention in crises, problems, and emergencies rather than attempting to provide a general model of prosocial behavior. It is our belief that it is not productive to attempt to apply one model to all prosocial behavior because (a) the *motivation* for different aspects of prosocial behavior may be quite different; and (b) the decision making that precedes the behavior differs across categories. In other words, we are dealing with different *processes* when we are dealing with intervention in the momentary problems of others on the one hand and volunteer work, cooperation among children, or choosing to enter a "helping profession" as one's life work on the other hand.

Much of this introductory chapter will necessarily deal with terminological and definitional questions. First, we will attempt to make clear the distinctions that are made among the various terms that are currently being used in the general area of research of which the study of intervention is a part. Then, we will specifically differentiate emergency intervention from other kinds of helping acts and further qualify those aspects of the emergency that will mainly concern us. In this connection, we will briefly present both the initial model with which we began in 1969 and the later model that has evolved—the development of which is presented in detail in the remainder of this volume.

The first terminological distinction we would like to make is between the broad category of prosocial behavior and other kinds of behavior—presumably the rest of the universe of behavior—which consist of antisocial and nonsocial acts. The main point to make in this regard is that what is considered to be prosocial behavior depends heavily on the culture in which it occurs and on the individual who is making the judgment. *Prosocial behavior* means no more (and no less) than behavior that is positively evaluated against some normative standard applicable to interpersonal acts. The first "Good Samaritan" laws requiring citizens to come to the aid of others were passed in Nazi Germany. Their initial intent was to require citizens to assist law enforcement officers. Certainly, Jews, Gypsies, Communists, and others who resisted the Nazi regime would not consider complicity with the SS as prosocial behavior. Nevertheless, it was designated as such by these laws. Prosocial behavior, then, is defined by society as behavior generally beneficial to other people and to the ongoing social system, although a great deal of disagreement regarding what is really prosocial can occur depending upon where one stands.

Another term that is frequently used within the general area of positive forms of social behavior is *altruism*. *Altruistic behavior* can be defined as behavior motivated solely by the desire to benefit another without the possibility of rewards for the self. A moment's reflection on this definition will lead to the conclusion that it is difficult, if not impossible, even to demonstrate the existence of altruistic behavior. Since some internalized system of self-reward is always a possibility, any behavior, no matter how objectively costly to the self and beneficial to another, and no matter how deliberately decided upon, can be interpreted as selfish by those totally committed to the economic model of the human being. In practice—that is, in the psychological and sociological literature—altruism has generally been operationalized in terms of acts that objectively provide no benefit to and often could harm the self while benefiting another. Included by most people in this category of behavior would be organ donation, blood donation when no insurance or payment is involved, heroic interventions that threaten real danger to life and limb, and lifelong commitments to the welfare of others that involve great self-denial.

Because of the ambiguities inherent in the definition of altruism and the overinclusiveness of the term *prosocial behavior*, most researchers have settled on *helping behavior* as the best term for this research area. We disagree with this usage because helping behavior still carries some connotation of intentionality and also implies a good outcome for the victim. Neither of these, however, is necessarily involved when a bystander intervenes in another's ongoing crisis.

Next we would like to define what we mean by *emergency*, *crisis*, or *problem* helping as compared to *institutionalized* helping. Institutionalized helping can best be seen as role behavior that is responsive to internalized needs and motives. The Red Cross volunteer who drives for the motor service on Mondays and Thursdays or the habitual blood donor who gives every 8 to 10 weeks are not responding to immediate external events but rather to their own internal schedules. The process by which such behaviors occur is so clearly different from the process by which emergency intervention occurs that we will not be dealing with institutionalized helping in this volume.

One clear defining dimension of emergencies and crises is that they happen suddenly and without warning. A second dimension that we believe must be included in the definition of an emergency is that there is a limited time during which a decision must be made if a bystander's response is to have a beneficial effect. That is, the decision process cannot be left open-ended; there is some time pressure. Our interpretation of the meaning of the term *emergency* appears to be shared by 522 undergraduate subjects who made judgments about 96 problem situations in a recent study by Shotland and Huston (1979). The strongest predictor of the judgment that the situation should be classified as an emergency is the characteristic "harm increases with time." Time pressure can come from several sources. One source may be the rapid deterioration of the victim's situation. The fire is approaching the children's bedroom, the explorer is waist deep in quicksand and sinking fast, or the rapist has the knife at the woman's throat and is dragging her into the bushes. In such cases, if a response is not made immediately, it will be useless because the victim will cease to exist or the crime will have been completed. Under rather less serious conditions, and those more like the ones generally studied by social scientists, the source of the time pressure is the actions of other people. The person with the problem or other bystanders will solve the problem themselves without your help. The other elevator riders or the "dropper" will pick up the pencils, other shoppers or the victim of the torn bag will pick up the scattered groceries, other subway riders will assist the collapsed passenger or he will revive on his own. Finally, there is the pressure of perceived social expectations. One cannot delay indefinitely a response to the door-to-door solicitor of charity in the same way one can put off a letter from the same organization. Added arousal, however, comes immediately with the time pressure; it is this that changes the process from a "cool" to a "hot" decision (Janis & Mann, 1977).

The distinction among the subcategories of helping situations—problem, crisis, and emergency—on which we will focus are along the dimensions of severity of consequences to the person in need and dependency upon outside assistance. The first dimension can go all the way from inconvenience, lost time, and mild annoyance to probable death or severe injury. The second dimension is related both to the nature of the crisis (e.g., dropped groceries, stalled car, assault) and to characteristics of the victim that determine his or her ability to cope (e.g., age, sex, infirmity). When a healthy young man drops groceries it is a minor problem; when a paraplegic in a wheelchair drops them, it is a crisis because he or she cannot cope alone. Again, in support of this second dimension as providing an important distinction between emergencies, crises, and problems, Shotland and Huston (1979) found that "outside help is necessary" is also a significant predictor of judgments regarding whether or not a situation is an emergency. We will try to use the terms *problem, crisis,* and *emergency* consistently in that order to indicate rough areas along these continua of relative severity of consequences and dependency on others.

Another reason we chose the title *Emergency Intervention* rather than *Helping in Emergencies* is that for us it carried an "amateur" connotation. Doctors, social workers, and the Red Cross *help* in emergencies; the person in the street *intervenes* in emergencies. It is this response of the untrained "innocent bystander" that is of interest to us. A major reason is, again, our focus on process. We are convinced that the emotional response of fortuitous bystanders to the crises and problems of others is critical in the determination of the behavioral response that they make. We feel that this will be particularly true in severe emergencies involving extreme time pressure and instantaneous onset without warning. Professional emergency helpers, such as doctors, nurses, fire fighters, fire rescue personnel, and police officers have had training and experience in such situations to the point that their emotional responses can be expected to be quite different from the rest of us, who are here designated as "amateur" helpers. Specifically, professionals have developed intellectualizing defenses against emotional arousal and have overlearned, habituated responses to specific kinds of emergencies such that at least no decision must be made regarding whether or not to act. A doctor in a police emergency, of course, is probably as much of an "amateur" as anyone else and a policeman may be relatively amateurish in dealing with a major fire. Nevertheless, professional helpers are clearly different from the rest of us in response to emergencies and crises for which they were trained. One extremely fruitful area for research, which we are planning eventually to pursue, is the developmental course of becoming a professional or paraprofessional emergency helper. At the end of this book, some suggestions will be made for educational programs that might help "professionalize" all citizens to some degree in response to certain kinds of relatively common emergencies.

In general, this book will be structured around the arousal:cost-reward model of response to emergencies originally proposed by Piliavin, Rodin, and Piliavin (1969). This model has two central components: (*a*) a motivational construct, vicarious arousal; and (*b*) a cognitive, decision-making component involving the calculation of costs and rewards contingent upon intervention or other courses of action. The book will attempt to present data that are relevant to the support or refutation of the model and to show how the model has changed and developed as we investigated it. The initial model was stated as follows:

> A model of response to emergency situations consistent with the above find-ings is currently being developed by the authors. It is briefly presented here as a possible heuristic device. This model includes the following assumptions: Observa-tion of an emergency creates an emotional arousal state in the bystander. This state will be differently interpreted in different situations (Schachter, 1964) as fear, disgust, sympathy, etc., and possibly a combination of these. The state of the arousal is higher (a) the more one can empathize with the victim (i.e., the more one can see oneself in his situation—Stotland, 1966), (b) the closer one is to the emer-gency, and (c) the longer the state of emergency continues without the intervention of a helper. It can be reduced by one of a number of possible responses: (a) helping directly, (b) going to get help, (c) leaving the scene of the emergency, and (d) re-jecting the victim as undeserving of help (Lerner & Simmons, 1966). The response that will be chosen is a function of a cost–reward matrix that includes costs associ-ated with helping (e.g., effort, embarrassment, possible disgusting or distasteful experiences, possible harm, etc.), costs associated with not helping (mainly self-blame and perceived censure from others), rewards associated with helping (mainly praise from self, victim, and others), and rewards associated with not helping (mainly those stemming from continuation of other activities). Note that the major motivation implied in the model is not a positive "altruistic" one, but rather a selfish desire to rid oneself of an unpleasant emotional state [p. 298].[1]

Several major issues in emergency helping behavior will be dealt with as we pursue this model throughout the book. The first question is that of the motivation behind intervention. In their 1970 book, Latané and Darley list a considerable number of motivations for helping in crisis situations and then leave the matter at that point. Various authors have argued that the motivations for helping inhere in the desire to conform to perceived social norms (Berkowitz, 1972), feelings of moral obligation crystallized in the situation (Schwartz, 1977), promotive tension, that is, the need to com-plete the goal-directed actions of a positively valued other (Hornstein, 1972), a need to restore equity (Walster & Piliavin, 1972), and vicarious emotional arousal in response to the observation of distress of the victim or other types of empathic response (e.g., Aderman & Berkowitz, 1970; Bat-son & Coke, in press; Piliavin et al., 1969; Stotland, 1966, 1969). We will argue that these motives operate in essentially the same way and are part of one process. Without some emotional response to the plight of the victim there will be no helping. This response can be of the "cool" variety, such as feelings of moral obligation, or of the "warm to hot" sort, as in promotive

---

[1] From I. M. Piliavin, J. Rodin, and J. A. Piliavin, Good Samaritanism: An underground phenomenon? *Journal of Personality and Social Psychology,* 1969, *13,* 289–299. Copyright 1969 by the American Psychological Association. Reprinted by permission.

tension and vicarious empathic response. We will discuss the conditions under which one can expect to see the various types of emotional arousal develop and their implications for action. Factors influencing the amount of emotion felt, such as personality, temporary mood, attention, and perceived "we-ness" between the bystander and the victim, will be discussed in this connection. We want to point out at the outset that we do not believe that emotional arousal is necessary to the generation of helping responses of a "considered" sort or for habitual helping. Such helping is likely to be purely intellectually motivated or the result of simple habit. For the overcoming of natural inertia under time pressure, however, we believe that an emotional "nudge" is needed. These questions will be addressed in Chapters 3, 4, and 7.

A second question we will address has to do with the direction of behavior in these situations. What controls the nature of the response? There are many possible actions to take in a crisis. As noted in the initial statement of the model, one can intervene directly or indirectly, or one can leave the scene. One can also employ physical or verbal assistance, effective or ineffective means, and real or fantasy solutions. In Chapters 5, 6, 8, and 9 we will consider three categories of variables: situational factors, social factors, and personal factors associated with the potential helper that can be seen to influence the cost–reward calculations. As noted above, these can also involve motivational constructs. For example, physical closeness to the emergency makes it easier to help but presumably also leads to higher levels of vicarious arousal because of exposure to more distress cues. Similarly, there is some evidence that being in a good mood is a facilitator of certain helping responses; this may lead to greater likelihood of empathizing, calculating costs differently, or both. Furthermore, several authors (e.g., Stotland, Mathews, Sherman, Hansson, & Richardson, 1978) suggested that there may be individuals more prone to empathize with others (a trait factor); others (e.g., Wilson, 1976) have proposed that trait factors may lead to differential cost calculations. Facilitating factors can work through the reduction of perceived costs across the board as well. There can be, to borrow Lofland's (1969) phrase, "facilitating hardware"— an emergency telephone or fire alarm box conveniently placed, for example. There also can be facilitative cognitive states such as having recently thought through an escape plan in case of fire (as we are urged in television spots not only to think about but to practice). Finally, there can be habitual ways of thinking and of analyzing situations that can be facilitative of or block response in rapid onset crises and emergencies, such as holistic, intuitive processing or low need for cognitive clarity.

In the course of our discussion of the decision process, we will raise, in Chapter 7, the question of "impulsive" helping. By now there has been enough research in these areas so that we know that responses to others' emergencies can be indefinitely delayed, or they can come in a split second. In much of the research carried out by the present authors, bystanders have, often against our firmly held expectations, plunged into helping acts extremely rapidly and on almost every occasion. The prevalence of this behavior under certain conditions, in contradiction to findings of prior research demonstrating the effectiveness of deterrents to such action, has lead us to consider the possibility, already alluded to, that the *process* by which one arrives at the helping decision is critical. Specifically, we are now wondering whether there may be two distinct processes by which one can arrive at a helping (or nonhelping) response: one rational and the other holistic, intuitive, nonrational, and impulsive. Or, if there are not two distinct, qualitatively different processes, is there a continuum from impulsive to considered helping along which the impact of situational, state, and trait variables have different effects? Our discussion of the impact of perceived costs and rewards contingent upon a helping act will be qualified by these considerations. There is little argument concerning the fact that many if not most helping acts are the outcome of calculations that resemble a cost–benefit analysis. The questions to be addressed in this connection are, first, are there conditions to which we can point under which these calculations are more or less likely to be performed in more or less completely "rational" ways? We also want to simply consider the evidence for and against the economic model of the helping decision.

In Chapter 10, we will summarize the current state of the model. To preview our development of the revised model and to present the reader with an organizational overview, we provide a schematic comparison between the original and our revised model in Figure 1.1.

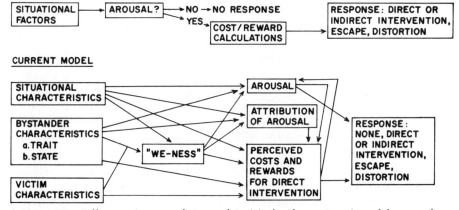

Figure 1.1. Differences in process between the original and current versions of the arousal: cost-reward model of emergency intervention.

In particular, our latest model has the following characteristics not present in the original model:

1. Rejection of a sequential model in favor of a simultaneous processing model
2. Explicit inclusion of iterative, cyclical effects, specifically concurrent and interactive effects between the arousal state occasioned by the emergency and the calculations of costs and rewards
3. Recognition of the importance of attribution of the cause and the interpretation of the nature of the arousal felt during the emergency for the occurrence of the helping response
4. Greater consideration to empathic determinants of response to victims' crises
5. Recognition of the relevance of state factors in the bystander to the determination of the helping response
6. Recognition that, under clear emergency conditions, costs for helping will have no impact or only portions of the cost–reward matrix will be attended to

After looking at the figure, the reader may initially be somewhat distressed at the added complexity of the new version of the model. Nevertheless, it must be realized that we are dealing with a complex problem. In just the past 20-year period, hundreds, possibly thousands, of studies have been conducted on helping behavior. Consequently, we have the data—most of the "parts of the whole" for understanding helping behavior—but we cannot recognize what the "whole" is. There is no relatively comprehensive model of helping behavior. It is, of course, quite unlikely that we have *the* answer either. We do, however, recognize the enormous complexity of the problem. Therefore, if it appears that we have sacrificed relative simplicity for inclusiveness, realize that we did it in the belief that it would be the most effective way of advancing research in this area at this time.

The major distinction between the original and the new version of the model represents a change from the basic premise of simple linear causality to the consideration of the general system of behavior. The systems approach (von Bertalanffy, 1955), in general, attempts to consider the mutual effects of several factors simultaneously. For example, increasing the costs for helping could not only have a direct effect on decreasing the likelihood of direct intervention, thereby increasing the likelihood of some other response, but could also have indirect effects on the level of arousal by motivating the bystander to reinterpret the situation as less severe. This, in turn, could reduce the costs for not helping. Throughout our discussions, then, we must always consider the principle of equifinality (von Bertalanffy, 1955). Very simply, the final outcome (e.g., direct intervention) may be reached from a variety of different initial conditions and in a variety of different ways. Consequently, our goal is to construct models and theories that successively approximate the complexity of the phenomenon we are trying to explain. In the last chapter, finally, we also present some policy suggestions based on our conclusions regarding the nature of the process by which interventions occur.

Based on our recent formalization, in the following chapters we will attempt to organize previous research, to present new research, to suggest new ideas, to open new areas of inquiry, and to encourage the orderly theoretical development of the area of helping behavior. Our model, therefore, is not meant to disprove other theories or necessarily to supersede them, but rather to stimulate further theoretical synthesis.

Aside from our desire to summarize and systematize the area of emergency intervention and to develop a predictive model for both theoretical and policy reasons, we have a supplementary purpose for writing this book. We mentioned it in the preface, but since many people do not read the preface we want to repeat it here. Consistent with our emphasis on process, we want to present the *development* of our model, not just a polished final version. Anyone who has tried to build a theory knows that it changes constantly in response to the influx of new data and one's insights concerning the new information. Yet, most books presenting a theory introduce the most recent version as if it had been etched in bronze and had sprung full-blown from the head of Zeus. Students may be intimidated by this and led to believe that their own sometimes sideways, sometimes backward efforts to progress toward understanding their own pet questions are somehow inadequate. We want to present a more realistic picture of how the process of theory development really occurs. A compromise has been necessary, of course. The way it really goes is so chaotic that this book would not have been readable if we had tried to be completely true to life. However, we have explicitly designed Chapter 2 to present the flavor of our "beginnings," and in Chapter 10 we have tried to present the ways in which the model has changed and developed and the process by which this has happened.

Origins and Early Tests of the Model and Other Approaches to Intervention

Most books reporting theoretically oriented research findings in the social sciences present a nicely articulated theory, model, or framework, followed by a well-orchestrated series of experiments, the primary purpose of which was (or is presented to have been) to test hypotheses explicitly derived from the theory. Often several investigators, working in separate laboratories, have pooled their energies in the interest of simultaneously questioning the efficacy of a theoretical model. These enterprises are intellectually exciting and are usually recognized as good science (Kuhn, 1970, refers to this process as "normal science"). Fortunately or unfortunately our own research reported in this volume initially did not represent this simultaneous interest in a common theoretical model. In truth, none of us set out to develop a theoretical model at all. At the University of Pennsylvania, Columbia, and later the University of Wisconsin, at Florida State, and at Delaware, and later at Colgate, we were each pursuing problems related to more idiosyncratic, largely empirically oriented interests either directly or indirectly related to emergency intervention or helping behavior. The findings from our several research projects first suggested the arousal:cost–reward model and then both provided support for parts of it and challenged other portions of it.

In this chapter, we will present the initial studies of the three research projects that have come together to produce the revised model that is fully presented in Chapter 10. We will begin with the Piliavin *et al.* research in the New York subway, since the initial model was generated there. We will briefly sketch the early Clark and Word studies, since they provided early support for the "impulsive helping" postulate of the model. Finally, we will introduce the early Gaertner work from which the concept of aversive racism was developed, because it showed in a very different context how important preconscious or preattentive processing can be in the determination of a helping or nonhelping response. The full integration of the Clark and the Gaertner and Dovidio work with the model comes in Chapter 6, Chapter 7, and finally Chapter 10; however, for the sake of our interest in presenting a case study of "the context of discovery," it seems appropriate to present the beginnings here.

Although the fact that we began with very different interests and have used different experimental paradigms on occasion makes comparisons difficult, we find that there are advantages as well. Since the development of the revised model represents a post hoc synthesis of findings obtained in the pursuit of diverse problems, the fact that similar, often unanticipated, results have appeared, apparently in spite of ourselves, seems to us particularly compelling. The synthesis provided by the revised model of our own researches, as well as the work of other investigators, represents an unusually broad-based empirical reality. We hope it will encourage others to tackle the task of model building.

Serendipity Rides the Subway

During the academic year 1967 to 1968, the first author of the 1969 "subway study" held an NIMH advanced post doctoral fellowship, with which he was studying social psychology at Columbia with Philip Zimbardo, Bibb Latané, and their students, most notably Judy Rodin. It was during this time that much of the research reported in Latané and Darley's (1970) *The Unresponsive Bystander: Why Doesn't He Help?* was being carried out. The evidence for the "bystander effect"—that is, the inhibiting effect of the presence of other bystanders on helping behavior—was becoming stronger as each new study was done. At that time several of us developed an interest in seeing whether some counteracting force might be found that could operate to increase helping, despite the presence of others. Macaulay (1970) and Bryan (1970) had demonstrated positive effects of helping models on generosity, Macaulay with adult donations to the Salvation Army, Bryan studying children's donations to other children. Bryan and Test (1967) had found similar effects on intervention in the common crisis of a flat tire on the highway. The intent of the first subway study was mainly to discover whether modeling could increase the likelihood of by-standers offering aid in emergency situations in which there were other bystanders, possibly providing a force counteracting the powerful "by-stander effect."

The question of the design and locale of the research was settled, as it frequently is, by the occurrence of a real-life event to one of the potential researchers who was riding the subway one day when a drunken passenger collapsed on the floor. Time passed; the man rocked back and forth on the floor of the car as the train hurtled over the poorly maintained roadbed; finally, realizing that there were no other potential Good Samaritans in the car, he got up, went to the man, and helped him to a seat. The beginnings of our model of helping in emergencies were starting to germinate from some of his subjective experiences, and the design of the first subway study was nearly complete by the time he reached his destination.

The first conclusion from this personal experience was that it certainly seemed as though diffusion of responsibility was operating in the situation. There were many people in the car, and no one helped for quite a long time. The long latency seemed to make the situation a good one for the in-sertion of manipulations designed to increase the speed and likelihood of helping, a necessary condition for a test of modeling manipulations. There also were structural features of the setting that made it potentially an ex-cellent laboratory, while maintaining the external validity of the field set-ting.

Design and Hypotheses of the First Subway Study

Since the first subway study was not based on a theory, no hypotheses were formally tested. The design involved two victim variables: race (black versus white) and source of the problem (illness versus drunkenness). The emergency was a simple collapse in the moving subway car. Two aspects of a Good Samaritan model, his or her latency to respond after the collapse and the area of the car from which he or she came, were also varied. There were control trials on which the model, although present, did not in-tervene.

The authors' expectations (based on a cost formulation) were that helping would be relatively infrequent and slow, that response would be less frequent when there were more bystanders, and that drunks and the black victim would be helped more infrequently and more slowly. The model who helped was expected to induce bystanders to intervene more frequently and to counteract the expected bystander effect. It was expected that models who responded more quickly would be imitated more because the actual bystanders would not already have responded with a covert rejection or derogation of the victim by the time help was offered; when the model came later, it was probable that they would have handled the situation by one of those other means.

The study has been reported elsewhere (Piliavin, Rodin, & Piliavin, 1969), so more details of procedure will not be given. Essentially, it was found, surprisingly at the time, that both a very high proportion of individuals helped and, especially with the ill "cane-carrying" victim, they helped extremely rapidly. On 62 of 65 trials, the "cane" victim was helped before 70 seconds had elapsed, which was the time at which the short latency model was programmed to arrive. On the other three "cane" trials, the model was able to help and a real bystander assisted him. The average latency of the helping response was 10 seconds. In fact, there were some trials on which the victim was helped *as* he fell. The drunk, however, did not fare so well. On only 9 of 38 trials did he receive help before 70 seconds, and on several trials he was not helped at all. While nearly all of the helpers of the cane victim had been sitting in the area close to him, on 7 of the 19 trials on which the drunk received help, the helper was someone from a distance.

Other findings that became relevant in the development of the model of helping behavior we are presenting concern, first, the responses other than helping that people made to the incident and, second, race and sex differences in helping. People can do many things other than help: leave the scene, avert their eyes, derogate the victim to justify not helping, talk to other bystanders about the incident, or simply sit and stare. For example, the number of people who left the critical area during the time in which the incident was taking place was noted. People left the area on many more drunk trials than cane trials, and more left on trials on which help took longer to arrive. Although these two factors are correlated, the researchers' subjective impression was that it was the tension of waiting for someone to do something that was the motivating force behind their exodus. The same pattern was found in the frequency of comments about the situation made by passengers in the immediate area around the observers. Much more was said about the drunk; more comments were also made on trials in which no one helped for more than 70 seconds, regardless of the cause of the collapse.

A second set of relevant findings for the development of the model deal with sex and race effects. Although there was no overall effect of the race of the victim on helping across the two emergencies there was a tendency for more helpers of the drunk to be of the same race as the victim as compared with the cane victim. When the concordance of race of victim and race of helper is examined for drunk trials alone, a highly significant relationship is obtained ($p < .01$). There was also a modest relationship between race of first and second helpers ($p < .05$). These findings were not reported in the published article. Thus race, although not strongly related to helping in this situation, is not totally irrelevant to people's actions. Sex of helper unquestionably is important in this setting; nearly 90% of helpers were men, in a population almost equally divided between men and women.

The most critical aspect of the results was the absence of any effect of the number of bystanders on helping behavior. The inhibiting effect of others had been proposed by Latané and Darley and supported in several well-known laboratory studies (Latané & Darley, 1970); it was expected to appear in the subway as well. The obtained effect was slightly in the opposite direction; the more bystanders there were, the greater was the likelihood and the speed of helping. These findings did not, of course, invalidate those found in the earlier studies.

> Two explanations can be suggested to account for the disparity between the findings . . . and those of Darley and Latané and Latané and Rodin. As indicated earlier in this paper, the conditions of the present study were quite different from those in previous investigations. First, the fact that observers in the present study could see the victim may not only have constrained observers' abilities to conclude there was no emergency, but may also have overwhelmed with other considerations any tendency to diffuse responsibility. Second, the present findings may indicate that even if diffusion of responsibility *is* experienced by people who can actually see an emergency, when groups are larger than two the increment in deterrence to action resulting from increasing the number of observers may be less than the increase in probability that within a given time interval at least one of the observers will take action to assist the victim. Clearly, more work is needed in both natural and laboratory settings before an understanding is reached of the conditions under which diffusion of responsibility will not occur [p. 297].[1]

The body of research that currently exists clearly indicates that what is now more generally referred to as a "bystander effect" is quite likely to occur under the majority of circumstances. However, this initial finding served as an important impetus to us and to others to more fully investigate the circumstances under which such effects do and do not occur and, more importantly, to speculate about the process underlying the helping decision generally.

Although reference to it was excised from the final version of the article, the difference in speed of response to the drunk and the cane victim had

---

[1] From I. M. Piliavin, J. Rodin, and J. A. Piliavin, Good Samaritanism: An Underground phenomenon? *Journal of Personality and Social Psychology*, 1969, *13*, 289–299. Copyright 1969 by the American Psychological Association. Reprinted by permission.

already aroused in the authors of that piece the suspicion that different processes might actually be underlying the decisions. In the initially submitted version of the Piliavin, Rodin, and Piliavin article, it was stated that

> The response to the cane victim was often virtually reflexive or so immediate as to suggest that helpers thought about little more than the fact that a young man might (1) be seriously ill and (2) sustain serious injury by lying helpless on the floor of the moving subway car. The delay of response to the drunk indicates a different process at work. Quite possibly, this delay resulted from the would-be helpers assessing the necessity to assist a person in threat of injury as against (1) the possibly distasteful moments such assistance to an inebriated person might provide and (2) the deserving character of a "drunk."

In the early version of the model of helping decisions that was included in the Piliavin, Rodin, and Piliavin (1969) article, no reference to this possibility was made.

Clarification of Some Problems Inherent in the Initial Model

The first version of the model, which we quoted in Chapter 1, was presented in the conclusions section of the Piliavin *et al.* (1969) article. It is very clearly a derivation from this first study and follows the points made in it very closely. The major unclarity in the model as first presented lay in the postulate, *Observation of an emergency creates an emotional arousal state in the bystander.* It was not specified whether the critical feature of the "state" was the arousal-activation aspect of it or the emotional interpretation of it. The three subhypotheses of the arousal postulate that were suggested at the time did not help to clarify the difficulty. Item one, stating that the more one can empathize the higher will be the state of arousal, carries an implicit assumption that the arousal state is interpreted sympathetically. The other two items seem to refer more straightforwardly to the level of arousal without reference to labeling. This confusion reflects the real unclarity the originators of the model had at the time concerning what the critical aspects of the motivational state really are. In part, that confusion was due to acceptance of the Schachter (1964) model of emotion, which allows for no differentiation of internal state associated with different emotions but does see the labeling—derived from situational factors—as crucial. That model has no room for considerations such as those we will now be dealing with, in which there may be at least two different arousal processes, defensive reactions and orienting responses, each possibly linked to unique action packages. Most importantly, since feedback from the viscera is slow, and over half the helpers in the cane condition responded in under 5 seconds, the sequence of arousal, then labeling, then action embodied in Schachter's model is not likely to be fully operating here. Instead, the response may be primarily due to an arousal process that is more central and neural in nature than is allowed for by Schachter. The effects over time, on the other hand, involving increasing distress with lack of response on the part of other bystanders, may well be appropriately understood in terms of some arousal–labeling–feedback process.

The second major problem with the model, which is inherent in the Lewinian paradigm that forms the metatheoretic background for much current social psychological theory, including ours, is that costs and rewards are as interpreted by the potential helper. This problem will remain with the model and can only be dealt with methodologically—and then only partially—by idiographic measurement. (The work of Schwartz, 1977, on personal norms and denial of responsibility provides an important step in the direction of being able to do this.) Without such measures, one must attempt to use cost manipulations that "clearly" will be perceived in the intended way by "most subjects." This problem does not make the model untestable, although it does provide the unfortunate opportunity (which devotees of the model generally find irresistible) to rationalize away "non-fitting" data after the fact. We have attempted to combat this temptation in Chapter 5, where we discuss the cost–reward issue in detail.

In summary, then, the first subway study led to the development of the initial form of the model to be pursued in this book. In its first form, it was vague about its central motivational construct, in the sense that it did not state whether "raw" arousal or arousal that had been cognitively labeled was meant, and it implicitly accepted the Schachter two-factor theory of emotion. However, the suggestion was present early that there might be two different processes operating under different stimulus conditions: one process that was relatively insensitive to such cost factors as race of the victim and the other process that was responsive to such factors. Finally, there was excessive vagueness about the nature of costs and rewards and how they could be identified a priori. The next study that was undertaken (Piliavin & Piliavin, 1972) was conducted to separate out the two major postulated categories of costs, which may have been confounded in the cane–drunk comparison: costs for helping and costs for the victim receiving no help. It was demonstrated in this study that (a) an a priori manipulation of costs for helping (blood versus no blood on the victim) had produced a difference in frequency and speed of helping; and (b) the bystander effect could be obtained in a field setting, at least with high costs for helping and a salient, suitable other potential helper (medical intern).

At this point (1972), the Piliavins attempted to formalize the model to a somewhat greater degree. In the course of doing so, they carried out a thorough review of the literature up to that time, and encountered the research of Clark and Word (1972) at Florida State. This research confirmed their findings that the "bystander effect" did not always occur and began to suggest under what circumstances it would not be found. Those findings also had strong implications for the developing model.

Falling Workmen and Electrical Malfunctions in Florida

Quite independently, Clark and Word had also decided to test the "bystander effect" with a lifelike emergency situation. Their studies combined the virtues of the field and the laboratory in that the experimenters were in control of the number of bystanders (not true in the subway), but the victim-to-be was not perceived as part of the experiment (not true in the Columbia studies). In their two initial studies (Clark & Word, 1972), the situation involved male subjects recruited for a study involving "sexual attitudes among students." Subjects were placed in a room to fill out a questionnaire. Somewhat later, a uniformed Florida State University maintenance employee, who had been seen working in the hall when subjects reported for the experiment, walked through the room carrying a ladder and a venetian blind. Three minutes later (the intervening time was filled with "working noises" from the adjacent room) he pushed over the ladder and pulled the venetian blind down from a 13-foot window. There were several variations in the number of bystanders present and in the clarity of the emergency.

In the first study the workman said, "Oh, my back, I can't move," 5 seconds after the crash and "Help!" 10 seconds later. He was helped on every trial, on the average in less than 10 seconds from the time of the crash. Whether the subject was alone or with others had no effect. In the second study, the verbal cues were omitted on half the trials. In this more ambiguous emergency, less helping overall was obtained, and the "bystander effect" appeared. In the unambiguous emergency, the results essentially replicated those of study one. There was a perceptible (and significant) effect of the presence of others on latency to respond, when the obtained latencies are compared with hypothetical ones derived from the alone conditions. The discrepancies are much smaller than those in the ambiguous condition, however.

A second pair of studies was carried out by the same investigators using a different type of emergency (Clark & Word, 1974). By this time they were aware of the Piliavin *et al.* model and were explicitly attempting to test the effects of costs for helping on both the occurrence of the bystander effect and the likelihood and type of helping (direct versus indirect) that occurred. In these two studies, subjects again reported alone or in pairs for a study of sexual attitudes. They were placed in a room, filled out their questionnaires, and were exposed to the emergency while leaving the experiment. The emergency involved a flash of light, sounds of falling equipment, an electrical "shorting out" sound, and variations in the presence of other cues such as screams and whether or not the victim was seen to fall or only heard. In one critical variation, physical danger to the potential helper was manipulated by whether or not the victim remained in contact with presumably "live" wires after falling to the floor.

The critical findings in terms of the impact of the development of the model were that (a) the "bystander effect" was obtained in only one comparison, involving a moderately ambiguous emergency; and (b) in the condition in which clear danger to the helper was a possibility, there was no decrease in the amount of direct intervention. In other words, in some conditions, costs for the victim receiving no help had no effect (the bystander effect did not occur) and in some cases obvious clear costs for helping did not deter helpers. A particularly important finding in the "danger" condition was that all but one of the subjects who touched the victim (which could have killed the helper had the emergency been real) indicated later that they had acted so quickly that no consideration was given to the possible harm involved.

On the basis of the review of the literature and particularly strongly influenced by the Clark and Word studies, Piliavin and Piliavin produced a module, "The Good Samaritan: Why *does* he help?" (unpublished, 1973), in which a revised and formalized version of the 1969 model was presented. The following section is taken directly from that manuscript, as an indication of our point of departure when setting out on the group venture that became this volume.[2]

Presentation of the Formalized Arousal:Cost-Reward Model

Within the model a *bystander* is defined as an individual who is fortuitously, accidentally, by misadventure exposed to an emergency occurring to another person previously unknown to him.[3] An *emergency* is defined as an event that involves or threatens to involve loss or damage to life or limb and that requires some intervention to prevent or contain.

---

[2] The only alterations we have made in the form of the model as it was presented in the module is to reverse and renumber Propositions III and IV for the sake of clarity of presentation and organization of the book and to insert dates for references that at the time had not been published. We have even retained the original sexist language.

[3] For the remainder of the book we will not constrain our definition of a bystander to someone who witnesses an emergency involving a "previously unknown" person. The a priori nature of the relationship between the bystander and the victim is not a critical part of the definition.

Proposition I: *Observation of an emergency arouses a bystander.*

 1a. *The degree of arousal is a monotonic positive function of the perceived severity of the emergency.*

 1b. *The degree of arousal is a monotonic negative function of the physical distance between the bystander and the emergency.*

 1c. *The degree of arousal is a monotonic positive function of the bystander's similarity to and emotional involvement with the victim.*

 1d. *The degree of arousal is a monotonic positive function of the length of the observer's exposure to the emergency, if no intervention occurs.*

Proposition II: *In general, the arousal occasioned by observation of an emergency becomes more unpleasant as it increases and the bystander is therefore motivated to reduce it.*

Proposition III: *The bystander will choose that response to an emergency that will most rapidly and most completely reduce his arousal, incurring in the process as few net costs (costs minus rewards) as possible.*

There are two basic categories of potential costs for the bystander: costs for helping and costs for the victim not receiving help. Costs for helping are those attendant upon the bystander making a direct helping response.[4] These include the following: personal danger, effort expenditure, time lost, embarrassment, exposure to disgusting experiences such as the sight of or contact with blood or other bodily fluids, wounds, seizures, or deformities, feelings of inadequacy if help is ineffective, and the value of any forgone rewards that are contingent upon activities which would have been interrupted or cancelled if help is provided. The second category of potential costs, those incurred for the victim receiving no help, contains two subcategories. First, there are costs attendant upon the bystander's personal failure to act, including rewards for helping possibly forgone, such as feelings of competence, self-congratulation, praise from others, thanks from the victim, money, or fame; and costs possibly incurred, such as self-blame for his inaction, public censure, or even prosecution as a criminal in some cases (Ratcliffe, 1966). Second, there are costs attendant simply upon the bystander's knowledge that the victim is continuing to suffer. These include continued and increasing unpleasant arousal and feelings of inequity Walster & Piliavin, 1972). We will refer to these as "personal costs for not

---

[4] Basically, these are costs and rewards incurred by the individual who helps directly. Some apply also to indirect helping responses (e.g., effort of phoning, time wasted, thanks from victim, etc.) but it can safely be said that whatever the perceived costs for making a direct helping response, the costs for making an indirect response will be less. Perceived rewards for a direct response may, however, be greater.

helping" and "empathy costs for the victim suffering" in any future reference to the subcategories.

Proposition IV: *There will be (a) special circumstances which give rise to
and (b) specific personality types who engage in rapid, impulsive, noncalculative "irrational" helping or escape behavior following observation of
an emergency.*

Proposition V: *On termination of contact with an emergency, the bystander's arousal will decrease monotonically with time, whether or not the
victim receives help. The rate of reduction will be a direct function of the
proportion of initial distress cues to which he is no longer exposed either
physically or psychologically.*

Three basic empirical predictions from the model are as follows:

1. As arousal increases, the probability of the observer making some
   response to the emergency increases.
2. Holding arousal constant, as costs for no help to the victim increase, the probability of helping as opposed to running away increases.
3. As costs for direct helping increase, the probability of direct intervention decreases and the likelihood of indirect help, flight, or psychological distortions of various kinds increases.

Given an emergency and an aroused observer, the following simplified
2 × 2 matrix (see Table 2.1) indicates the observer's most likely response as
a function of costs for direct help and costs for no help.

The most complicated prediction in this diagram is that in the upper
right cell. Presumably, with at least moderate arousal and with costs for no
help relatively high, the bystander has a need to do *something*, yet high
costs for direct intervention preclude that response. In the case of high
costs, the bystander should be in very strong conflict between his need to
help and his fear or distaste for doing it, or, in some cases, the physical impossibility of it. Our prediction is that he can solve it either by seeking an
"institutional helper" (policeman, doctor, etc.) or by psychologically altering the costs attendant upon the victim receiving no help. The bystander
can do this by redefining the situation as not an emergency or the victim as
someone who deserves no help. These redefinitions lower costs for no help
and allow the bystander to leave the scene or return to his interrupted activity. There are, however, situations in which the bystander will regard
help from any source as impossible and will be unable to use the set of redefinitions just mentioned. That is, he *knows* that people are suffering and

they cannot conceivably be made to seem to deserve it. Under these circumstances, the decrease in arousal over time (see Proposition V) will be slower than in other conditions. Furthermore, bystanders are more likely to experience hysteria and other symptoms of great stress such as those seen under disaster conditions (Barton, 1969).

It is obvious that the model as presented in the 1973 module is clearer in some ways than the original heuristic in the 1969 article. The unclarity of the nature of "arousal" is still present, however, both in the lack of specificity regarding its physiological aspects and whether it must be interpreted as arising from the emergency, as "empathy," etc. Specific predictions are made concerning the effects of increases in the two kinds of costs, and indirect helping is predicted to occur under high costs for helping and high costs for the victim receiving no help. Note that in this version of the

Table 2.1

Predicted Modal Responses of Moderately Aroused Observer as a Joint Function of Costs for Direct Help and Costs for No Help to Victim[a]

		Costs for direct help		
		Low	High[b]	
	High	Direct intervention	Indirect intervention or ⟶	Redefinition of the situation, disparagement of victim, etc., which lowers costs for no help, allowing
Costs for no help to victim	Low	Variable: will be largely a function of perceived norms in situation		Leaving the scene, ignoring, denial

[a] From J. A. Piliavin and I. M. Piliavin. The effect of blood on reactions to a victim. *Journal of Personality and Social Psychology*, 1972, 23, 235–261. Copyright 1972 by the American Psychological Association. Reprinted by permission.

[b] There are some situations, generally those in which victims themselves are very likely to perish, such as severe fires, explosions, cave-ins, and ship accidents, in which the costs for helping become so high that they will be perceived as total, incalculable, or infinite. That is, the bystander perceives—often correctly—that he would be almost certain to lose his own life in any attempt to save the victims and that all possible aid has already been summoned. Under these limiting conditions, the actions and reactions of bystanders will deviate somewhat from those predicted here. First, the great severity of the victim's crisis and the likelihood that it was due to fate rather than to his own actions preclude his being derogated. On the other hand, to the extent that a portion of the bystander's discomfort in emergencies derives from his belief that he "should" take action, the perceived impossibility of successful help should reduce his discomfort somewhat. On balance, in such circumstances, bystanders should experience great discomfort but be unable to dissipate it through any of the responses shown here. Often crowds will gather under these conditions.

model, the qualification in regard to the matrix presented is explicit: It assumes "an emergency and an aroused bystander."

Preattentive Processing and the Wrong Number Technique

The final set of researchers who became involved in studies closely related to the arousal:cost–reward model, Gaertner and Dovidio, began with a central interest in racism, not in helping at all. Gaertner and Bickman (1971) used helping behavior as an unobtrusive measure of prejudice in their creative "wrong number technique." Black and white callers called black and white respondents with the story that they were stranded on the highway and were attempting to call "Ralph's Garage" but had reached the respondent by mistake. As had been predicted, white respondents helped blacks significantly less than they helped whites. (Interestingly, blacks did not discriminate against whites.) Perhaps a more intriguing trend in this study is that, discounting the victim's race, whites hung up prematurely (i.e., prior to the victim's opportunity to explain that he had used his last dime) more frequently than blacks. Also, overall, females hung up more frequently than males. In terms of racial discrimination, only white males and black females hung up prematurely more frequently on black rather than on white victims.

In a second study, Gaertner (1973) pursued the implications of the "premature hang-ups" further. Respondents were selected from the rolls of the Liberal and Conservative parties in New York City, and were again called by a black or white stranded motorist. Among respondents who stayed on the line long enough to hear the request for help, Conservatives were far more likely to discriminate against the black victim by refusing to call Ralph's Garage for him. However, Liberals on the whole were more likely to hang up prematurely than were Conservatives, and they were particularly likely to hang up prematurely on a black victim. Furthermore, it was among the young Liberals—who were least likely to discriminate overtly by refusing to help—that the race difference in premature hang-ups was most significant.

What is the relevance of this line of research for the arousal: cost–reward model? It is one of several other suggestive sets of findings that have led us—much farther down the road—to postulate an initial nonconscious "preattentive" processing of situations that alerts the bystander that his or her help may soon be needed or that the situation is not one of consequence. Gaertner, with Dovidio, has pursued this issue into the emergency area, continuing to use race of the victim as the critical variable. Those studies are presented in detail in Chapter 6, where we first demonstrate that there are physiological as well as behavioral consequences for such pre-judgments. The findings of their 1977 article on the "subtlety of white racism" have also suggested the importance of seemingly minor situational variations for the processing of help-requiring situations and, ultimately, for the behavioral outcome.

SUMMARY

The origins of the arousal:cost–reward model as it emerges in this volume are mainly in the early subway studies, which, however, had even earlier theoretical underpinnings in the area of deviance. Other early con-tributions came from the research of Clark and Word in Florida, which em-phasized the possibility of less "rational" and calculative determination of the helping response than was first postulated by the initial "economic" model presented in Piliavin, Rodin, and Piliavin (1969). Gaertner and Dovidio's data on subtle forms of racism provided another strong sugges-tion that nonconscious processes—of a kind quite inconsistent with the in-dividual's expressed values—might operate in the determination of the ulti-mate outcome in emergencies.

Other Approaches to Intervention

Before we proceed through the postulates of the model, we wish to review various models, prior to and concurrent with, our model of inter-vention.[5] We are not examining other models with an eye to proving all of them wrong as a first step in the process of setting ours up to be proved right. Rather, we wish to explore the common themes regarding the nature of the helping act that show up consistently in the thinking of many dif-ferent people.

---

[5] Readers who are not familiar with the broader aspects of the area of prosocial behavior are referred to the following sources for the essential background: J. Macaulay and L. Berko-witz, *Altruism and helping behavior* (1970); B. Latané and J. Darley, *The unresponsive by-stander: Why doesn't he help?* (1970); *The Journal of Social Issues, Volume 28*(3), edited by L. Wispé (1972); D. Krebs, Altruism: An examination of the concept and a review of the litera-ture, *Psychological Bulletin*, 1970, *73*, 258–302; E. Midlarsky, Aiding responses: An analytic review. *Merrill-Palmer Quarterly*, 1968, *14*, 229–260; and four recent volumes from Academic Press: L. Wispé (Ed.), *Positive forms of social behavior* (1978); E. Staub, *Positive social behavior and morality, Vol. I: Social and interpersonal influences* (1978); E. Staub, *Positive social behavior and morality, Vol. II: Socialization and development* (1979); and J. Grzelak and V. J. Derlega (Eds.), *Living with other people: Theories and research on cooperation and helping behavior* (in press).

THE NORMATIVE APPROACH TO PROSOCIAL BEHAVIOR

The recent upsurge of social scientific interest in positive forms of social behavior began around 1960 with a series of theoretical and empirical articles dealing with norms. Gouldner (1960) proposed that there is a universal principle or norm that makes "two interrelated, minimal demands: (1) people should help those who have helped them, and (2) people should not injure those who have helped them [p. 171]." More empirically, Berkowitz (e.g., Berkowitz & Friedman, 1967; Goranson & Berkowitz, 1966) has demonstrated that this norm does seem to operate in work settings and also, interestingly, that its strength is related to the social class background of the participants, indicating that there may be a Western capitalist bias embodied in the principle.

Related to the "norm of reciprocity" is the work of Walster (now Hatfield) and her colleagues (1972, 1978) relating equity theory to helping behavior. Essentially, she suggests that, to the extent that one perceives that one is in a relationship with another person, there will be a felt pressure for the ratio of inputs and outcomes of the two participants to be balanced. This can impel one to give aid to a person in need (increase their outcomes) or to devalue them as individuals (decrease their inputs) in an attempt to make the relationship appear to be equitable. Her research has provided support for these ideas, while Gergen, Ellsworth, Maslach, and Seipel (1975) have replicated the findings cross-culturally. However, as with Berkowitz's reciprocity research, the equity approach has been applied only in nonemergency situations.

The cross-cultural consistency in acceptance of some form of reciprocity brings us to our first brush with the possible innate determinants of prosocial behavior. There are at least four kinds of data that one can use to argue that a behavior has an innate component:

1. It occurs before socialization can have an impact (not easy to assess in this regard).
2. It is influenced by variations in hormones or other bodily secretions (no argument can be made here).
3. It has a widespread occurrence cross-culturally (Gergen's data suggest this).
4. It is found, with minimal confounding from culture, in related animal species.

Kropotkin, in a book entitled *Mutual Aid* (1902/1914), proposed that reciprocity must have been built into the social species of animals because of its obvious survival value. Building on the much earlier statements of Kessler (1880), he proposed in addition to, but not in place of, the "law of

mutual struggle," a "law of mutual aid," which he saw as far more important for the survival and the progressive evolution of the species. He emphasized that he did not mean to make the motivation one of love or sympathy, which would "reduce its generalizability and importance." Rather,
he says,

> It is not love to my neighbor—whom I often do not know at all—which induces
> me to seize a pail of water and rush towards his house when I see it on fire; it is a
> far wider, even though more vague feeling or instinct of human solidarity and
> sociability which moves me . . . an instinct that has been slowly developed among
> animals and man in the course of an extremely long evolution [p. 21].

Trivers (1971), a member of the new "sociobiology" group, has recently elaborated upon Kropotkin's conceptualization. In a reaction against
those who claim that helpful or altruistic behavior could not convey adap-
tive advantages on the individual (although it might increase the "inclusive
fitness" of its progeny) he has proposed a reciprocity model. Trivers claims
that mutual helpfulness can indeed benefit the helpful individual in a "you
scratch my back, I'll scratch your back" fashion. The simplest example is
that of food sharing. In a community of chimpanzees in which each individual alerts the others when sources of food are found, each individual
will benefit. Reciprocity, then, is the medium through which such altruistic
behavior develops and is maintained. This model would appear to have
less to do with emergency intervention, however, and more to do with
"considered" helping. It is unlikely that heroic self-sacrifice could evolve
through reciprocity, although the quote from Kropotkin suggests that he
did not rule out such areas of mutual help from his considerations.

The reciprocity norm, or equity principle, does not move us too far in
the direction of confronting the essential question in the helping area, that
of whether altruism per se exists. This has always created grave theoretical
difficulties for American psychologists, given their firm grounding in the
law of effect and various forms of reinforcement theory or hedonism.
Gouldner (1960) suggested that the norm of reciprocity does not apply for
individuals who cannot reciprocate for reasons of dependency. Berkowitz
(1972; Berkowitz & Daniels, 1963) proposed that under such conditions
there exists as well a norm of social responsibility. In pursuing the idea of
the norm of social responsibility, investigators discovered more and more
qualifications that had to be added to it, such as the locus of responsibility
for the problem, the sex of the person in need and of the potential helper,
and the direction of attention or with whom one identifies. In this series of
investigations, it became quite clear that there is no strong behavioral
adherence to such a general norm, although individuals may give strong
verbal support to it, like Americanism, motherhood, and apple pie.

The normative approach to helping behavior has fallen into disuse because it was too general to provide for accurate behavioral predictions. Schwartz's (1977) model, to be discussed in the following section, is its intellectual heir. It is an improvement because it emphasizes individual norms and because it makes explicit both a motivational construct related to adherence to the norm and some mechanisms individuals employ to deny the applicability of a norm under certain conditions. Broad, general normative approaches, however, are no longer considered to be very valuable for the understanding of prosocial behaviors.

DECISION-MAKING MODELS

There are, in addition to the model we present in this book, two other models that approach helping behavior as a kind of decision making. The event that provides the opportunity for intervention or for the performance of helping behavior is a stimulus, in many ways no different from many other occurrences, that is perceived by a bystander as requiring his or her attention. The decision-making process is then begun. Latané and Darley presented their version of this process in their 1970 book. Essentially, their model involves a decision tree, a sequence of decisions that must be made, if an individual is to intervene in another's crisis, problem, or emergency. The steps are as follows:

1. Notice or attend to the event.
2. Decide whether the event is an emergency.
3. Decide on the degree of one's personal responsibility.
4. Decide on the specific mode of intervention.
5. Implement the intervention.

They suggest that bystanders move from one decision to the next, except that some cycling may take place. For example, in order to justify inaction at Step 3, one can go back and change the decision at Step 2. They also suggest the possibility of blocking or becoming "transfixed at the decision point [p. 122]." These suggestions are made speculatively in the last chapter of their book, and no one to our knowledge has taken up these suggestions to the extent of actually trying to probe into the nature of the decision process in emergency helping. Conceptualizing the problem as a decision, however, is rather generally agreed upon.

Schwartz (1977) has modified and expanded the Latané and Darley decision-tree model. Specifically, the steps in his model include:

1. *Activation:* the perception of the need of another and the apprehension of some responsibility to become involved.

2. *Obligation:* norm construction and generation of feelings of moral obligation.
3. *Defenses:* assessment of costs, evaluation of probable outcomes, and, if a particular response does not clearly optimize the cost considerations, reassessment of the situation by denial of other's need, denial of personal responsibility, or denial of the suitability of norms.
4. *Response:* action or inaction.

There are three major changes from the Latané and Darley model embodied in Schwartz's version. First, Schwartz goes into much greater detail in his discussion of the steps. Second, his model explicitly allows for cycling or reevaluations of earlier steps in the sequence. Finally, the Schwartz model provides for a specific motivational construct—feelings of moral obligation—that gives the bystander a reason to intervene. The Latané and Darley model presented the framework for the decision process without postulating one specific motivation that might lead people to proceed through the specified steps. They suggested a number of motivational constructs; however, they did not incorporate one into the actual model. In the Schwartz model, feelings of moral obligation are or are not aroused by the helping opportunity, and the reward for action is increased self-evaluation as a result of adherence to one's moral standards. Although we happen not to agree that this is the primary motivational force behind helping in a crisis, it is a promising decision model.

EMPATHIC AROUSAL MODELS

Many researchers in the general area of prosocial behavior have postulated some form of identification with, sympathy for, vicarious emotional arousal in response to, or empathy with the person in need as the motivational construct underlying the performance of helping acts. Aronfreed (1970) and Aderman and Berkowitz (1970) were the earliest in experimentally investigating the possible links between taking the role of the other emotionally and helping behavior. Aronfreed and Paskal (1966) demonstrated that children who had learned to associate the emotional state of another with their own feeling would act to relieve distress or facilitate joy for the other person for no extrinsic reward. In fact, children lost rewards in order to do so. Aderman and Berkowitz (1970) showed clearly that attention was important; those subjects told to empathize with the petitioner in a help-requiring scenario helped more than those who were told to empathize with the person being asked for help.

None of the investigators cited above suggested an innate basis for the empathic-arousal–helping relationship. Aronfreed, in fact, explicitly presents a learning paradigm within which the reward value of the altruistic response can be established. In general, the possible existence of "purely altruistic" helping as a natural disposition, based only on empathic identification with the suffering victim, as noted above, has always provided theoretical difficulties for American psychologists and biologists.

Clearly, the present authors also take the view that emotional arousal in response to the distress of others plays a central role in intervention. However, we place ourselves in the "nativist" camp to the extent that, with Hoffman (1977a), we believe that the best evolutionary guess is that the human being is "set" or "programmed" for *both* altruistic and selfish responses (not to mention sexual and aggressive reactions). Campbell (1965) discusses this possibility in a section of his Nebraska Symposium article headed "ambivalence as optimal compromise." Discussing this paper in his 1972 article, he summarizes his earlier position, "In it . . . I argued that natural selection could produce opposed genetic tendencies, and that ambivalence was a better resolution of opposed utilities than was averaged indifference to novel objects. I argued that in man . . . genetically determined altruism or bravery were in a similar ambivalent balance with genetically determined selfishness or cowardice. . . [p. 31]." His 1972 position has changed, as he indicates, "I now believe that these self-sacrificial dispositions, including especially the willingness to risk death in warfare, are in man a product of social indoctrination, which is counter to rather than supported by genetically transmitted behavioral dispositions. . . [p. 23]." Later he concludes, "while I will stick to this position in the present paper both for reasons of conviction and clarity, *a mixture of both sources of ambivalence is of course possible* [p. 31; italics added]." In his most current position, Campbell (1978) contends that because humans are genetically unlike the social insects (who are mostly sterile and who thus do not experience genetic competition among themselves), altruism is logically unlikely to occur, since the altruist will be evolutionarily disadvantaged by the selfless act.

We do not wish to be more doctrinaire than Campbell. His last statement is likely, given the complexities of the human organism, to turn out to be the truth of the matter. For now, for heuristic purposes, we will, however, adhere to the nativist position. It is, after all, clear that altruistic or self-sacrificing behavior can be genetically programmed in social species since we see it in the social insects. The law of parsimony suggests that we not simply rule out the possibility of its presence at some less rigidly programmed level in the higher vertebrates, including *Homo sapiens.* Our argument will be that innately programmed altruistic responses to victims perceived as "we-group" are possible, although one of the many functions of socialization is to eliminate such forms of immediate, impulsive responding in favor of delaying tactics that bring in the higher cognitive functions. However, we suggest (and in Chapter 7 we will pursue the idea) that under certain relatively clear-cut sets of triggering conditions intervention will sometimes occur very rapidly, in response to the initial impulse, and before the "socialized" delay can be imposed.

In the next few chapters, we will proceed through the postulates of the model as presented in this chapter, providing strong evidence in support of the model but also data that suggest modifications. Finally, in Chapter 10, we will return to our subsidiary didactic purpose and try to show a little more of the process by which we arrived at our current theoretical stance.

Chapter 3

Arousal in Response to
the Crises of Others

The model, as it was originally formulated, was quite vague about the nature of the very central construct of arousal. When we developed the model, we implicitly accepted the unitary, undifferentiated conceptualization of arousal that is inherent in the Schachter (1964) model of emotion. (Social psychologists, who unfortunately tend to be uninformed about the complexitites of central nervous system functioning, commonly accept this as the only type of arousal system.) Thus, our assumption was that arousal per se would be activating, but not directional. The implication was, however, that the observation of another's crisis would most likely be subjectively experienced as unpleasant, and would therefore serve as a drive state. That is, arousal would motivate a person to do *something*, but it would not inherently lead to approach or avoidance of the victim as the preferred route of drive reduction. This chapter, then, will examine the concept of arousal in relation to the original development and our subsequent redevelopment of the model of bystander responsiveness.

The Nature of Arousal

Current thinking among psychophysiologists (Cohen & MacDonald, 1974; Graham & Clifton, 1966; Lacey, 1967; Lacey & Lacey, 1970, 1973;

33

Lynn, 1966; Routtenberg, 1968; Sokolov, 1963) is that there are two basic arousal systems that operate in some ways antagonistically and in other ways cooperatively in regulating the organism's alertness, responsiveness to environmental stimuli, and readiness for action. Routtenberg (1968) designated these systems simply as Arousal Systems I and II. System I is generally identified with the ascending reticular activating system, which begins in the medulla and serves the main function of alerting the cortex and preparing the organism to act. System II is associated with the limbic system, originates "higher up" in the brain, and affects the determination of the direction in which the organism will go. Thus, within a Hullian framework, System I has been associated with "drive" effects and System II with "incentive" effects.

The theoretical interpretation of the two systems and their relationship need not be restricted to a Hullian framework, however. The Laceys (Lacey, 1967; Lacey & Lacey, 1970, 1973) conceptualize the two arousal systems as functioning in the service of information processing. In particular, they see the control of attentional processes as central. In the Laceys' framework, heart rate response is critical; it serves not only as a measure of the way attention is directed but also, through feedback, as a source of control over central processes. Specifically, when the organism gathers necessary information by attending to external events, heart rate *decelerates*, blood pressure decreases, and feedback to the reticular activating system produces an increase in the frequency and a decrease in the voltage of the electrical activity of the cortex. Thus, to facilitate the intake of information from the environment, internal "noise" within the organism is minimized. When the individual needs to facilitate internal processing (e.g., doing mental arithmetic) or to prepare for activity, however, a quite different pattern of physiological response occurs. Heart rate and blood pressure *increase,* and feedback to the reticular activating system reduces the frequency and increases the voltage of EEG waves. Thus, the impact of external stimuli on the organism at this time is attenuated.

From a slightly different theoretical perspective, Sokolov (1963; Lynn, 1966) also identified two distinct patterns of physiological activation. Fortunately, these findings can be assimilated with the theoretical models of Routtenberg and the Laceys. In particular, these two patterns are called the orienting response (OR) and the defense reaction (DR). They can only be definitively differentiated when multiple channels of physiological measurement are employed, since it is the relationship among the channels that identifies them. The orienting response is characterized by an increase in skin conductance, peripheral vasoconstriction, heart rate decrease, pupillary dilation, and cephalic vasodilation. The defense reaction is characterized by an increase in skin conductance, by peripheral and cephalic vasoconstriction, heart rate increase, and pupillary constriction. Consistent with both Routtenberg's and the Laceys' formulations, the orienting response is generally related to openness to external stimulation and cortical activation whereas the defense reaction is involved with the sympathetic mobilization of the organism.

It is important to note that across the three different theoretical formulations of Routtenberg, the Laceys, and Sokolov, psychophysiologists have consistently identified two functionally distinct arousal systems. Thus, now aware of the research suggesting this important distinction, we have attempted to include a more comprehensive consideration of the nature of arousal in the most recent revision of our model.

In particular, what is the relationship among these theoretically related systems and empirically demonstrated response patterns? There seems to be a relatively consistent relationship among the orienting response, Routtenberg's System I, and the cortical facilitation heart rate process proposed by the Laceys. This type of arousal system functions to heighten an organism's sensitivity to novel stimulation, to direct an individual's attention, and to facilitate information intake. The orienting response (as we will generally refer to this system) habituates rapidly, however. If nothing new happens after a few trials, the organism ceases to respond. Either a change in stimulation or an increase in the intensity of stimulation is then required to recapture attention. Lynn (1966) claims that the affective reaction to the orienting response is an "agreeable rise in excitement and interest," but that sympathetic activation does not occur to any significant degree. The implication of this arousal system for bystander responsiveness will be discussed in more detail in Chapter 9.

In addition, there seems to be a relatively straightforward relationship among the defense reaction, Routtenberg's System II and the Laceys' "gating out of stimuli" through heart rate increase. In particular, the defense reaction arousal pathway arises in the amygdala—a part of the nervous system involved in emotion. The pathway to action for this type of arousal system is quite rapid and direct and may involve fleeing, attacking, or freezing. In addition, the defense reaction does not readily habituate, as one might expect if it is functional for survival. Apparently, it is this type of arousal system that social psychologists typically associate with the arousal component of emotion. Thus, we give it precedence in our model. The remainder of this chapter will deal primarily with the importance of the defense reaction in bystander responsiveness.

Before we proceed with our discussion of bystander responsiveness, however, we will first briefly consider how defense and orienting responses are produced. Sokolov (1963) presents a very clear and useful diagram (see Figure 3.1) showing the relationship between the strength of stimulation and these two types of response (in comparison to no response). In general, as a stimulus increases from threshold to moderate intensity the likelihood of occurrence of an orienting or "What is it?" response increases. Beyond the moderate level of stimulation, the likelihood of a defense reaction begins to increase and the probability of an orienting response decreases. Sokolov states, "Within limits, any increase in the stimulus intensity increases the stability of the orientation reaction. Any further increase in intensity weakens the . . . orientation reflex, and accelerates its displacement by the defence reaction [p. 50]." Describing Figure 3.1, he says, it

> shows the results of 20 applications each of electrocutaneous stimuli of a fixed intensity. It is clear that, while initially the orientation reflex is brought into operation by a stimulus of only 2 arbitrary units in intensity and the defence reflex by a stimulus of 17 units, after 16 applications only the stimuli of 7–9 arbitrary units are capable of producing the orientation reflex and those of 9–10 units give rise to defence reaction [p. 50].

Intensity, however, is not the only characteristic that relates to the occurrence of orienting responses. Novelty, unexpectedness, or a change in ongoing stimulation can also lead to orienting. Essentially, only "threat," as indexed by strong stimulation, can produce the defense reaction. The relevance of the defense reaction to bystander responsiveness in emer-

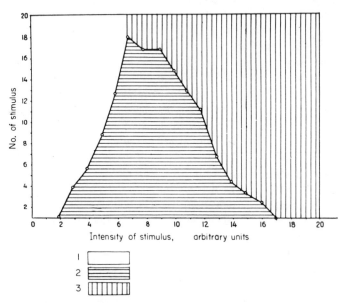

Figure 3.1. Relationship between orienting reflexes and defensive reflexes produced by electrodermal stimuli of various strengths. Subject O.S., March 1956. 1—Zone of no reaction. 2—Zone of orienting reactions. 3—Zone of defensive reactions. [From Sokolov, 1963.]

gencies, situations that involve threat of harm to another, will now be discussed.

The Nature of Physiological Response to the Crises of Others

Our model proposed that the motivation behind intervention in emergency or crisis situations was "arousal." There are two basic questions to be answered concerning this central motivational construct; these correspond to Propositions I and II of the model. First, is the observation of an emergency arousing to bystanders, and second, is such vicarious arousal (assuming that it does indeed occur) a causal factor in the motivation of intervention into the emergency?

The first of these questions is one of those mundane questions psychologists ask that lay individuals can already answer from their own experience. We have all seen another person take a fall—trip on the stairs perhaps—and have ourselves taken a rapid inspiration and felt our hearts accelerate. Even more frequent, in our entertainment-oriented culture, is our intentional seeking of vicarious arousal experiences through fantasy; movies, television, even the written word, through our well-developed imaginative processes, can lead us to share the emotional experiences of imaginary people.

Such "anecdotal" evidence, however, has never deterred psychologists from a question in which they were interested. ("Obvious" facts frequently turn out to be false, actually.) Furthermore, the more complete answering of the question certainly requires systematic investigation. First, it is important to know the nature of vicarious responses to others' crises. We have noted that our original formulation of the nature of the arousal postulated in the model was vague. With a greater sophistication regarding the two types of arousal systems, we are now of the opinion that emotional arousal such as is indicated by a defense reaction is more precisely what we intended when we spoke of this motivating force. That is, it is not merely attention to the crisis of another (i.e., an orienting reaction) that will suffice to galvanize intervention. Rather, the bystander must be actually emotionally aroused in a way that is at least akin to (although perhaps not as intense as) the feelings he or she would have if involved in the crisis personally. The question to be addressed in this chapter is, therefore, "What is the nature and extent of vicarious response to another's distress?" More specifically, we will attempt to show that, at least at reasonably high levels of severity, the response of bystanders to the emergencies of others more nearly resembles an emotional defense reaction than it does an orienting response. In the course of our presentation, it will be argued that with less severe emergencies, with less identification with the victim, and under certain other circumstances, the response is likely to be more like an orienting reaction. Our conclusion, however, is that for realistic situations of perceived high severity, the response of bystanders to others' crises approximates the kind of defense reaction they would make to their own emergency.

Problems of Physiological Measurement

Before we directly address the research on arousal, we must first consider some of the important methodological issues in the measurement of arousal.[1] In particular, we must discuss, albeit superficially, the way in which we propose to identify the occurrence of a defense reaction as distinct from an orienting response. Earlier in this chapter we noted that these two responses could not be distinguished on the basis of only one channel of information, unless that channel was heart rate. That is, the best single indication of orienting as compared to defense lies in whether the heart decelerates (orienting) or accelerates (defense) in response to the stimulus of interest. Unfortunately, hardly anyone who has studied response to the crises of others has used heart rate changes as their measure. Most have used the psychologist's favorite measure, the galvanic skin response (GSR). And they have used it in all sorts of different ways. In discussing what we propose to do about this problem, we will first present evidence, from the extensive work of the Mandlers, that GSR responses indeed do not appear to measure the same thing as heart rate and other circulatory measures, and then we will discuss some differences between measures of GSR that may give some hope for the use of that channel of information after all.

The Mandlers and their colleagues (Mandler, Mandler, Kremen, & Sholiton, 1961) have used a wider range of channels and more measures calculated from each channel than do most other investigators into physiological response. The major finding of importance to us in the Mandler *et al.* investigation is that the galvanic skin response measures do not correlate well, and, in fact, in some cases correlate negatively, with heart rate, blood flow, and temperature, which all relate to circulatory system func-

[1] There are a multitude of methodological difficulties in the measurement of physiological response. The interested reader can refer to Lang (1971) or Strong (1970). Briefly, one must keep in mind (a) that one is dealing with an extremely complicated system; (b) that many measures are sensitive to environmental variations as well as emotional events; and that (c) the initial state of the subject is also extremely important (see Benjamin, 1963). In the research to be discussed, one major problem is the difference between researchers in what is counted as "a response," even when using the same measure.

tion. Furthermore, a summary physiological response omitting the GSR correlated better with verbal disturbance (a measure of emotionality) than did the summary measure that included the GSR scores. The two GSR measures correlated +.596 and +.361 with subjects' scores on the Taylor Manifest Anxiety Scale, long considered to be a measure of general activation rather than a measure of emotionality. Similar to the recent conceptualization of arousal, Mandler *et al.* conclude that, "In the light of the lack of consistency between the GSR and the other physiological indices, it might be useful to distinguish between two processes: emotionality and activation. Considering the GSR as a measure of activation . . . and the other measures as an index of emotionality, these findings may be seen to be fairly consistent [1961, p. 14]." On the basis of the Laceys' "gating" hypothesis (not referred to in the Mandler *et al.* monograph), one might indeed conclude that, when psychological threat is involved, heart rate measures should relate to perceived "threat" and emotionality in the suggested way, while GSR would be insensitive in discriminating between "interesting" stimuli and threatening ones, yielding deflections to both.

Must we therefore ignore all of the studies involving vicarious arousal that have used GSR as their measure of response in our attempt to determine whether the nature of vicarious arousal is an orienting or a defense reaction? Not necessarily. There is an indication that certain of the measures of electrical activity in the skin are more closely related to general activation (reticular activating system) whereas others are more nearly measures of true emotionality. Specifically, Edelberg (1967) suggests that both rate of spontaneous skin resistance responses (SRRs) and basal levels of resistance are measures of general activation while the *magnitude* of response to specific stimuli may reflect an emotional response to those stimuli. Furthermore, since a characteristic of the orienting response (in whatever channel measured) is that it habituates rapidly, for studies involving the repeated presentation of another's crisis (e.g., a series of presumed shock deliveries) the extent to which the GSR continues to occur at about the same magnitude would strongly suggest that it reflects a defense reaction rather than an orienting response. ("One shot" GSRs will still provide ambiguous information.) Finally, we propose that successful conditioning of the GSR to, for example, a buzzer signalling shock to the victim is also strong evidence of an emotional reaction.

In the remainder of the chapter we will present various bits of evidence, moving, naturally, from the weaker to the stronger, in support of the proposition that it is possible for bystanders to experience a vicarious defense reaction to the emergency of another. First we will briefly present research that demonstrates that observers are affected—either to the extent of showing GSRs or having instrumental responses speeded up or amplified

—but that cannot demonstrate that the effect is specifically a defense reaction. We will then move to discuss research that demonstrates either classical or instrumental conditioning of the vicarious response in ways that strongly indicate the presence of real emotion. Finally, we will discuss the work of Lazarus and of his coworker Alfert, which shows quite clearly that defense reactions can be obtained to fantasy materials and that these responses strongly resemble defense reactions of the same individuals to personal threat. At the end of the chapter, we present work from our own laboratories showing defense reactions of bystanders to "real" emergencies.

Research Showing Arousal of Indeterminate Nature

Ezra Stotland (1969; Stotland, Sherman, & Shaver, 1971) has carried out an extensive series of experiments attempting to demonstrate the existence of empathic physiological response to the experiences of others. His research has employed a number of different situations, including observation of peers undergoing "diathermy treatments" described as painful or pleasant, failure experiences, fear of loss of status, etc. They have used a variety of different instructional sets: Imagine yourself in his or her position, imagine what it is like to be him or her, and so forth. The measures used, unfortunately, have been a palmar sweating index and a peripheral vasoconstriction measure. Palmar sweat is a rather insensitive measure, compared to skin conductance. Skin-conductance changes involve preparatory stages in the sweat-secreting process, while palmar sweat changes require a further set of steps. Both measures are also very greatly affected by temperature and humidity, and no controls for these were available. The sweat measure is also plagued by sex differences. Finally, both measures, even if they worked well, are indices only of sympathetic innervation.

Results of these investigations are extremely complex and inconsistent from one study to another. Sometimes an effect was found on the sweat measure, sometimes on the vasoconstriction measure. There was a tendency to find more responsiveness among males and among later-born subjects. One is left with the distinct impression that under some circumstances, physiological response on these two measures occurs in subjects watching others undergoing emotionally arousing experiences. However, there are no firm conclusions that can be drawn. Considering the time and effort that was expended on this series of studies, it is a very disappointing outcome. One very basic problem with the entire series of experiments, in our opinion, was that the experiences of the observed individuals were not presented with enough vividness.

A considerable number of studies have employed a paradigm in which observers watch a confederate apparently receiving electric shocks. Most of these studies have used some measure of change in skin resistance of the observer as the physiological index (Bandura & Rosenthal, 1966; Berger, 1962; Geer & Jarmecky, 1973; Haner & Whitney, 1960; Tomes, 1964). Craig and Lowery (1969) employed both GSR and heart rate. In all of these studies subjects showed skin conductance increases on observation of the distress cues provided by an ostensibly shocked other. These responses, generally referred to as "instigated emotional responses," occur from the outset of the training sessions. They do not have to be developed through a training program. However, in some studies the GSR does habituate somewhat. The Craig and Lowery study found heart rate decreases concurrently with the skin conductance response, a finding further suggestive that an orienting response, rather than a defense reaction, was occurring. Thus it is possible that the responses in most of these studies were orienting reactions rather than defense responses.

Two studies (Craig, 1968; Craig & Wood, 1969) employed observation of another undergoing a cold pressor experience (immersing his or her hand in ice cold water) and employed both skin conductance and heart rate. Again, these investigators suggest that the responses are indicative of an orienting response. Finally, Craig and Weinstein (1965) took skin conductance measures from subjects observing another undergo repeated failure experiences; in one condition the failure was followed by shock. Skin conductance increases were found regardless of whether or not observers believed that shock was applied to the victim, and these responses habituated somewhat over time. Thus, the general conclusions to be drawn from all of these studies is that individuals do clearly demonstrate physiological responsiveness on exposure to other people undergoing presumably emotionally arousing experiences. It is not clear whether this arousal should be best characterized as activation, namely, an orienting response, or a truly emotional or defense reaction.

A few other studies employed dependent measures presumed to reflect heightened arousal by virtue of past findings in experimental psychology. Four studies used reaction time (Baron, 1970a,b; DiLollo & Berger, 1965; Weiss, Buchanan, Altstatt, & Lombardo, 1971) in situations involving observation of another person receiving electric shock. In the Weiss et al. study the connection between watching the shocked person and reaction time was completely disguised. Subjects set dials to "evaluate" the observed person's motor performance and then pushed a series of buttons to "register" their evaluations. The responses of experimental subjects, who observed a shocked performer, showed faster latencies than did subjects observing a nonshocked performer from Trial 2 through the end of the session. In the DiLollo and Berger (1965) study, subjects were told to respond as fast as possible when a needle on a dial deflected. In half the cases, the needle indicated shock delivery to the observed person; in half it signalled the start of the trial. Crossed with these instructions was a second manipulation, namely, whether the observed person moved her arm. Subjects in the "shock–move" condition responded significantly faster from Trial 2 to the end, although it was made clear that no relief from the shock would accrue to the victim by virtue of their actions. Both of these studies suggest a higher level of drive or activation among subjects watching a person who displays distress in response to shock. Two studies by Baron (1970a,b) are the only ones that present anomalous results; in both, the shocked confederate performed the same reaction time task as the subject. Our interpretation of these data is that the situation was changed by the introduction of the potential for competition. Finally, Kobasigawa (1965) studied speed and amplitude of response to a buzzer that signaled the end of a trial for an observed person. There were three kinds of trials: success, failure far from the goal, and failure near the goal. Subjects (first grade boys) showed both faster and stronger reactions on "failure near the goal," consistent with prior research showing increasing drive with closeness to a goal.

Conditioning Vicarious Emotional Responses

A higher level of activation among subjects observing an emotionally aroused person seems to be well demonstrated in the studies cited above. The more interesting questions, however, remain to be explored. Does this increased "drive level" behave like other drives? Can the vicarious emotional response be conditioned like a first-order emotional response? Is it "the same" as directly instigated arousal? And, finally, can it be used to motivate the learning and performance of instrumental responses as is required by Proposition II of our model?

Two different conditioning paradigms have been employed in exploring the drive properties of vicarious arousal: classical conditioning and instrumental conditioning. In classical conditioning, a stimulus that normally does not elicit a response, the conditioned stimulus (CS), is repeatedly paired with a stimulus that normally does, the unconditioned stimulus (UCS). The sequence is CS–UCS followed by the unconditioned response (UCR). After repeated pairings, the UCR, or some portion of it, comes to be elicited by the CS alone. This conditioned response is referred to as the CR. Chains of responses can be built up in this fashion such that a stimulus–response sequence that was trained, rather than innate, can serve as the unconditioned stimulus–response pair upon which yet other responses can now be learned. (This only happens under certain specified circumstances.)

Berger (1962) presents a very clear analysis of the paradigm as applied to vicarious instigation and conditioning. For simplicity, assume a situation in which a subject is observing another person receiving electric shock. The observer already has (whether because it is innate or because of previous conditioning is not relevent here) a tendency to respond emotionally when he or she perceives or infers an emotional response in another individual. What the observer sees is a signal indicating shock delivery to the victim and then a pain response from him or her. This pain response serves as a cue that the victim is experiencing emotional arousal (referred to as an unconditioned emotional response, or UER by Berger) and this perceived arousal serves as a UCS for an emotional reaction from the observer. Over trials, if this response operates like the response of the shocked individual, it will come to be associated with the signal, and becomes the conditioned emotional response (CER). That is, it will move up in time and begin to occur before the observed pain reaction. Using essentially this paradigm, several studies have demonstrated that observers do condition in this fashion (Bandura & Rosenthal, 1966; Berger, 1962; Craig & Lowery, 1969; Craig & Weinstein, 1965; Tomes, 1964). These studies indicate that the conditioning takes place only if the observer does indeed infer an emotional reaction in the victim. The results of these conditioning studies generally demonstrate the drive properties associated with witnessing the problem of another person.

Vicarious Arousal and Instrumental Conditioning

We do not intend to pursue the question of the link between arousal and actual helping until Chapter 4. Thus, it is difficult to know where we should bring in the research showing that vicarious arousal can activate instrumental responses that relieve the suffering of "victims" *under circumstances not defined as emergencies* and, in particular, in situations in which the observer does not know that "helping" is being measured. We have chosen to discuss it here, since these studies seem to speak more directly to the nature of the arousal than to the link between arousal and helping in real emergencies.

The work of Weiss and his colleagues (1971; Weiss, Boyer, Lombardo, & Stich, 1973) is the most elegantly conceived for the purpose of showing how vicarious arousal (unfortunately not directly measured) behaves like other drive states to energize action to relieve the other's distress. In his series of experiments, Weiss has attempted to demonstrate not only that

"people will help others who are in need, despite the absence of an exter-
nally administered reward for the altruistic person," but far more
significantly that "people will actually learn an instrumental conditioned
response, the sole reward for which is to deliver another human being from
suffering [1971, p. 1262]." In a series of five experiments, two reported in
the 1971 article and three in the 1973 report, he also demonstrates that
"there is a profound similarity between altruistic and conventional, non-
altruistic drives and reinforcers [1973, p. 397]" by manipulating parameters
of the "altruistic reward" in a classical escape–learning paradigm.

The basic Weiss experimental situation involves an observer who believes her or his task is to evaluate the performance of a subject who is doing a motor task under stress induced by electric shock. The performer is
enclosed in a booth, and the setup is such that highly realistic evidence of
suffering can be produced, including sweating, although the performer is
actually not being shocked. All studies involved the observer setting a
series of dials to evaluate the performer and then recording the evaluation
by pressing a button. The button press provided a 10-second respite from
shock for the performer, and from exposure to the performer's pain cues
for the subject. Speed of pressing the button was the instrumental response
being conditioned. The elegance of the design lies in the completely masked
measure; subjects had no idea that helping behavior was being studied.

Within this basic situation, Weiss has varied many of the standard
parameters used in the exploration of drive strength: partial versus continuous reward (shock to the victim is turned off on 50% or 100% of trials),
magnitude of reward (shock to the victim stays on, is turned down, or is
turned off), and stimulus intensity (victim receives continuous versus inter-
mittent shock). The effects of all these variables are as expected from the
literature on drive state. The authors conclude that their findings strongly
support the existence of an aversive state being aroused by observing the
suffering of another, "without . . . any necessary implication that all
altruistic behavior is aversively motivated [1973, p. 397]." They add that
there is considerable anecdotal evidence that their subjects were under
stress and were truly concerned with the welfare of the confederate. "Subjects sweat visibly and show other signs of strain, subjects frequently express distress, saying that they wish they could do something to help the
stooge . . . in one instance we were obliged to let the subject drive the
'shaky' stooge home [1973, p. 397]." Finally, two studies in which some
subjects were made aware of the contingency between their behavior and
the reward to the other person have also been carried out (Baron, 1970b;
Geer & Jarmecky, 1973). In both, subjects who believed that their response
turned off the shock reacted more quickly than did those who believed

their response to be irrelevant. In the Geer and Jarmecky (1973) study, an overall effect of shock intensity on reaction time was also found.

Evidence for a Clear Defense Reaction to Fantasy Materials

Lazarus (1966) reports on a series of studies (e.g., Lazarus, Opton, Nomikos, & Rankin, 1965; Lazarus, Speisman, Mordkoff, & Davison, 1962) in which subjects watched films involving physical mutilation. One film, *Subincision*, portrays a series of crudely performed genital operations on teenage aboriginal boys. The other, *It Didn't Have to Happen*, presents a series of three carpentry shop accidents, two involving bloody finger lacerations and the last portraying a workman being impaled by a flying board. Both films are subjectively experienced as unpleasantly arousing, and physiological responses were strong. Figure 3.2, taken from Lazarus *et*

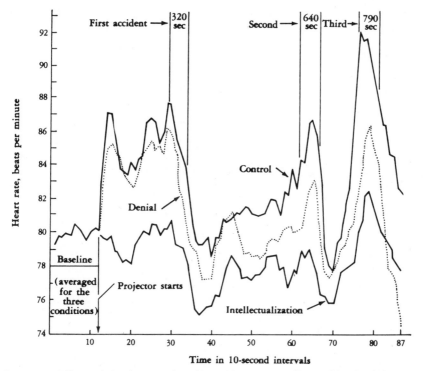

Figure 3.2. Effects of the shop accident film on heart rate, influenced by the defensive orientations of denial and intellectualization. [From R. S. Lazarus, E. M. Opton, M. S. Nomikos, & N. Rankin, The principle of short-circuiting of threat: Further evidence. *Journal of Personality*, 1965, *33*, 622–635. Copyright © 1965 by Duke University Press.]

al., 1965, shows heart rate responses across the course of watching the accident film. The pattern appears to be best described as a defense reaction, since both skin conductance level (not presented here) and heart rate show increases at the three accident incidents. The three curves presented are from three different cognitive orientation conditions. Note that, although the general level of arousal decreases from the control condition to the denial condition (which states that the characters are actors) to the intellectualization condition (which tells subjects to analyze the safety appeals being used by the foreman), a defense reaction, rather than an orienting response, seems evident at each critical incident in all conditions.

Relationship between Vicarious and Direct Arousal

It is essential to our argument that vicarious arousal energizes emergency intervention that we be able to demonstrate that, at least under vivid, realistic circumstances, vicarious responses resemble personal defense reactions. The best demonstration of the relationship comes from the dissertation research of Alfert (1966; as quoted by Lazarus, 1966). She presented portions of the *It Didn't Have to Happen* mill accident film (Incident 2) as her vicarious threat situation. All subjects were also exposed to a direct threat: a period of time filled with clicks presented at 5-second intervals that, they were told, would be followed by electric shock. Both the accident sequence and the direct threat involve a period of unpleasant expectation, so they are quite similar. Presentation of film and shock threat were counterbalanced, and subjects were allowed time between conditions to return to physiological baselines. Skin conductance and heart rate were taken at 10-second intervals.

The results show clear defense-type reactions to both film and threat of shock, with highly significant increases in both skin conductance and heart rate, although the response to threatened shock is greater on both measures. What is demonstrated by this result is that it is possible to obtain vicarious defense reactions but that they may be less intense than personal ones. Furthermore, the data clearly show a relationship between the magnitude of response to personal and vicarious threat. That is, there is consistency across situations for individual response patterns. Separately for shock–film and film–shock order of presentation, three of the four correlations are significant, and all four are positive. In summarizing her results, Lazarus claims

> The results provide strong evidence that the dynamics of vicarious and direct threat are indeed comparable. The pattern of affective change was similar in both. The correlation of threat and stress reactions between the vicarious and direct

threat conditions was substantial. In other words, subjects who reacted most to one, tended to preserve their position of intense reaction in the other. There is evidently a great deal in common in the psychodynamics of vicarious and direct threats [1966, p. 51].

Although different subjects were involved in the vicarious and real situations, the research of Berkun, Bialek, Kern, and Yagi (1962) is also relevant to this question. Unfortunately, along with the severe ethical problems involved in their research, the physiological measures they used— 17-hydroxycorticosteroids in the urine and eosinophil cell counts in the blood—are comparable to nobody else's. Thus we will mention their research only briefly.

The Berkun et al. (1962) study is unique in that it employed servicemen in highly realistic stress situations that simulated battle conditions. Subjects were exposed to apparent personal danger from a flying emergency, reported radiation, a forest fire, and misdirected artillery fire and were required to perform complex electronic repair operations on a radio in order to be "rescued" in the last three of these. Self-reports of distress and behavioral deterioration could thus be related to physiological measures. Unfortunately, although the measure of adrenocortical secretion shows a stress reaction to have occurred under all four situations in which the servicemen were placed in perceived danger, and these differences were paralleled by differences in self-reported fear and in behavioral deficits, correlations between the measures are not given. The eosinophil measure was taken in the last three situations, with mean differences in the expected direction but large variabilities precluding finding significant differences.

In addition to the simulated combat situations, these investigators used one other test condition. This was a situation in which subjects were led to believe that they were in some way responsible for the injury of a fellow soldier in an explosion. Self-report measures and performance measures both indicated that this situation was highly stressful for subjects. Overall, in fact, in comparison to the personal threat conditions, it produced the highest level of stress, as indexed by self-report, and a level of deterioration in complex motor performance that was second only to being potentially under artillery fire. Results with the physiological measures of stress, the problems of which have been discussed, were inconclusive. Nonetheless, they do not indicate that lower levels were present among those in the "vicarious" condition. These data are at least consistent with the suggestion from Alfert that patterns of response to vicarious arousal are similar to those obtained under personal threat.

There are two other studies, the results of which are inconsistent with those of Alfert and Berkun et al. They are by Craig (1968; Craig & Wood, 1969) and, as with the Craig and Weinstein study cited earlier, they present certain methodological difficulties. The physiological measures are very well done. However, the stressor is one involving actual "insult to the body," which, as pointed out earlier, leads to the confounding of physical with emotional stress responses. The Craig and Wood (1969) study involved counterbalancing direct and vicarious experience in a simple 2 × 2 design. Subjects were measured (on log skin conductance and heart rate) in anticipatory and test periods for each experience (vicarious and direct). Direct experience led to more increase in skin conductance than did vicarious experience. The heart rate data are even more striking. Whereas the direct experience led to increases in heart rate, the vicarious experience led to no change when it came first and to considerable decrease when it came second. This decrease is clearly confounded with relief at being over and done with the cold pressor test. Nevertheless, the pattern, even in the vicarious–direct sequence, suggests that the vicarious experience is more like an orienting response, whereas the direct experience resembles a defense reaction. The Craig (1968) study finds smaller differences in heart rate between vicarious, imagined, and direct experiences under "test" conditions and no differences under "anticipation." The GSR effects are still present across conditions at both time periods. Interestingly, the "imagination" condition resembles the direct experience more closely than the vicarious experience, although both are presumably "mental" events. The effects of order are still a problem, and the author does not present all of his means. The means that are presented, for skin conductance, show essentially no differences between conditions for the test situation when only the first experiences are compared.

Based on the results of these studies, we are left with the distinct possibility that the vicarious experience of a bystander is likely to be a less intense version of the direct response. However, they may sometimes be qualitatively different. For example, when the severity of the situation is relatively low, the response of the victim may be one of defense, while the reaction of the observer may be orienting—primarily reflecting interest. When the crisis is severe, however, the vicarious experience, like the direct one, is likely to be a defense reaction. Consequently, the behavior of a victim can critically affect the nature of bystander response; loud screams of pain or cries for "Help" or emphatic appeals may effectively change the response of the observer from intellectual interest into emotional involvement. Finally, when the severity of the situation is minimal, both the direct and vicarious experience is likely to be in the orienting range. Both the victim and the observer will be activated but not strongly emotionally instigated, and rational decision making without emotional pressure should be possible. Essentially, then, we are suggesting that the direct–vicarious difference simply places the individual at a different point on Sokolov's stimulus-intensity dimension (refer to Figure 3.1), which can lead to differing probabilities of no response, an orienting response, or a defense reaction.

Arousal in Emergency Situations

The model of helping in emergencies that we have proposed states that the observation of the occurrence of an emergency involving another person is physiologically arousing, that this arousal state may become aversive, and that the bystander is then motivated to reduce it. One way to effectively reduce the arousal, clearly, is by helping the victim. Since it is the vicarious response that is aversive and the response is contingent upon one's knowledge of and exposure to the other's distress, the most direct way to end one's vicarious distress is typically to end the victim's troubles. However, there are often difficulties in obtaining direct physiological measures under emergency conditions. Thus, we have had to rely mainly on studies investigating observation of another's distress under less spontaneous circumstances. There are, though, two sets of studies with which we are familiar in which physiological measures were taken on individuals exposed to relatively realistic emergency situations. These studies were done in the laboratories of the Piliavins and of Gaertner and Dovidio. The measures used in many of these studies were far from sophisticated, since at the time the studies were conducted, neither were the investigators. Thus, the Piliavin studies employing skin resistance responses will be presented in relatively incomplete detail or with current knowledge that the method used may obscure or lose much information. In addition, although these studies generally involved more complicated designs, we will primarily discuss the effect of an emergency on bystanders who witness it alone, in order to provide the reader with the most direct test of emergency impact. Fuller discussion of the potential mediating effects of other factors will be presented in later chapters.

STUDY 1: THE IMPACT OF A "FALLEN WOMAN" ON PHYSIOLOGICAL RESPONSES

The first study we did that employed physiological measures was conducted by Byeff (1970). This study was done for a senior honors thesis at the University of Pennsylvania. The experiment was described to subjects as a study of physiological responses to movies seen on television. Briefly, subjects were either tested alone, in side-by-side pairs, or two at a time in separate rooms. The emergency was both seen and heard on a television monitor by half the subjects. For the other subjects, the emergency was heard through the wall. Thus, the audio–visual version of the emergency was very clear; the audio-only presentation, ambiguous. In the audio-visual version, subjects (all males) saw a young woman, who they had been told was next door setting up the movie, enter the television picture, set up the projection screen, climb on a chair to pull up the top of the screen, and then fall over, out of sight, with a crash (the "fallen woman" emergency). Subjects in the audio-only conditions only heard the accompanying noises.

A continuous GSR record was available on one subject for each trial for the 3 minutes preceding the emergency, and for however long the subjects left the electrodes on afterward.[2] The "pre-emergency" period was divided into three 1-minute segments and basal resistance was taken at the beginning and the end of the 3 minutes. The number of spontaneous skin resistance responses for each minute was counted and their average height in millimeters was calculated. The second 1-minute segment, the last segment not associated with the occurrence or aftermath of the accident, served as baseline for our later calculations. Although, as noted earlier, there is controversy concerning the meaning of different GSR measures, there is a general agreement (Edelberg, 1967; Katkin, 1966; Stern, Winokur, Graham, & Graham, 1961) that this rate of spontaneous skin resistance reflects general activation, as does base level. As a second GSR measure, the height of the first peak on the GSR record within 5 seconds after the crash was scored. This initial response may more nearly represent a truly emotional reaction to the event, although it can not definitively be classified as a defense reaction without evidence of nonhabituation or concurrent heart rate increase. Subsequent data, however, do support this interpretation.

In order to present the clearest picture of subjects' physiological responses to an emergency, independent of the potential influence of other witnesses, only the conditions in which the subject believed that he was the only witness will be considered at this point. The effect of the face-to-face or the known but unseen presence of another bystander will be discussed in Chapter 6. Although no formal adaptation period was provided, subjects in the alone conditions showed a nonsignificant increase in skin resistance (increased relaxation) across the waiting period. Figure 3.3, then, presents the peak height measures at three critical points during the course of the experiment: (a) the 1-minute baseline period; (b) the minute segment ending with the occurrence of the emergency; and (c) the postemergency period.

---

[2] This study was conducted using a machine of now-unknown manufacture and operating characteristics. At the present time we do not know what type of electrodes were used, what kind of electrode paste or jelly was employed, and whether or not subjects washed their hands. The sensitivity settings varied from about 1.6 to about 2.2 K ohms per millimeter of pen deflection.

As illustrated in Figure 3.3, there is a highly significant difference ($p < .01$) between the height of the first GSR peak after the emergency and the average height of spontaneous peaks produced during the baseline period. There is also a general increase ($p < .05$) in the rate of spontaneous skin resistance response over baseline. Thus, the "fallen woman" emergency appeared to elicit both an orienting and a defense reaction from subjects. Furthermore, as depicted in the figure, the audio–visual presentation generally generated a greater responsiveness than the audio-only emergency between the preaccident and postaccident periods ($p < .05$). Certainly, the audio–visual emergency should be more emotionally arousing than the audio-only presentation, even though the amount of noise (which relates to startle) is the same. In summary, then, the data from the Byeff study indicate quite clearly that the observation of an emergency in a laboratory can indeed create physiological responses typically associated with strong emotional reactions.

THE IMPACT OF ANOTHER "FALLEN WOMAN" AND CRIMINAL VICTIMIZATION

During the spring and summer of 1974, we conducted additional studies in order to further investigate the arousal hypothesis. In these studies (Piliavin, Piliavin, & Trudell, 1974, unpublished) male subjects again reported for an experiment on the physiological effects of movies on television. The major differences from the Byeff study were that subjects actually saw a movie in this case, with the emergency occurring afterward,

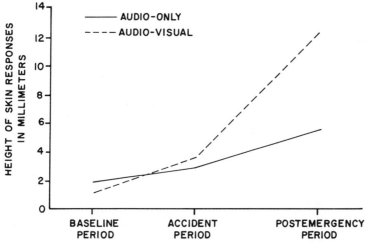

Figure 3.3. Height of galvanic skin responses before, during, and after the emergency. [From Byeff, 1970.]

and that two different emergencies were used. One was the "fallen woman" emergency, staged in a very similar way to the audio–visual presentation in the Byeff study except that the projectionist falls while taking the projection screen down after the movie. The other emergency was a theft, perpetrated by an unknown bearded young man, followed by a physical struggle when the projectionist attempts to restrain the thief from absconding. As in the Byeff study, some subjects were tested alone while other subjects were tested in pairs. Finally, subjects were wired for both heart rate and GSR, which yielded both height and rate measures.[3] Again, at this time we will only present the results of the alone condition (combined across spring and summer data collection periods, $N = 139$), since it provides the most straightforward demonstration of the impact of the emergency.

Four different measures of physiological arousal were taken in this study: rate of spontaneous skin responses, amplitude of first GSR peak after the "point of clarity" of the emergency, average height of GSR peaks, and heart rate. The baseline period for our purposes here will be taken as the last 2 minutes of the film. The time between the end of the film and the "point of clarity"—the time at which the nature of the emergency becomes clear—was 26 seconds for the fallen woman accident and 73 seconds for the theft. Rates were adjusted to rates per minute for comparability, however. These four measures show a consistent pattern of change associated with witnessing the emergency. As in the Byeff study, observation of the emergency generated increases, relative to baseline, in both the rate of spontaneous skin response ($p < .001$) and in the height of the first peak following the emergency ($p < .03$). The effect on the average height of GSR peaks after the emergency was less pronounced ($p = .18$). Also, for the argument of a defense reaction that we have been making, the heart rate data are crucial, and quite unequivocal. The overall cardiac response to the emergency was one of acceleration ($p = .002$). For illustrative purposes, height of GSR peaks and heart rate are presented across the time span of the experiment in Figure 3.4. In this figure we have presented separate lines for the "fallen woman" and the thief emergencies to demonstrate their similarity.[4]

[3] The physiological recordings were done on a two-channel Lafayette recorder (76400 solid state amplifier) with chrome-plated electrodes (76602) and K-Y sterile lubricant. Subjects washed their hands before electrodes were applied. Since there were only two recording channels, when subjects were tested in separated pairs, one was randomly assigned to have his heart rate measured and the other his GSR. Dummy transducers of the other kind were also attached, so subjects thought both measures were being obtained in all conditions. Sensitivity was adjusted so that 1 millimeter of pen deflection indicated a change of about .5 K ohms (a sensitivity setting of 3 on the machine).

[4] Each data point in Figure 3.4 represents the number of subjects for whom measures were available at that point in time. Due to the practical difficulties associated with obtaining

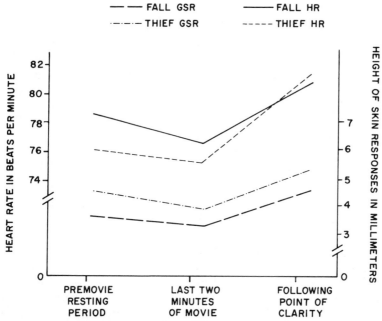

Figure 3.4. Heart rate in beats per minute (indexed on the left vertical axis) and GSR in millimeters (indexed on right vertical axis). GSR is average height of peaks for premovie and movie periods, and height of the *first* peak after point of clarity. [From Piliavin, Piliavin, & Trudell, 1974.]

Clearly, on both measures there are consistent increases from baseline to the point of clarity through the postemergency period. Thus, the data are quite unequivocal in demonstrating the arousing effects of emergencies. The newly added measure, heart rate, appears to give results similar to those obtained with skin resistance, both in this study and in the Byeff study. This strongly suggests that the pattern of response obtained in both studies reflects a defense reaction, indicative of emotional involvement, rather than only an orienting response, reflecting interest.

THE IMPACT OF "FALLEN CHAIRS" ON
PHYSIOLOGICAL AROUSAL

During the years 1974 to 1978 we conducted a similar research program, investigating physiological and behavioral responses to emergencies,

---

physiological measures while an emergency occurs, the number of subjects for whom records were available generally declined from the premovie resting period to the postemergency response period. The significance tests were, of course, based on subjects for whom both baseline and postemergency data were obtained.

at the University of Delaware. In general, these studies shared a common paradigm. Female subjects were introduced to an experiment investigating the "physiological synchrony" theory of ESP. Consequently, they became involved in an ESP task with another person, a black or white female confederate, in another cubicle. During the task, the confederate interrupted the procedure, mentioned a stack of chairs that needed to be straightened, and then stood to fix them. A short period later, the subject heard over the intercom system the sound of chairs crashing to the floor accompanied by the cries of the victim, "They're falling on me. . .(scream) . . . (scream) . . . (scream) . . ." followed by prolonged silence.

During the emergency, subjects' heart rates were monitored using radiotelemetry. This procedure had two major advantages. On a theoretical level, unlike GSR, a single channel of cardiac response would allow us in this emergency context to distinguish between an orienting response (heart rate decrease) and a defense reaction (heart rate increase). More practically, the use of biotelemetry permits cardiac monitoring without limiting the subject's mobility. A heart rate measure was calculated on the mean heart rate for each second in each of four periods: (a) a baseline period, 1 minute immediately prior to the confederate's interruption of the ESP procedure; (b) a 15- to 25-second period, depending on the specific study, in which the procedure was interrupted and the emergency occurred; (c) an initial 10-second period following the emergency (for those subjects who tried to help the victim during this initial period, the measure was based on the period prior to the subject standing); and finally, (d) an overall postemergency period, which was concluded after 180 seconds or, for those subjects who intervened, 1 second prior to their standing. Notice that the overall postemergency period included the initial 10-second period. Again, although the designs of these studies were typically complex, at this time we will focus only on the impact of the emergency on solitary bystanders.

In one experiment (Gaertner, Dovidio, & Johnson, 1979a), female subjects were presented with an emergency over a closed circuit television. Briefly, the black or white female confederate mentioned the stack of chairs, and then stood to fix them out of camera range. After the screams and the loud crash, the victim fell back into camera view and collapsed, apparently unconcious, to the floor among the fallen chairs. She remained motionless on the screen for the remainder of the emergency period. A total of 18 subjects whose heart rates were continuously monitored witnessed these events alone.

Throughout the course of the experiment, subjects exhibited systematic changes in heart rate. Specifically, subjects' heart rates decreased significantly ($p < .02$) from baseline (83.68 beats per minute) to the period in which the ESP task was interrupted (77.32 beats per minute). Participants apparently exhibited an orienting response to this curious deviation from the anticipated procedure. Interest, though, quickly changed to emotional activation. During the initial 10 seconds after the occurrence of the emergency, bystanders' heart rates increased ($p < .04$) to 82.07 beats per minute. Therefore, based on the theoretical framework provided by Routtenberg, the Laceys, and Sokolov, a defense reaction, emotional involvement, dominates subjects' postemergency responses. Since 89% (16 of 18) of the subjects intervened within 11 seconds of the occurrence of the accident, the expected further increase in heart rate over time could not be assessed in this study. There were no significant differences in the level or pattern of cardiac responses associated with the race of the victim.

In another pair of studies, we again investigated the responses of female subjects to the same "chair crashing" emergency; in these, however, subjects could only hear the accident over the intercom system. In the first of the studies ($N = 32$), the victim was either a black or a white female, and no significant effects for race were obtained when subjects were the only bystander. The cardiac responses, plotted throughout the critical periods of this study (Gaertner & Dovidio, 1977) are presented in Figure 3.5. In general, there was a decrease in heart rate from the baseline to the interruption period. Although this difference by itself is not statistically significant, it does parallel the orienting response obtained with the audio–visual emergency. Furthermore, subjects' post emergency responses again reflect emotional activation. Heart rate increased ($p < .001$) from the interruption period to the initial 10 seconds of the postemergency period, and heart rate throughout the entire postemergency was generally greater ($p < .01$) than cardiac level during the initial 10 seconds. Furthermore, consistent with our hypothesis that arousal continues to increase as a function of the length of time the observer is exposed to the emergency, 83% (20 of 24) of the subjects who had response times greater than 10 seconds showed greater heart rate after the initial postemergency period than during it. A final set of comparisons revealed that heart rate was significantly greater during the initial and entire postemergency period than during the baseline period ($p = .001$). The results of this study, then, continue to demonstrate quite unequivocally a strong defense reaction generated by witnessing an emergency.

We subsequently conducted another study (Gaertner et al., unpublished, 1979b), which replicated, in part, the above procedures. This time 25 female subjects who believed that they were the only witness heard the emergency involving the black or white victim. The results of this study,

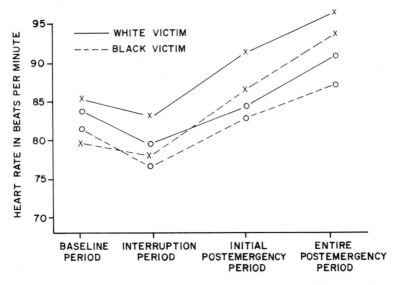

Figure 3.5. Heart rate in response to the "falling chairs" emergency (Gaertner & Dovidio, 1977, indicated by X's; Gaertner, Dovidio, & Johnson, 1979b, indicated by O's). [From S. I. Gaertner & J. F. Dovidio, The subtlety of white racism, arousal, and helping behavior. *Journal of Personality and Social Psychology*, 1977, *35*, 691–707. Copyright 1977 by the American Psychological Association. Reprinted by permission.]

also illustrated in Figure 3.5, strongly parallel our earlier findings. Although there were no significant effects associated with race of the victim, there was a significant decrease ($p < .001$) from baseline to the period in which the ESP procedure was interrupted. Heart rate then increased ($p < .01$) to the initial 10 seconds of the postemergency period. Also, heart rate during the entire postemergency period was greater than cardiac level during both the first 10 seconds ($p < .01$) and baseline ($p < .01$). Finally, arousal again appeared to be a function of the length of time subjects were exposed to the emergency. Eighty-three percent (19 of 23) of the subjects for whom data were available experienced faster heart rate after the initial 10-second postemergency period than during it.

Across three studies employing a similar paradigm, then, we have obtained an extremely consistent pattern of cardiac response. Bystanders initially demonstrate an orienting response, reflected by heart rate deceleration, when the established task procedures are disrupted. As the gravity of the situation is realized, however, a defense reaction, manifested by heart rate increase, becomes the dominant response. Intellectual interest is replaced by emotional involvement. Finally, the longer the bystander is exposed to the emergency, the greater is the arousal that is generated.

Summary

The results of a wide variety of studies discussed in this chapter offer a clear and consistent picture of bystander arousal. Very simply, bystanders do respond physiologically to the need and victimization of others. Although the response may be one of interest, an orienting response, it may also be one of true emotional activation, a defense reaction. In fact, the findings of studies from our own labs, conducted over a 9-year period and using a variety of paradigms, subject populations, experimenters, and physiological measures, clearly demonstrate that it is the defense reaction that dominates bystander response to "emergency-like" situations. The experience of an emergency, therefore, is not solely a cognitive or intellectual one, but rather may involve a strong emotional component as well.

Chapter 4

Arousal and the Helping Response

In the preceding chapter we have presented what we consider to be convincing evidence that the observation of another's emergency is physiologically arousing to the bystander. We have argued that for realistic, compelling crises the qualitative nature of this arousal state bears more resemblance to a defense reaction than to an orienting response. That is, the response appears to have the "fight or flight" characteristics exhibited in defense reactions to one's own crises. In this chapter, we will present evidence that this arousal state can, and often does, energize a helping response.

It is important to note as we begin our argument that the response made to an emergency will also be determined in part by the perceived costs and rewards in the situation. We will go into those factors in detail in Chapter 5. In this chapter, for simplicity, we will restrict our analyses to relatively straightforward situations that are, in the model, optimal in predisposing the aroused bystander to choose a helping response—situations characterized by high costs for not helping and low costs for helping. We will certainly not attempt to go into the complexities of the interactions produced in designs manipulating costs, rewards, and personality characteristics.

In developing our case, we will again, as in Chapter 3, move from weak to strong evidence. The first section will explore characteristics of the emergency presumed to relate to the degree of arousal. In particular, we will discuss data supporting two of the subhypotheses of the basic arousal postulate: namely, the effects of severity of the emergency and physical proximity of the victim on emotional responsiveness to the victim's crisis. The clarity of the emergency will also be discussed as an important factor affecting arousal. Then, we will examine research that shows greater helping in response to more severe, clearer, and closer emergencies. Finally, in the last section, we will present more recent, direct evidence relating arousal to helping and arguing that arousal is a causal factor in intervention.

Factors Affecting Arousal

SEVERITY

It is likely that an observer will infer greater pain and distress from greater reactivity of victims of electric shock or from knowledge that higher levels are being delivered. Thus, many of the studies discussed in Chapter 3 also suggest that observers' arousal is a function of severity. For example, Berger (1962), across three studies, consistently found more conditioning, an indirect indicator of vicarious arousal, among subjects who saw a reactive "shocked" performer as compared to a nonreactive one. Similarly, Tomes (1964) found greater GSR conditioning and greater vicariously instigated emotional response among subjects who saw a reactive as compared to a nonreactive performer. Replicating the earlier work, DiLollo and Berger (1965) obtained differences in reaction time as a direct function of the reactiveness of a victim to shock, and also found evidence that suggests that this effect may be attributable to differences in perceived severity. Even more direct evidence indicating increased arousal as a function of severity, however, is provided by Geer and Jarmecky (1973). Consistent with the previous research, Geer and Jarmecky found more rapid reaction times and higher nonspecific GSR levels among subjects who believed that the victim was receiving more painful electric shocks.

Using a quite different experimental paradigm, Lazarus (1966; Lazarus et al., 1962, 1965) also demonstrated the effect of perceived severity on arousal. Although no tests for statistical significance were reported, visual inspection of Figure 3.2 reveals that the heart rate is considerably faster in response to the "impaling" accident (Accident 3), in which a man dies, than in either of the prior minor accidents involving finger lacerations (Accident 1) and losses (Accident 2). In the control condition, the difference in heart rate between the severed finger accident and the impaling incident is almost six beats per minute, although, in general, adaptation to stress occurs across the viewing of this and other stressful films. Additional demonstration by Lazarus and his colleagues of the effects of perceived severity on arousal is provided by the results associated with the "denial" manipulation.

CLARITY

Whereas severity concerns the degree of potential injury to a victim, manipulations of clarity (or, conversely, ambiguity) involve variations in the quantity and/or quality of cues emitted from an emergency of a given level of severity. Common manipulations of clarity include the presence or absence of verbal cues of distress (e.g., Clark & Word, 1972, 1974; Yakimovich & Saltz, 1971) or the audio-only or audio–visual presentation of an accident (e.g., Clark & Word, 1974). Drawing from the literature on perception, these varied manipulations may generally be considered as examples of "stimulus degradation." Since the theoretical distinction between severity and clarity has not typically been articulated, researchers have rarely attempted to empirically isolate the effects of the two factors.

One study from our own laboratories (Gaertner & Dovidio, 1977, Study 2) does suggest that the presence of screams can strongly affect subjects' self-reports of arousal in response to an emergency. In one condition, female subjects involved in an ESP task overheard the sound of a stack of chairs crashing to the floor accompanied by the screams of the partner, "They're falling on me . . . (screams)." For subjects in another condition, the sound of crashing chairs also interrupted the ESP procedure, but screams were absent. Consistent with the propositions of our model, subjects who were presented with the additional distress cue of screams, compared to subjects who were exposed to the same emergency without screams, experienced significantly greater upset and responded with more symptoms of autonomic arousal ($p < .01$), based on postexperimental reports. A second study from our lab performed by Sterling (1977, Study 3) provides an even more direct test of the proposed relationship between the quantity of cues and the degree of psychophysiological arousal experienced in response to an emergency. For this investigation, biotelemetry was used to monitor male subjects' heart rates while the emergency occurred. Based on this more sophisticated methodology, Sterling found that subjects who heard a groan of pain after a victim "inadvertently" caused a ladder and toolbox to crash to the floor exhibited significantly ($p < .05$) greater elevation in heart rate ($M = +6.07$ beats per minute) than did witnesses who heard the same emergency without groans ($M = + .35$ bpm).

Byeff (1970) also presented subjects with an audio–visual or an audio-only emergency. As we mentioned in Chapter 3, male subjects were exposed to a woman's fall from a chair while attempting to set up a projection screen. This emergency was either overheard through the walls of the experimental cubicle or heard and seen via a television monitor. Again, consistent with our previous research, subjects showed greater arousal in response to the clear audio–visual emergency than to the ambiguous audio-only emergency. Analyses of covariance, controlling for baseline,[1] revealed a main effect for emergency on both the magnitude of the first GSR peak ($p < .03$) and the average height of peaks that occurred within 1 minute after the accident ($p = .06$). Thus, clarity of an emergency and arousal were related across three different experimental paradigms employing subjective, heart rate, and GSR measures.

DISTANCE

Although physical proximity to a victim theoretically could affect a bystander's level of arousal, either by providing a greater quantity of cues (e.g., being able to see blood or hear cues that could not be detected at a distance) or by increasing the quality of the cues (e.g., the intensity of the screams or moans or the vividness of the blood), there is no published literature relating distance from the victim to arousal. Nevertheless, our theoretical framework, reinforced by the recent empirical evidence relating clarity and arousal, would continue to suggest a direct relationship between proximity and arousal.

Factors Affecting Helping Behavior

If arousal is an important motivator of a helping response, as we propose, then one might expect that the same conditions that generate high levels of arousal should, in general, also elicit relatively high levels of helping behavior. Thus, we will continue to present evidence of an arousal–helping relationship by discussing studies that, although not directly measuring arousal, do demonstrate that clearer, closer, and more severe emergencies produce greater helping behavior.

SEVERITY

Several empirical studies have demonstrated a direct relationship between the severity of an emergency and bystander responsiveness. For example, in Chapter 3, we mentioned two laboratory studies, Weiss *et al.*

---

[1] Unless otherwise indicated, analyses of the physiological measures controlled for baseline rates. Tests for mean differences were based on analyses of covariance; linear relationships were based on partial correlations.

(1971) and Geer and Jarmecky (1973), in which subjects observed victims apparently receive shocks of different levels of severity. In both studies, victims who were ostensibly receiving higher-intensity shocks displayed more severe pain cues. Both studies demonstrated that subjects helped more rapidly when the victim was in greater pain. Thus, consistent with our theoretical framework, the more severe the distress of the victim, the more helpful observers were.

Ashton and Severy (1976), in an attempt to test directly the model being discussed here (as well as a prediction based on the Yerkes–Dodson law) presented subjects with three levels of severity in a "falling bookcase" emergency. They found that the latency of response was significantly longer in the low-severity than in high- or moderate-severity conditions; the latter two conditions, however, did not differ significantly from each other. Both the linear and quadratic trends were significant. Using a field setting, West and Brown (1975) also found a systematic effect of severity on helping behavior. In their study, a female undergraduate approached a male passerby outside the student health center with a story about being bitten by a laboratory rat, needing a tetanus shot, and not having enough money. As expected, a highly significant main effect of severity, manipulated by the presence or absence of a "blood-soaked" gauze bandage over the "wound," was obtained for the amount of money donated. Most recently, Shotland and Huston (1979) had experimenters approach people either getting into or out of their cars in a campus parking lot with a request that they "drive me home to Boalsberg" for one of four reasons. Two reasons were defined as "nonemergencies"; the other two reasons were defined as "emergencies." The emergencies were clearly more severe: needing an insulin shot or having to get back to a roommate who had just taken too many sleeping pills versus needing allergy medicine or wanting to get back to a roommate who was depressed. The drivers acquiesced to the request 64% of the time for "emergencies" and 45% of the time for "nonemergencies."

Finally, Staub and Baer (1974) carried out two field studies in which apparent severity of a victim's condition was varied. Results of the two studies, however, were contradictory. In these studies, a victim collapsed on the sidewalk, either grabbing his chest (bad heart condition) or his knee (bad knee condition). In the first study, more subjects helped in the bad knee condition, while in the second study subjects were more likely to help the victim with a bad heart than the victim with a bad knee. The authors attempt to explain these obviously contradictory results as follows: "This discrepancy may be due to differences in the exact conditions of the experiments or to differences in the characteristics of the confederates [p. 282]." Thus, except for Staub and Baer's first study, empirical research demonstrates that greater severity is generally related to greater helping behavior, as well as greater arousal levels.

As we discussed previously, the clarity of an emergency has been manipulated by varying both the quantity and quality of cues associated with the event. In general, studies investigating the effects of ambiguity on helping vary the number of cues by exposing some subjects to an emergency with screams or cries of some kind while presenting other subjects with the same emergency without sounds from the victim. Research along this line has consistently demonstrated a direct relationship between clarity, or conversely ambiguity, and helping behavior. For example, Yakimovich and Saltz (1971) had subjects working on a questionnaire when a maintenance man, who was washing the windows, apparently fell from his ladder to the pavement below and injured his ankle. Although most of the subjects rushed to the window, only 29% of the subjects actually offered assistance to the victim. However, when the workman also made a cry for help during the accident, the percentage of bystanders who helped increased substantially, to 81%. Similarly, Clark and Word (1972) found that the presence of verbal pain cues during the emergency also increased bystander intervention dramatically. When the victim gave verbal cues of distress, 100% of the subjects intervened to help; when the distress cues were absent, less than one third of the bystanders, 30%, helped the victim. Thus, as ambiguity increases, helping behavior decreases.

The verbal cues accompanying the emergencies in the studies by Yakimovich and Saltz and by Clark and Word may have increased helping behavior in two ways. Firstly, the explicit cries for help by the victims may have clearly defined for bystanders what the appropriate response to the situation *should* be. That is, the cry "Help!" from a victim clearly defines the response the victim would like to have the bystander make. A second possibility, though, is that the cries of distress by the victim provide additional cues to bystanders allowing them to interpret the situation as one in which a person is injured, and thus enhancing the emotional impact of the situation. This latter explanation suggests that quantity of pain cues mediates helping behavior at the more basic level of vicariously experiencing the situation as an emergency.

Consistent with the notion that an increase in the quantity of cues emitted from the emergency may increase the impact of the emergency, Clark and Word (1974) in another study found that screams, even without an explicit plea for assistance, were sufficient to create increases in bystander intervention. In this study, the victim was working on electrical apparatus in a corner of the laboratory and out of the subject's view. During the emergency the victim apparently received a serious shock simulated by a flash of light, a dull buzzing noise, and a "shorting out" sound emanating from the equipment. In one condition these sounds were accompanied by cries of pain, while in a more ambiguous situation there were no human distress sounds. Among subjects exposed to the emergency alone, those who heard the victim's exclamations of pain were twice as likely to intervene than those who heard the same emergency without shouts. In a second part of the article, Clark and Word replicated this finding. Bystanders who were the only witnesses helped the victim 75% of the time when the victim cried out while only 13% of the subjects helped when no pain cues accompanied the emergency. Thus, sounds from the victim were sufficient to cause large increases in responsiveness even without a specific request for assistance.

Clarity has also been manipulated by presenting some subjects with an emergency that they could both see and hear and others with the same emergency, but only with auditory cues. For example, in their 1974 study, Clark and Word included a situation in which subjects not only heard the worker receive a severe electrical shock but also visually witnessed the event. In the first part of the study, subjects who heard and saw the accident helped the victim 100% of the time, compared with the 36% rate of helping for subjects who only heard the same emergency. In a second part of this study, this difference was replicated, although it was less pronounced. Similarly, Byeff (1970) found that subjects were more likely to intervene in a "fallen woman" emergency if they could both see and hear the incident (52%) than if they could only hear the accident (36%). Tilker (1970), using a Milgram teacher–learner paradigm, also found that subjects were more likely to disobey the experimenter and stop the "teacher" from shocking the "learner," a socially responsible behavior, when they had audio–visual feedback from the victim than when the only cues were auditory. Finally, Solomon, Solomon, and Stone (1978) found, across both laboratory and field studies, that audio–visual emergencies elicit more helping behavior than similar audio-only situations.

DISTANCE

Although the effects of severity and clarity on emergency helping have been well documented, the effect of physical distance has received surprisingly little empirical attention. In the Staub and Baer (1974) study, manipulation of ease of escape also reflected differing distances. In the difficult escape conditions, the confederate collapsed 40 *feet* in front of the subject on the same side of the road, while in the easy escape condition, he collapsed 40 *yards* away from the subject on the opposite side of the street. Consistent with our theoretical framework, greater distance produced less helping both when the confederate feigned a bad knee (14% versus 56%) and a bad heart (42% versus 84%). Unfortunately, though, distance and ease of escape are confounded in this study.

The only study of which we are aware that has attempted to specifi-cally vary the "immediacy of cues" aspect of physical distance is an unpub-lished study from our lab carried out by Lorraine Broll. Distance was varied by placement of a video camera focused on the victim from either a very short distance, such that the victim's face filled the screen, or from a farther distance, such that the victim was seen from the top of the head to the waist. The situation was not an emergency in the usual sense; rather, it was presented as research into the supervisor–worker relationship. In par-ticular, the subject–supervisor could choose to prevent the confederate-worker from being shocked, but would lose money if he or she did so. There was, however, no direct effect of camera distance on helping.[2] It is likely that the difference in quantity of cues due to distance in this par-ticular experimental context was quite small.

In their 1979 study, Duval, Duval, and Neely introduced the term *tem-poral proximity* to describe the variable they have manipulated, which leads to increased willingness to help victims of adverse social conditions. Their manipulation involved showing the subject his or her image on a television screen either immediately before or after a movie about the group in question or 4 minutes before or after the movie. Subjects in the "immediate" conditions felt more responsible, volunteered more time, and pledged more money. The authors suggest a "unit formation principle of temporal proximity [p. 1776]" as an explanation. We would suggest that this temporal proximity may operate to bring the potential helper "closer" in a way similar to the operation of physical distance.

Interpreting the Arousal–Helping Relationship

The research we have presented thus far has consistently demonstrated that as severity and clarity of an emergency increase (a) subjective and physiological arousal increase; and (b) helping behavior increases. The

[2] Although there was no main effect of camera distance on helping, there was some evidence that relative costs to the victim had more impact at the close distance, while costs to the supervisor (the subject) had more impact at the far distance. Also, the correlation between Schwartz's AR scale (measuring tendency to deny or accept responsibility to help) and number of helps is + .62 in the close condition and essentially zero in the distant condition. These cor-relations do not differ significantly with such a small number of subjects; however, they do provide some evidence that the closer camera distance led to more involvement of the subject with the victim's need.

process by which these factors increase helping is still problematic, however. That is, although arousal and helping seem to be related, cognitive factors may also be operating. For example, bystanders who hear a cry for help or a scream of pain may be more likely to define the situation as one requiring assistance than if these additional cues were absent. Differences in helping behavior, therefore, could be explained solely in terms of cognitive factors, such as concern with personal costs for not helping (e.g., guilt or blame), without recourse to an explanation involving underlying psychophysiological arousal. In this section of the chapter, then, we will attempt to demonstrate more directly the relationship between arousal and helping. Again moving from weak to stronger evidence, we will introduce studies that measured helping behavior and used post hoc cognitive and arousal measures. Next, we will present several investigations that measured both arousal and helping as they occurred. Finally, the mediating effect of arousal on intervention will be addressed by a series of studies that attempted to manipulate the amount and/or perceived source of arousal that subjects experienced.

POST HOC MEASURES OF AROUSAL

A few studies, primarily from our own labs, manipulated the clarity or severity of an emergency and also attempted to assess subjects' reactions to the situation by using postexperimental responses. For example, evidence of a relationship between arousal and intervention was initially suggested by a post hoc internal analysis conducted by Clark and Word (1974). In their study, subjects exposed to the audio-visual emergency were more likely to report being upset than were subjects presented with an audio-only accident. Furthermore, subjects who reported being upset, regardless of condition, were more likely to help than subjects who did not report being upset.

A study by Sterling (1977, Study 2), as part of his dissertation, provides further indication of a relationship between arousal and helping. This study, mentioned earlier, was designed to investigate the effects of feelings toward the victim (anger or no anger) and clarity on helping behavior. Clarity was manipulated by having subjects see and hear or just hear an emergency in which a heavy toolbox apparently fell and injured another "subject." The results of this study were consistent with previous research that varied the quality of cues associated with an emergency. Although there were no main effects or interactions associated with anger, there was an effect for the type of emergency to which the subject was exposed, ($p <$ .08). Seventy-six percent of the subjects who saw the victim bent over and moaning among scattered tools and books offered help, while only 53% of the subjects whose view of the victim was obscured by a cardboard partition intervened. Furthermore, based on subjects' responses during a postex-perimental session, there appeared to be a direct relationship between arousal and helping. Although subjects who saw the emergency did not describe the situation as more serious nor more certainly involving injury to the victim than did subjects who only heard it, they did rate it as more arousing ($p < .05$). Also, there was a significant relationship between how aroused subjects reported themselves to be and how quickly they inter-vened to help ($r = .51$). However, relationships of a similar magnitude were also obtained between the assessment of the seriousness of the situa-tion and helping ($r = .51$) and between certainty that the victim was hurt and helping ($r = .57$).

The previously discussed Gaertner and Dovidio (1977, Study 2) in-vestigation, which manipulated the presence or absence of screams associ-ated with a "crashing chairs" accident, also measured helping behavior, as well as how upsetting, arousing, and serious the emergency was. Consis-tent with previous findings, subjects exposed to the emergency with screams as compared to subjects presented with the emergency without screams helped the victim more often (96.3% versus 65.0%) and evaluated the incident as more arousing, upsetting, and serious. Furthermore, cor-relational analyses revealed significant relationships between latency to in-tervene and subjects' reported upset ($r = -.36$), arousal ($r = -.34$) and perceived seriousness ($r = -.31$). The more upsetting, arousing, and seri-ous subjects described the event to be, the more quickly they responded.

Using a quite different procedure, Piliavin, Piliavin, and Broll (1976) similarly found a direct relationship between the amount of assistance the victim received and the clarity of an emergency. In this study, subjects either saw an entire scenario in which a victim either fainted or fell, or they saw only the aftermath of the fainting spell or accident. For the "whole scenario" conditions, a bystander, descending a staircase in a classroom building, saw the victim fall dramatically down the stairs or slump to the floor in a faint. In the "aftermath" conditions, the subject came upon the victim either lying in the stairwell slowly returning to consciousness (faint aftermath) or sitting up rubbing his or her ankle (fall aftermath). The fall–faint emergencies did not differ in their help-eliciting potential. The dif-ference between aftermath and whole scenario conditions, however, was very large. Victims received help in 12.5% of the aftermath conditions as compared to 88.9% of the full scenario trials ($p < .001$). Thus, there is clearly an important difference between seeing the event unfold and coming upon the victim after the fact. Obviously, the bystander who sees the entire incident has more information to facilitate recognition of the immediate need for assistance. It is also quite likely that viewing the entire scenario is much more arousing.

Naturally, one cannot take physiological measures under field conditions. In order to attempt to discover whether the emotional impact of the scenario as compared to the aftermath conditions could have mediated differences in helping behavior, Piliavin, Piliavin, and Broll (1976) carried out an "as if" study in the lab. Subjects were requested to role play, that is, to assume that they were in a classroom building, going down stairs, and that they "witnessed the following scene. . .". Subjects, with GSR recording electrodes attached, were then shown a videotape of one of the emergency sequences. Immediately after, they were asked to answer a series of questions: "What would you do?" "What happened?" "What caused it?" and "How sure are you?" Then they were shown a second and finally a third emergency sequence. Each subject saw at least one aftermath and one scenario, and the order was counterbalanced. The height of the first GSR peak produced by the subject within 5 seconds after the emergency was used as the measure of the emotional impact of the accident.

Since GSR is widely variable across individuals and since the order of presentation could exert a contaminating influence, we examined the difference in subjects' responsiveness to the first two emergency sequences they viewed within each of the three order categories: (a) scenario first, aftermath second; (b) aftermath first, scenario second; and (c) both films of the same category (i.e., aftermath–aftermath and scenario–scenario). The category in which subjects see the same type of sequence, then, allows for the assessment of habituation and/or sensitization effects.

Although there was a significant relationship between the category of viewing sequence and relative GSR responsiveness ($p < .03$), the only group to show an increase, on the average, for the second film was the group that saw the entire scenario sequence second. Indeed, comparisons demonstrate that the aftermath scenario group was different from both the scenario–aftermath ($p = .05$) and the same category group ($p < .05$). Thus it appears that, controlling for habituation effects, subjects were more aroused while viewing an emergency sequence involving the entire scenario than when watching only the aftermath.[3] It is likely, therefore, that the difference in helping obtained in the field study between these two conditions is in part due to their differential arousal value.

To briefly summarize the literature on ambiguity of an emergency and helping behavior, then, as the situation becomes less ambiguous, there is a monotonic increase in bystander intervention. In addition, as the situation

[3] Another way to look at these data, ignoring order effects, is to consider the subjects who saw films in different categories and responded differently to them, and ask what proportion reacted more strongly to the scenario film. There are 37 subjects who fit this description. Twenty-eight, or 75.7% reacted more strongly to the scenario film. Chi-square for this comparison (McNemar, 1955, p. 229) is 9.76, $p < .01$. Because it controls for the effect of habituation, this comparison also seems to be an accurate representation of the true difference. Which specific film was seen first seems not to be important.

becomes unambiguous, bystanders are both more likely to define the situation as one in which help is needed and more likely to exhibit greater arousal. Furthermore, both bystanders' perceptions of the degree of severity and the magnitude of self-reported arousal are directly related to speed of intervention.

STUDIES MEASURING HELPING AND AROUSAL

If arousal is an important factor influencing helping behavior, as we propose, then arousal and bystander responsiveness should be related, particularly in low-cost-for-helping/high-cost-for-not-helping situations. Therefore, for now we will limit our discussion to only those portions of studies measuring helping behavior and arousal in which the subject believes that he or she is the only witness to a relatively unambiguous emergency involving a victim of the same sex and race. Thus, for studies in which many factors were manipulated, we will primarily be discussing the situation that most resembles an experimental "control" condition.

Although the sample sizes are relatively small, since we are often considering only one condition of a much larger investigation, the results appear quite consistent across studies. Even when the frequency of help is high and the range of responses is restricted, arousal and latency of intervention are directly related. For example, in a study mentioned earlier (Gaertner & Dovidio, 1977, Study 2), female subjects overheard a female victim scream as a stack of chairs apparently crashed down upon her. Ninety-five percent of subjects (19 of 20) who were lone witnesses intervened in the emergency. As in past research, apathy does not seem to occur under these circumstances. Furthermore, consistent with our theoretical framework, subjects' postexperimental reports suggested a direct relationship between upset and latency of intervention ($r = -.37$) and between self-report of autonomic arousal and latency ($r = -.36$). The more upset and aroused subjects reported themselves to be, the more quickly they intervened to help. Not too surprisingly under these emergency conditions, upset and arousal were strongly correlated ($r = .79$), suggesting that the arousal generated by the emergency was subjectively labeled as upset.

Using a similar paradigm and emergency, Gaertner and Dovidio (1977, Study 1) conducted another experiment in which subjects' cardiac response was measured as the indicator of psychophysiological arousal. Again, a generally high rate of helping, 83% (13 of 16 subjects), was obtained and self-report of upset and latency of intervention were directly related ($r = -.38$). In addition, physiological arousal as measured by subjects' cardiac response to the emergency was significantly related to latency ($r = -.58$). The greater the upset and the heart rate elevation of bystanders, the more quickly they intervened to help. Upset and physiological arousal were strongly related ($r = +.59$), as in the previous study. Gaertner, Dovidio, and Johnson (unpublished, 1979b) subsequently replicated these procedures and also measured heart rate. Although only 12 subjects were studied in the alone condition, increase in heart rate and latency of intervention were related with equivalent magnitude ($r = -.58$).

Two other studies in which both the procedures and the emergency were somewhat modified have replicated our earlier demonstrations of the relationship between heart rate and helping. In one (Gaertner et al., 1979a), female subjects were again presented with a "crashing chairs" accident. Subjects in this study, however, could both see and hear the emergency over closed circuit television (actually a videotape). These quite unambiguous circumstances elicited a very high degree of helping behavior. One hundred percent (12 of 12) of bystanders intervened, with a mean latency of 7.2 seconds. Nevertheless, even with a restricted range of response times, a relationship between heart rate increase and latency of intervention, of nearly the same magnitude, was obtained ($r = -.60$). Sterling (1977, Study 3), using male subjects and a different emergency context, obtained similar results. Near the conclusion of his experiment, the subject heard a male victim in a nearby cubicle groan in pain as a toolbox, tools, and ladder crashed to the floor. Sixty-three percent (5 of 8) of the subjects intervened. Correlating the difference between baseline heart rate and rate after the emergency with latency, Sterling found the same relationship between physiological arousal and helping ($r = -.44$). Unfortunately, in neither of these last two studies were subjective measures of upset available. Nevertheless, across five different studies conducted over a period of 4 years, subjective and cardiac measures of arousal were strongly and consistently related to the latency of bystander intervention. Furthermore, it appears that this arousal, generated in response to the victim's apparent plight, was generally experienced by bystanders as a negative emotional state of upset.

Three other studies also investigated bystander intervention and recorded physiological measures of arousal. In the two studies conducted by Piliavin, Piliavin, and Trudell (1974), introduced in the previous chapter, male subjects were wired for GSR, yielding both height and rate measures. In the experiment, subjects, viewing a television monitor, were shown a neutral movie or a movie with aggressive or sexual content intended to arouse them. In the low-cost emergency condition (the only one we are presently considering) subjects then saw the projectionist fall while taking down the projection screen. Again, although the designs were more complicated and we will be discussing them in more detail elsewhere, only the alone-subjects/neutral-movie conditions will be considered here. The major procedural difference between the two studies for these conditions is that Study 1 was conducted in the spring and Study 2 was run in the summer.

Across the two studies ($N = 12$), latency of intervention was related to emotional arousal as measured by both average height of GSR responses in the period immediately following the accident ($r = -.77$) and the height of the first GSR peak after the emergency became clear ($r = -.43$). Latency and general activation, measured by the rate of spontaneous skin responses following the emergency, were also correlated ($r = -.40$). Overall, the more aroused subjects were, the more quickly they intervened. Thus, in a different experimental paradigm utilizing different physiological measures, a significant relationship between arousal and intervention was again obtained.

The Byeff (1970) investigation is the only study that manipulated the clarity or severity of an emergency for which data on helping and physiological arousal are both available. As we mentioned earlier, subjects in response to the audio–visual as compared to the audio-only presentations were generally more helpful (52% versus 36%) and more aroused, based on height of the first GSR peak to occur within 5 seconds after the emergency ($p < .03$) and the average height of GSR peaks for 1 minute after the incident ($p = .06$). In addition, for lone bystanders ($N = 30$) across audio and audio–visual emergencies, initial arousal (height of the first GSR peak) and latency of intervention were significantly correlated ($r = -.52$). Latency and average peak height were correlated $-.50$. It also appears that the arousal experienced by the bystander is a partial mediator of the audio–audio-visual effect on helping. Although, for "alone" subjects, the type of emergency and latency of intervention were related ($r = -.26$), the partial correlation between emergency type and latency, controlling for the potential mediating effects of arousal, was reduced substantially ($r = -.14$). Thus, although the effect of audio–visual versus audio-only emergencies on helping may have some influence independent of arousal, through, for example, its effects on judgments of the need for intervention, much of its impact seems to be mediated by arousal. Finally, when the relationship between initial arousal and latency is explored within audio-only and audio–visual conditions separately, similar relationships exist. For the audio-only emergency, the correlation of latency with first peak GSR was $-.36$; for the audio–visual accident, it was $-.53$. Using the average height of the GSR over the first minute after the emergency as the measure of emotional arousal, the correlation within the audio-only condition was $-.54$ and within the audio visual condition was $-.48$.

AROUSAL, ATTRIBUTION, AND HELPING

Over several studies, substantial evidence consistently demonstrates a strong relationship between psychophysiological arousal and bystander intervention. Encouraged by these findings, quite independently, we began to initiate studies that were designed to manipulate the amount and/or perceived source of arousal.

In order to investigate more directly the effect of arousal on bystander responsiveness, Piliavin, Piliavin, and Trudell (1974, Study 1) adopted an excitation–transfer paradigm frequently used in the study of aggression (Donnerstein, Donnerstein, & Evans, 1975; Zillman, Katcher, & Milavsky, 1972). Briefly, male subjects ($N = 82$), participating individually, were told that the experiment involved physiological responses to television movies. Consequently, during the experimental session subjects were wired for GSR, were informed that they could remove the electrodes themselves at the end of the movie (to facilitate response to the subsequent emergency), and then were shown a 6–8-minute movie segment. Five movie clips, intended to elicit three levels of arousal, were used. In particular, subjects viewed either a neutral, a mildly violent, a mildly sexually arousing, a strongly violent, or a strongly sexually arousing film clip.

At the end of the movie, when the projection room was visible on the television monitor, one of two emergencies occurred. In the "fall" emergency, a female projectionist, attempting to let down the movie screen, fell with a crash from a stool and then moaned and swore about having hurt her leg. In the "thief" emergency, subjects viewed a bearded young man steal money from the projectionist's cash box. She then returned, discovered the crime, and confronted him. A struggle continued until the screen went blank, as if the participants had knocked over the camera. Both emergency sequences lasted approximately 4 minutes after the end of the movie.

The experimenter observed the subject's reaction to the emergency through a one-way mirror and rated his degree of suspicion or belief at that point. As soon as the subject emerged from his room, or 4 minutes after the end of the movie if he did not come out, the experimenter explained to him that the emergency was part of the experiment and asked him to make some ratings and then to talk about his reactions. Specifically, sources of suspicion were probed. He was then debriefed fully.

In general, it was predicted that subjects would be less likely to intervene in a high-cost-for-helping (thief) incident than in a low-cost-for-helping (fall) emergency. In addition, since arousal and intervention were hypothesized to be directly related, the residual arousal generated by the sexual and aggressive movies was expected to facilitate responsiveness, relative to the neutral film condition, in the low-cost-for-helping "fallen woman" emergency. In the thief emergency, however, the impact of high costs for helping was expected to mitigate the arousal effect. In fact, the extent to which subjects who were inhibited from helping by the potential personal consequences of intervening in a theft labeled their arousal as fear, the added film-generated arousal would then be expected to reduce helping, relative to the neutral film control group. Thus, a Movie × Emergency-Type interaction was anticipated for helping behavior.

As expected, the cost manipulation reliably affected bystander intervention. Subjects in the thief conditions, as compared to subjects in the fall conditions, were less likely to help (15% versus 38%) and had longer latencies (107.15 versus 84.17 seconds). No main effect for movie nor the anticipated Movie × Emergency interaction was obtained. Closer examination of the measures of emotional arousal (height of GSR peaks), however, revealed no differences in physiological arousal experienced between the types of movie viewed. Furthermore, subjects viewing the neutral film were not less aroused than other subjects either immediately before the incident or following the emergency. The manipulation of the amount of arousal subjects exhibited was apparently not successful.

In addition to potentially affecting the amount of arousal subjects experienced, the presentation of the sexual or aggressive movie might also have influenced subjects to misattribute emergency-generated arousal to the film—the direction opposite the intended manipulation. The less arousal subjects attributed to the accident, the less likely they should be to respond to the emergency. Additional analysis of subjects' postexperimental responses, though, revealed that although subjects presented with the aggressive or sexual movie reported the film to be more arousing than did subjects with the neutral film, subjects did not differentially attribute arousal to the emergency. Thus, the movie had no reliable effect on the arousal experienced by subjects or on attribution of arousal to the emergency, and had no reliable effect on intervention.

Next, in order to more closely examine the relationship between arousal and helping, correlations within the "fallen woman" and thief emergencies and across film conditions were conducted. Recall that, although arousal and helping were predicted to be related for low-cost emergencies, the effect was expected to be less pronounced—even nonexistent or inversely related—in the high-cost thief incident. For the fall conditions ($N = 21$) latency was related to emotional arousal as measured by the height of the first peak ($r = -.42$) and the average height of peaks ($r = -.65$). Latency and general activation, represented by rate of GSR peaks, were less strongly related ($r = -.24$). The correlations within the thief conditions ($N = 16$) were only slightly different (height of first peak, $r = -.37$; average height of peaks, $r = -.42$; rate of peaks, $r = +.21$).

Although these relationships are weaker, they are still stronger than expected.

It appears that the effects of high cost for helping may be more complicated than originally anticipated. Specifically, high cost for helping may have a direct effect, inhibiting subjects from intervening despite the high costs for not helping. It may also have the indirect effect of motivating subjects to escape the high-cost-for-helping–high-cost-for-not-helping dilemma by seeking some alternative interpretation to the situation that relieves the necessity for intervention. For example, subjects in the thief condition were more likely to be rated by the experimenter as suspicious and to report being suspicious ($p < .01$) after the experiment. Subject suspicion does not necessarily invalidate the study. In fact, Latané and Darley (1970) also report that subjects often seize this excuse as a means of denying responsibility. Nevertheless, to the extent that this rationalization successfully relieves the bystander's dilemma, a reduced arousal state should accompany subjects' reports of suspicion. Indeed, across all conditions in the study, emotional arousal, as indexed by average peak height following the emergency, was inversely related to suspicion ($r = -.23$). The more suspicious subjects were, the less arousal they experienced. Of course, these results are only suggestive and our conclusions are speculative. Nevertheless, the consistency with which this pattern of redefinition later occurred in our data leads us to a more detailed discussion in Chapter 5 of the cyclical and indirect effect of high costs for helping.

In another experiment investigating the relationship between arousal and bystander responsiveness, Sterling (1977, Study 3) adopted a different excitation–transfer paradigm also frequently used in the study of aggression. Specifically, male subjects ($N = 54$), who reported for an experiment concerning the effects of physical distraction on following instructions, performed in one of three exercise conditions (either 10 push-ups, 5 push-ups, or in a control condition, no push-ups). Subjects then overheard, through an intercom system, a male confederate mutter something while "accidentally" jostling a ladder. A loud crash followed. In the ambiguous emergency condition subjects heard the crash followed only by silence; in the relatively unambiguous emergency condition subjects heard the crash, moans of pain, and then silence. In addition, heart rate was monitored throughout the study using biotelemetry.

In general, the exercise was intended to provide subjects with both an additional source of arousal and a potential attributional alternative. Specifically, it was expected that in an unambiguous emergency involving exclamations of pain, the salience of the situation would lead subjects to attribute their arousal, including residual excitation due to exercise, to the emergency. Exercise, therefore, was expected to facilitate bystander intervention based on the assumed direct relationship between arousal attributed to an emergency and bystander responsiveness. In an ambiguous situation, without sounds indicating pain, misattribution of arousal from the exercise to the emergency is less likely to occur. In fact, since the exercise experience itself provides subjects with an alternative attributional source for emergency-generated arousal, it was expected that exercise could actually decrease helping behavior when the emergency was ambiguous. Therefore, an Exercise × Emergency-Type interaction was anticipated.

In general, the results of the study were supportive of the predictions. Exercise did arouse the subjects. Prior to the emergency, the mean change in heart rate was .34 beats per minute for the no-excercise group, +9.89 beats for the moderate-excercise condition and +12.55 beats for the high-exercise groups. The pattern of data on helping, in addition, was quite consistent with the hypothesized relationship between attribution of arousal to an emergency and bystander responsiveness (see Figure 4.1). The expected interaction between level of exercise and type of emergency approached significance ($p = .08$). For the emergency with pain cues, subjects in the high-exercise condition helped most quickly while subjects in the moderate- and no-excercise conditions helped about equally. Furthermore, when there were no moans associated with the emergency, exercise tended to inhibit bystander intervention. In this situation, subjects in the high-exercise condition intervened most slowly, subjects in the moderate-exercise group were the next slowest, while subjects in the no-exercise group helped most quickly. Furthermore, when latencies for only those subjects who decided

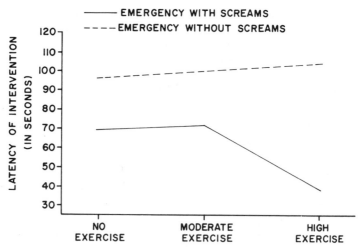

Figure 4.1. The effect of prior exercise on the response to an emergency with or without screams. [From Sterling, 1977, Study 3.]

to intervene during the critical 2-minute period were analyzed, the Emergency × Exercise interaction was more pronounced ($p < .05$).

Since it was hypothesized that it is the attribution of arousal, rather than the overall level of arousal per se, that critically affects helping behavior, separate correlations between heart rate increase and latency of intervention were conducted for subjects who heard the emergency with and without pain cues. If the facilitative effect of excercise on helping that was obtained among subjects who heard moans was mediated by the misattribution of residual arousal to the emergency, then a direct relationship between arousal and helping would be expected. Consistent with these expectations, the greater the increase in heart rate from baseline, the faster subjects helped ($r = -.47$). Furthermore, this relationship is similar in magnitude to comparable correlations obtained between psychophysiological arousal and helping in the previous studies.

Taking the implications of the attributional framework one step further, if the inhibitory effect of exercise in the emergency without moans is due to the misattribution of emergency-generated arousal to the exercise experience, then little relationship between the overall level of arousal and helping would be expected. That is, if arousal is attributed primarily to the exercise, then responding to the emergency would be perceived as having little instrumental value for reducing arousal. In fact, the correlation between arousal and latency under these conditions revealed only a slight, positive relationship ($r = +.18$). There was a weak tendency for subjects who were more aroused to intervene more slowly. This suggests the importance of an intervening attributional mechanism. The difference between the correlations in the clear and ambiguous conditions is, of course, significant.

To further pursue the investigation of attributional effects on helping behavior, another study was conducted. A more detailed account of this study may be found in Gaertner and Dovidio (1977, Study 2). In the Sterling study just discussed, the exercise experience provided subjects with both an attributional alternative to the emergency and an additional source of arousal. The Gaertner and Dovidio experiment was designed to explore the effects of misattribution of arousal on helping by exposing subjects, prior to the emergency, to a stimulus that had no inherent arousing properties but which subjects believed could be a source of arousal. Thus, misattribution effects could be isolated from the residual excitation effects suggested in Sterling's study.

In particular, if, prior to an emergency, people are administered a placebo described as having side effects associated with arousal, they may misattribute arousal generated by the emergency to the pill. If misattribution occurs, then, according to the arousal model of bystander responsiveness, responding to the emergency would not be instrumental in reducing the unpleasant emotional state. Thus, subjects given the opportunity to misattribute the source of arousal to a placebo would be expected to intervene less readily than subjects administered a placebo described as having nonarousing, irrelevant side effects.

The findings of Nisbett and Schachter (1966), however, suggest that the degree of ambiguity in the situation may be a critical factor in mediating attributional effects. Their results indicate that there are limits to the extent that a person could misattribute arousal to an artificial source. The range is apparently bounded on the lower end by situations that elicit at least some arousal, and at the upper limit by situations that generate extremely high levels of arousal. Since unambiguous emergencies have been demonstrated to generate higher levels of arousal than ambiguous emergencies, it was expected that misattribution of arousal would be less likely in an unambiguous emergency and thus would have a less pronounced effect on bystander responsiveness.

As in the previous studies, each of the subjects ($N = 160$, females) was led to believe that she was in an ESP experiment. In particular, subjects were informed that a purpose of the study was to determine if certain substances could increase receptivity to ESP messages. Consequently, before administering a placebo, the experimenter provided the subjects with a list of symptoms that were supposedly related to the pill. For half of the subjects, the symptoms were associated with arousal (e.g., increase in the heart rate), while for the other half of the subjects they were described as nonarousal symptoms (e.g., dull headache). Ambiguity of the emergency was manipulated by the presence or absence of screams associated with the chair-falling accident. Finally, the race of the victim (either black or white) was manipulated.

The results suggested that the attribution manipulation was successful. Although subjects receiving the arousal placebo description did not differ from subjects with the nonarousal description in the total number of arousal symptoms reported, subjects who received the arousal placebo description attributed more arousal to the placebo alone ($p < .02$), more arousal to the placebo in part ($p < .01$), and less arousal to the emergency ($p = .05$) than subjects who believed that the placebo would have nonarousal side effects.

Consistent with the previous studies, the overall analysis of variance on the latency of intervention revealed a significant effect for the type of emergency ($p < .001$). Furthermore, in support of the proposed causal relationship between arousal and responsiveness, this analysis demonstrated that subjects receiving the arousal description of the placebo helped the victim significantly more slowly than did subjects with the nonarousal placebo description ($p < .02$). The Emergency × Placebo-Description interaction was not statistically significant when all the subjects were considered ($p < .16$).

In order to provide a test of the arousal model that was uncomplicated by race of victim effects, a test of simple effects was conducted involving only those subjects with a white victim. This analysis revealed a significant Emergency Type × Placebo-Description interaction ($p < .05$), as illustrated in Figure 4.2. Analogous to the findings of Nisbett and Schachter (1966), there was no difference in helping due to the opportunity to attribute arousal to the pill when the situation was unambiguous. However, in the ambiguous emergency situation, subjects given the opportunity to attribute their arousal to a placebo helped the victim significantly more slowly than did subjects not provided with this attributional alternative ($p < .01$). These results were indeed supportive of the proposed causal relationship between arousal and helping. Subjects helped faster when helping could be instrumental in reducing the unpleasant state of arousal.

Furthermore, the manipulation of attribution of arousal affected bystanders' motivation to respond to the emergency independent of their cognitive evaluation of the situation. Although the description of the

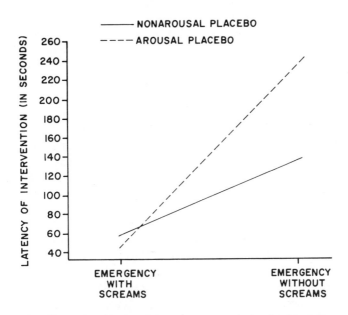

Figure 4.2. The effects of ambiguity of the emergency and placebo description on the latency of helping responses for subjects with a white victim. [From S. L. Gaertner & J. F. Dovidio, The sublety of white racism, arousal, and helping behavior. *Journal of Personality and Social Psychology*, 1977, 35, 691–707. Copyright 1977 by the American Psychological Association. Reprinted by permission.]

arousal symptoms associated with the placebo systematically influenced helping behavior, no comparable pattern was obtained for subjects' ratings of the seriousness of the situation, the amount of help needed by the victim, and the certainty that the victim was injured. Similarly, there was no consistent relationship between the extent that subjects attributed arousal symptoms to the placebo and their descriptions of the emergency situation. This result suggests that the differential degree of helping exhibited by subjects was not mediated solely by different perceptions of the situation. Misattribution appears to have directly influenced helping behavior. Thus, the pattern of results obtained in this and previous studies strongly supports the proposed causal relationship between arousal and bystander responsiveness to an emergency.

The consistency of our results over a period of years and across several different emergencies, cover stories, rooms, recording techniques, and experimenters increases our confidence in the reliability and validity of our findings. It is even more encouraging when other researchers provide additional support indicating the generalizability of our findings. For example, two studies involving less "emergency-like" situations have also demonstrated a relationship between arousal and helping. In the Krebs (1975) experiment, subjects observed a performer play a roulette game. Half of the subjects believed that the performer won money and received electric shock as he played the game; half believed that he performed a cognitive and motor skills task. The results revealed a relationship between subjects' physiological response, indexed by several different measures (e.g., GSR, heart rate, blood pulse volume), and subsequent helping behavior. Although this study does not necessarily demonstrate a causal relationship, it is entirely consistent with our findings. Furthermore, an earlier study by Harris and Huang (1973b) suggests that arousal may be a determinant of helping in minor crises as well. In their study, subjects, while working on mathematics problems, were exposed to noise described either as having arousing or nonarousing side effects. During the session, a female confederate with a bandaged knee entered the subject's room, began to ask a question, and then tripped over a chair. She then fell to the ground, gripping her knee and moaning. Similar to the results we obtained with respect to attribution and arousal, Harris and Huang (1973b) found that subjects who had the opportunity to misattribute their arousal to noise offered less help than subjects who believed the noise had only nonarousing effects. Therefore, the studies by Krebs and Harris and Huang, using quite different experimental contexts, yield results supportive of our own.

More recently, Coke, Batson, and McDavis (1978) investigated the effects of arousal and the nature of this arousal on nonemergency helping. In particular, they proposed a two-stage model of empathic motivation of helping. First, taking the perspective of a person in need increases a person's emotional response to a situation. Second, this empathic emotional response increases an individual's motivation to reduce the need of the other person. Thus, this model, like the one we have been exploring, suggests that a helping response is based on the need to reduce an emotional state.

In their first study, Coke *et al.* had subjects listen to a newscast about a college senior who had recently lost her parents in an automobile accident. One independent variable was a perspective-taking manipulation designed to affect subjects' emotional involvement in the situation. In an attempt to encourage emotional involvement, half of the subjects were asked to imagine themselves as the victimized senior; in order to limit emotional involvement, the other half of the subjects were instructed to concentrate on the broadcasting techniques. The second independent variable concerned the opportunity to misattribute arousal to a placebo. Prior to hearing the newscast, half the subjects were administered a placebo described as having arousing side effects and the other half of the subjects were given a pill described as producing relaxing symptoms. As Coke *et al.* had predicted, subjects who presumably experienced arousal due to taking the perspective of the victim and who did not have the opportunity to attribute arousal to the placebo helped the most. Furthermore, consistent with our theoretical framework, subjects who experienced arousal due to perspective-taking and who had the opportunity to misattribute arousal to the "arousal" placebo helped significantly less than did subjects with the "relaxing" placebo. It appears, then, that even in this less immediate situation of need, arousal that is attributed to the victim's need is a critical determinant of helping behavior.

Coke *et al.* also designed a second study to investigate the nature of the arousal subjects experience in a nonemergency situation. Subjects in this study heard an appeal for help from a graduate student in the School of Education. Since she could not afford to pay for subjects, she was asking for volunteers for her master's thesis research project. In addition, all subjects were attached by electrodes to a machine described as measuring GSR. Half the subjects then received false feedback during the newscast indicating that they were quite aroused; half the subjects received feedback suggesting no significant emotional reaction. At the end of the broadcast, subjects were asked how they felt from 1, indicating "not at all," to 7, indicating "extremely," on 23 items describing emotional states. Five of these items were related to "empathic concern": softhearted, empathic, warm, concerned, and compassionate. Three items were scored as related to "personal distress": alarmed, troubled, and upset. Finally, later on in the study subjects were asked to volunteer time for the graduate student.

The results revealed, as predicted, that subjects who experienced high-arousal feedback volunteered more time to help the graduate student than subjects who received low-arousal feedback. Furthermore, to investigate the nature of the arousal that affected subjects' behavior Coke *et al.* explored the relationships between the personal distress items and the empathic-concern items and helping. In this situation, the mean of the personal distress items was not significantly related to helping behavior. However, it is unlikely that subjects who were alarmed, troubled, or upset would attribute these rather extreme feelings to a graduate student's need for volunteer subjects. Unfortunately, there was no direct measure in this study of whether subjects attributed their emotional arousal to the need of the other or to the likely unexpected increase in apparent arousal as indicated by false GSR feedback. When the mean of the empathic-concern measures of emotional arousal was analyzed, though, a relationship with helping was obtained ($r = +.59$). Subjects who experienced greater emotional arousal that could be attributed to the other's need were more likely to help. Although Coke *et al.* interpret their results within a different theoretical framework, we see their results as compatible with our own. Emotional arousal that was presumably attributed to the need of another was directly related to subjects' responsiveness.

Summary

Although the label of psychophysiological arousal experienced by witnesses of the need of another person may differ with the context, the relationship between arousal and helping seems quite generalizable. It is further encouraging that the effectiveness of the emotional response for eliciting help is not limited to such unpleasant emotional experiences as disgust, shame, and fear; more subtle emotions such as concern and compassion also increase responsiveness.

Chapter 5

Costs, Rewards, and
the Helping Decision

The idea that actions are in part determined by actors' perceptions of their potential costs and rewards is hardly original. The application of this "economic man" idea in the area of helping behavior has been recognized and used as a post hoc explanation for nonintervention in many pieces of research. Beginning with three studies in 1969 (Epstein & Hornstein; Piliavin, Rodin, & Piliavin; Wagner & Wheeler), it has also been manipulated. In this chapter we will examine the current status of our knowledge concerning the effects of costs and rewards on helping behavior.

Propositions III and IV of the model of helping behavior that provides the framework for this book deal with the impact of costs and rewards on helping. In particular, Proposition III stated that the bystander will choose that response to an emergency that will most rapidly and most completely reduce his or her arousal, incurring in the process as few net costs (costs minus rewards) as possible. Proposition IV stated that there will be (*a*) special circumstances that give rise to and (*b*) specific personality types who engage in rapid, impulsive, noncalculated "irrational" helping or escape behavior following observation of an emergency. Our interest in the impact of costs and rewards originated in past work in the area of deviance (Briar & Piliavin, 1965; Piliavin, Hardyck, & Vadum, 1968; Piliavin, Vadum, & Hardyck, 1969). The similarity between the process of making a

decision to commit a crime and that of deciding to intervene to help someone may not initially be obvious, but we believe it is there. In both cases,
we feel that the evidence is strong that most acts are committed after a rational (though not necessarily conscious and deliberate) decision process in
which the consequences of acting versus not acting are weighed and the
rewards from the action are deemed to be worth the potential costs.
However, in both areas, some acts are committed "on impulse," "in the
heat of the moment," under circumstances that strongly suggest that a less
than complete assessment of the potential costs of the action have been
made. In the crime and delinquency area, these circumstances are recognized in the law as justifying a plea of reduced responsibility, temporary in-
sanity, etc. Temporary states of the person (drug-induced or brought on by
passions) are predominant reasons behind such pleas. Permanent states are
also used, such as "mental disease or deficiency," the XYY syndrome, or
the "menstrual distress syndrome."

This chapter and the following chapter will examine the basic
cost–reward proposition and the relationship of social factors to costs.
Then, in Chapter 7, we will move to Proposition IV and address the possibility that certain situations predispose most individuals to disregard
aspects of the cost–reward considerations and engage in "impulsive"
responses to help-requiring situations.

The Nature of Costs and Rewards

As we stressed in our Chapter 2 we are, like most social psychologists,
phenomenologists at the core. With W. I. and D. S. Thomas (1928) we
believe that "If men [sic] define situations as real, they are real in their consequences [p. 572]." Thus, our analysis is based on costs as perceived by
the bystander, not as they might "objectively" be assessed by some uninvolved social scientist. This conceptualization naturally leads to some
difficulty in attempting to predict from the model. As a result, most researchers in this as in other social psychological areas attempt to set up
situations in which "most people's" assessments will be similar. One can
then assume that much of the variability in response to those "clear" differences in manipulated costs is attributable to differences in interpretation.
It is a rare study in which attempts are actually made to assess the
bystander's interpretations of the situation in any meaningful way.

Although it is somewhat of an oversimplification, in our model we
have set up two general categories of potential costs and rewards for the
bystander: those that are contingent upon his or her making a direct helping response and those that would result were the victim to receive no help.

As is the usage in economics, costs include the value of rewards foregone. The first category, personal costs *for* helping, involves negative outcomes imposed directly on the benefactor and includes (but is not restricted to) the following: physical danger; effort expenditure; embarrassment; exposure to disgusting experiences such as seeing or having contact with blood and other body fluids, wounds, seizures, and deformities; close proximity to disliked others or members of disliked groups; feelings of inadequacy if help proves ineffective; time lost; and the value of rewards contingent upon activities that could have been performed in the time taken up in helping. Rewards for helping include feelings of efficacy, admiration from others, thanks from the victim, fame, awards, or possibly money. Both costs and rewards for helping indirectly (i.e., by calling the police, by drawing the victim's attention to the problem, etc.) will generally be less (specifically, physical danger and effort expenditure are generally lower in indirect helping, and feelings of efficacy, admiration, fame, etc. will also be less likely), but many of the same factors are involved.

The second general category of costs, namely costs attendant upon the bystander's knowledge that the victim has received *no* help, conceptually contains two subcategories. Most researchers do not operationally separate these subcategories, but we will attempt to do so in our discussion. There is first a set of "personal costs" for *not* helping, that is, negative outcomes imposed directly on the bystander for failure to intervene. These include self-blame for one's inaction, public censure, recriminations from the victim, and in some countries even prosecution as a criminal (Ratcliffe, 1966). These "personal costs" are the "flip side" of the set of rewards *for* helping discussed above.

The second subcategory of costs for the victim receiving no help is unrelated to bystanders' actions on behalf of the victim, but depends solely on their knowledge that the victim is continuing to suffer. In particular, these "empathy costs" involve internalizing the need or suffering of the victim and include a continued and perhaps increasing level of unpleasant arousal related to the perceived distress of the victim and associated feelings of inequity or unfairness (Walster & Piliavin, 1972).[1] Both personal

---

[1] Theoretically, "costs *for* helping" could also be subdivided into "personal" (directly affecting the bystander) and "empathy" (affecting the bystander through the internalization of the other's needs) costs. However, we have decided not to present a formal discussion of empathy costs *for* helping, since it has received neither prior empirical nor previous theoretical attention. This category, though, could exist in practice. For example, an individual may be inhibited from helping based on the belief that assistance could cause the *other* person embarrassment. See the sex difference in helping a depressed other (Enzle & Harvey, 1979) for a possible place where this could be occurring.

costs and empathy costs are strongly influenced by personal characteristics of the bystander: the former by the person's feelings of personal moral obligation (Schwartz, 1977) and the latter by the individual's tendency to empathize (Stotland, Mathews, Sherman, Hansson, & Richardson, 1978). These costs for the victim receiving no help are associated with the subjective aspect of arousal.

The Role of Costs and Rewards in the Decision Process

The original model with which we began our work assumed that the bystander first notices an emergency and is to some degree aroused as a result of his or her observation of it. At this point the bystander (if he or she is not the impulsive type who has already responded) enters into a decision process involving a matrix of perceived costs and rewards like that shown in Table 5.1. Several specific predictions can be made by reference to this table. First, given that a perceived real need for help exists, as costs for direct intervention decrease, the probability of direct intervention increases. This is the straightforward "economic man" model prediction. As

Table 5.1

Predicted Modal Responses of Moderately Aroused Observer as a Joint Function of Costs for Direct Help and Costs for No Help to Victim[a]

| | | Costs for direct help | |
		Low	High
Costs for no help to victim	High	Direct intervention	Indirect intervention or ⟶ / Redefinition of the situation, disparagement of victim, etc., which lowers costs for no help, allowing
	Low	Variable: will be largely a function of perceived norms in situation	Leaving the scene, ignoring, denial

[a] From J. A. Piliavin and I. M. Piliavin. The effect of blood on reactions to a victim. Journal of Personality and Social Psychology, 1972, 23, 253–261. Copyright 1972 by the American Psychological Association. Reprinted by permission.

costs for intervention increase, not only does the probability of direct intervention decrease, the variability of bystanders' responses should increase. Presumably, with at least moderate arousal and with costs for no help relatively high, the bystander has a need to do something; yet, high costs for direct intervention preclude that response. In the case of high costs, bystanders should be in a very strong conflict between their need to help and their fear or distaste for doing it, or, in some cases, the physical impossibility of it. Our prediction is that they can solve this conflict either by seeking an "institutional helper" (policeman, doctor, etc.) or by psychologically altering the costs attendant upon the victim receiving no help. Bystanders can do this by redefining the situation as not an emergency or the victim as someone who deserves no help. These redefinitions lower costs for no help and allow bystanders to leave the scene or to return to their interrupted activity.

A second straightforward prediction, also based on the "economic man" model, is that as costs for the victim receiving no help increase, the probability of the bystander helping in some way increases. However, this prediction probably holds only at low levels of cost for helping. In this connection, it must be mentioned that the reward value of helping to the bystander may be different depending on the method of intervention selected. Silverman (1974) has suggested that, particularly for men, direct intervention will generate large ego rewards, due to the confirmation provided for a "John Wayne" self-image. Indirect intervention does not provide the same "kick." It should be added here that indirect intervention is also likely to be slower. Bystanders faced with a high-cost situation with a very needy victim can decrease their own arousal faster by derogating the victim or by reinterpreting the situation as one in which help is not needed than by indirect help. Thus at high levels of cost for helping, one might find relatively less help as victim's need and its contingent cost for not helping increase. These are empirical considerations.

The remainder of this chapter will be organized as follows: First, we will discuss research that either can be reconceptualized as involving differential costs for direct intervention or that was specifically designed to test the effects of such costs. This section will be structured by type of costs (e.g., danger, time lost, money expended, etc.). Second, we will examine research that relates to the impact of costs for the victim receiving no help. Research on victim "deservingness," assignment of responsibility to the bystander, and surveillance will be reviewed. We will not deal with the issue of "diffusion of responsibility" and group influence effects. That aspect of costs will be dealt with in Chapter 6: The Social Context of Helping. Finally, the few studies in which both costs for and for not helping have been varied will be examined, and the specific predictions concerning the "high–high" cell of the matrix will be addressed.

Costs for Helping: Personal Costs for Helping

PSYCHOLOGICAL AVERSION

The first subway study (Piliavin, Rodin, & Piliavin, 1969) was not designed as a test of the cost–reward postulate of the model. Rather, the model was developed largely as a result of the findings from that study. Thus the data can only be seen as consistent with the model in that context. Furthermore, costs for helping, costs for not helping, empathy, arousal, and attribution of responsibility for the victim's plight are all hopelessly confounded in the design. The "cane" victim in that study received far more help ($p < .001$) than did the "drunk." It would be hard to argue against the notion that helping a drunk would be more costly (in terms of effort, disgust, possible danger, embarrassment, etc.) than helping an obviously infirm individual. Unfortunately, the cane–drunk manipulation can also be interpreted as a manipulation of costs for the victim receiving no help. A drunk is typically seen as responsible for his own plight and "only drunk," that is, not in a truly needy state. Perceived costs for his receiving no help should therefore be less (see Schopler & Matthews, 1965). Bystander response to the victim's plight can readily be that of redefining the situation as not an emergency and denigrating the victim. Another finding of the Piliavin, Rodin, and Piliavin (1969) study also supports this latter hypothesis. The researchers found that helping is more frequent and more rapid to a drunk of one's own race than to a drunk of the opposite race. A not unreasonable interpretation would be that there is greater uncertainty concerning the way an out-group member might act, particularly one who already evidences some lack of control, and the negative affect felt in closely approaching him constitutes a cost for helping. This finding however, is also subject to another interpretation within the model. That is, by Proposition I, arousal should be greater for an emergency occurring to an in-group member.

The Piliavin and Piliavin (1972) "blood study" was intended to clear up the confounding of costs for helping and costs for the victim receiving no help that was present in the previous study. In this experiment, all victims were white and used canes. On half of the trials, the victim as he fell let a thin trickle of what appeared to be blood slip from his mouth; on the other half of the trials he did not. It was assumed by the investigators that the presence of blood would increase the costs of assisting the victim, since contact with blood for most people is unpleasant. Thus the "blood" condition is the high-cost condition and the "no-blood" condition is the low-cost. It was further assumed that the presence of blood would, in addition, either increase the costs of not helping the victim (since blood is generally regarded as a sign of seriousness) or, at the minimum, not decrease such costs. An increase in costs for not helping in the model leads to more help, while an increase in costs for helping should lead to less help. Thus, a confounding of this sort would work against our hypothesis rather than in concert with it, as in the 1969 study. The results revealed that the bloody Philadelphia victim is responded to more rapidly than the drunk in New York, indicating that there are more deterrents for helping the drunk, but the bloody victim is also responded to more slowly than the nonbloody victim, showing a significantly greater cost for helping a bleeding victim (see Figure 5.1). A suggestive anecdote recorded during the "blood study" involved two teenage girls who got up on seeing the victim fall; one then said, "Oh, he's bleeding!" and both sat down again.

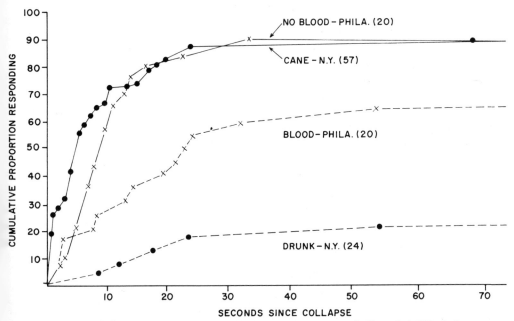

Figure 5.1. Direct intervention as a function of time up to 70 seconds. [From J. A. Piliavin & I. M. Piliavin, The effects of blood on reactions to a victim. *Journal of Personality and Social Psychology,* 1972, *23,* 253–261. Copyright 1972 by the American Psychological Association. Reprinted by permission.]

The third study in the "subway series" was designed to eliminate the remaining possible confounding of two kinds of costs for helping in the blood study. Disgust, fear, or discomfort felt at the sight of blood might be only one way that the manipulation had increased costs for helping. A second kind of cost could be an "incompetence cost." That is, the blood might have suggested to some bystanders that the victim's condition was a more serious one, leading them to feel that they would be unable to help successfully. This interpretation would lead to higher perceived costs for intervention in the "blood" condition. Nevertheless, we wanted to pursue the idea of "disgust costs," or, at least of costs that were simply related to the act of approaching the victim closely. We thus decided to use a physical stigma not suggestive of any kind of serious medical problem, but one that would lead people to avoid interaction with the afflicted person (Goffman, 1963).

This third study (Piliavin, Piliavin, & Rodin, 1975) actually used two independent cost manipulations and a manipulation of presence of a medically competent individual who could serve as someone to whom responsibility could be diffused. The stigma used as one form of costs for helping was a "port wine stain" birthmark (applied by the use of stage makeup) on the victim's left cheek. The other cost manipulation (which proved ineffective) was the point on the subway run at which the collapse of the victim occurred: just before the last stop (thus potentially causing all passengers in the car to consider that they might lose time from their end-of-journey pursuits were they to help) or just before the third from the last stop (presumably causing only those who were going to get out there to consider that they would be inconvenienced by helping). On half of the trials, an "intern" was near the spot where the victim fell. On the other trials the confederate bystander was in the same location wearing ordinary street clothes. The stigma manipulation had a significant overall impact on the proportion of trials on which the victim was helped. The unmarked victim received help on 86.4% of 59 trials, while the stigmatized victim was helped on only 60.7% of 61 trials.

Two other studies have employed a physical stigma in an emergency, crisis, or problem situation, one by Samerotte and Harris (1976) and the other by Ungar (1979). Samerotte and Harris had a confederate drop a stack of envelopes in a shopping mall under three conditions: normal, injured (large forearm bandage), and injured and stigmatized (bandage plus eye patch and theatrical scar). The presence of the bandage increased helping over the "normal" level by 65% to 27.5%; the eye patch and scar reduced it again to the "normal" level. Ungar had confederates who did or did not wear an eye patch ask people for directions on a subway platform. Another confederate then gave incorrect directions. The results indicated that subjects were less likely to help the stigmatized person than the nonstigmatized person when helping required chasing the victim who was already walking away. In summary, the presence of blood or physically stigmatizing conditions can depress helping behavior. Combining these studies with the results of the initial "cane–drunk" comparison provides good support for "disgust costs" as a deterrent to helping.

POSSIBLE PHYSICAL HARM

A closely related cost, and one that was likely also to have been involved in the "drunk" condition of the first subway study, is possible physical harm. In many real-life emergencies this is an important deterrent to bystander intervention. In the real-life incident that began the upsurge in social scientists' interest in helping in emergencies—the Kitty Genovese incident—it was clearly a major factor. There are difficulties involved in manipulating physical danger in such a way as to both convince subjects of the reality of the incident and protect their safety. Thus all research that has manipulated physical costs such as pain or potential assault have been done in laboratories or at least in closely patrolled hallways in academic buildings. The problems of external validity are thus clearly present. Furthermore, most research has not involved interpersonal threat, but rather willingness to accept electric shock as the cost of helping another experimental participant.

Midlarsky and Midlarsky (1973) manipulated costs by the level of shock subjects would have to take in the process of helping another presumed subject finish his work. The work consisted of moving various metal objects on an electrically charged surface, and the dependent variable was the number of items the subject touched. The effect of costs was significant but accounted for relatively little variance (2%) in comparison to other variables (e.g., competence explains 45% of the variance). The authors suggest that the difference in shock level was probably perceived as relatively insignificant. It should also be noted that the crisis can also be seen as greater at the higher shock levels, potentially confounding bystander arousal and perceived costs for the victim receiving no help with the cost manipulation in such a way as to perhaps cancel out the impact of costs.

McGovern (1976) used an experimental situation in which male subjects could prevent a female confederate from having to take a shock by pushing a particular button. When the costs for performing this response was to receive the shock themselves, subjects were less likely to push the button. However, when the confederate specifically asked them to do so, the cost effect disappeared. Both of these studies suggest that pain is a deterrent to helping, a less than remarkable finding. In contrast, though, Clark and Word (1974) found no difference in response to a clear, dangerous, and apparently very arousing electrical emergency in which the victim was still in contact with presumably live wires and the same clear emergency in which the victim was free of the wires. Nearly 100% helping occurred in both conditions. Had the dangerous emergency been real, the considerable proportion of helpers who responded by touching the victim might well have been killed. (This finding will be discussed in more detail in Chapter 7, where we cover impulsive helping.)

In a study by Piliavin, Piliavin, and Krutsch (1973, unpublished) and two studies by Piliavin, Piliavin, and Trudell (1974, unpublished), which are referred to in Chapters 3 and 4, subjects watched arousing or nonarousing films and then were exposed to one of two emergencies. One was a "fallen woman" emergency, in which costs for helping were minimal. The other was a theft followed by a struggle between a male and the same female victim; costs for intervention in that case would involve possibly confronting this demonstrably violent individual. The differences between rates of intervention in the "fall" and "thief" conditions of all three studies were highly significant ($p < .001$ in all cases). Suspicion was uniformly higher in the thief conditions, as well. This result does not necessarily invalidate the thief condition. Recall that Latané and Darley (1970) have demonstrated that subjects who were made to feel responsible for two children playing next door thought the violent fight the children got into was a fake, while subjects who did not have responsibility thought it was real. Our model suggests that under high costs for helping, the preferred mechanism for handling one's arousal will be to distort the situation in such a way as to perceive it as a nonemergency requiring no action. Since the two emergencies in the Piliavin et al. studies were not the same (as they were in Latané and Darley) we cannot argue forcefully that our finding of greater suspicion in the thief condition is a response to perceived responsibility under high costs. We believe that to be the case, however. In contrast to the previous findings, Austin (1979) found no effect of the specifically manipulated size of a thief on intervention.

Finally, the literature contains three studies involving physical assaults that bear careful scrutiny because of the current increased concern over the recently discovered high rates of rape and wife beating. Borofsky, Stollak, and Messé (1971), in an "as if" study which was, however, apparently compelling, exposed subjects to a psychodrama involving a fight that appears to "get out of hand." The fight was between same sex or opposite sex individuals; in the male–female fight, sometimes the male was the aggressor, sometimes the female. The rate of intervention was uniformly high except by male subjects in the fights in which a man was attacking a woman.

Shotland and Straw (1976) have followed up this initial finding with a series of five experiments. The first study involved a highly believable staged fight in which a man attacked a woman in an elevator, which opened on the floor where subjects had been left alone to finish an experiment. The major independent variable was whether the couple were presented as strangers ("Get away from me, I don't know you.") or as married ("I don't know why I ever married you."). A total of only 4 of 21 subjects intervened in the "married" fight, while 13 of 20 took action with the strangers, a highly significant difference. Male and female subjects were equally likely to intervene, and direct intervention was the most likely response.

The remaining four studies involved showing videotapes of the fights to other groups of subjects, in order to come up with an interpretation of the results. Suggestive findings include the following:

1. The possibility of injury to the woman is perceived as greater in the "stranger" fight (higher costs for not helping).
2. Both men and women expect that intervention would result in the potential helper being attacked more often in the "married" fight (higher costs for helping).
3. Subjects of both sexes feel more responsibility to intervene and think the victim wants their help more in the "stranger" fight (higher costs for not helping).
4. When videotapes are shown in which reference to the nature of the relationship between the combatants has been edited out, 67% of subjects spontaneously suggest that the couple have some relationship.

In this connection, a third study should be mentioned here briefly. Anderson (1974) found 100% intervention by both individuals and groups of subjects in a simulated rape which was clearly an attack by a stranger.

The results of these three pieces of research are clear. In cases of physical assault by a man on a woman, costs of intervention are perceived as high. Bystanders tend to assume that there is a relationship between the people, unless it is clear that there is none. Other costs of intervention are then conjured up that justify not intervening in an intimate relationship. The results of the Shotland and Straw research do not show a difference between males and females in this regard; the original Borofsky et al. study did. The implications for the public attitudes concerning the rights of married women are disturbing (see Gelles, 1972; Martin, 1977).

EFFORT AND TIME

The economic definition of costs includes "rewards foregone." Helping is an act that takes time. Thus, it is possible that helpers will lose benefits that could have accrued to them were they to have continued on their way to whatever appointments they had. Only three emergency studies and one nonemergency study have investigated the impact of potential time loss on helping. As noted above, the Piliavin, Piliavin, and Rodin (1975) study employed a manipulation intended to involve such costs. There was no effect on rate or speed of helping as a function of the manipulation.

Darley and Batson (1973), on the other hand, found a highly significant effect of a more specific "hurry" manipulation. Subjects who were told that they had ample time before they had to deliver a speech were far more likely to help a person slumped in a doorway on their route than were those who were told they could barely make it to the appointment on time. Batson, Cochran, Biederman, Blosser, Ryan, and Vogt (1978) manipulated both the importance of the experiment to which the subject was going and how late he was. The intent of the study was to test whether it was the self-preoccupation associated with being in a hurry or rather the conflict over whom to help (the experimenter or the victim) that leads to less helping when people are rushed. The data rather conclusively demonstrate that hurry leads to less help only when subjects are going to an important appointment. Thus it appears, interpreting these data in cost terms, that the effect is due to the costs that are attendant upon being late to the appointment. Although the data do not clearly rule out lack of attention or self-preoccupation as possible determinants of the "hurry" effect under some circumstances, they do provide strong support for the "rewards foregone" or "costs incurred" interpretation. Using a nonemergency situation, Feldman and Rezmovic (1979) found, in analyzing various characteristics of the 72 cities in which they rang a phone booth until someone answered, that the only significant predictor of answering was the "degree of movement" of the population. They interpret their results as a "hurry" effect.

The conclusion we draw from these studies is that the major cost in the Batson "hurry" research is the loss of the experimenter's good will or social approval. In the subway study, it may well have been that most subjects just were not in a hurry or, if they were, what they were hurrying to would not involve any great loss of social rewards. It is also possible that the time to help the subway victim was perceived as minimal (which in actuality, it usually was). The evidence from the two Batson studies is convincing; the time and effort that would have to go into providing assistance to another person is a factor in whether aid will be offered. The findings of Feldman and Rezmovic (1979) are also consistent with this interpretation.

MONEY EXPENDED OR FOREGONE

Anyone who conducts psychology experiments for a living knows that people are more willing to help experimenters—by being subjects—if they are paid for doing so. (They are also more likely to volunteer the less time the study will take and the less pain and anguish it will involve.) Very few studies of helping behavior, however, seem to have directly manipulated money to be won or lost as a cost manipulation, and none has been done using a situation one would call an emergency.

Wagner and Wheeler (1969) solicited a $25 donation from 144 Navy enlisted men for one of two needs, with the cost manipulation involving a one-time deduction from the next week's paycheck (high cost), versus a one-dollar-per-week deduction, for 25 weeks (low cost). A modeling manipulation was also used. For our purpose here, the major finding was a highly significant effect of the cost variable representing about a 50% increase in the amount donated under low cost. It should be noted here that the effect is one of perceived costs, since the total amount to be deducted was the same in both cases. We know from much research in experimental and developmental psychology, however, that the value of a reward in the immediate present is psychologically much greater than the value of the same reward in the future. The same is apparently true of costs.

Other research using money has dealt not with the amount of money requested from a helper but rather the amount of reward foregone. Schaps (1972) employed as a cost variable how many customers were present in a shoe store and used salesclerks as subjects. (Time spent with one customer means commissions lost from other sales if there are so many customers that one cannot help them all.) There was a nearly significant overall effect of costs on an index of helpfulness made up of the number of pairs of shoes shown, the number of trips to the stockroom, and the time spent with the customer.

Bleda, Bleda, Byrne, and White (1976) found a highly significant effect of potential loss of money on likelihood of turning in a cheater. Subjects in a "cooperative" condition, whose fate was linked to that of the cheater, were far less likely to turn him or her in than were those who were independent or in a competitive relationship. There are two other studies involving money costs (Epstein & Hornstein, 1969; Piliavin, Piliavin, & Broll, 1974, unpublished), which will be discussed in the last section of this chapter because they also involve costs for the victim receiving no help.

POTENTIAL SOCIAL SANCTIONS OR
LOSS OF SOCIAL REWARDS

From a very early age, many of the most rewarding experiences we have are social, and the most severe punishments can come from withdrawal of love and social approval. Violation of rules generally carries with it social disapproval, and sometimes other sanctions as well. Staub (1970a, 1971, 1974) investigated the effect of giving permission or forbidding subjects to enter an adjacent room on subsequent level of helping in an emergency that occurred there. In particular, Staub (1970b) explored developmental trends in emergency helping behavior. Upon finding a cur-vilinear trend, with kindergarteners and sixth-graders helping the least and first-, second-, and fourth-graders helping the most, instead of the expected linear increase in prosocial behavior, Staub proposed that increased socialization involving prohibitive norms may have inhibited sixth-graders from interrupting their task and helping the victim. Consequently, in a series of studies (Staub, 1971; 1974) he explored the effects of implicit and explicit rules on bystander intervention. For example, in one study (Staub, 1971), seventh-graders heard a crash in an adjacent room accompanied by the cries, sobs, and the call for assistance of a 7-year-old girl. Consistent with Staub's theoretical framework, 50% of the subjects who had earlier received explicit permission to enter the adjoining room offered direct or indirect help to the victim while only 15% of the subjects who received no instructions concerning the room helped. Similarly, in a second study of seventh-graders, students who received explicit permission to enter the room exhibited more help (91%) than subjects who received no informa-tion (36%) or previous explicit prohibitions (46%). Staub therefore con-cluded that explicit rules could significantly affect bystander responsiveness and that no information for children may be functionxlly equivalent to prohibition. With adults, however, Staub (1971) found a slightly different pattern. Although subjects in the permission group (83%) helped more often than subjects in the prohibition group (61%), the results of the no-information group (89%) most closely resembled the permission group. Nevertheless, as Staub (1974) articulates, the general pattern of findings in-dicates that both children and adults "are highly sensitive to the explicitly stated expectations of others and respond to these eapectations even if, as a consequence, they deviate from presumably socially highly valued norms which prescribe that one should help those who need help [pp. 316–317]."

Three other studies have found support for this effect of having per-mission to engage in the helping act or being prohibited from it on rate or speed of helping. Ashton and Severy (1976) found faster intervention in a "falling bookcase" emergency among those given permission to go next door. McGovern (1976) employed a "social threat" for intervening to pre-vent shocks to the confederate. As with threat of shock, as noted earlier, this prohibition was effective until subjects received a direct request from the confederate to intervene. Finally, Pavlos (1971), in a study of children's response to a feigned heart attack on the part of a teacher, found a signifi-cant effect of reward (manipulated by emphasizing that leaving the room would *not* prohibit them from winning candy bars) on helping.

Another type of possible negative social sanction for helping is blame for help incompetently offered. Competence, as a personal trait, is related to helping, as we will show in Chapter 8. Situations may also vary, however, in the extent to which they suggest the need for special abilities and thus promise to provide negative outcomes to one who might incompetently intervene. The difference in rate of intervention in the "blood" versus the "no-blood" conditions of Piliavin and Piliavin (1972) could be interpreted along these lines just as easily as along the "disgust costs" suggested earlier. Consistent with this possibility, Staub and Baer (1974, Experiment 1) found less help to a victim of an apparent heart attack than to a victim of a knee problem under conditions where escape from the situation was easy. In a nonemergency helping study, Benson (1978) manipulated both potential social approval and the risk of failure and measured the rate of volunteering to make "poll-taking" phone calls. As predicted, there were main effects for both variables, such that the most helping was obtained under low risk of failure and high opportunity for social approval. Other than these studies, there is no direct evidence for the role of possible blame for helping incompetently on rate of intervention. In general, the research discussed in this section suggests that potential social sanctions for inappropriate or incompetent intervention in the crises of other can operate as a cost for helping.

Potential Rewards for Helping

So far, we have discussed only costs in our presentation of the cost–reward postulate. Are there no rewards to helping? One of the strongest sets of findings in social psychology are those linking similarity of beliefs, shared group membership, and physical attractiveness to liking. It is assumed that interacting with liked others is more rewarding than interacting with disliked others. Thus the findings, to be discussed in the next chapter, regarding in-group versus out-group membership and helping, cross-sex helping, racial effects on helping, and physical attractiveness and pleasantness of the person in need of help can all be viewed as involving different degrees of reward for helping. That is, the same characteristics that lead to a greater likelihood of empathizing with the victim should also lead to more reward when one helps.

Only a few studies have looked at other rewards in the helping situation. In a nonemergency study (Wilson & Kahn, 1975), subjects were offered one of two levels of monetary compensation for agreeing to stuff envelopes or make phone interviews. There was only a borderline effect of this variable; furthermore, the effect was found only among female subjects. Bickman (1976) varied the pleasantness of a supermarket clerk in a study of shoplifting. The manipulation did not significantly influence the rate of reporting the crime (although the rate was lowest with a "nasty" clerk) but it did affect to whom the subject reported the theft if she chose to report it. Eight of nine reporting subjects in the "pleasant" condition reported to the clerk whose behavior was being varied rather than to other store personnel. In the control and "nasty" conditions 5 of 11 and 2 of 6 helpers reported to her rather than telling someone else or intervening directly. A second study in the same research report showed no effect of the pleasantness of a person who was dealt with on the phone on the likelihood of reporting a crime. These data suggest that the unpleasantness of the clerk did not deter reporting. It altered the form that the reporting took where there was choice; where there was no choice, it did not affect the response. Katz, Farber, Glass, Lucido, and Emswiller (1978) manipulated interpersonal pleasantness and handicap and found that with the physically normal confederate helping (agreeing to be interviewed) was greater with a pleasant demeanor. An inexplicable reversal was found in the handicapped condition.

McGovern, Ditzian, and Taylor (1975) investigated the effect of positive reinforcement for a helping response on subsequent helping. In this study, a female confederate asked male subjects to take a shock for her. If they did, she said "thank you" in the reinforcement condition and said nothing in the control condition. The majority, 75% of the subjects, did take the shock when asked. On 11 subsequent trials, thanked subjects were far more likely to volunteer to take shock in place of the confederate than were those who had not been rewarded for their prior help. Thanked subjects also later rated the confederate as more fair, good-humored, good, and brave than did unrewarded subjects.

Finally Paulhus, Shaffer, and Downing (1977) found an increase in behavioral intentions to continue giving blood among "veteran" blood donors whose altruistic motives had been made salient. This effect was not found among first-time donors. Donors read paragraphs that discussed either altruistic motives, self-serving motives, both kinds of motives, or neither, before giving blood. After donating, they were asked their intentions regarding future giving. The interpretation of the results of this study is that the primary reward for giving blood, for prior donors, is the satisfaction of altruistic motives. When these are made salient, giving blood is more rewarding and the intention to give again is strengthened. The effect cannot occur for first-time donors because they have no previous experience of reward in the situation of which to be reminded.

Overall, the results reported in this section provide strong support for the part of Proposition III that states that helping will be reduced when costs for helping increase and increased when rewards are provided. We will now turn to studies involving costs for the victim receiving no help.

Costs for the Victim Receiving No Help

What do we expect to find as costs for the victim receiving no help increase? Recall the matrix presented earlier in this chapter; the effect of costs for the victim receiving no help will depend upon the level of costs for helping. When costs *for* helping are low to moderate, helping should increase as costs for the victim receiving no help increase. With high costs for helping, however, victims are predicted to receive indirect help or no help at all. In the latter case, the arousal engendered by observing the victim's distress will likely be handled through derogation of the victim or other reinterpretations of the situation as "not an emergency," or one that is not one's responsibility. Ironically, then, those situations in which need is greatest will often be those in which help is least likely to be received. In this section, we will discuss the overall effects of costs for the victim receiving no help without regard to this distinction. Most of the research, after all, has not involved really high levels of cost to the potential bystander. In a later section we will consider studies in which the potential for high costs of both kinds exists. We are also omitting, in this section, discussion of research that has systematically varied both kinds of costs. Again, those studies will be dealt with later in the chapter.

In discussing costs for the victim receiving no help, we will attempt to consider the two subcategories, empathy costs and personal costs, separately, although in practice the same factor could affect both simultaneously. Empathy costs, costs to the bystander associated with internalizing the need or suffering of the victim, are often related to the unpleasant arousal state experienced by witnessing an emergency or crisis of another. Consequently, empathy costs are affected by all of the factors discussed in Chapter 3 where we dealt with arousal and in Chapter 4 where we specifically examined the effects of severity, clarity, and closeness to the victim. In general, anything that increases the impact of the victim's distress on the bystander will of necessity also increase the empathy costs attendant upon the victim receiving no help. The more clear and more severe the emergency is, the more unpleasant and costly the continued suffering of the victim will be for the bystander. Severity and clarity, though, may also affect personal costs for not helping, that is, the costs or sanctions imposed directly on the bystander for not intervening in the crisis of another. For example, self-blame or censure from others is likely to be greater for not helping a person who has been physically injured than for not intervening in behalf of a person who dropped groceries on the sidewalk. This "problem" of multiple effects of some independent variables has forced us to reconsider certain aspects of the original model to which we will return in

Chapter 10. A discussion of the effects of severity, clarity, and closeness will not be included here since they have been considered in detail previously.

There is one other situational factor that we see as affecting both "empathy costs" and "personal costs" for the victim receiving no help. This factor is the "deservingness" or "innocence" of the victim. Victim innocence or deservingness may have two effects. We are more likely to identify with deserving victims, leading to higher arousal and higher empathy costs. Furthermore, with blameless and truly innocent victims it is difficult to employ victim derogation as a means of evading responsibility and reducing personal costs.

There are also situational factors that influence "personal costs" alone. These include all of the factors that focus responsibility on an individual or assist him or her in evading responsibility for action. Being officially designated as one "in charge" is the most obvious of these. Also, surveillance by others who cannot help can make one more attentive to social norms and thus either increase or decrease the "personal costs" for not intervening. Knowledge of the presence of others who could also help can allow "diffusion of responsibility" and thus decrease "personal costs." Finally, actually being in the presence of other bystanders adds further complications, since combined with surveillance and the possibility of diffusion is a social influence effect; one bystander can use the inaction of the others to help define the incident as not a crisis, thus removing all responsibility to act. These social effects will be discussed in Chapter 6.

EFFECTS OF VICTIM DESERVINGNESS AND NEED

Most of the research on victim deservingness has been done in non-emergency, laboratory research settings (e.g., Schopler & Matthews, 1965). Many victim characteristics to be discussed in Chapter 7 could also be interpreted in terms of "deservingness" and could be brought in here. We will refer only to a few examples that seem particularly clear. First, there is the original "drunk versus cane" manipulation from the first subway study (Piliavin, Rodin, & Piliavin, 1969). Drunks can certainly be written off as less deserving of our help than the handicapped. As noted in an earlier chapter, however, deservingness is confounded with costs for helping in that study.

Several studies have also explored the effect of the dependency of the victim on helping behavior (e.g., Berkowitz & Daniels, 1963, 1964; Clark, 1976; Daniels & Berkowitz, 1963; Gruder & Cook, 1971; Harris & Meyer, 1973; Midlarsky, 1971; Pandey & Griffitt, 1977; Schaps, 1972). These experiments typically demonstrate a direct relationship between dependency and helping. For example, Baker and Reitz (1978), using a wrong number technique, found that "blind" confederates received more help than "non-blind" confederates and that high-dependent individuals were helped more than low-dependent persons. Two additional studies conducted in super-markets manipulated "legitimacy of need" and observed another shopper's willingness to help by providing 10 cents (Bickman & Kamzan, 1973) or a salesclerk's willingness to help by allowing the person to have an item when they were 30 cents short on the price (Field, 1974). In both cases, help was less likely when the item was less needed (cookie dough, beer) than when it was more necessary (milk, antiseptic ointment for a burned baby). Both empathic arousal and personal costs for not helping could be involved in greater willingness to help those perceived as having the "legitimate" needs.

There are two other articles to be discussed under the heading of vic-tim need. In two experiments, Enzle and Harvey (1979) manipulated victim's mood and studied the response of subjects given the opportunity to help by providing positive experiences to the other (giving chances for a drawing, choosing particularly nice music for the other to hear). In both, female subjects provided more "help" to depressed than to nondepressed same-sex others; males did not. The research is of interest mainly because of the sex difference in what is perceived as need. In another article, Austin (1979) manipulated the amount of harm done by a thief (using the value of items stolen) and found main effects in several replications; the more harm to the victim, the more likely was the bystander to intervene. He also found sex differences such that the amount of harm was less important for female bystanders. Taking these two findings together, one could tentatively con-clude that female bystanders become sensitive to the needs of others at a lower level of distress. This is consistent with the role expectation of nur-turance for women. In the cost framework, it should be more costly, in terms of self-concept, for females to ignore others' needs, just as it is more costly for both sexes to ignore higher levels of harm.

EFFECTS OF FOCUSING RESPONSIBILITY

Focusing of responsibility on a bystander and/or surveillance by others should create higher personal costs for nonintervention. We will discuss the surveillance studies first, followed by the research that has directly focused responsibility on the bystander. There are only a few studies that have investigated the effect simply of a subject's knowledge that others can observe him or her on helping. The possibility of social sanctions for inaction are clearly present under such circumstances, and this can function as a cost for not helping. (Surveillance could of course also serve as a cost for helping if helping is seen as inappropriate. Such circumstances are probably rare.)

Several studies have been done involving problem, crisis, or emergency helping situations and surveillance. Two (Konečni & Ebbesen, 1975; Ross, 1971) involve the impact of the presence of children on helping. As noted above, the physical presence of adults involves a complex of potential effects: social influence, diffusion of responsibility, and surveillance. One would assume that the first two do not operate when the other bystanders are children. In neither of these studies, however, was a facilitative surveillance effect found. In the Ross study, adult bystanders in the presence of children actually responded somewhat more slowly than did bystanders who were alone, although the "diffusion" effect was not as large as the effect of the presence of adults. (The effect of adults was significant; the effect of children was not.) In the Konečni and Ebbesen study, the presence of children made no difference; two bystanders with a child responded no more slowly than one person with a child to a "fallen person" crisis. Again there was no evidence that presence of a child increased helping, as the surveillance argument would suggest. Gottlieb and Carver (1980) have carried out a study that relates to surveillance, although it does not involve the opportunity for observation at the time of the helping act. In a replication and extension of the Schwartz and Clausen (1970) research, bystanders to an epileptic siezure emergency were led to believe that they would or would not meet for a second discussion. Those in the "future interaction" condition helped more rapidly. Furthermore, no diffusion of responsibility effect was found among members of those six-person groups.

Three articles, involving four experiments, have reported effects of surveillance by others in response to crime. In all of these, the other bystander(s) could also have helped; surveillance opportunity is manipulated independently of this, however. Bickman and Rosenbaum (1977) staged shoplifting incidents in supermarket checkout lines. The results are complex, but there is no overall effect of surveillance on reporting. The other two crime studies are by Schwartz and Gottlieb (1976; 1980, Experiment 1) and both involve a combined theft and assault that takes place in the course of a laboratory experiment. In the 1976 study, the emergency is heard; in the more recent study it is vividly seen on television (presumably live, actually on tape). In the 1976 study, 65% eventually help; in the more recent study, 89%. There is an effect in both studies of the awareness other participants have of the subject's actions or presence. In the 1976 study, this effect occurs only in the second half of the response period; that is, it appears to be those subjects who do not respond or respond slowly when they believe themselves to be anonymous who are impelled to action by the fact that their actions can be observed. In the later study, the effect is found in both halves of the response period, but it is more marked during the second half.

The final surveillance experiment involving a crisis is Schwartz and Gottleib again (1980, Experiment 2). In this experiment the crisis is a seizure rather than a crime, and the surveillance effect is again found. In this case, it occurs early and then reverses at just about the point of clarity; anonymous subjects respond very little before clarity, and not all of them eventually help. Those whose presence is known help quite a bit before but very little after the point of clarity. At the conclusion of the 1980 article, the authors argue convincingly against a simple interpretation of "evaluation apprehension" as the sole mediating process. (Evaluation apprehension is essentially the process involving the arousal of personal costs for not helping.) Instead, they present an analysis suggesting a combination of "detachment"—which would correspond to lowered "empathy costs"—and evaluation apprehension as the best explanation for their complex findings. Since both are components of costs for not helping, the Schwartz and Gottlieb research as a whole is highly consistent with the model being presented in this volume.

In a recent nonemergency donation study, Satow (1975) found that more money was given to a psychology student research fund by subjects observed through a one-way mirror than by those working in a room with no mirror. The effect was stronger among those scoring high on the Marlow–Crowne social desirability scale. Finally, Enzle and Harvey (1977) found main effects of both recipient awareness and third-party surveillance on donation of chips to an experimental participant who was "down on her luck." In all of these studies, increased objective self-awareness (Duval & Wicklund, 1972) is a possible alternative intervening process. However, since knowledge that one is being observed theoretically always leads to heightened self-awareness it would be difficult to devise a situation in which this was not a confound.

In summary, research has found clear effects of "publicity" on nonemergency, low-cost helping situations (Satow, 1975; Enzle & Harvey, 1977). In emergency situations, though, the effects of surveillance are somewhat more complex. Surveillance by other potential helpers (or by a child) seems to reduce the tendency to diffuse responsibility (Konečni & Ebbesen, 1975; Ross, 1971; Schwartz & Gottlieb, 1976; 1980, Experiment 1). However, it sometimes reduces or slows the helping response (Bickman & Rosenbaum, 1977; Schwartz & Gottlieb, 1980, Experiment 2). A good deal more must be investigated about the role of anonymity as compared to surveillance before these effects can be understood.

A more direct way to manipulate personal costs for not helping is to instruct the subjects differentially in regard to the degree of their responsibility. Several studies have quite effectively done this. Tilker (1970), in his study utilizing the Milgram situation (a "teacher" who gives more and more severe shocks to a "learner" who makes many errors), gave an "observer" total responsibility, ambiguous responsibility, or no responsibility for the conduct of the "learning session." Among subjects in a low-ambiguity condition (audio–visual feedback) 100% of the "totally responsible" subjects stopped the experiment; only 30% of those whose responsibility was unclear did so. Staub (1970) found that more children intervened in an emergency when they were specifically made responsible than when they were not.

Two studies have investigated the effect of subjects' acceptance of responsibility for others' possessions on their behavior in potentially risky help-requiring situations. Moriarty (1975) had confederates ask either other sun bathers at Jones Beach or people lunching in Manhattan automats to watch possessions for them. In the control group subjects were not asked, although their attention was attracted to the possessions being left. Among "responsible" subjects, 94% and 100% intervened to stop a thief in the two settings, while only 20% and 12.5% of control subjects did so. In a similar study, Shaffer, Rogel, and Hendrick (1975) had an experimenter ask students studying in a campus library to be responsible for belongings or merely left the belongings unattended. Sixty-seven percent of those asked to watch but only 12.5% of those not asked intervened in the subsequent attempted crime.

Two studies manipulated responsibility by actually blaming the bystander for the victim's plight. Samerotte and Harris (1976) had a confederate either brush against the target bystander or not and then drop a stack of envelopes. In the first condition, the confederate accused the subject of having caused the accident; in the second, he merely said, "I've dropped. . . ." Fifty-two percent of those blamed versus 38% of those not blamed helped picked up the envelopes, a significant difference.

In a rather more dramatic experiment, Schwartz and Ben David (1976) led some male subjects to believe that they were responsible and led others to think that the female experimenter was responsible for the escape of a "septic rat" who was potentially dangerous. The setting involved, ostensibly, research on "training people to control their heart rate," through the process of training rats to modify their heart rates. Subjects were in a separate room from the rats, and they were warned that giving shocks to the rat of over a second in length could be dangerous. This set the stage so that the "blame" manipulation could be employed. Part way through the series of shocks by the subject to the rat, the female experimenter, for the neutral condition, screamed "What happened? The rat escaped!" To blame either the subject or herself, the experimenter substituted, "What did you do?" or "What did I do?" for "What happened?"

As predicted, the three groups of subjects all differed significantly in rate of helping. More of the blamed subjects helped as compared to the condition in which the experimenter said "What happened?" and fewer of those who thought the experimenter was responsible helped (both at $p <$ .01). The authors discuss their results as probably involving at least two kinds of "personal costs" for not helping (although they do not use that term): public and private. These can be seen as equivalent to guilt and shame, and they involve first, the experimenter's response and second, the person's own response in terms of moral censure. The authors suggest that the manipulation should lead to differences in both kinds of costs across conditions. Furthermore, there should be individual differences based on a person's tendencies to accept or deny responsibility. Consistent with this notion, the authors found a significant within-cells average correlation between the responsibility denial scale and speed of response to the emergency.

In the preceding sections, both clarity and being given responsibility have been shown to relate to increased helping. Theoretically (see Table 5.1), personal costs for *not* helping will be high for a person made responsible, so he or she should feel more pressure to do *something* than should a person not "put in charge." Clarity may operate by blocking the alternative of denial of responsibility, thereby maintaining high costs for nonintervention. Thus, the response of the bystander under these conditions is typically one of intervention. In a more ambiguous emergency, one susceptible to multiple interpretations, the response could also be one of cognitive distortion or reinterpretation of the situation. For example, in a study run by Rodin, reported in Latané and Darley (1970), subjects overheard two children fighting in the next room. Of 12 subjects "put in charge" only three, or 25%, later claimed to have thought the fight real. All but one of eight subjects not responsible for the children thought it was real (88%). Only one subject in each condition intervened. In a similar brief report Staub (1970a) found that among nonhelping "responsible" subjects, there was a significant amount of denial that anything had happened in the next room at all. This form of distortion can clearly serve to mitigate the pangs of conscience among subjects made responsible. Nonresponsible subjects, having less reason to do something because of lower costs for the victim receiving no help, do not need to distort the situation. It is the opinion of the present authors that the relatively high level of suspicion found in many laboratory studies of bystander response can be attributed to this need to evade responsibility for action.

Costs for Helping and Costs for the Victim Receiving No Help, Combined

Let us return to the matrix presented in Table 5.1, and review what we have said so far. In general, we have found decreasing help with increasing costs for direct intervention. In addition, we have found increasing help with increasing costs for the victim receiving no help. The matrix presented in Table 5.1, however, suggests that there should be an interaction between these two variables. Specifically, the matrix predicts a direct relationship between costs for no help to the victim and intervention when costs for helping are low, but no definite prediction can be made as costs for helping increase.

A number of studies have tried to vary both kinds of costs simultaneously. Typically they have found complex interactions that differ from study to study. We will first briefly review two that did not: Bloom and Clark (1976) and Schwartz and Ben David (1976). Bloom and Clark, in a study specifically designed to test the cost–reward model, found no effects of either costs for helping (consequences to a blood donor of a special kind of donation versus an ordinary one) or costs for not helping (how critical was the need of a hemophiliac for blood). About half of those approached to give actually volunteered (16% eventually gave), but response was unrelated to either kind of costs. The only explanation that can be advanced is that blood donation may be a very particular type of response, one with a unique kind of cost, such that variations in the personal costs or need have little effect.

The second study (Schwartz & Ben David, 1976) found two strong main effects. This experiment was mentioned earlier in the "costs for not helping" section, where it was noted that the effect of blaming the subject for the escape of a dangerous rat was to speed up the helping response, while the effect of the experimenter's blaming herself was to slow helping. In that study, costs for helping were also varied by attributing to subjects either high, average, or low levels of ability to deal with rats. Presumably, costs are lower as ability to cope is higher. There was a highly significant main effect of attributed ability to handle rats on rate of helping, and there was no interaction between the two kinds of costs. This is one of only a few studies in the entire group that could be called an emergency experiment.

Two of the subway studies (Piliavin & Piliavin, 1972; Piliavin, Piliavin, & Rodin, 1975) varied both costs for helping and costs for the victim receiving no help. Costs for not helping were manipulated in both studies by presence or absence of a nonreactive programmed "intern" bystander. It was assumed that he would serve as an appropriate person to whom to "diffuse responsibility"; his programmed inaction, if he was taken as a guide, could also serve to help bystanders interpret the situation as not an emergency. The results for both studies, presented in Table 5.2, indicate an interaction such that helping was particularly decreased by the combination of high personal costs for helping and low costs for not helping.

Aside from the studies just discussed there are six other studies that have manipulated both costs for helping and another variable that can be interpreted as costs for the victim receiving no help (Clark, 1976; Epstein & Hornstein, 1969; Harris & Meyer, 1973; Piliavin, Piliavin, & Broll, 1974, unpublished; Schaps, 1972; Schwartz, 1970). None of these is an emergency study and there is a great range of experimental designs and kinds of helping responses employed. Schaps studied shoe salesmen, and the helping response was time given to a customer. Clark's helping response was volunteering to read to a blind student. Harris and Meyer asked people to sign a petition. Schwartz studied willingness to donate bone marrow. Epstein and Hornstein and Piliavin *et al.* used saving another experimental participant from shock.

There is one common finding that runs through all six of the above studies. Under low personal costs *for* helping (e.g., the shoe store is not crowded, preventing each shock to the other loses you only 2 cents, the probability that you will be called to actually donate bone marrow is

Table 5.2

Percentage of Trials on Which Victims Received Help and Mean Latencies in Seconds: Blood and Birthmark Studies[a][b]

Costs for not helping	Blood Study (1972) Costs for helping		Birthmark Study (1975) Costs for helping	
	Low	High	Low	High
High (no intern)	87.5 (8)	85.7 (7)	87.9 (33)	71.9 (32)
	17.3	22.66	12.32	21.34
Low (intern present)	100.0 (6)	71.4 (7)	84.6 (26)	48.3 (29)
	6.00	30.69	14.21	29.56

[a] From I. M. Piliavin, J. A. Piliavin, and J. Rodin. Costs, diffusion, and the stigmatized victim. *Journal of Personality and Social Psychology*, 1975, *32*, 429–438. Copyright 1975 by the American Psychological Association. Reprinted by permission.

[b] Ns are given in parentheses. First figure in each cell is percentage helping; second figure is latency of helping in seconds.

1/1000, the blind student is right on campus, or you will hear a nasty buzzer if you do not help), a relatively high level of assistance is given when costs for the victim receiving *no* help are high. Again, the ways in which costs to the victim were operationalized differ across studies. In Harris and Meyer and in Schaps, dependency manipulations were used. In Clark, the blind student was either about to have three exams (high cost) or was just keeping up with daily reading assignments (low cost). In the Schwartz study the vividness of the need of the potential recipient was varied. In Epstein and Hornstein and Piliavin *et al.* similarity of the shock recipient to the helper—and therefore presumably "empathy costs"—was varied. Piliavin *et al.* also varied the level of shock, and the two manipulations appeared to be additive.

On the other hand, little can be said about the effect of costs for the victim receiving no help as costs for helping increase. Over all the studies, the rate of helping decreases as costs for helping increase. But in several of the experiments there are peculiar cross-over interactions (e.g., Epstein & Hornstein found significantly more helping for the dissimilar than the similar victim under high costs for helping), while in other studies the effect of costs for not helping simply becomes less pronounced. Clearly more research is needed before we will understand the processes that underlie the complex effects that take place when both costs to the self and costs to the other are high.

Order Effects in Helping Research

We are aware of only two studies in which the order of manipulations of costs was varied. One of these was the Bloom and Clark (1976) study in which no effects of costs for helping or of costs for not helping were found. Similarly, no effect of the order in which the two were presented was found.

Langer and Abelson (1972) carried out two studies in which costs for not helping were varied by the "legitimacy" of a request (presumably one does not feel bad about turning down an illegitimate request). Costs for helping were not directly manipulated. Rather, the potential helper's attention was initially drawn either to the victim's need ("I'm in a terrible state.") or to the potential helper's decision ("Can you help me?"). Presumably under the latter circumstance, personal costs *for* helping should be attended to first. In both studies, the most helping was found in the "legitimate need, victim-oriented" cell, and least in the "illegitimate need, victim-oriented" cell. These findings for order are consistent with the previous analyses, if one assumes less weight is given to personal costs for helping when attention is directed toward the victim. That is, in "victim orientation" there is an effect of the victim's need; in "target orientation," where the bystander is likely to think about his own needs, there is no effect of the victim's need. In support of this interpretation, Austin (1979) suggests, in explaining the lack of impact of his manipulation of costs *for* helping in a "high harm" theft, that bystanders "focus on costs for not helping, and ignore the risk of physical danger [p. 2115]."

The "High-High" Cell: Real Emergencies

The upper right corner of the simplified 2 × 2 presentation of the cost–reward matrix (Table 5.1) is of particular interest. This is likely to be the cell in which many real-world emergencies occur (e.g., the Kitty Genovese case). The prediction from the model is for either an indirect helping response to be made, for the subject to redefine the situation, or for him or her to derogate the victim.

TYPE OF HELP OFFERED

Given high costs for the victim receiving no help (i.e., there is a clear emergency and injury to the victim is likely) it is predicted that as costs for helping increase, the likelihood of indirect as compared to direct helping will increase. Most research on helping has not specifically investigated the way in which helping is offered. Often, following the tradition of dissonance theory experiments, only one of several possible responses is made available or there is only one conceivable way to help (e.g., by picking up dropped objects or by giving blood). Other researchers have used scales to measure intensity of helping; generally they have viewed direct helping as "higher" on these scales (e.g., Harris & Huang, 1973; Howard & Crano, 1974).

There have been 14 experiments, to our knowledge, that have explicitly examined the incidence of direct as compared to indirect helping. Twelve of these are listed in Table 5.3 in decreasing order of incidence of indirect help. The other two studies are the subway collapse experiments (1969, 1975). In both, direct helping was nearly 100% of all helping, but the data are currently difficult to reconstruct fully.

The situations used in these 14 studies, most of which have been previously discussed, are all clearly crises or emergencies. They range from simple collapses or falls to more frightening occurrences such as electrical accidents, seizures, and physical assaults. The percentage of help received varies from 48% to 100% across the studies. The results of these studies are

Table 5.3

Studies Examining Determinants of Direct and Indirect Help

Study	Situation	Subject sex	Percentage helping overall	Percentage helping indirectly	Comments
Schwartz and Gottlieb (1980, Expt. II)	Audio-visually presented seizure	F	92%	82%	Phone available (done at night)
Schwartz and Gottlieb (1976)	Audio-only: theft, physical attack	M	65%	67%	Bell to summon experimenter (done at night)
Ashton and Severy (1976)	Audio-only: falling bookshelves	F	91%	55%	E location explicitly stated
Clark and Word (1974, Expt. I)	Electrical emergency	M	70%	37%	E location vague
Schwartz and Gottlieb (1980, Expt. I)	Audio-visually presented theft, physical attack	M and F	89%	35%	Phone available (done at night) anonymous Ss help less and help indirectly more (52% versus 79%)

Study	Situation	Sex			Comments
Clark and Word (1974, Expt. II)	Electrical emergency	M	65%	29%	E location vague
Shotland and Straw (1976)	Male attacks female	M and F	44%	24%	Phone available
Schwartz and Clausen (1970)	Audio-only seizure	M and F	68%	18%	E location known both sex (F more) and information (none more) affect level of indirect help
Byeff (1970, unpub.)	Audio or audio–visual fall	M	45%	16%	Alone Ss more likely to help indirectly than Ss in separated pairs (36% versus 0%)
Piliavin and Piliavin (1972)	Collapse in subway	M and F	85%	9%	Indirect help all in blood condition
Clark and Word (1972, Expt. I)	Audio falling workman	M	100%	0%	In pairs, one would help directly, the other indirectly; E location vague
Clark and Word (1972, Expt. II)	Audio falling workman	M	100% high ambiguous; 30% low ambiguous	0%	Same as Expt. I

not easy to systematize. One thing is, however, clear: Our straightforward prediction that as costs for direct intervention increase, the incidence of indirect helping should also increase is wrong.

In only a few of the studies were costs specifically manipulated. In the Clark and Word (1974) electrical emergency research, danger (operationalized by the victim being in contact with the presumably live wires) did not affect the likelihood of direct as compared to indirect help. In the Ashton and Severy (1976) "falling bookcase" experiment, neither manipulated competence nor permission to go next door affected the type of help offered. In fact, those told not to enter the room were more likely to do so, if they helped at all (and they did help less) by a margin of 62% to 49% (not significant). On the other hand, more indirect help was given in the "blood" condition of the Piliavin and Piliavin (1972) subway study than in the presumably lower-cost "no blood" condition (the difference was not significant).

When one compares across studies, which is a dangerous practice because there are so many differences, there is some evidence that personal costs for helping are related to increased use of indirect helping. The electrical emergency studies and the three studies involving physical attacks all fall in the top half of Table 5.3; that is, they are among the studies in which indirect helping is somewhat more likely. Similarly, clarity concerning the nature of the problem (and, thus, costs for helping) seems to be involved if we compare the Schwartz and Gottlieb (1980, Experiment 2) and the Schwartz and Clausen (1970) seizure experiments. In the former, subjects had no idea what was wrong with the person; most later speculated a drug problem or "being carried away by ESP." In the latter, subjects knew the victim was an epileptic. There was, in that study, a further manipulation involving information about what to do in the event of a seizure; subjects receiving this information were more likely to intervene directly.

On the other hand, the evidence suggests that indirect helping may be related to personal costs for *not* helping as well as to personal costs *for* helping. The only two studies involving all female subjects show 82% and 55% indirect helping, and Schwartz and Clausen found more indirect helping among females than among males. These sex differences may reflect a combination of lower personal costs for not helping for females, based on cultural expectations, and higher personal costs associated with helping by females, given the nature of the emergency. In addition, Schwartz and Gottlieb (1980, Experiment 1) found more indirect helping among anonymous subjects than among those known to another bystander, and Byeff (1970) found more indirect helping among alone subjects than among subjects run in separated pairs but who were aware of each other's presence. This kind of manipulation may operate to increase costs for not helping directly, since one is "on stage."

The final consideration in attempting to summarize these studies involves assessing the relative availability of the direct and indirect helping responses. If the direct response is obvious and its effect reasonably certain, while the indirect response is hard to make and of uncertain effectiveness, one would not be expected to choose an indirect action. In all three of the studies in which indirect helping was the preferred response (over 50% of helpers chose it), indirect helping responses were made salient; a phone or a bell to summon the experimenter was explicitly pointed out or the experimenter's room number and location were stated. In only 4 of the other 11 experiments was similar information provided.

Only one study (Penner, Dertke, & Achenback, 1973) has systematically varied the availability of indirect helping while holding constant the possibility for direct helping. In 1970 Florida instituted a "flash" system in which passing motorists could report a stranded motorist by blinking their lights three times at special signs set up along selected highways. Performing this act can be interpreted as indirect helping. The other possible helping response is a direct one, namely stopping to offer help. "Flash" and "nonflash" highways were used and stranded motorists varying in race and sex were planted. Since most passing motorists were Southern white males, the presumably least costly (most rewarding) type of assistance is helping a white female. On the nonflash highway, in fact, white females were more than five times as likely to receive direct help (the only possible kind) than was any other category. On the "flash" highways, the percentage of direct helping was reduced for white females—apparently some potential direct helpers "flashed" instead—but their overall level of receiving help was the same. The addition of the possibility of indirect help greatly benefited the "higher cost" category of victims, however. Over 9% of cars passing now helped white males (as compared to 1.4% when only direct helping was possible) and over 5% of cars now helped stranded blacks (as compared to 1.4%). These data strongly suggest that costs can be involved in type of help, and that indirect help will be provided under high cost for helping if the opportunity is explicitly made available.

Our tentative conclusions, based on this entire group of studies, are as follows. As suggested by Silverman (1974), the most salient response for most people in most emergencies seems to be direct intervention. If for some reason, such as high costs for helping, they are inhibited from making a direct helping response, bystanders are likely simply not to help. Only if an indirect response is made clearly available (e.g., on the "flash" highway) is it likely to be used. The indirect response can then be substituted for inaction, which is more common in response to high costs. However, even an apparently obvious method of indirect help may be forgotten "in the heat of the moment." For example, in the Shotland and Straw (1976) "attack" study, a nearby police phone was used by only one subject.

There are clear policy implications of this essentially negative finding, which we shall address in the final chapter. As a preview, we will simply note that there is one institutionalized form of indirect helping known to everyone: the fire alarm box. Nobody thinks they should try to put out a fire by themselves. Strategies and hardware for institutionalizing indirect forms of helping in other types of emergencies could certainly be developed.

DEROGATION OF THE VICTIM AND DISTORTION OF THE SITUATION

It is very difficult to know when the costs for helping have become sufficiently high to lead us to expect disparaging of the victim or redefinition. Furthermore, most research on helping in emergencies has not been designed in such a way as to facilitate these tendencies. There is one body of research, however, that presents the opportunity to study these two responses by the simple expedient of making a helping response impossible but making the bystander watch what is happening to the victim. This is the work of Lerner and his colleagues and others who have used his paradigm. Lerner has presented the hypothesis that people have a need to believe in a just world, and that observation of the suffering of innocent victims disconfirms this belief, causing the person to engage in behavior designed to reconfirm it. The basic prediction is the following: If the bystander cannot alleviate the suffering, he or she must disparage the victim, thus making the world right again—a world in which only evil people suffer. Lerner (1974) reviews the studies from his own laboratory as follows:

> When given the opportunity, the vast majority of subjects 'voted' to end the victim's suffering and have her compensated. When they had no such power, however, the majority reduced the attractiveness of the 'innocent' victim. The degree of condemnation was determined by the amount of injustice they were seeing: the longer the suffering, the greater the condemnation. . . If, on the other hand, they believed that the victim would be compensated sufficiently by the experimenter in the end, there was no condemnation (Lerner and Simmons, 1966; Lerner, 1970; Lerner, 1971) [p. 342].

Other studies (Chaikin & Darley, 1973; Johnson & Dickinson, 1971; Lincoln & Levinger, 1972; MacDonald, 1971; Stokols & Schopler, 1973) have also found that subjects who cannot intervene to assist an "innocent" victim will denigrate the victim. In most cases, the results demonstrate, as Lerner has hypothesized, that the more innocent the victim the higher are the costs for his or her receiving no help, in terms of the observers' feelings about their responsibility to intervene. However, if one continues to make the victim even more innocent (Piliavin, Hardyck, & Vadum, 1967) or makes the subject think specifically of the victim as being a victim of misfortune (Simons & Piliavin, 1972) subjects do not use this technique for lowering costs for not helping. Rather, they choose to distort the situation in various ways. In the Simons and Piliavin (1972) study, 13 of the crucial 19 subjects who thought they were watching "a victim of misfortune" chose to believe it was taped rather than live. This was a higher level of "suspicion" than was shown in any other condition. Similarly, 9 of 13 subjects in the condition in the Piliavin et al. (1967) study in which a "truly innocent victim" was manipulated either rejected the reality of the experiment or perceived the victim as not really suffering. No more than 30% of subjects in any other condition behaved in this fashion. Furthermore, those who distorted the situation did not derogate the victim; those who derogated the victim did not distort the situation. Thus, the subject's dilemma was alleviated by systematic reinterpretation of one sort or another.

We are still at a loss with the current form of our model to know how real-world bystanders respond when watching an emergency in which the victims are completely beyond anyone's help—they are doomed, like a child being eaten by an alligator or the crew of a submarine trapped hopelessly below the surface of the sea. Such totally innocent victims are not typically derogated, yet their suffering can hardly be minimized and there is no experimental manipulation to suspect. We presently feel that such bystanders will have no recourse. They simply suffer and wait until their arousal decreases with the inexorable passage of time.

In the foregoing discussion we have intentionally omitted the large group of studies investigating the reaction of actual harm-doers to their victims, because our specific concern has been with the response of the "innocent" bystander. Interestingly, most of the research on actual victimizers is consistent with what we have presented on the uninvolved bystander. In particular, those studies show clearly that when it is too costly, or when it is impossible, for an unintentional harm-doer to compensate a victim, he or she is very likely to derogate the victim (see Walster, Walster, & Berscheid, 1978).

Summary and Conclusions on Overall Effects of Costs and Rewards

There is strong support in the literature for both aspects of costs having an effect on helping behavior. Help that is likely to be costly to the benefactor in terms of psychological distress, money, time, or rewards foregone is in general less likely to be offered. The effects of costs for the victim receiving no help are equally clear: Needy victims receive more help and victims receive more assistance when responsibility is focused on the bystander. Many of these effects must be qualified, and in Chapter 10 we will present some modifications of the model by which some of the exceptions can be subsumed. Here the primary qualifications we want to emphasize are the following:

1. Costs for the victim receiving no help seem to be predictably related to helping only when costs for helping are relatively low.
2. Costs for helping are related to intervening only at moderate to high levels of costs for the victim receiving no help. If costs for the victim receiving no help are low, help is so low that there is no variance to which to relate costs for helping.

The most difficult area for prediction is currently that in which both costs for helping and costs for the victim receiving no help are high. Contrary to our initial expectation, indirect help is not the most typical response. Nevertheless, the results across several studies are sufficiently systematic to allow some additional speculation at this point. In general, bystanders caught in a high–high dilemma do seem to choose (not necessarily with conscious awareness) the response that will most rapidly and completely relieve their unpleasant arousal state. Although there are many different types of responses a bystander can select, there seems to be an order of preferred alternatives in the high–high situation.

We now propose, albeit speculatively, the following process. Given a bystander's *initial* perception of high costs for helping and high costs for the victim receiving no help, the first most likely response is one of cognitive reinterpretation. In particular, the bystander, whose attention is largely focused on the plight of the victim, first attempts to reduce the perceived costs for not helping. Similar to the process that Lazarus (1968) proposed concerning coping with perceived threat, reinterpreting the costs for not helping relieves the bystander's dilemma in a way that effectively reduces the bystander's unpleasant arousal state. Lowering the costs for not helping may be accomplished by redefining the situation as one in which help is unnecessary (e.g., "The situation is not *really* serious."), diffusing responsibility (e.g., "Someone else will intervene."), or derogating the victim (e.g., "He got what he deserved."). With high costs for helping and lowered costs for not helping, bystanders are less likely to intervene.

Indeed, there is research that suggests that cognitive reinterpretation is more likely to occur in emergencies when the costs for helping are high than when they are low. Piliavin, Piliavin, and Trudell (1974) found that subjects presented with a high-cost "thief" emergency were more likely to question the reality of the event than were subjects exposed to a low-cost "fallen woman" accident. Piliavin, Piliavin, and Rodin (1975) observed greater diffusion of responsibility when a victim had a large facial birthmark than when a victim had no stigma. Similarly, in an experiment by Gaertner and Dovidio (1977, Study 1) white bystanders were more likely to diffuse responsibility when the victim was black than when the victim was white. Also, as discussed in the previous section, several investigators have found that subjects who cannot intervene will denigrate an apparently "innocent" victim.

If reinterpretation or distortion of the costs for the victim receiving no help are precluded by the clarity or the nature of the emergency, bystanders are then likely to reevaluate the costs for helping. In reappraising the situation, the bystander may decide that the costs for helping are not so high as to allow another person's suffering without attempting to help. Thus, the costs for helping are reduced relative to the costs for not helping, and the bystander becomes likely to intervene. Although there is little evidence directly showing this reinterpretive process, several studies demonstrate high levels of intervention in high-cost helping situations in which the need for assistance is clear and/or in which diffusion of responsibility is not possible. For example, Clark and Word (1974) observed 100% helping in a very graphic but potentially dangerous electrical accident. Darley and Latané (1968) found that although subjects, given the opportunity, readily diffused responsibility in an epileptic seizure emergency, 100% of the subjects who witnessed the emergency alone intervened. Similarly, Gaertner and Dovidio (1977, Study 1) showed that although bystanders were more likely to diffuse responsibility with black than with white victims, they exhibited high and equivalent rates of helping when they were the only witness to the emergency. When unable to diffuse responsibility, bystanders apparently decided that the costs for helping a black victim were not sufficiently high to preclude intervention.

It is possible that a bystander in the high–high dilemma will be unable to effectively reinterpret either the costs for helping or the costs for the victim receiving no help. For example, an only witness to a victim trapped in a blazing building would not likely misinterpret the severity of the situation nor would the bystander likely risk certain injury by entering the fire. It is under these conditions—continued high costs for helping and high costs for not helping—that indirect help becomes likely. It is critical, however, that the bystander *perceive* that indirect help is possible. As we mentioned earlier, given the prominent nature of the emergency event in the bystander's attentional focus, bystanders may fail to consider this option unless the mechanism for indirect assistance (e.g., a firebox) is also prominent. If the bystander does not perceive indirect help as a viable alternative, then the bystander's dilemma continues, and the bystander does not intervene. Furthermore, to the extent that personal costs for helping remain high, leaving the scene may be even more costly than no response. Under these conditions, bystanders can only wait until the emergency is resolved, one way or another.

We propose this sequence of steps in resolving the high–high dilemma only tentatively. Although these steps seem to describe the results of many studies, few studies directly explore the issue. In addition, the order of the sequence of alternatives may vary with social or personal factors. For instance, although the results of the studies in which the bystander and the victim were unacquainted suggest that reinterpretation of the costs for not helping is the first likely response, perhaps in an emergency involving a loved one the costs for helping would be first distorted and lowered. Also, the sequence of steps may be cyclical and iterative. After cognitive reinterpretation and indirect help are unsuccessful, further attempts at reinterpretation may be made. We feel, though, that the sequence we have outlined may provide a useful theoretical basis for future research elucidating the process with which the high–high dilemma is resolved.

Chapter 6

The Social Context of Helping

In this chapter, we shall discuss the effects of the presence of others and the process by which others influence the likelihood of intervention, while integrating these findings with the arousal:cost–reward model. We shall also consider effects associated with the interpersonal relationship between the bystander and the victim. Both the presence of others and the nature of the bystander–victim relationship seem to affect cost–benefit considerations and arousal. The findings also suggest that arousal and cost factors are often not mutually exclusive and independent components. That is, the value of one can affect the value of the other.

The Presence of Others

We are now brought to the best-known and most discussed set of studies in the area of helping behavior: studies that examine the effects of the presence of other bystanders on emergency intervention. In our discussion, the effects of the presence of other witnesses will be related both to cost consideration and arousal factors. In particular, Latané and Darley (1970, 1976) have suggested that the presence of other bystanders can affect an individual's response to an emergency in three ways. First, the presence of others, or simply the believed ability of others to intervene, may allow an individual to diffuse the responsibility for helping and also the guilt and blame for not helping (Darley & Latané, 1968). Diffusion of responsibility effects, then, generally inhibit helping. Second, the reactions of other witnesses to an emergency can provide a bystander with information about the seriousness of the situation. For example, analogous to Sherif's (1936) classic study of informational social influence, passive bystanders can lead a potential benefactor to believe that the situation is less severe than originally anticipated, and thus reduce the likelihood of intervention (e.g., Latané & Rodin, 1969). Similarly, active and involved witnesses can lead a bystander to believe that the situation is relatively more serious and therefore increase the likelihood of helping. Third, concern for the evaluation of others, frequently termed normative social influence (Deutsch & Gerard, 1955), can critically affect a bystander's likelihood of intervention depending on the bystanders' beliefs about what others consider to be normatively appropriate (Schwartz & Gottlieb, 1976).

DIFFUSION OF RESPONSIBILITY

Diffusion effects are associated with the question of "Who should help?" and require only that a bystander believe that someone else could help. Several studies (see Table 6.1) have demonstrated that the awareness of the presence of other capable bystanders inhibits or delays intervention (Bickman, 1971; Darley & Latané, 1968; Horowitz, 1971; Schwartz & Clausen, 1970; Schwartz & Gottlieb, 1976). For example, in the classic study of Darley and Latané (1968), subjects, believing that they were the only witness or among two or five bystanders, overheard a person suffer an apparent epileptic seizure. During a discussion of college life, the victim became increasingly loud and incoherent, choking and gasping and crying out for help before lapsing into 6 minutes of silence. The results, consistent with the diffusion hypothesis, revealed that before the end of the epileptic fit 85% of the alone subjects helped, while only 62% of the subjects believing that one other witness was available and 31% of the subjects believing four other bystanders were present intervened. Schwartz and Clausen (1970) replicated these results, finding that 100% of the female subjects who were alone intervened to help a seizure victim while only 33% responded with assistance when they believed that four other bystanders were present.

Although the diffusion hypothesis has generated a considerable amount of research, there appears to be some confusion about the concept. In introducing the concept of diffusion of responsibility to the area of bystander intervention, Darley and Latané (1968) argued that when several bystanders are present "the pressures to intervene do not focus on any one of the observers; instead the responsibility for intervention is *shared* among all the onlookers and is not unique to any one [p. 378]." As a result, the likelihood of any one bystander intervening is reduced. There is another distinct process, which has not heretofore been differentiated from "diffusion," which we will call "dissolution of responsibility." Darley and Latané also argued that if the behavior of other bystanders cannot be observed, the bystander "can assume that one of the other bystanders is already taking action to end the emergency. Therefore his own intervention would be redundant—perhaps harmfully or confusingly so [p. 378]." Thus, "diffusion" implies that responsibility is accepted, but shared, while "dissolution" suggests that the bystander's responsibility is dissolved by rationalizing that someone else has already helped. Most researchers, however, do not distinguish between the two processes and refer to both as "diffusion of responsibility". In some studies, bystanders are given continuous access to events in the victim's location after the emergency, enabling the subject to realize that no other bystander has yet intervened. Under these conditions, diffusion of responsibility rather than dissolution of responsibility seems to more accurately characterize the process.

Recently, in reviewing the literature on diffusion of responsibility, Schwartz and Gottlieb (1976), making another distinction, have argued that "pure diffusion" effects can only be isolated when the bystander believes that "others are present and that neither he/she nor they are aware of each other's responses [p. 1189]." That is, when subjects are aware of the response of others informational social influence may also be operating. When the subject believes that others can monitor his or her response, concern for the evaluation of others can influence the response to the emergency. Thus, for many of the studies in which the number of bystanders has been manipulated but bystanders were aware of each other's presence (Darley & Latané, 1968; Latané & Dabbs, 1975; Latané & Rodin, 1969; Piliavin, Rodin, & Piliavin, 1969; Smith, Smythe, & Lien, 1972), diffusion effects were not independent of other forms of social influences. Schwartz and Gottlieb (1976), however, did demonstrate a "pure" diffusion of responsibility effect when male subjects believed that others were present but were mutually unaware of each other's behavior. Specifically, 92% of the subjects who were alone, but only 45% of the subjects who believed that others were present intervened to help a victim injured in theft. Thus, the belief that others can intervene, independent of other types of bystander effects, can strongly influence helping behavior.

In the remainder of our review of the literature, we will not generally make the distinction between diffusion, dissolution, and pure diffusion effects. Many studies, in fact, involve more than one of the processes. For example, in the classic Darley and Latané (1968) investigation, a diffusion effect appeared during the first 120 seconds in which the subject heard the

Table 6.1

Effect of Number and Type of Nonvisible Bystanders on Percentage of Subjects Who Help in Various Emergencies[1]

	Alone	Together: same sex (unless note 1)[6]	Together: mixed sexes (unless note 2) + others[6]	Special conditions
Studies with female subjects				
Epileptic seizure studies				
Latané and Darley, 1970 (Percentage responding by end of fit)	85 (13)	62 (26)*[2]	31 (13)*	75 (28)[a] 75 (12)[b]
Schwartz and Clausen, 1970 (Percentage ever responding)	100 (13)	—	35 (12)*	25 (12)*[c]
Schwartz and Gottlieb, 1980 (Expt. 2, Percentage responding by 100 sec) Subject's presence:				
Known	42 (12)	42 (12)		
Unknown	50 (12)	17 (12)*		
Bookcase or chairs falling studies				
Bickman, 1971 (Percentage responding by 60 sec)	80 (15)	40 (15)*		74 (15)[d]

Gaertner and Dovidio, 1977 (Expt. 1)				
White victim	81 (16)		75 (16)[3]	
Black victim	94 (16)		38 (16)[3]	
Violent theft study				
Schwartz and Gottlieb, 1980 (Expt. 1, Percentage responding by 90 sec)				
Subject's presence:				
Known	80 (15)	93 (15)		
Unknown	87 (15)	27 (15)*		
Studies with male subjects				
Epileptic seizure studies				
Darley and Latané, 1970 (Percentage responding by end of fit)		69 (13)[3]		
Schwartz and Clausen, 1970 (Percentage ever responding)	67 (12)		50 (12)	57 (14)[c]
Horowitz, 1971 (Percentage ever responding)	55 (40)		42.5 (40)[3]	20 (20)[*,e] 65 (20)[f]

(continued)

Table 6.1 *(continued)*

	Alone	Together: same sex (unless note 1)[6]	Together: mixed sexes (unless note 2) + others[6]	Special conditions
"Fallen woman" emergencies Byeff, 1970 (unpub.) (Percentage responding in 3 min)				
Audio only	40 (15)	35 (22)		28 (15 pr)*ᵍ $E = 64$
Audio–visual	53 (15)	59 (22)		47 (15 pr)* $E = 78$
Piliavin, Piliavin, and Trudell, 1974 (unpub.) (Percentage ever responding)				
No arousal	73 (11)	86 (7 pr) $E = 93$		
Prearoused	83 (18)	40 (10 pr)* $E = 97$		
Violent theft studies Piliavin, Piliavin, and Trudell, 1974 (unpub.) (Percentage ever responding)				
No arousal	20 (10)	33 (6 pr) $E = 36$		
Prearoused	33 (18)	0 (10 pr)* $E = 55$		
Schwartz and Gottlieb, 1976 (Percentage ever responding)	92 (13)	45 (14)*⁵		93 (14)*ᵏ 62 (13)*ᵏ

Schwartz and Gottlieb, 1980

(Expt. 1, Percentage responding by 90 sec)

Subject's presence:

Known	80 (15)	73 (15)	42 (12)[j]*
Unknown	80 (15)	87 (15)	

* "Diffusion" effect is significant at $p < .05$ or better.

[1] Number of subjects in parentheses.

[2] For half of subjects, other is female; for other half, other is male. The effect is the same.

[3] Other bystander(s) is (are) female.

[4] Others are all males.

[5] Subject believes he is not under surveillance and cannot hear others: a "normal" type of "one other" condition—no evaluation apprehension, no social influence.

[6] This column includes subjects run with programmed nonreactive bystander-stooges (number of subjects in parentheses) and naive pairs of subjects (number of *pairs* in parentheses). E = expected number of pairs who would help based on rate of helping by alone subjects. E is calculated by $1 - (1 - P)n$, where P is proportion helping in alone condition, n is number of naive bystanders in group.

Special conditions footnotes:

[a] One other bystander, a female friend of the subject.

[b] Three other bystanders; the real subject met the victim in the hall before the experiment.

[c] Three other bystanders, one with special competance to help (emergency room experience)

[d] One other bystander who cannot help for reasons of physical location.

[e] Subjects are fraternity members (half of the subjects in Column 3).

[f] Subjects are members of social service organizations (the other half).

[g] Subjects are in face-to-face pairs (social influence manipulation).

[h] Subjects believe they are under surveillance (evaluation apprehension).

[i] Subjects believe they are under surveillance and also that they can hear others' response (evaluation apprehension + social influence).

[j] Subjects believe they are *not* under surveillance but that they can hear others' response (social influence).

seizure and could also hear that no one intervened. After the first 2 minutes, a dissolution effect occurred as the subjects heard only silence when the microphone switched to the next bystander–discussant. This silence probably led many subjects to believe that someone else had already intervened. Unfortunately, it is difficult to determine what process was actually operating in most studies due to confounds inherent in the design, ambiguities in the published procedure, or data reported in a way that precludes isolating the different effects. Consequently, following the popular convention, we will generally refer to these investigations as diffusion studies.

Bickman (1971, 1972) and Korte (1969) independently tested an extension of the diffusion of responsibility hypothesis. Specifically, they investigated whether diffusion is affected by the perceived ability of the other bystander(s) to help or whether the mere presence of other bystanders is sufficient to produce the inhibition effect. Theoretically, bystanders cannot diffuse (or dissolve) responsibility if they believe that the other bystanders are physically unable or unwilling to intervene. In Bickman's research (1971, 1972) subjects believed that the other bystander to the emergency was located in another building some distance away from the victim and themselves and thus was unable to help, or, alternatively, was in an adjacent cubicle and therefore could intervene. The emergency consisted of the subject hearing a bookcase apparently fall on the victim. In Korte's (1969) study, subjects believed that the other bystanders were strapped inextricably to their chairs or were freely mobile. The emergency involved an apparent asthma attack to the experimenter.

Both Bickman and Korte reported that subjects whose fellow bystanders were unable to help intervened 13% more frequently than bystanders who believed that others could intervene. In Bickman's study, subjects in the "not able" and "able" conditions helped 90% and 77% of the time, respectively, whereas Korte's subjects helped 50% and 37% of the time, respectively. Furthermore, Bickman reported that subjects in the "not able" other bystander condition helped faster than subjects in the "able" other bystander condition and also that there were no differences in the speed of helping between subjects witnessing the emergency alone and subjects together with an unable bystander. Therefore, diffusion of responsibility does not seem to occur unless the bystander believes that someone else witnessing the emergency is capable of intervening.

Further exploring the diffusion process, Bickman (1971, 1972) reasoned that the diffusion of responsibility effect would be greatest when the emergency was perceived as moderately serious. If the situation was extremely serious, then the severity of the event might preclude looking to see if anyone else is around or whether others are qualified to help. (We will discuss this implication further in the next chapter under the topic of "impulsive" helping.) If, on the other hand, a bystander was to receive a "no-help-needed" definition of the situation and accept it, no diffusion effect could occur since there was no responsibility to diffuse. However, if the situation was perceived as one in which help might be needed, the bystander should be in maximum conflict. The situation would not appear so unambiguously serious that the bystander would ignore the presence of others, nor would the potential emergency seem to be of trivial consequence. Hence, diffusion should be greatest when other bystanders suggest that help may be needed.

The results, as expected, indicated that the difference between the "able" and the "not-able" conditions was greatest when the other bystander suggested that help *may* be needed. However, this difference was marginally significant. Korte also obtained the largest difference between "able" and "not able" conditions when the confederate offered a "help-may-be-needed" definition. His findings also failed to reach traditionally acceptable levels of statistical significance. Nevertheless, the fact that two investigators obtained an identical pattern of results suggests that the phenomenon is real.

Initially, we agreed with Latané and Darley (1970) that the diffusion process primarily affected personal costs for not helping the victim. When a bystander is the only witness to an emergency, he or she bears 100% of the responsibility for helping and 100% of the blame for not intervening. When an individual can diffuse responsibility onto other bystanders, these personal costs for not helping are lower. Diffusion of responsibility, however, can also affect empathic costs to the extent that a bystander truly believes that another person will intervene in the emergency. That is, the belief that someone may help should relieve a bystander's empathic distress (i.e., arousal) associated with the victim receiving no help.

Since the impetus for research on diffusion of responsibility has primarily come from cognitive models of bystander intervention, most research has focused on the personal cost aspect and little research has investigated the physiological correlates of the diffusion process. Two studies, though, Piliavin, Piliavin, and Trudell (1974) and Gaertner and Dovidio (1977, Study 1), did observe a diffusion of responsibility effect while measuring subjects' physiological response to the emergency. In Piliavin et al. (1974), subjects, alone or together in separated pairs, viewed an arousing or nonarousing film sequence prior to witnessing an emergency. The results revealed that the helping behavior of previously aroused bystanders was inhibited by the presence of another bystander, whereas no diffusion effect was obtained for those who previously viewed a nonarousing film. In addition, where diffusion occurred, arousal, as measured by

GSR, also tended to be lower. Perhaps prior viewing of the arousing film sequence presented bystanders to the emergency with an attributional dilemma such that the source of their arousal was relatively unclear compared to those who viewed the nonarousing film. Thus, these results seem to be consistent with the Bickman (1971, 1972) and Korte (1969) findings that indicate that diffusion of responsibility occurs more frequently when an emergency is ambiguous.

The other study, Gaertner and Dovidio (1977, Study 1) investigated the diffusion process while measuring subjects' heart rates. Although the design of this previously discussed study is more complex, we will consider in detail at this time only those issues that focus directly on the relationship between arousal and helping. To briefly review the procedure, female subjects overheard an emergency in a nearby room in which a black or white fellow participant in an ESP study was accidently struck by a stack of falling chairs. Screams from the victim accompanied the incident. During this emergency, subjects were led to believe that they were the only bystanders or one of three separated bystanders who could not communicate with each other. (To the extent that subjects believed, as intended, that the microphone was damaged during the accident, this study most likely represents a dissolution of responsibility process.)

Three sets of dependent variables were recorded in the study. First, whether or not the subjects helped (within 3 minutes) and the latency of intervention, assigning 180 seconds for nonhelpers, were measured. Second, heart rate was monitored. Third, during a postemergency period subjects were asked to rate (a) how sure they were that the victim was hurt; (b) how much help they believed the victim needed; and (c) how serious they assessed the situation to be. On similar scales, self-report measures of arousal and upset were obtained.

Analyses revealed that subjects who had the opportunity to diffuse responsibility helped the victim less frequently (56.3% versus 87.5%, $p < .02$) and less quickly ($p < .01$) than did subjects who heard the emergency alone. A multivariate analysis of subjects' assessments of the seriousness of the situation, degree of help needed, and certainty of injury revealed no effect. This result is quite consistent with the original Darley and Latané formulation of the process of diffusion of responsibility. That is, diffusion can only occur after the bystander has recognized that help is needed. The analysis of the heart rate measure, though, did reveal a diffusion of responsibility effect ($p < .06$). Paralleling the helping measures, cardiac responsiveness was greater when subjects were alone than when they believed that others were present ($+12.95$ versus $+6.62$ beats per minute). Thus, these results suggest the potential mediating effect of arousal on helping.

To further explore the relationship between arousal and helping, correlational analyses were performed. Consistent with our theoretical framework, significant correlations between latency and change in heart rate ($r = -.61$) and latency and degree of upset ($r = -.31$) were obtained. Thus, the greater the psychophysiological impact of the emergency, the faster the bystander responded. Furthermore, although these correlational analyses do not directly address the issue of causality, subsequent analyses do provide increasing support for the proposed causal relationship between arousal and helping. In particular, there is a strong indication that the arousal that preceded the decision to intervene was directly related to the speed of intervention. Although the median response time was 52 seconds, cardiac responsiveness during the first 10-second period following the emergency was directly related to the time to intervene ($r = -.56$). Therefore, there appears to be a direct relationship between bystander responsiveness and the immediate impact of the emergency.

In addition, a greater proportion of subjects who believed that others were present displayed a decrease in heart rate than did subjects who believed that they were alone (40.62% versus 18.75%, $p < .10$). Indeed, the finding of greater likelihood of heart rate deceleration when bystanders believe that others are present is consistent with the hypothesized diffusion (or dissolution) of responsibility process. The diffusion concept implies that the bystander is in a temporary state of confusion, looking for information and therefore orienting towards other people to resolve the dilemma of whether or not to intervene. Thus, the results of this study are compatible with earlier findings (e.g., Lacey & Lacey, 1970, 1973) that demonstrated that heart rate deceleration is often associated with the intake of information from the environment, an orienting response, whereas acceleration often accompanies preparation for action, a defense reaction.[1] Physiological arousal involving heart rate increase is generally indicative of emotionality. Thus the subjects who were alone should have been subjectively experiencing greater distress, which, in our model, should predict greater likelihood of taking some kind of action quite independent of any "diffusion" or "dissolution" of responsibility effect.

Why should being alone lead to more subjectively experienced emotion and arousal? The finding is at least consistent with the percep-

---

[1] Similarly, 40.62% of the subjects with black victims showed heart rate deceleration, while only 18.75% of the subjects with white victims decelerated in heart rate ($p < .10$). This finding is consistent with the indirect attitudinal process model, which we will discuss in more detail later in this chapter, that proposes that a white bystander with a black victim is motivated to seek information that will justify noninvolvement and avoid the attribution of racist intent.

tual–motor theory proposed by Leventhal (1974, 1980).[2] In his model, unlike that of Schachter (1971), arousal is not a factor in the *creation* of the subjective experience of emotion, but rather a consequence of it. Subjective emotion is the result of the integration of feedback from facial muscles involved in the expression of emotions with information concerning the situation. If this integration occurs *out of awareness*—that is, if the person is not directing his or her attention towards the self—the experience will be one of subjective emotion. If the individual is attending to his or her own expressive behavior, however, the subjective experience of emotion is decreased or destroyed altogether. According to the theory of objective self-awareness (Duval & Wicklund, 1972), the presence of others is one factor that can lead an individual to turn his or her attention from the outside world toward the self. To the extent that subjects who are with others are more objectively self-aware, then, we would expect them to experience less emotion.

Another set of analyses was performed to determine if the diffusion of responsibility effect on helping was mediated by arousal or whether the effect was independent of arousal. As suggested by Coke, Batson, and McDavis (1978), two stepwise multiple regressions were performed to provide a path analysis. In one analysis, the effect associated with the independent manipulation of the believed presence of others was entered first, followed by the measures of psychophysiological arousal (heart rate and self-report measures of upset and arousal); in the second regression analysis, arousal measures were entered first and the manipulation was entered second. Therefore, the extent to which the variance in helping accounted for by psychophysiological arousal overlapped with the effect of the manipulation could be assessed by comparing the contributions of the manipulation before and after the effects of arousal were considered. Thus, any increase in the explanation of helping behavior associated with the manipulation after arousal was considered would be an indicator of its effect over and above the possible mediating effects of arousal.[3]

When the effect of the manipulation was entered into the equation

[2] Given the incisive analyses of Schachter's theory by Leventhal (1974, 1980) and the recent nonreplications of Schachter and Singer (1962) by Maslach (1979) and Marshall and Zimbardo (1979), we are adopting the Leventhal model rather than the Schachter model of the generation of emotional response. We will discuss Leventhal's model in greater detail in our analysis of "impulsive" helping in Chapter 7.

[3] Two other studies, Byeff (1970) and Piliavin, Piliavin, and Trudell (1974), investigated diffusion of responsibility and measured bystanders' physiological responses. Byeff (1970) did not obtain a reliable diffusion effect. Piliavin *et al.* (1974) did find an inhibition effect associated with the presence of others, but physiological measurement was particularly unreliable in the diffusion conditions. Consequently, similar regression analyses were not meaningful for these other two studies.

after the arousal measures, there was a substantial decrease in its effect. When entered into the equation first, the manipulation explained 16.0% of the variance in helping. However, when entered into the equation second, the manipulation only accounted for 4.6% of the variance, a nonsignificant proportion, beyond the effects of arousal. The arousal factors, though, exerted a significant effect when considered before (44.7%) and after (33.3%) the manipulation was entered. Thus, the relationship between arousal and helping was generally strong, and the effect of the manipulation of the believed presence of others on helping appeared to be mediated by arousal. Incidentally, when a similar set of analyses were performed to assess the potential mediating effects of subjects' assessment of the seriousness, degree of injury, and certainty of injury, the manipulation of the believed presence of others was statistically significant both before and after the ratings were considered. These path analyses, then, suggest not only that changes in psychophysiological arousal accompany the process of diffusion of responsibility, but also that arousal has a critical mediating effect on helping behavior. Apparently, diffusion affects both personal costs and arousal factors.

The pattern of results across the studies presented in Table 6.1 suggests that diffusion of responsibility effects are typically more pronounced for females than for males. Examination of the only two studies that have employed both sexes of subjects in all conditions is particularly informative. Schwartz and Clausen (1970) and Schwartz and Gottlieb (1980, Experiment 1) both found statistically significant diffusion effects for females but not for males. Although Schwartz and Gottlieb (1980) do not report the sex differences, males and females appear to respond differently. In the "together–presence-unknown-by-others" condition (which Schwartz and Gottlieb consider to represent a "pure diffusion" situation) males showed only a nonsignificant tendency to diffuse responsibility. For females, the effect was statistically reliable. This generally consistent pattern of sex differences may be attributable to generally higher personal costs for not helping associated with cultural expectations for males. It is also possible that for many emergency situations males may perceive the personal costs for helping to be lower. For example, to the extent that assistance requires physical strength (e.g., moving a large bookcase), the costs for intervening may be relatively higher for females than males. Thus, perceived high costs for helping may, in general, be an important facilitator of the diffusion effect. As we discussed in Chapter 5, bystanders caught in a high-cost-for-helping–high-cost-for-not-helping situation frequently resolve their dilemma by reinterpreting the necessity of their involvement. Believing that someone else will or has helped is one such rationalization. Supportive of this notion, in violent theft emergencies (see Table 6.1), involving particularly high costs for helping, diffusion effects occur for both male and female bystanders. Unfortunately no currently available studies adequately explicate the dynamics underlying the sex differences in diffusion of responsibility.

SOCIAL INFLUENCE: INFORMATIONAL AND NORMATIVE

The face-to-face presence of others has important effects on emergency intervention (see Table 6.2). Typically, subjects in the studies of these effects were male. For the theft studies, the Wilson (1976) study, and the Solomon, Solomon, and Stone (1978) study, however, the subjects were of both sexes. The Gaertner (1975) and the Gaertner, Dovidio, and Johnson (1979a) studies used only female subjects.

Two additional studies, Bickman (1972), using female subjects, and Howard and Crano (1974), are not listed in the table because they do not present data in percentages. The findings, however, are quite consistent with those presented in the table. In the Bickman study (1972), subjects were not physically together. The naive subject, speaking over an intercom to another supposed bystander, was exposed to a crash and an apparent injury to a third group member. The programmed other bystander then verbally defined the situation as either not an emergency, possibly an emergency, or definitely an emergency. Speed scores increased as the definition as an emergency became clearer. This manipulation accomplishes verbally what the "two subjects together" or "programmed inactive bystander" conditions of the more typical experiments are assumed to do nonverbally. The Howard and Crano (1974) research involved a theft staged in a library, a student union lounge, or the union grill. Naturally occurring groups of two or more were less likely than lone individuals to respond by either stopping the thief or volunteering to identify the thief when directly questioned. Percentages are not given; the data are presented in terms of a 0–3 scale of degree of help. The findings, although difficult to interpret due to lack of random assignment of subjects to group versus individual conditions, demonstrate a group inhibition effect.

Informational Social Influence

A considerable amount of this research has demonstrated the importance of others in influencing the bystander's impression of the severity of the emergency and in consequently influencing helping behavior. In particular, the presence of nonresponsive bystanders, likely leading a potential benefactor to a no-help-needed definition, typically decreases intervention substantially. For example, Latané and Darley (1970) conducted an experiment in which subjects, while completing a questionnaire, were exposed to

Table 6.2

Effect of Number and Type of Visible Bystanders on the Percentage of Subjects Who Give a Helping Response in Various Emergencies[1]

	Alone	One other bystander[2]	More than one, special
Thefts			
Latané and Elman (In Darley and Latané, 1970), lab study	24 (25)	19 (16 pr)* $E = 42$	
Bonnarigo and Ross (In Darley and Latané, 1970), liquor store	65 (48)	56 (48 pr)* $E = 87$	
Shaffer, Rogel, and Hendrick, 1975, Expt. II, in library			
Committed	75 (16)	50 (16)*	
Uncommitted	32 (16)	0 (16)*	
Attempted rape			
Anderson, 1974, lab study	100 (31)		100 (9) three-man groups
Faints, falls, and crashes			
Latané and Rodin, 1969, in lab	70 (26)	7 (14)* 40 (20 pr)* $E = 91$	70 (20 pr)* $E = 91$ [a]
Smith, Smyth, and Lien, 1972, in lab	65 (20)	5 (20)*[3]	35 (20)[b]
Smith, Vanderbilt, and Callen, 1973, in lab		7 (15)*[3]	20 (15)[b] 60 (30)[c]
Wilson, 1976, in lab	75 (69)		38 (61)*[d] 83 (66)[e]

(continued)

133

Table 6.2 *(continued)*

	Alone	One other bystander[2]	More than one, special
Byeff, 1970 (unpub.), in lab			
Audio	40 (15)	28 (15 pr)* $E = 64$	
Audio–video	53 (15)	47 (15 pr) $E = 74$	
Solomon, Solomon, and Stone, 1978, in lab expts.			
Audio	30 (52)	15 (54 pr)* $E = 51$	
Audio–video	67 (52)	68 (53 pr) $E = 89$	
Same authors, field study			
Audio	62 (8)	50 (8 pr)* $E = 86$	
Audio–Video	100 (8)	100 (8 pr) $E = 100$	
Gaertner, 1975, in lab (Audio)			
White victim	100 (10)		90 (10)
Black victim	100 (10)		30 (10)
Gaertner, Dovidio, and Johnson, 1979a, in Lab (Audio-video)			
White victim	100 (12)		100 (11)
Black victim	100 (10)		80 (10)
Injuries to workmen Clark and Word, 1972, in lab			
High ambiguity	30 (10)	20 (10 pr)* $E = 51$	41 (10 four-man groups)* $E = 84$
Low ambiguity	100 (10)	100 (10 pr) $E = 100$	100 (10 five-man groups) $E = 100^f$

	¹	²	
Ross, 1971, in lab	83 (6)	16 (6)*	
Ross and Braband, 1973, in lab	64 (14)	35 (14)	
Darley, Teger, and Lewis, 1973	90 (10)	20 (10 pr)* $E = 99$[4]	80 (10 pr) $E = 99$[g]
Electrical emergency			
Clark and Word, 1974			
Expt. I and II: High ambiguity	16 (19)	44 (8 pr) $E = 28$	
Expt. I: Moderate ambiguity	36 (11)	50 (8 pr) $E = 59$	
Expt. II: Moderate ambiguity	75 (8)	75 (8 pr)* $E = 94$	
Expt. I and II: Unambiguous	95 (19)	100 (16 pr) $E = 100$	

* Percentage is significantly less than expected on the basis of response in the alone condition at at least $p < .05$. Entries are the percentage of subjects ever responding to the emergency with a helping response, as defined by the experimenters.

[1] Number of subjects in parentheses.

[2] This column includes subjects run with programmed nonreactive bystander-stooges (number of subjects in parentheses) and naive pairs of subjects (number of pairs in parentheses); E = expected number of pairs who would help based on rate of helping by alone subjects. E is calculated by $1 - (1 - P)n$, where P is proportion helping in alone condition, n is number of naive bystanders in group.

[3] The bystander-stooge is presented as being similar to the subject before the experiment.

[4] The naive subjects are seated back-to-back.

Special conditions footnotes:

[a] Subjects are pairs of friends.

[b] Programmed nonreactive bystander-stooge is presented as dissimilar to subject before experiment.

[c] Bystander-stooge is programmed to act alarmed. Similarity–dissimilarity was manipulated but had no effect, and conditions have been combined here.

[d] There are two programmed nonreactive bystander-stooges.

[e] There is one nonreactive and one active helping bystander-stooge.

[f] Subjects run in groups of five.

[g] These naive subjects are seated face-to-face.

a steady stream of smoke that would fill the room within 6 minutes. Subjects experienced the incident alone, together with two passive confederates, or together with two other naive subjects. Although 75% of the subjects experiencing the emergency alone reported the incident within 6 minutes, only 10% of the subjects with the passive confederates and 38% of the subjects in the groups responded. Furthermore, subjects who did not report the incident expressed little emotional concern. They uniformly rejected the idea that it was a fire and accepted a "nondangerous incident" definition of the situation. Obviously, then, the presence of other bystanders had powerful effects upon subjects' interpretations of the event and their responsiveness. Nevertheless, as in Sherif's (1936) and others' studies of informational social influence, subjects at the end of the study denied that they were influenced by the others.

In a subsequent study, Latané and Rodin (1969) demonstrated similar bystander inhibition effects under quite different emergency circumstances. In this experiment, subjects overheard a female in an adjacent room stand on a chair to reach a stack of papers located on the top of a bookcase. A loud crash, accompanied by screams and moans, followed. Seventy percent of the subjects who heard the emergency alone intervened to help, while only 7% of the subjects with a passive confederate responded. Inhibiting effects of the presence of a stranger or a friend were also present, but were less pronounced. In particular, the victim received help only 40% of the time when a pair of strangers overheard the emergency. Furthermore, anecdotal evidence reported by Latané and Rodin suggests the importance of informational social influence: "When strangers overheard the emergency, they seemed noticeably confused and concerned, attempting to interpret what they heard and to decide a course of action. They often glanced furtively at one another apparently anxious to discover the other's reaction yet unwilling to meet eyes and betray their own concern [p. 200]." In addition, subjects' postexperimental responses suggested that the presence of others influenced subjects' definition of the situation. Subjects who intervened reported that they did so because the fall sounded serious or because they were uncertain as to what happened and felt obliged to investigate. However, although many noninterveners were also uncertain of what happened, many (46%) concluded that it was not serious. Thus, it appears that in emergency situations in which some ambiguity exists, the presence of other bystanders may inhibit helping by subtly leading individuals to interpret the situation as less severe.

Investigators have continued to generate evidence suggesting the importance of others in defining the nature of an emergency. For example, Ross (1971), using an "injured workman," found that 83% of the subjects who witnessed an emergency alone intervened while only 16% of the subjects with a passive bystander helped. Darley, Teger, and Lewis (1973) similarly found that a victim received help 90% of the time when there was one bystander, but only 20% of the time when there was a pair of naive bystanders seated back-to-back. Two studies reported by Latané and Darley (1970) demonstrate the bystander inhibition effect under quite different circumstances. Studies by Latané and Elman and by Ross and Bonnarigo both found that the presence of others significantly reduced the frequency with which a theft was reported. Howard and Crano (1974) present similar findings.

Recently, studies have also focused more directly on the importance of information provided by others. Clark and Word (1972) demonstrated that subjects were more likely to intervene in a nonambiguous emergency involving verbal cues of distress than in an ambiguous emergency without verbal cues. Furthermore, under nonambiguous emergency circumstances, victims were no less likely to receive assistance from groups of naive bystanders than from bystanders who witnessed the emergency alone. The victim received 100% help in all conditions. When the emergency was ambiguous, increasing the relative importance of information provided by nonresponsive others, the victim received help relatively less often when bystanders witnessed the emergency in groups of two or five than when they were alone.

Using an alternative approach to explore the informational effect of others on bystander responsiveness, Smith, Smythe, and Lien (1972) manipulated the similarity of a confederate to the subject. Consistent with previous research, subjects in the presence of a nonresponsive confederate were significantly less helpful (20%) than subjects who were alone (65%). Furthermore, as one might expect based on social comparison theory, the inhibiting effect was most pronounced when the confederate had been presented as similar to the subject. Interestingly, when the confederate in a subsequent study was programmed to act alarmed (Smith, Vanderbilt, & Callen, 1973), subjects' rate of helping (60%) was equivalent to the alone condition in the earlier study and was unaffected by the degree of similarity with the other bystanders. Wilson (1976) found that although two passive confederates significantly decreased subjects' intervention (38%) compared to subjects who were alone (75%), the presence of one active confederate increased the rate of responding (83%).

Bickman (1972) provides even more direct demonstration of the informational effect of fellow bystanders on intervention in an emergency. In this study, a confederate located in a separate room provided the subject with a crisis, possible crisis, or noncrisis definition of the situation. The manipulation of information produced dramatic results on the speed of intervention ($p < .001$). Subjects who heard the crisis definition helped fastest, subjects who heard the noncrisis explanation helped slowest, with the possible-crisis definition group helping at an intermediate rate. Similarly, Borges and Penta (1977) found that subjects were more likely to intervene when a confederate expressed concern for a victim than when the confederate said nothing (75% versus 16%). Finally, Staub (1974) conducted a study in which information defining the situation was volunteered by confederates in a face-to-face setting. During the study, female subjects heard a crash in an adjoining room, followed by a female's cry for help. In one condition, the confederate suggested to the subject, "That sounds like a tape recording. Maybe they are trying to test us. . . ." In another condition, the confederate emphasized the seriousness of the situation by responding, "That sounds bad. Maybe we should do something, " and then prepared to enter the adjacent room. Two control groups were also included. Some subjects were exposed to the emergency alone while other subjects overheard the accident in pairs. Consistent with earlier findings, subjects who heard the confederate reinforce the severity of the situation helped most, 100%. Intermediate levels of helping were obtained from subjects who witnessed the emergency alone, 93%, or in pairs, 60%. Subjects with confederates who minimized the seriousness of the situation were least likely to help, 25%. Thus, there appears to be considerable evidence demonstrating that one way in which the presence of other bystanders can affect intervention is by influencing the perceived clarity or severity of the emergency.

If one type of effect of the face-to-face presence of others can be attributable to differential perceptions of the clarity and severity of the emergency, then it is possible that both personal costs for not helping and empathic costs for the victim receiving no help may be affected. To the extent that the presence of others leads a bystander to interpret the situation as less critical, he or she should feel less social pressure to intervene and should anticipate less blame for not helping. Thus, personal costs for not helping would be lower. In addition, empathic costs should also be reduced. That is, it is likely that a decrease in arousal accompanies the no-help-needed conclusion frequently reached by subjects in the face-to-face presence of others. Indeed, anecdotal evidence from the series of studies conducted by Latané and Darley indicated that subjects, upon defining the situation as nonserious, exhibited little "emotional concern." Only the study of Byeff (1970), however, directly measured arousal under these conditions.

In the Byeff investigation, some subjects were the sole bystander to the "fallen woman" emergency, while other subjects witnessed the emergency together in face-to-face pairs. The results, consistent with previous research, revealed a social inhibition effect ($p < .05$) on the rate of intervention in the "together" condition. "Together" subjects also tended to respond more slowly than "alone" subjects (speed score difference, $p = .11$). In addition, supportive of our foregoing discussion, "together" subjects also exhibited significantly less arousal ($p = .05$), as indexed by the height of the first GSR peak following the accident, than "alone" subjects. Thus, the social influence inhibition effect hypothesized to occur in the face-to-face presence of others apparently was accompanied by a decreased level of bystander arousal. Across "alone" and "together" conditions, arousal and latency were again correlated, $r = -.40$. Unfortunately, subjects' cognitive assessments of the seriousness of the emergency were not recorded systematically.

Normative Social Influence

Although the process of normative social influence (i.e., concern for the evaluation of others) has received little explicit empirical attention in the emergency helping behavior literature compared to informational social influence and diffusion of responsibility, its importance has been suggested by several investigators. For example, Latané and Darley (1970) described audience inhibition effects in which an individual believes that others are aware of his or her responses and desires to optimize their evaluations. More recently, Schwartz and Gottlieb (1976) renamed this process evaluation apprehension in order to avoid any directional connotation. That is, normative social influence (or evaluation apprehension) could conceivably either facilitate or inhibit bystander responsiveness. If individuals feel an obligation to help when others are in trouble (Heberlein, 1975) and believe that other people share this norm (Bickman, 1971), then the belief that others are aware of their response should facilitate bystander intervention. If, however, a person both believes that others are aware of his or her behavior and witnesses a unanimously nonresponsive reaction of the group, then the individual may come to believe that intervention is not appropriate in that situation. As suggested by Gaertner (1975), the uniformly nonresponsive group establishes a norm of nonintervention. Thus, in many of the studies involving the face-to-face presence of bystanders (Latané & Dabbs, 1975; Latané & Rodin, 1969; Ross & Braband, 1973; Smith, Vanderbilt, & Callen, 1973), both normative and informational social influence may have been operating to inhibit helping behavior.

One experiment conducted by Schwartz and Gottlieb (1976) was designed to isolate normative social influence effects; in it the responsiveness of bystanders who believed that others were either aware or unaware of their behavior was compared. Consistent with their expectations, Schwartz and Gottlieb found that bystanders were more likely to intervene when others were aware of their actions (74%) than when others were unaware (39%). Furthermore, subjects' postexperimental reports indicated that realizing that others would be aware of whether or not they intervened increased bystanders' own sense of obligation as well as their thoughts about what others expected of them. A more recent investigation by Schwartz and Gottlieb (Study 1, 1980) replicated the finding that in an unambiguous emergency, evaluation apprehension can enhance responding. In this study, subjects whose presence was known to others were more likely to help and more likely to report a sense that others expected them to help than were subjects who believed that their presence was unknown to others.[4] It appears, then, that implicit norms of social responsibility, when focused on the bystander, may increase the likelihood of intervention.

In order to further investigate normative social influence during emergencies and to explore its psychophysiological effects, we conducted another study on bystander intervention (Gaertner et al., 1979a). The procedure for this study was generally similar to our investigation of diffusion of responsibility. Female subjects participated in an ESP task and ultimately witnessed a chair-crashing incident. Subjects, however, were in the actual physical presence of three female confederate bystanders who remained passive and uniformly nonresponsive during the 3-minute period that followed. In addition, in order to minimize the effect of informational social influence, an unambiguous situation was created in which subjects witnessed the chair-falling incident on closed-circuit television. Specifically, after the screams and the loud crash, the black or white victim fell into the camera's view and collapsed, apparently unconscious, to the floor among the fallen chairs. The victim remained motionless for the remainder of the emergency period.

Although the bystander inhibition effects on helping were predicted to be similar to the results we obtained under diffusion of responsibility conditions, we anticipated that the different processes underlying diffusion and normative social influence effects would be reflected in subjects' psychophysiological responses. When bystanders are isolated from other potential helpers and have the opportunity to diffuse responsibility, they may come to believe that somebody else is already helping. A reduced level of arousal, therefore, characterizes the process of diffusion of responsibility. For subjects who witness a relatively unambiguous emergency in the face-

[4] In a seizure emergency that developed slowly (Schwartz & Gottlieb, 1980, Study 2,), the effect of being known to others was more complex. During the ambiguous phase of the emergency, anonymous bystanders responded more slowly than those known to other witnesses. After the emergency became clear, anonymous bystanders tended to respond more quickly. Schwartz and Gottlieb suggest that subjects who had still not responded when the need became unequivocal probably interpreted the inaction of other bystanders as indicating that others expected the subject *not* to intervene.

to-face presence of uniformly nonresponsive bystanders, however, heightened emotionality was expected to reflect their conflict between helping the victim or conforming to the group.

Replicating previous studies, subjects helped the victim more quickly when they were alone than when they were in the presence of others ($p <$ .01). Across the conditions, the rate of intervention was uniformly high (80%–100%), indicating extreme clarity of the emergency. It was therefore expected that the inhibiting effect of other bystanders would be due to normative influence, rather than informational influence in which a no-help-needed definition would be suggested. Consistent with this hypothesis, the analysis of subjects' ratings of the severity of the victim's injury showed no effect associated with the manipulation of the presence of others. Thus, the obtained pattern of helping behavior for subjects in the alone and together conditions could not be attributable to differences in their definitions of the situation.

Subjects' psychophysiological responses were also supportive of the conformity hypothesis. The analysis of subjects' cardiac response after the emergency revealed a main effect for the presence of others ($p <$ .01). The effect, however, was different than the arousal pattern previously obtained for diffusion of responsibility. Consistent with the hypothesized normative influence generated by the passive behavior of other bystanders, subjects experienced a greater increase in heart rate when they witnessed the emergency with others than when they witnessed it alone. Within-cell correlations between latency of intervention and postemergency heart rate revealed negative relationships for subjects who were the only witness to an emergency involving a white ($r = -$ .60) or a black ($r = -$ .23) victim. The greater the heart rate, the more quickly subjects intervened. However, for subjects in the presence of a uniformly nonresponsive bystander group and for whom conflict-generated arousal was hypothesized, positive correlations were obtained for both white victim ($r = +$ .65) and black victim ($r = +$ .57) conditions. Thus, in the situation in which conformity pressures were likely operating, the greater the level of arousal, the more hesitant subjects were to intervene.

It appears, then, that normative social influence in emergency situations may affect personal costs for helping, personal costs for not helping, and arousal. If the perceived social forces favor intervention, the presence of others increases the personal costs for not helping and increases the anticipated rewards for helping. If, however, the bystander expects social censure for intervention, the presence of others increases the costs for helping. Thus, normative influences may more often place subjects in a dilemma than do informational social influence or diffusion processes. When perceived censure increases the costs for helping while the continued suffering of the victim and internal conflict increase the bystander's unpleasant state of arousal (thereby increasing costs for the victim receiving no help), the situation becomes one represented by the "high–high" cell of the 2 × 2 cost matrix presented in Table 5.1. In order to relieve the dilemma, the bystander is likely to engage in one of the processes outlined in the previous chapter: cognitive reinterpretation, direct intervention, indirect help, or no response.

SOCIAL INFLUENCE AND DIFFUSION OF RESPONSIBILITY: A COMPARISON

There are only two available pieces of research in which the design allows for a direct comparison between diffusion and social influence effects within the same study. The two studies are Byeff (1970) and Schwartz and Gottlieb (1976). The studies give us somewhat different but not contradictory information. Diffusion and social influence appear to be dynamically distinct processes that operate at different times in determining bystander response to an emergency.

In the Byeff (1970) study, subjects, either alone, in separated pairs, or together in face-to-face pairs, witnessed a "fallen woman" emergency presented with audio-only or audio-visual cues. Cumulative response curves for this experiment are presented in Figure 6.1. In the clear, audio-visual emergency, subjects in the "separated" condition behaved similarly to alone subjects; in fact, a slightly higher proportion of them

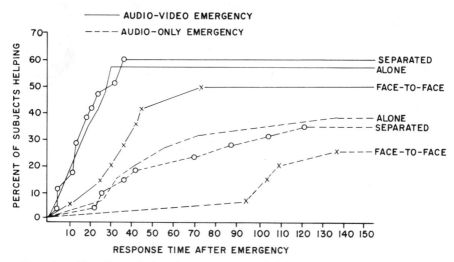

Figure 6.1. The effects of alone, face-to-face, and separated-pairs bystander conditions on intervention in audio-visual and audio-only emergencies. [From Byeff, 1970.]

responded by the end of the emergency. In the "together" condition, pairs
of subjects exhibited an inhibition effect. In terms of actual responses, they
were slower to respond than "alone" subjects, and a somewhat lower
percentage of them eventually helped. As indicated in Figure 6.1, this inhibition effect in dyads occurred immediately after the onset of the
emergency. In the ambiguous, audio-only condition, "separated" subjects
again behaved very much like "alone" subjects, although there is a suggestion of a diffusion effect between 30 and 120 seconds. During this period,
"separated" subjects responded consistently more slowly than "alone" subjects. As shown in the "together" conditions, there is, however, a very large
informational social influence effect, which again occurred at the onset of
the crisis. "Together" subjects responded more slowly than "alone" subjects
throughout the postemergency period.

Schwartz and Gottlieb (1976) have also compared social influence and
diffusion effects. Cumulative response curves for their five conditions are
presented in Figure 6.2. In this study, which involved a violent theft and
thus some danger, there was both an early effect of social influence (see the
mutually aware condition) and a later effect of diffusion (see the mutually
unaware condition). The interpretation Schwartz and Gottlieb propose is
that the two manipulations operate at different points in the decision pro-

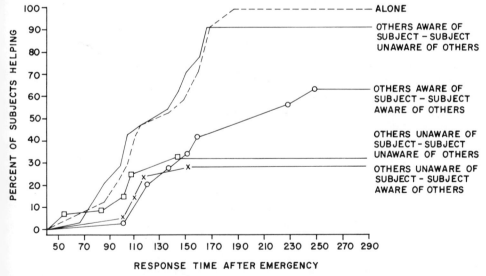

Figure 6.2. The effects of the subject's being aware of the behavior of the other bystanders
and other bystanders' being aware of the subject's behavior on bystander intervention in a
violent theft. [From S. H. Schwartz & A. Gottlieb, Bystander reactions to a violent theft:
Crime in Jerusalem. *Journal of Personality and Social Psychology,* 1976, *34,* 1188–1199. Copyright 1976 by the American Psychological Association. Reprinted by permission.]

cess. Informational social influence has its effect as bystanders are attempting to interpret the situation: "Is it an emergency? Is any action required?" Diffusion, they suggest, has its effect later in the postemergency period as bystanders attempt to determine their personal responsibility after deciding that the event requires action.

In summary, the results of several independent investigations of normative and informational social influence and diffusion of responsibility as well as the findings of Byeff (1970) and Schwartz and Gottlieb (1976) support the notion that informational social influence, normative social influence, and diffusion of responsibility are dynamically distinct processes as initially proposed by Latané and Darley (1970). Informational social influence typically exerts its effect soon after the onset of the emergency. It primarily influences bystanders' interpretation of the situation, and thus their experience of the event as an emergency. Diffusion of responsibility, if it occurs, appears later in the postemergency sequence, apparently after the bystander has defined the event as an emergency, and seems to be related to the decision of what personal action to take. Normative social influence effects also occur later and are related to concern about the evaluation of others. These processes, as we suggested earlier, appear to relate to both cost–benefit considerations and arousal factors.

The Nature of the Bystander-Victim Relationship

Similarity and feelings of closeness to the victim are proposed to increase the bystander's potential for empathic arousal as well as the values within the cost–benefit matrix. Using the extreme example, it is difficult to deny that an emergency occurring to one's own child would be more arousing and failure to intervene more costly than the same emergency involving a total stranger.

In terms of empathic arousal we seem more likely to put ourselves in the place of a victim we perceive to be like us, or one whom we know and have ties with than to do so with a stranger or with a person perceived to be different. A series of pioneering studies by Stotland and his colleagues (Stotland, 1969) demonstrated that instructions to imagine how a suffering or joyous person was feeling (as opposed to instructions merely to watch this person), as well as similarity to this other person, indeed increased the magnitude of an observer's empathic arousal as measured by changes in palmar sweating and vasoconstriction. With greater methodological refinement, Krebs (1975) replicated the finding that similarity to a person observed to be experiencing pain or pleasure is associated with greater psychophysiological arousal (heart rate, vasoconstriction, and skin conductance). Self-report measures of empathy (e.g., how did you feel while waiting for the performer to receive a punishment?) showed similar results. Krebs, however, followed the similarity–empathic arousal process one step further by providing his subjects with an opportunity to offer assistance to the performer at considerable cost (electric shock) to themselves. Consistent with the hypothesis that similarity facilitates higher levels of empathic arousal, which in turn mediates helping, Krebs reported that people who experienced the highest levels of empathic arousal were more self-sacrificing and helpful than subjects receiving experimental treatments associated with lower levels of empathic arousal. In a similar vein, Aderman and Berkowitz (1970) and Coke, Batson, and McDavis (1978) have demonstrated the mediating role of empathic arousal (using self-report feelings) induced by the observational set to imagine the self in the place of another in helping in nonemergency situations.

Taken together, the studies by Stotland (1969), Krebs (1975), Aderman and Berkowitz (1970), and Coke *et al.* (1978) offer support for the proposition that similar victims generate higher magnitudes of vicarious arousal and helping because it is easier to identify with their circumstances than with those of dissimilar victims. Unfortunately, there is a paucity of psychophysiological findings, particularly with respect to emergency situations, that directly address this issue. Nevertheless, there is an abundance of research demonstrating that bystanders are more likely to offer assistance to similar than dissimilar others. Few of these studies involved intervention in emergency situations, however.

Hornstein and his colleagues (Hodgson, Hornstein, & LaKind, 1972; Hornstein, 1972, 1976; Hornstein, Masor, Sole, & Heilman, 1971; Sole, Marton, & Hornstein, 1975) have applied an extension of the Lewinian tension system construct in an attempt to understand the causes of prosocial behavior. Hornstein and his colleagues propose that people often help one another for the purpose of reducing promotive tension, defined as tension aroused by the awareness of another's interrupted goal attainment. That is, our own need state can become coordinated to that of another, which then motivates behavior intended to reduce this tension. It is proposed that perceived similarity to the other, which increases interpersonal attractiveness and which may also increase the feeling of "we-ness," must characterize the relationship with the other person before promotive tension can be aroused. In support of this reasoning, Hornstein *et al.* (1971) arranged for pedestrians in a Jewish section of New York City to find two open envelopes clipped together, apparently dropped by accident. One envelope contained a questionnaire that indicated that the stranger's attitude toward the Mid-East crisis was either pro-Israeli or pro-Arab. Earlier extensive pilot work established the efficacy of this manipulation of perceived similarity and interpersonal attractiveness of the stranger in this Jewish area (see also Byrne, 1971). The contents of the second envelope, a check and a contribution card indicating whether the enclosed contribution to the "Institute for Research in Medicine" was the second or ninth in a series of 10 planned contributions, set the stage for an elegant test of Lewinian assumptions about psychological tension.

Hornstein *et al.* hypothesized that the interrupted goal attainment of liked others would be completed (i.e., the lost envelope would be mailed) more often when the contributors were close to completing their goal of 10 donations. That is, tension or arousal would be greatest for liked others when their goal attainment was more imminent, while for disliked others, nearness to the goal was expected to be irrelevant. As expected, pedestrians mailed the charitable contribution in behalf of the pro-Israeli stranger more frequently when he was close (86.7%) rather than far (53.3%) from his goal. There was no difference in the proportion of pedestrians helping the pro-Arab stranger when he was close (44.8%) or far (53.6%) from his goal. In addition, the envelope containing the questionnaire expressing the pro-Israeli opinion (69%) was returned more frequently than pro-Arab questionnaires (30%), lending further support to the relationship between similarity and prosocial behavior. With regard to the effects of belief similarity, Hornstein (1978) points out that dissimilar strangers, although less attractive, did not seem to stimulate an aversive, intentionally harmful response. Instead, dissimilarity did not allow for the development of promotive tension or arousal, which for similar others seemed to mediate helping behavior.

Brewer's (1979) review of ingroup bias in the minimal intergroup situation (see Billig & Tajfel, 1973; Dion, 1973; Rabbie & Horwitz, 1969; Worchel, Andreoli, & Folger, 1977) concludes that members of outgroups are not necessarily deprecated relative to nondescript, undifferentiated others (i.e., those who are neither members of ingroups or outgroups). However, ingroup members are perceived as "better" than members of both outgroupers and the nondescript. Consistent with Hornstein's findings, members of outgroups do not automatically engender feelings of hostility and destructiveness. There is a bias for ingroup favoritism, not outgroup rejection.

The manner in which similarity mediates helping is still elusive, however. Similarity of belief increases interpersonal attractiveness, but it may also give rise to feelings of general promotive interdependence relating to mutuality of fate. These feelings, then, may bind the self and others together with a sense of "we-ness", independent of interpersonal attractiveness. The findings of Sole *et al.* (1975) speak to this issue. The procedures were basically identical to the study discussed earlier except the questionnaire contained four issues rather than only one and the pedestrians were led to believe that the stranger was always close to his goal of 10 contributions to the medical charity. After extensive pretesting of attitudes within the neighborhood in which the envelopes were to be lost, five levels of similarity were established (i.e., 0%, 25%, 50%, 75% and 100%).

When the beliefs of the stranger concerned important issues, any deviation from 100% similarity reduced helpfulness sharply in a stepwise fashion. There were no reliable differences in helping among the 0%, 25%, 50%, and 75% similarity conditions, although each group helped less frequently than the 100% similarity group. Nevertheless, pilot work established that attractiveness of the stranger increased monotonically with increases in similarity on these important issues. In other words, although the 75% similar stranger was more attractive than the 0% similar stranger, there was no difference in the amount of help accorded these people. When the beliefs of the stranger involved unimportant issues, subjects responded quite differently. Overall, helping was considerably lower. Moreover, when unimportant issues constituted the basis for similarity, helping increased monotonically with the proportion of similar beliefs, but attraction to the stranger was not affected by the similarity manipulation. Thus, degree of similarity, not attraction, seemed to constitute the basis for helping.

The stepwise effect for helping when important issues were varied and the finding that similarity, not attraction, related to helping when unimportant issues were varied suggests that similarity permits the formation of we–they categorizations, which then affects the arousal of promotive tension. Hornstein (1978), however, claims that the role of attraction cannot be discounted entirely because it is possible that a threshold for attraction (beyond 75% agreement on important issues) might be required for the arousal of promotive tension. With unimportant issues, even complete similarity does not seem to generate very high levels of promotive tension given that helping overall was quite low. Obviously though, the we–they interpretation for the arousal of promotive tension is the most parsimonious.

The feeling of "we-ness," leading to more positive ingroup behaviors, seems to increase when people share a common fate, particularly if that fate is highly arousing and stressful (Lanzetta, 1955; Mulder & Stemerding, 1963; Sherif, Harvey, White, Hood, & Sherif, 1961). Campbell and Levine (1972) and Collins (1970) have suggested that external threat increases awareness of ingroup identity. With greater awareness of ingroup identity, members should be more likely to experience sympathetic identification with each other's needs, leading to an increase in prosocial behavior. A study by Dovidio and Morris (1975) nicely supports this reasoning. These investigators prepared subjects to participate in either a highly stressful study involving electric shock or a less stressful word association experiment. Then, a confederate of the experimenter was introduced as someone waiting to participate in the same study as the subject or in some other study (involving shock or word association). During the waiting period the confederate, apparently by accident, knocked over a container sending 100 pencils to the floor of the laboratory. Thus subjects were provided with an opportunity to help the confederate although no direct request for assistance was made.

The results indicated a main effect for common fate but also a Fate × Stress interaction. Basically, subjects under high stress who shared a common fate with the confederate helped more frequently than low-stress-common-fate subjects; however, high-stress subjects with a confederate of dissimilar fate were less helpful than low-stress–dissimilar-fate subjects. The pattern of means suggested that sharing a similar stressful experience increases ingroup identification and also the awareness of the needs of ingroup members, while the experience of stress alone (high-stress–dissimilar-fate increases the salience of one's own needs. Shared or similar fate, however, regardless of stress, seems sufficient to arouse some sympathetic identification, promotive tension, or empathic arousal coordinated with the needs of the other. Batson, Pate, Lawless, Sparkman, Lambers, and Worman (1979) have provided partial replication of these results using a game situation in which "disaster" can strike either player. Similarity of the confederate and personal threat of disaster to the subject were varied. An interaction was obtained such that threat affected sharing behavior only with the dissimilar victim. The authors suggest that "we-ness" leads to sharing with the similar victim regardless of whether or not the subject is concerned about his own future need. With the dissimilar victim, however, sharing occurs only when the subject may want reciprocation.

A number of other studies, discussed below, varied the degree of belief similarity between the potential benefactor and recipient of nonemergency assistance but did not vary or directly measure any dimension of arousal. Generally, these studies report positive relationships between similarity and helping across a variety of interpersonal situations. We will describe some of these researches because of their potential relevance to empathic tension arousal (as opposed to alarm, distress, and upset) and also because their generally consistent pattern of findings presents a marked contrast to studies that varied racial similarity between bystander and victim, which will be discussed in the next section. In addition, these studies of bystander–victim similarity also have relevance to the cost–benefit considerations of the model.

As emotional involvement, a sense of "we-ness," similarity, or attraction to the victim increases, the benefits associated with helping as well as the costs for not helping, both personal and empathic, are proposed to increase monotonically. Furthermore, the costs for helping should be less for similar than for dissimilar victims if only because the bystander would be more confident of the consequences associated with interacting with a similar victim. Also, the empathic costs for not helping dissimilar victims might be lower given that the bystander may be less concerned for the victim's well-being, while personal costs for not helping might also be lower since the social censure for not intervening may be expected to be less. Thus, the arousal:cost–reward model unambiguously predicts that emotional involvement, similarity, and "we-ness" should increase the likelihood of prosocial responding.

The literature presents a relatively consistent picture supportive of the similarity–helping prediction, which could have been derived from a number of theoretical perspectives. Furthermore, the advantage given victims similar to the bystander seems to occur across a wide variety of situations. Baron (1971), for example, reported that a face-to-face request was granted more frequently to a person of similar beliefs who expressed positive attitudes toward the potential benefactor relative to a person who had dissimilar beliefs and who earlier had ridiculed the subject's character. This effect was especially strong for moderate and large (i.e., very costly) favor requests. Gross, Wallston, and Piliavin (1975) also found that people were more willing to accede to a request from a third party in behalf of a pleasant than unpleasant experimenter. Similarly, Pandey and Griffitt (1974) demonstrated that subjects, when solicited indirectly by a third party, more readily helped a person with similar than dissimilar beliefs. Support for the similarity–helping prediction is also obtained in situations in which help is not explicitly solicited. Karabenick, Lerner, and Beecher (1973) observed that voters leaving a polling place more frequently stopped to help pick up campaign materials dropped by placard-carrying campaign workers supporting the bystander's own preferred candidate (assessed afterward by a second experimenter) than campaign workers supporting the opposition's candidate. Similarly, Ehlert, Ehlert, and Merrens (1973) reported that university students encountering a parked automobile with its headlights on more frequently turned the headlights off when the automobile had no bumper sticker than when a bumper sticker proclaimed the probably unpopular campus views, "Support the Black Panthers," or "America—Love it or leave it." Reykowski (undated manuscript A), a Polish researcher, also reports the similarity–helping relationship. Specifically, he cites research by Karylowski (unpublished, 1973) indicating that subjects increased their production rates for similar partners and decreased their work rates for dissimilar partners. Karylowski (1976) reports a similar finding (which may be the same study).

In further support of the hypothesis that similarity of beliefs, a sense of "we-ness", or attractiveness is related to helping, some investigators found that people are more likely to comply with a direct request for a small favor (e.g., "Can you give me two nickels for a dime?") from a person dressed more similarly to themselves (Emswiller, Deaux, & Willits, 1971; Harris & Baudin, 1973; Raymond & Unger, 1972). In addition, physical attractiveness of the victim seems to promote increases in prosocial responding. Benson, Karabenick, and Lerner (1976) reported that people who found a lost graduate school application form in an airport phone booth were more likely to mail these materials when an attached photograph was that of an attractive than that of an unattractive applicant. West and Brown (1975) also found that males were more helpful to an attractive than unattractive coed when she asked for money to treat a serious wound. However, a less severe wound did not produce differences between helping attractive and unattractive victims. Research also indicates that brief personal contact between a potential helper and a recipient either during (Lindskold, Forte, Haake, & Schmidt, 1977) or prior to the helping opportunity (Baer, Goldman, & Juhnke, 1977) can facilitate helping behavior.

Although similarity and interpersonal attraction are generally potent variables, their effects are sometimes mitigated by other factors introduced into the situation. For example, Macaulay (1975) found that familiarity with a victim seemed to override likability. Also, Regan (1971) reported that the desire to reciprocate a favor reduced the effect of liking on helping. In addition, the need to avoid publicly appearing vindictive toward a disliked other seemed to promote relatively high levels of helping (Goodstadt, 1971; Nemeth, 1970). In terms of the general picture, though, the finding (at least in nonemergency situations) relating helping to belief similarity, a sense of "we-ness" between a potential benefactor and recipient, and attractiveness support the hypothesis that these interpersonal factors increase the likelihood of prosocial responding.

RACE AND HELPING

Since emotional involvement, similarity, and a sense of "we-ness" seem to facilitate prosocial behavior, predictions concerning the effects of racial similarity seem straightforward (particularly in view of the evidence that without additional information, racial dissimilarity often leads to the assumption of belief dissimilarity [Stein, Hardyck, & Smith, 1965]). It would be expected that:

1. Racially similar victims would be helped more readily than racially dissimilar victims.
2. Greater levels of arousal would be experienced when witnessing emergencies involving racially similar than dissimilar victims.
3. The effects in 1 and 2 above should be more pronounced among bystanders scoring relatively high on prejudice inventories.

An examination of the 20 or so studies relating racial similarity to the victim and helping, particularly for white bystanders, does not offer strong and consistent support for any of the above predictions. Some research has indeed reported that whites are less likely to help black victims than white victims (Benson et al., 1976; Clark, 1974; Franklin, 1974; Gaertner, 1973; Gaertner & Bickman, 1971; Graf & Riddell, 1972; West, Whitney, & Schnedler, 1975). Other research, however, found that, depending upon the experimental treatment, blacks are helped either less frequently or as frequently as white victims (Farra, Zinser, & Bailey, 1978; Gaertner, 1975; Gaertner & Dovidio, 1977; Gaertner et al., 1979a; Piliavin, Rodin, & Piliavin, 1969). In addition, some investigators report, depending upon experimental treatment, that blacks are helped *more* frequently than white victims (Dutton, 1971; Dutton & Lake, 1973; Dutton & Lennox, 1974; Katz, Cohen, & Glass, 1975; Katz, Glass, Lucido, & Farber, 1979; Thayer, 1973). Finally, a few studies failed to observe any differential effects of the victim's race on helping (Bickman & Kamzan, 1973; Lerner & Frank, 1974; Wegner & Crano, 1975; Wispé & Freshley, 1971).

Furthermore, although we are aware of only two studies that examined the issue (Gaertner & Dovidio, 1977; Gaertner et al., 1979a), arousal among white bystanders, as measured by changes in heart rate upon witnessing an emergency, was not consistently greater on behalf of racially similar victims than for racially dissimilar victims. Also, the effects of a victim's race on emergency helping have not generally been related to the bystander's measured racial attitude (Gaertner, 1975; Gaertner & Dovidio, 1977; Gaertner et al., 1979a).

In addition, the effect of racial dissimilarity sometimes appears to be mediated by the race of the potential benefactor. Some studies demonstrate that the victim's race seems to have greater impact on the prosocial behavior of white compared to black bystanders (Gaertner & Bickman, 1971; Graf & Riddell, 1972; Thayer, 1973; Wispé & Freshley, 1971). Nevertheless, Wegner and Crano (1975) found that black college students were more likely to assist a black than a white student pick up computer cards and West, Whitney, and Schnedler (1975) reported that black motorists were more likely to help a black than a white motorist in distress. The pattern in the West et al. (1975) study, however, suggested problack rather than antiwhite sentiment. Thus, the helping behavior of white bystanders toward racially similar and racially dissimilar victims does not generally mirror the findings when beliefs alone constitute the basis of similarity. We believe that the theoretical orientation concerning contemporary racial attitudes proposed by Gaertner and Dovidio (1977), which integrates nicely with the arousal: cost–reward model, can account for this discrepancy.

THE NATURE OF RACIAL ATTITUDES

A number of investigators have accumulated evidence that supports Myrdal's (1944) conclusion regarding the conflicted nature of white America's attitudes toward blacks and other minorities (Katz, 1970; Katz et al., 1975; Katz, Glass, & Cohen, 1973). These investigators have characterized the racial attitudes of most whites as neither uniformly favorable nor all negative, but as ambivalent. Also, we (Gaertner, 1976; Gaertner & Dovidio, 1977) suggested that the racial attitudes of many people who claim low racial prejudice may best be characterized by a special type of ambivalence, that is, aversiveness (Kovel, 1969). The aversive type is characterized by a conflict between negative feelings toward blacks, which are not always consciously salient, and a conscience that seeks to dissociate these feelings from a nonprejudiced self-image. More typically, this aversive attitude involves a sense of discomfort and uneasiness. One cause of this discomfort is that in interracial situations many whites seem motivated to avoid acting inappropriately. In our society, race and ethnic origin have been too often declared to be inappropriate, unfair criteria, by themselves, with which to justify negative responding. Just as subjects appeared to be concerned with maintaining a nonvindictive public image in the Nemeth (1970) and Goodstadt (1971) studies, we propose that people are concerned with protecting a nonbigoted self-image. Based on this theoretical framework, then, we propose that most low-prejudice-scoring people and even many high-prejudice-scoring people are not likely to view themselves as prejudiced to the extent that they would act negatively toward someone based merely on the fact of that person's race. In fact, the importance of people maintaining a relatively egalitarian, open-minded self-image also represents a key link, as we see it, to the arousal: cost–reward model.

Our orientation suggests that racial attitudes are more typically expressed in rationalizable, rather than in overt, ways. Thus, we propose that in addition to the personal costs incurred for not helping a white victim, there is a special cost associated with not helping a black victim. This framework, therefore, suggests that whites are more likely to discriminate in situations in which failure to respond favorably could be attributable to factors other than the person's race. In terms of the arousal:cost–benefit model, the proposed indirect attitudinal process does not simply or directly minimize emergency-generated arousal or raise the costs associated with helping or decrease costs for not helping black victims. Rather, it is proposed that the victim's race affects helping by differentially modifying the personal costs imposed by other elements that enter the cost–benefit analysis. Thus, variables that ordinarily increase costs for helping or decrease personal costs for not helping are believed to be more exaggerated for black than for white victims. In an emergency, this proposed indirect attitudinal process is hypothesized to differentially increase the saliency and potency of those non-race-related factors that would justify becoming personally involved, even if the victim were white. However, when no non-race-related justification to avoid intervention is readily available, white bystanders are expected to behave either without regard for the victim's race or to respond even more favorably toward blacks, in order to avoid the special cost associated with the potential self-attribution of bigoted intent.

The work of Dutton and his colleagues (Dutton, 1971, 1973; Dutton & Lake, 1973; Dutton & Lennox, 1974) has shown that whites may be more helpful toward blacks than toward whites to protect or reaffirm a liberal, nonprejudiced self-image. This "extra" helpfulness, which consisted of donating more money to black than to white panhandlers, among subjects whose egalitarian self-image was threatened, served to preclude more costly assistance on behalf of a Brotherhood Week campus campaign. Liberal, egalitarian subjects whose self-image was not threatened and who were not solicited by black panhandlers felt least compelled to participate in the Brotherhood Week campaign. Evidently, helping blacks may reflect an effort at reaffirming a nonprejudiced self-image. When the self-image is not threatened, however, these whites are not particularly interested in behaving in a manner consistent with their espoused values. A recent article by Katz *et al.* (1979) provides data that also fit this interpretation. Some subjects were induced to compose and read a critical personality assessment of a black or white confederate. Feedback from the experimenter indicated that the confederate had been quite upset by the negative evaluation. Subjects were later asked to help the confederate with a class assignment. A Race × Criticism interaction revealed that the most help was offered in the black–criticism condition. Another study reported in the same article used a physically handicapped versus a physically normal confederate manipulation and found the same pattern of results. This is consistent with a recent study by Snyder, Kleck, Strenta, and Mentzer (1979), which suggests the same sort of ambivalence toward the handicapped as we are proposing exists regarding blacks.

Our own research was designed to test the proposed manner in which racial attitudes affect helping behavior among white bystanders. Basically, our strategy has been to arrange for high- and low-prejudice-scoring white bystanders to witness emergencies involving a black or white victim. We varied the presence of non-race-related factors that bystanders could use to justify nonintervention without necessarily threatening their nonbigoted self-images. Given our assumptions regarding the ambivalence of racial attitudes among both high- and low-prejudice scorers, we did not really expect to observe any differences between these groups, except in one particular instance in which the emergency was extremely compelling. Since we were interested in the effects of emergency-generated arousal, heart rate changes as a function of the victim's race were obtained in some of the studies. We will describe this research briefly here, attending only to findings that relate to race and victim effects on arousal, arousal attribution, and helping.

In Gaertner and Dovidio (Study 2, 1977), discussed in Chapter 4, subjects witnessed either an ambiguous or unambiguous emergency after ingesting a placebo described as having arousal or nonarousal side-effects. Both of these variables were expected to differentially affect the bystanders' responsiveness to the situation as a function of the victim's race. White female bystanders were expected to help black female victims less readily than white victims only when the emergency was ambiguous. Since this situation could more easily be interpreted as one in which help is not needed, failure to intervene could be attributed to the fact that helping is not necessary. However, racial discrimination would not be expected for the unambiguous emergency unless the bystander had some other non-race-related rationale that would reduce her motivation or perceived necessity to intervene, as might be the case for bystanders given the placebo described as having arousing side-effects. If motivation to intervene is related to its instrumentality to reduce arousal and if emergency-generated arousal has the opportunity of being misattributed to the pill, subjects with the arousal placebo would be expected to help less readily than those without this misattributional alternative. In general, misattribution effects on helping were expected to be greater for black than for white victims since the opportunity to misattribute emergency-generated arousal could provide an alternative appraisal of the situation for bystanders motivated not to intervene—without threatening their nonbigoted self-images.

The pattern of results was generally supportive of the predictions. Without an opportunity to misattribute emergency generated arousal (i.e., the nonarousal placebo group), black victims were helped less quickly than white victims when the emergency was ambiguous (means were 196 versus 148 seconds). During the unambiguous emergency, however, black victims were helped as quickly as white victims (63 versus 64 seconds). Furthermore, when the emergency was unambiguous, black victims were helped more slowly than white victims only by subjects given the opportunity to misattribute the source of arousal to the placebo (114 versus 64 seconds).

Another study (Gaertner & Dovidio, 1977, Study 1) concerned the likelihood that diffusion of responsibility would occur more readily for black than for white victims. In this study, the presence of other white bystanders, whom the high- and low-prejudice-scoring white female subjects could neither talk to nor observe, was introduced so as to present half of the subject bystanders with a non-race-related rationale to avoid personal intervention: the belief that one of the other bystanders may intervene. As expected, the race by alone–together interaction ($p < .01$) indicated that when other bystanders were believed to be present, black victims (37.5%) were helped *less* frequently than white victims (75%). However, bystanders believing themselves to be the only witness to the "falling chairs" emergency, helped black victims (93.8%) slightly *more* frequently than white victims (81.3%). An exact replication of this procedure in a subsequent study (Gaertner et al., 1979b) obtained nearly identical findings. Furthermore, the physiological responses of subjects paralleled the results of the helping behavior (see Footnote 1). Alone bystanders seem genuinely concerned about the well-being of blacks, both psychophysiologically and behaviorally; however, in the presence of a non-race-related rationale to remain inactive (i.e., the presence of others) there is no longer the same evidence of personal concern. Bystanders in the presence of others, nevertheless, need not attribute their failure to intervene to racial antipathy.

Further studies (Gaertner, 1975; Johnson, Gaertner, & Dovidio, 1978, Study 2) demonstrated once again that alone bystanders, overhearing an emergency, did not discriminate against black victims. Black and white victims were each helped 100% of the time in both studies. However, in the face-to-face presence of three nonresponsive confederate bystanders, black victims were helped 30% in the 1975 study and 46.7% in the 1978 study while white victims were helped 90% and 92.3% of the time, respectively. The race by alone–together interaction was statistically reliable ($p < .02$ and $p < .05$) in each study. Thus, the social influence inhibition effect occurring in the face-to-face presence of others was more pronounced for black than for white victims. Unfortunately, these studies do not permit us to distinguish between informational and normative social influence effects.

A subsequent study (Gaertner *et al.*, 1979a) was designed to isolate normative social influence effects. The avoidance of deviant status in a group of nonresponsive others may be a priority that has greater potency and influence for black than for white victims. Thus, as a function of the victim's race, white bystanders may differentially succumb to conformity pressures not to intervene. In this study, an audio–visual presentation of the emergency was introduced to minimize the likelihood that the bystanders would misinterpret the severity of the victim's situation. Following the "falling chairs" emergency, the victim was seen to lie motionless for the duration of the postemergency period. In this study, for the first time, we expected to observe some effect for the bystander's prejudice score. We suspected that even in the presence of nonresponsive fellow bystanders, the continuous video image of the unconscious black victim might be too compelling for low-prejudice scorers to ignore without threatening their more egalitarian self-images.

In terms of frequency measures of helping, almost 100% of the subjects across all conditions helped regardless of the victim's race. However, in terms of latency to intervene, bystanders helped less quickly in the presence of others than alone ($p < .01$) and, overall, black victims were helped more slowly than white victims ($p < .03$). Furthermore, the predicted race by alone–together interaction ($p < .05$) indicated that in the presence of nonresponsive other bystanders black victims were helped more slowly than white victims (58.2 versus 16.6 seconds, $p < .01$), while alone bystanders helped blacks and whites equally quickly (11.2 versus 7.8 seconds). A marginally significant three-way interaction ($p < .09$) suggests that the interactive effect of race and presence of others is less pronounced for low- than for high-prejudice-scoring bystanders. In addition, the different types of social influences affecting bystanders seem to be reflected in bystanders' subjective and psychophysiological responses to emergencies (see pp. 127–131 and 138–142 in this chapter). Subject self-reports of perceived severity and psychophysiological arousal suggested that the inhibiting effect of other passive bystanders was due primarily to conformity pressures not to intervene. Furthermore, these conformity pressures may have been appreciated differently based on the race of the victim and the prejudice of the subject. In general, the results of our own research support the hypothesized indirect attitudinal process by which the victim's race affects the helping behavior of white bystanders. In terms of the arousal: cost–reward model, it seems that the victim's race influences helping by differentially affecting the costs imposed by other, nonracial elements that enter the cost–benefit matrix. Therefore, discrimination against black victims seems to occur more readily when failure to intervene can be attributed to factors other than the victim's race.

NONRACIAL ELEMENTS AND HELPING

A further examination of the helping behavior literature involving manipulations of the victim's race reveals, at least for white bystanders, an apparently systematic relationship between the occurrence of discrimination against black victims and the presence of nonracial elements that reduce the personal costs for not helping. Consistent with the indirect attitudinal model these nonracial elements seem to have an especially strong impact when the victim is black.

Studies Reporting That White Bystanders Discriminate against Black Victims

Discrimination in helping black, relative to white, victims has been found in a number of investigations. In all of these studies, the costs for not helping were low. For example, Bryan and Test (1967) reported that white passers-by less frequently contributed to a Salvation Army kettle when solicited by a black than by a white solicitor. Since not helping could be attributable to a number of factors, the solicitor's race would not have to be the salient rationale for the decision not to contribute. In addition, in their first subway study, Piliavin, Rodin, and Piliavin (1969) observed that only with the drunk victim was a race effect obtained, not with the cane-carrying victim. It seems that the personal costs for not helping were lower for the drunk because (a) he can have been perceived to have been more responsible for his dilemma; and (b) his condition can be perceived as less serious. In addition, responsibility to help was never solely focused on one particular bystander.

In other research, whites discriminated against blacks (identifiable by dialect) after receiving a telephoned "wrong number" request for assistance from an apparently stranded motorist (Franklin, 1974; Gaertner, 1973; Gaertner & Bickman, 1971). The presumed presence of passing motorists, patrolling police, and roving service vehicles perhaps allowed a potential benefactor to disregard the necessity for his or her personal intervention. The anonymity afforded the recipient of a wrong-number telephone call, as well as the ease with which it could be terminated, also serves to lower many of the personal costs for not helping. Studies by Graf and Riddell (1972) and West, Whitney, and Schnedler (1975) reported that white motorists stopped less frequently to offer assistance to black than to white motorists standing alongside a disabled vehicle. This roadside situation also offers the bystander nonracial elements that could lower the cost for not helping, including the driver's relative anonymity and the presence of other potential helpers.

Finally, Benson *et al.* (1976) found that subjects discriminated against black students in their willingness to mail a graduate school application "found" in a public phone booth in a busy airport. The presence of other potential helpers, the subject's degree of anonymity, the ease of leaving the materials where they were found, and the physical absence of the victim all seem to combine so as to render the personal costs associated with not helping reasonably low.

Studies in Which White Bystanders Do Not
Discriminate against Black Victims

A number of studies reported either no effects for the victim's race or a reverse discrimination effect in which whites offered higher levels of assistance to black than to white victims. In these studies, the situational contexts typically contain fewer nonracial elements that can be used to rationalize nonintervention. Also, in many of these contexts, not helping seems especially rude and inappropriate, which, according to our theoretical framework, is the type of behavior whites attempt to avoid in interracial situations.

Several studies in which a confederate dropped objects, apparently by accident, nearby or directly in front of the subject found no difference in the frequency of help black and white victims received (Lerner & Frank, 1974; Wegner & Crano, 1975; Wispé & Freshley, 1971). Although the victims in these studies did not verbalize a request for assistance, the personal costs for not helping are higher than, for example, when passing motorists could anonymously speed by a disabled vehicle. In these studies, the bystander is within 10 feet of the incident and must practically step over the fallen objects as well as the victim to avoid helping. Furthermore, given the typically low costs for helping, not helping seems especially inexcusable. In addition, a reanalysis of the Wispé and Freshley (1971) data indicated that although black victims were helped as frequently as white victims, blacks received mainly perfunctory, token-like levels of assistance relative to the more extensive help given to white victims ($p < .10$).

Several studies using explicit requests for assistance report that black victims are helped as often or more often than white victims. In this category are studies by Dutton (1973), Dutton and Lake (1973), Dutton and Lennox (1974), and Thayer (1973). Direct, personalized, face-to-face requests that require little time for deliberation may render not helping awkward and thus more costly relative to other contexts. Also, responsibility is focused on the bystander and anonymity is precluded. Katz *et al.* (1975) also obtained a reverse discrimination effect when whites were telephoned, personally identified by name, and asked, with a nonassertive appeal, to participate in a consumer survey by either a white (63.1% helped) or black male (74.6% helped) identifying himself as a member of the

(Negro) students' Self-Help Program at the City College. In terms of the indirect attitudinal process, whites, when approached with a polite appeal, may have been more helpful with the "Negro" than with the "white" to avoid the attribution of bigotry that could accompany refusal given the relative lack of non-race-related justifications to avoid participating.

It appears, then, that racial dissimilarity, unlike dissimilarity along other dimensions, does not generally lead to less frequent helping. Among white bystanders, discrimination against black victims seems to occur more readily when there is a decreased likelihood that negative responding would be attributed to bigoted intent. When personal costs for not helping are low, black victims are helped less than white victims; when personal costs for not helping are moderate or high, black victims receive as much help or more help than white victims. Thus, the ambivalent nature of white America's attitudes toward blacks and official norms condemning racial bigotry seem to modify the otherwise straightforward cost-benefit considerations associated with bystander–victim dissimilarity.

The Social Context of Helping: Summary and Implications

In summary, the presence of other bystanders, as well as the interpersonal relationship between the bystander and the victim, appears to affect *both* the values within the cost–reward matrix and the bystander's level of emotional arousal. For example, the presence of unseen or passive bystanders, leading an individual to define the incident as less severe or providing the opportunity to diffuse responsibility, reduces both the perceived necessity for intervention and the emotional impact of the event. The formation of a we-group may both increase promotive tension and decrease the perceived costs for helping. Thus, the same factor can affect different processes in the model simultaneously.

In addition, the pattern of findings obtained across several studies suggests that arousal and cost–benefit factors may not be sequential, orthogonal determinants of bystander behavior. Rather, they may be involved in a feedback network in which each affects the values of the other. As we discussed in Chapter 5, increased arousal increases the empathic costs for the victim receiving no help. Also, for bystanders believing that others are present, the rationalization that someone else has already intervened reduces the perceived costs for not helping and may subsequently reduce bystander arousal. Thus, although the parameters of these interrelationships are not fully understood, given the paucity of research in this area, there is sufficient evidence to warrant considerations of these possibilities in our revised model and in future research.

Chapter 7

Impulsive Helping

Thus far in this book we have examined the first three general propositions of the arousal:cost–reward model. In this chapter, we will investigate Proposition IV of the model, which states that under certain special circumstances and for specific personality types there will be rapid, impulsive, noncalculative, "irrational" helping or escape behavior following observation of an emergency. This proposition was developed in response to the observation in the initial subway study that in many cases bystanders jumped up immediately and intervened, on occasion catching the victim before he hit the floor. Thus, bystanders seemed not to be going through any very involved conscious decision process.

Our suspicion that, under some circumstances, very rapid helping that is unresponsive to costs would occur was only strengthened when we became acquainted with the Clark and Word (1974) "electrician" studies. It was predicted, in their experiment involving potential danger to the helper, that the preferred response would be indirect help, namely, seeking an institutional helper such as a fire fighter or campus security officer. The manipulation of danger, however, had no effect on the type of helping; the same proportion of subjects in danger and nondanger conditions helped directly. A considerable number of subjects in the danger condition put their hands on the victim, an act that seemed not to be deterred by the presence of potentially lethal electric shock to the bystander. At that point we speculatively added this postulate, which suggests that under certain *specifiable* circumstances and for certain personality types there would be rapid, noncalculative, "impulsive" helping, that is, helping in which certain potentially relevant aspects of the physical and social environment appear to be ignored. We did not intend, however, that the postulate serve as an "escape hatch" to make the model impervious to disproof. Thus, the first question that we wish to address in this chapter is whether we can theoretically specify and empirically identify some situational characteristics of emergencies in which such immediate, "unthinking" actions seem most likely to occur.

The circumstances under which we initially observed "impulsive" helping seemed to be those in which high levels of arousal were immediately engendered in the bystander. In attempting to specify situational characteristics that trigger impulsive helping, then, we first looked at the subpropositions of Proposition I of the model. These state that severity (and, as we have later modified it, clarity), physical proximity to the victim, and emotional involvement with and similiarity to the victim all increase the arousal experienced by the bystander. We also chose to look at the apparent loudness of the event (on the belief that startle leads to arousal) and the physical posture of the bystanders (assuming that an impulsive motor response is more likely if one is standing or moving already). We also chose to look at the sex of the bystander, since males are reputed to be more impulsive. Finally, we looked at "reality," in the expectation that situations in which there was any opportunity for the subject to doubt that the event was a crisis would not lead to impulsive responding.

The empirical analysis to be presented proceeds as follows:

1. Delineation of the universe of studies we will refer to as emergency helping studies (as opposed to problems—we think that this process occurs primarily under emergency circumstances).
2. Designation of studies within that group as cases of "impulsive" and "nonimpulsive" helping.
3. Investigation of differences in situational characteristics between these studies and those in which less impulsive helping occurs.
4. Discussion of how the potential costs to the bystander appear to operate differently in the two kinds of situations.[1]

Table 7.1 includes all of the studies that we believe fit our rather stringent definition of emergency situations. As the reader will recall, our

---

[1] A preliminary version of this analysis was presented at the International Congress of Psychology in Paris, 1976, in a paper entitled "Impulsive Helping, Arousal, and Diffusion of Responsibility."

definition of an emergency is an event of rapid onset occurring to another individual in which outside assistance is needed to prevent the victim's condition from deteriorating rapidly. For further control in our analysis we have excluded studies in which the subjects were children or in which subjects were themselves threatened by the emergency. Finally, only experiments in which over 50% of subjects help are used in this analysis. Hopefully, situations too ambiguous to be perceived as emergencies by most subjects are ruled out by this procedure.

Definition of "Impulsive" and "Nonimpulsive" Helping Studies

Within this group of studies, we have designated as "impulsive helping" studies those that involve 85% to 100% of subjects helping and help that is rendered, on the average, in under 15 seconds. Empirically it is the case that very rapid helping is correlated with a high percentage of overall response to the emergency; that is, in studies in which one observes 100% or close to 100% helping across trials, one also tends to see very rapid helping. Thus, we have also included in the group of studies referred to as "impulsive helping studies" (see Section A of Table 7.1) experiments in which very rapid or almost 100% help is received but in which the other piece of data is not available.

Nonimpulsive helping studies are defined as those in which the percentage helping is over 50% but not over 85%, or in which help is received more slowly than in 15 seconds (see Section B of Table 7.1 for these studies). There is necessarily some arbitrariness in the inclusion or noninclusion of studies in the impulsive helping group. For example, the definition of when an emergency "begins" will differ widely between studies. Similarly, since these experiments are done in a wide variety of different settings, the actual physical ability of subjects to respond within any given length of time is in part determined by the ecology of the surroundings.[2]

The two sections of Table 7.1 are organized with the names of the authors and the date of the study in the first column, then a brief discussion of the type of emergency, then any special conditions such as whether the subject is alone, with other naive subjects, or with a programmed stooge. The percentage of subjects helping is in the next column. The latency of

[2] In counting the studies, we have included as separate studies separate conditions of the same study if they present clearly different emergencies to the bystander. For example, in Clark and Word's (1974) studies, the nondangerous electrical emergency and the dangerous electrical emergency are presented as two separate studies, since the situation is perceptibly different. Also, an experiment in which in one condition the bystander has never seen the victim before and in another condition he or she *has* seen the victim before is counted as two separate studies.

Table 7.1

Studies on Helping in Emergency Situations: Part A — Impulsive Helping Studies and Part B — Nonimpulsive Helping Studies

Authors and nature of emergency	Study number	Special conditions	Helping Percentage	Helping Latency (sec)	Diffusion?	Subjects' sex	Situational variables[a] 1	2	3	4
Part A. Impulsive helping studies. *Defined as either average latencies under 15 seconds in at least one condition or over 85% helping (due to absence of one or another datum and the known correlation between the measures)*										
Piliavin, Rodin, and Piliavin, 1969; "cane" victim, collapse in subway	1	—	91	10	—	MF	x	x	x	x
Piliavin and Piliavin, 1972; "cane" victim, collapse in subway	2	—	93	11	—	MF	x	x	x	x
		Intern in car	100	6	no	MF	x	x	x	x
Piliavin, Piliavin, and Rodin, 1975; "cane" victim, collapse in subway	3	—	88	12	—	MF	x	x	x	x
		Intern in car	85	14	no	MF				
Piliavin, Piliavin, and Broll, 1976; falling downstairs, fainting	4	—	89	10	—	MF	x	x		x
Clark and Word, 1972; injured workman cries "Help!" (low ambiguity conditions)										
Experiment I	5	Subject alone	100	9	—	M	x	x	x	x
		Two naive subjects	100 (pairs)	9	no	M				
Experiment II	6	Subject alone	100	7	—	M	x	x	x	x
		Two naive subjects	100 (pairs)	8	no	M				
		Five naive subjects	100 (groups)	10	no	M				
Darley, Teger, and Lewis, 1973; injured workman, "Oh, my leg!"	7	Subject alone	90	12	—	M				
		Two subjects face-to-face	80 (pairs)	17	no	M			x	x
		Two subjects back-to-back	20 (pairs)	17	yes	M			x	
Anderson, 1974: attempted rape of experimenter	8	Subject alone	100	—	—	M	x	x	?	
		Subjects in three-man groups	100 (groups)	—	no	M				

	#	Condition	%	N		Sex				
Clark and Word, 1974; electrical malfunction emergency										
Experiment I										
Nondangerous	9	Subject alone	100	—	—	M		x	x	x
		Subjects in pairs	100 (pairs)	—	no	M		x	x	x
Dangerous	10	Subject alone	91	—	—	M		x	x	x
		Subjects in pairs	100 (pairs)	—	no	M		x	x	x
Experiment II: dangerous	11	Subject alone	88	—	—	M		x	x	x
		Subjects in pairs	100 (pairs)	—	no	M		x	x	x
Bickman, 1974; bookcase falls on other subject										
Defined as emergency	12	Other bystander unable	—	7	—	F		x		
		Other bystander able (to help victim)	—	12	no	F				
Defined as possible emergency	13	Other bystander unable	—	10	—	F				
		Other bystander able	—	27	yes	F				
Staub, 1974; woman next door falls off ladder, "Oh, my leg!"	14	Subject alone	93	—	—	F		x		?
		Two naive subjects	60 (pairs)	—	yes	F				
	15	Subject and stooge	100	—	no	F		x		?
		(with various definitions of the situation, all positive)	82	—	no	F				
			67	—	yes	F				
			75	—	no	F				
Staub and Baer, 1974; man collapses on sidewalk, holding chest	16	Escape difficult	88	—	—	MF		x	x	x
		Escape easy	(42)	—	—	MF				
Moriarty, 1975	17	Theft of radio, Jones beach	95	—	—	MF			x	x
	18	Theft of suitcase, automat, NYC	100	—	—	MF			x	x
Gaertner, 1975; chairs falling on other subject, "Scream"	19	Subject alone, white victim	100	8	—	F				x
		Subject alone, black victim	100	16	—	F				
		Subject with others, white victim	90	—	no	F				
		Subject with others, black victim	30	—	yes	F				

(continued)

Table 7.1 (continued)

Authors and nature of emergency	Study number	Special conditions	Helping		Diffusion?	Subjects' sex	Situational variables[a]			
			Percentage	Latency (sec)			1	2	3	4
Wilson, 1976; crash next door	20	Subject alone								
A. Experimenter, "Oh my foot, it's broken!" (Note: latency is median for all Ss, not just for helpers.)		Esteem-oriented	96	12	—	MF				x
		Middle-oriented	65	27	—	MF				
		Safety-oriented	55	91	—	MF				
		Two stooges (both passive)								
		Esteem-oriented subject	71	14	yes, but	MF				
		Middle-oriented subject	23	no help	yes	MF				
		Safety-oriented subject	17	no help	yes	MF				
B. Behavior of stooge defines as emergency (says "Jesus Christ! What was that?")	21	Two stooges (one helps, other does not)								
		Esteem-oriented subject	86	10	no	MF	x	x		
		Middle-oriented subject	95	10	no	MF				
		Safety-oriented subject	71	12	no	MF				
Solomon, Solomon, and Stone, 1978; collapse of woman in laundry room of apartment building (seen)	22	Subject alone	100	—	—	MF	x	x	x	x
		Two naive subjects	100 (pairs)	—	no	MF				
Gaertner, Dovidio, and Johnson, 1979a; Chairs falling on other subject, "Scream!" (audio-visual)	23	Subject alone, white victim	100	8	—	F	x	x		
		Subject alone, black victim	100	11	—	F				
		Subject with others, white victim	100	16	no	F				
		Subject with others, black victim	80	58	yes	F				

Part B. Nonimpulsive helping studies. *Helping occurs in 50%–85%, with latencies over 15 seconds in most cases*

Authors and nature of emergency	Study number	Special conditions	Helping		Diffusion?	Subjects' sex				
			Percentage	Latency (sec)						
Darley and Latané, 1968 (1970);	1	Subject alone	85	52	—	F				
A. Epileptic seizure of other subject		Subject and friend	75	58	no	F				
		Subject and stranger	62	93	yes	F				
		Subject, four strangers	31	116	yes	F				

B. Subject meets victim before experiment	2	Subject, four strangers	75	69	no	F	x
Latané and Rodin, 1969; female experimenter falls	3	Subject alone	70	40	–	M	x
		Subject and two friends	70 (pairs)	36	no	M	
		Subject and two strangers	40 (pairs)	130	yes	M	
		Subject with stooge	7	–	yes	M	
Schwartz and Clausen, 1970; epileptic seizure of other subject (third condition is four strangers, one medically competent)	4	Subject alone	N.A.	28	–	F	
		Subject and four strangers	N.A.	60	yes	F	
		S, 4 (1 competent)	N.A.	115	yes	F	
		Subject alone	N.A.	54	–	M	
		Subject and strangers	N.A.	57	no	M	
		S, 4 (1 competent)	N.A.	58	no	M	
Yakimovich and Saltz, 1971; workman falls off ladder outside	5	Cries "help"	81	–	–	M	x
		Does not	(29)	–	–	M	x
Bickman, 1971; bookcase falls on other subject in experiment	6	Subject alone	80	30	–	F	
		Third subject can't help	80	45	–	F	
		Third subject can help	53	80	yes	F	
Bickman, 1972; bookcase falls on other subject. "No emergency" defined by third	7	Third subject can't help	–	50	–	F	
		Third subject can help	–	37	no	F	
Ross, 1971; accident to workman in next room (when stooges, they are programmed to be calm)	8	Subject alone	83	48	–	M	x
		Subject, child stooges	50	39	yes?	M	
		Subject, adult stooges	16	184	yes	M	
Ross and Braband, 1973; same design as Ross, 1971	9	Subject alone	64	61	–	M	x
		Subject and one normal adult	35	41	yes	M	
		Subject and one blind adult	28	116	yes	M	
Byeff, 1970; falling projectionist on television monitor	10	Subject alone	53	16	–	M	
		Two subjects, separated	59	28	no	M	x
		Two subjects, together	47 (pairs)	32	yes	M	
Piliavin, Piliavin, and Trudell, 1974, unpublished; falling projectionist on TV—just watched arousing (A) or nonarousing (NA) brief movie clip	11	Subject alone (NA movie)	73	18	–	M	x x
		Two subjects apart (NA movie)	86 (pairs)	24	no	M	
		Subject alone (A movie)	83	26	–	M	
		Two subjects apart (A movie)	40 (pairs)	25	yes	M	

(continued)

Table 7.1 (continued)

Authors and nature of emergency	Study number	Special conditions	Helping Percentage	Helping Latency (sec)	Diffusion?	Subjects' sex	Situational variables[a] 1	2	3	4
Piliavin and Piliavin, 1972; collapse in subway—"blood" victim	12	—	79	19	—	MF	x	x	x	x
		Intern in car	43	60	yes					
Piliavin et al., 1975; collapse in subway—"birthmark" victim	13	—	72	21	yes	MF	x	x	x	x
		Intern in car	48	40	yes					
Smith et al., 1972; ill experimenter, no loud crash	14	Subject alone	65	13	—	M				
		Subject with stooge	20	12	yes	M			x	
Smith et al., 1973; ill experimenter, loud crash	15	Subject, alarmed stooge	60	19	no	M				
		Subject, calm stooge	13	30	yes	M			x	
Staub and Baer, 1974; street collapse, victim holding knee	16	Escape hard	56	—	—	MF	x	x		x
		Escape easy	(14)	—	—	MF				?
Staub, 1974; apparent fall from ladder in next room	17	Permission to go	72	—	—	F				
		No information	78	—	—	F		x		
		Prohibition	33	—	—	F				
Clark and Word, 1974; electrical emergency, moderate ambiguity	18	Subject alone	75	—	—	M	x		x	x
		Two naive subjects	75 (pairs)	—	yes	M				
Schwartz and Ben David, 1976; escaped "septic rat"; experimenter places blame on subject, chance, or self; competence of subject to handle rats has been manipulated; experimenter screams and is frightened	19	Blame subject:								
		Competent subject	100	33	—	M				
		Neutral subject	88	71	—	M		x		
		Incompetent subject	75	87	—	M		x		
		Blame chance:								
		Competent subject	88	61	—	M				
		Neutral subject	75	106	—	M				
		Incompetent subject	50	148	—	M				
		Blame self:								
		Competent subject	75	84	—	M				
		Neutral subject	50	136	—	M				
		Incompetent subject	50	156	—	M				

	Situation	%	No.	Clarity	Sex	1	2	3	4
20	Schwartz and Gottlieb, 1976; theft of tape recorder and fight								
	Subject alone	90	60	—	M				
	Subject, others (not audible)	70	45	yes?	M				
	Subject, others (audible)	48	65	yes	M	x	x		?
21	Schwartz and Gottlieb, 1980; violent theft seen on TV monitor (Experiment I)								
	Subject alone:								
	S is anonymous	90	35	—	MF				
	S known to victim	80	30	—	MF				
	Others present:								
	S is anonymous	80	35	no	MF				
	S known to all	90	95	yes·	MF				
22	Gaertner and Dovidio, 1977; chairs falling on other subject, audio only, with screams (Experiment I)								
	Subject alone: white victim	81	62	—	F				
	Subject alone: black victim	94	45	—	F				
	Subject with others: white victim	80	63	no	F				
	Subject with others: black victim	38	89	yes	F				
23	Same situation, all subjects are alone, emergency with screams (Experiment II, A)								
	No placebo: white victim	95	63	—	F				
	No placebo: black victim	95	64	—	F				
	Placebo: white victim	100	50	no[b]	F				
	Placebo: black victim	86	114	yes[b]	F				
24	Same situation, all subjects are alone, emergency *without* screams—high ambiguity (Experiment II,B)								
	No placebo: white victim	85	148	—	F				
	No placebo: black victim	65	196	—	F				
	Placebo: white victim	55	254	yes[b]	F				
	Placebo: black victim	55	237	no[b]	F				
25	Solomon, Solomon, and Stone, 1978 Collapse in laundry room (not seen)								
	Subject alone	62	—	—	MF	x		x	x
	Two naive subjects	50 (pairs)	—	yes	MF				
26	Three laboratory faints and crashes, combined (seen)	67	—	—	MF	x		x	x
	Subject alone	67	—	—	MF				
	Two naive subjects	68 (pairs)	—	no	MF				

[a] Situational variables: 1. Subjects physically in motion, or at least some of them standing. 2. Extreme clarity, defined as (a) victim is visible, (b) victim calls for help, (c) someone defines situation as an emergency. 3. Prior acquaintance with victim (saw or interacted before emergency). 4. Reality, defined as (a) field study or (b) victim clearly is not part of experiment, if lab study. (A ? indicates ambiguity regarding the latter point or that *perpetrator* of emergency is not part of the study).

[b] Since the studies do not provide pair or group conditions, there is no opportunity for diffusion of responsibility, per se. We see the placebo as providing an alternative rationale for one's arousal, however, leading to the opportunity to reduce costs for not helping by cognitively reducing the perceived severity. Thus we see the process as being the same. Note that in study 23, the subjects seem to have already done this with the black victim, even without the placebo, because of the greater ambiguity of the situation. Thus they do not do it significantly more when they have the placebo.

169

response to the emergency is in the next column, and whether or not diffusion of responsibility occurs (if possible) is noted in the next column. The last four columns note the presence or absence of four different situational variables suggested as having some impact on the occurrence or nonoccurrence of impulsive helping.

The analysis of the relationship between these four situational variables and impulsive helping is presented in Table 7.2. One variable shows up as rather strongly related to impulsive helping. This is clarity of the situation, operationally defined as the victim either being visible to the bystander as the emergency is occurring, the victim calling for help, or as someone in the experiment clearly defining it as an emergency. Two other factors are significantly related: (a) reality, defined as the study being done in a field setting or having as its victim a person who is from outside the experiment; and (b) whether bystanders have any prior experience with the victim, either in the form of observation or actual social contact. One other variable seems to bear some relationship to impulsive helping, although the relationship is not statistically significant. This is the physical position of the bystanders—namely, whether at least some bystanders are standing or walking as compared to sitting.

We have given each of the studies reviewed one "point" for each of these variables; that is, studies can receive from zero to four points depending upon the clarity and reality of the situation, the physical position of the subjects, and the degree of prior contact with the victim. The mean number of such points for the studies characterized by impulsive helping is 2.48, with the median being 2, while the mean number of points for the studies characterized by less impulsive helping is 1.31, with a median of 1. When these scores are dichotomized at the overall median, a chi-square of 7.56 (p < .01) is obtained for a comparison of the impulsive with the nonimpulsive studies. Two other variables, the loudness with which the event occurs and the sex of the subjects in the experiment, were found to be unrelated to the impulsive versus nonimpulsive distinction. Although we are convinced that severity is also an important factor, we were unable to find a sufficiently clear, observable criterion on which to judge severity across such different situations. Similarly, it proved impossible to determine the distance between the victim and the bystander in most cases. Thus, we have had to omit these variables from the analysis.

Interpretation of the Process by Which "Impulsive" Helping Occurs

We have discussed four features of the environment that may contribute to bystanders' making "impulsive" responses to the emergency. There are, however, several possible uses of the word "impulsive." Here we

Table 7.2
The Relationship of Selected Situational Variables to "Impulsive" Helping[a]

	Variables																		
	Conductive posture			Clarity			Prior contact			Reality			"Impulse points"		
	Yes	No	Total	Yes	No	Total	Yes	No	Total	Yes	No	Total	0-1	2-3	Total
"Impulsive" helping studies	9	14	23	17	6	23	17	6	23	14	9	23	6	17	23
"Nonimpulsive" helping studies	5	21	26	9	17	26	12	14	26	8	18	26	17	9	26
Totals	14	35	49	26	23	49	29	20	49	22	27	49	23	26	49
Chi-square	1.49 (corr.)			7.56			3.89			4.47			7.56		
p-value	n.s.			< .01			< .05			< .05			< .01		

[a] Variables: *Conducive posture* = Subjects moving or at least some of them standing. *Clarity* = Victim visible, clearly cries "Help!" or someone defines situation as an emergency. *Prior Contact* = Bystanders saw or met victim before event. *Reality* = Bystanders cannot see victim as being part of an experiment. *"Impulse Points"* = Each study receives one point for each "yes" on the four variables examined.

intend to imply a rapid, driven, almost reflexive response that appears to be insensitive to potential costs in the situation. For example, many subjects who helped directly and unsafely in the Clark and Word (1974) dangerous electrical emergency, when asked afterwards whether they realized that what they were doing was dangerous, replied, "Yes, I knew but I didn't think about it," or "I acted too fast to be able to think about the consequences." In this study, although the costs for intervention are clearly present to an objective observer, they apparently had little impact on the behavior of the involved bystanders.

There are several other studies in the impulsive group in Table 7.1 that can easily be characterized as potentially dangerous to helpers and in which 100% of the bystanders intervened. The study by Anderson (1974), for example, involved an attempted rape in which the perpetrator sounded very tough and in which the subjects who gallantly rushed out of the experimental room to intervene could very easily have been physically assaulted. There are also two thefts carried out by Moriarty (1975) in which it is certainly possible that the intervening bystanders could have had distinctly negative outcomes for their heroics.

The second feature of impulsive helping seems to be that subjects are ignoring the presence of other potential bystanders who could help. That is, in response to these emergencies, the fact of the presence or absence of others who might either (a) define the situation as a nonemergency; or (b) provide normative expectations for nonintervention; or (c) themselves help (allowing subjects to diffuse responsibility) appears not to be entered into whatever calculations go on in determining the response to be made. Table 7.3 presents the relationship between the occurrence of a "bystander inhibition effect" and the "score" given each of the experiments presented in Table 7.1 (omitting 11 studies that did not have conditions involving the possibility of diffusion). Note that in the "high-point" studies bystanders seem to ignore high costs for helping, and they are not responsive to the lowered personal costs for not helping due to the presence of other potential helpers. Bystanders appear to attend solely to the plight of the victim; that is, the level of severity as it affects bystanders' arousal and the potential empathic costs for the victim receiving no help seem to overwhelm other determinants in galvanizing witnesses into action.

An important question that remains has to do with the process by which these apparent emotional factors dominate more "rational" considerations. In this connection, we must turn to the experimental psychology literature and to the literature in the sociology of deviance—on the surface an odd pair of bedfellows. First, a number of years ago Easter-brook (1959) demonstrated that in the very basic physiological sense, under high levels of drive (which we are of course arguing are present in "im-

Table 7.3

Relationship between Variables That Lead to Impulsive Helping and Presence or Absence of the "Diffusion of Responsibility Effect"[a]

	"Impulse points"							
	Studies using male subjects or both sexes					Studies using only female subjects		
	4	3	2	1	0	2	1	0
Diffusion occurs in some conditions	2	2	3	7	2	1	3	4
Diffusion does not occur	6	2	3	0	0	0	2	1
Totals	8	4	6	7	2	1	5	5

	For experiments with male subjects only			For all experiments		
	3–4 points	0–2 points	Total	2–4 points	0–1 points	Total
Diffusion occurs in some conditions	4	12	16	8	16	24
Diffusion does not occur	8	3	11	11	3	14
Totals	12	15	27	19	19	38
x^2 (corrected)	4.24, $p < .05$			5.54, $p = .02$		

[a] Eleven studies in which no opportunity for diffusion is present are omitted.

pulsive" helping situations) the focus of attention of subjects was narrowed to the fovea and that peripheral stimuli simply did not register. Peripheral stimuli, therefore, were not considered in the determination of subjects' responses. Other research since then has supported this finding while changing somewhat the interpretation. M. V. Eysenck (1977) states

> A major finding has been that aroused subjects pay less attention to information in the visual periphery than unaroused subjects. However, as was pointed out by Hockey (1970, 1973), the peripheral visual cues usually had little or no relevance to the subject's primary task. When these two factors were unconfounded (e.g., Cornsweet, 1969), it appeared to be the case that the main effect of high arousal is to increase the attentional bias towards the primary task at the expense of the secondary task. Broadbent (1971) concluded that, "the aroused system devotes a higher proportion of its time to the intake of information from dominant sources and less from relatively minor ones" (p. 443) [p. 174].

In connection with the "impulsive" helping studies, what subjects seem to be focusing on, as their "primary task," is extricating the victim from his or her plight. Note that one of the factors that seems to be predictive of impulsive helping is prior acquaintance between the observer and the victim. We propose that if this prior knowledge becomes a strong friendship or love relationship, the likelihood of impulsive helping will increase still further, due to increased arousal, as well as greater likelihood of seeing the other's problem as highly salient. In an article on helping behavior, Lynch and Cohen (1978) make a very similar point, but are more specific regarding the features of helping situations to which they expect the potential helpers to attend. They attempted to predict the probability of helping (in one experiment) and how bad people would feel if they did not help (in a second study). Stimulus conditions were varied along continua of seriousness. Their results did not fit a simple additive subjective expected utility model, indicating that certain features received more attention than others. Lynch and Cohen suggest that their results demonstrate that bystanders give heaviest weight to consequences with extreme implications. Most specifically, they suggest that the salience of certain costs leads to a lack of processing of other features of the situation.

Thus, a unique aspect of emergency situations is that they are both attention-getting and arousal-generating. If the arousal is sufficiently high, the bystander's attention becomes focused primarily on the plight of the victim and, consequently, on the costs for the victim receiving no help. Personal costs *for* helping become peripheral and are not attended to. Therefore, the impulsive helping behavior that may appear irrational to an uninvolved observer who considers *all* the apparent costs and rewards may be a quite "rational" response for a bystander attending primarily to the costs for the victim receiving no help.

Lofland, in *Deviance and Identity* (1969), presents an analysis of the process by which individuals are caught up in aggressive deviant actions that we think bears a great deal of similarity to the process we are proposing for impulsive helping. His most relevant analysis is his discussion of what he calls "deviance among normals." The distinction he makes is critical to the relevance of his theorizing about the commission of deviant acts to our theorizing about helping. He says, "the category is . . . intended to denote those acts that are either a *first* occasion or a relatively unpracticed and isolated or episodic occurrence [p. 39]." He contrasts this category with that of repeated deviant acts that have "become practiced, routine and unremarkable [p. 39]" and may be role-related. The distinction Lofland is making here is exactly the distinction we made in an earlier chapter in separating "amateur" helping from practiced, institutional helping or habitual helping in non-emergency situations. Lofland's approach is particularly relevant to our discussion of impulsive helping in that he is concentrating on the facilitators of deviant acts, as we have just been attempting to discover the situational features that facilitate impulsive helping.

Lofland's Model of the Defensive Deviant Act

Lofland's model for facilitation of performance of a first defensive deviant act has three sequential and cumulating stages. He stresses that the deviant act is not an inevitable outcome of beginning the sequence; there are dropouts at each stage. The three stages are as follows:

1. An event defined as a threat occurs.
2. A state of "psycho-social encapsulation" ensues that involves decision making under social and temporal pressures.
3. Finally, there is "closure upon an act," which can be facilitated by combinations of places, hardware, others, and certain self-definitions that "make the deviant act the most objectively and subjectively available action [p. 41]" at that moment in time.

As an actor moves through the stages, alternative possible actions are closed off at each phase.

THREAT

Threat can come from either physical sources or from perceived danger to one's sources of self-esteem. Threat in our model of helping comes, of course, from the perception of danger or difficulty for another person. It can be increased or multiplied by a bystander's state of arousal at the time of occurrence of the event, of course, and it is not impossible that self-esteem might also be involved.

ENCAPSULATION

The most critical aspect of the Lofland model for our theorizing about rapid (and particularly impulsive) helping is Step 2, encapsulation. He states:

> Under conditions of threat and of a consequent high anxiety level, Actor may come to have a kind of fixation upon the threat itself, wherein he desires to remove or render harmless as quickly as possible that which is threatening . . . .

The actor appears to become . . . relatively open and responsive to threat-reducing management efforts which have the character of being short-term, simple, and close to hand or proximate [p. 50].

The actor's focus of attention becomes narrowed to the threat. Lofland discusses the factors that are facilitative of moving into an encapsulated state under conditions of threat, and identifies three: (a) suddenness, uniqueness, or unexpectedness of the event in relationship to the actor's experience, background, and training; (b) time pressure; and (c) the perceived behavior and expectations of others.

Lofland argues that unexpectedness increases the emotional impact of an event, leading it to be defined as more threatening than the same event would be if it could have been foreseen. It is the increased threat, then, that leads to the encapsulation. As we have mentioned, there is considerable evidence from experimental psychology (Berkun, Bialek, Kern, & Yagi, 1962; Broadbent, 1971; Easterbrook, 1959) that something like "encapsulation" does indeed occur under increased drive, arousal, activation, or whatever one may wish to call it.

With regard to the importance of time pressure, Lofland proposes that "the greater the available time in which to stall, the less the likelihood of encapsulation . . . . Ideally the threat should require immediate defensive action, as appears to be the case in many episodes of homicide [Wolfgang, 1958, p. 59]." In longer-decision-time situations, there is more opportunity to change one's fixation from the threat to long-term implications, and, particularly importantly, the pressure to decide immediately is not adding arousal to what is already there. Furthermore, there is more chance that others will intervene in the behavior sequence.

The final facilitating factor in the encapsulation process is the behavior of other people. If others in the situation suggest alternatives to the one on which one's attention is riveted, they can break down the encapsulation process. If, on the other hand, the other bystanders do not intervene and, particularly, if they are perceived as having expectations that the actor will take the action, encapsulation is increased. In the helping situation, similar effects may be noted. One of the most replicated findings is that the presence of others usually slows responding. Schwartz and Gottlieb (1976, 1980) recently demonstrated that the inhibiting effect of the presence of others is greatly decreased when other bystanders can monitor the individual's behavior but the individual cannot monitor the behavior of the other bystanders. In Lofland's terms, such a condition should facilitate one's attention to the expectations of those others for appropriate action, while eliminating any possibility for the bystander to use their behavior to modify his or her own behavior.

CLOSURE

The final stage in Lofland's proposed three-stage model is closure upon the act. He discusses four classes of facilitators of closure. All have at least some relevance to the helping situation. The first is facilitating places, by which he means mundane aspects of the ecology. In the case of helping, we would have to consider the layout of doors, corridors, the location of official helpers such as police, etc. The research of Staub and Baer (1974) has demonstrated an increased likelihood of helping a "heart attack" victim if there is no convenient way to "escape," as defined by the arrangement of streets on which the "attack" was staged. The second category of facilitators, somewhat related to the ecological setting, is "facilitating hardware." Objects accessible to a bystander may be used in helping and thus may promote intervention. Fire boxes are the most obvious example of "hardware" facilitating prosocial behavior.

The third category of facilitators of closure is, again, "others" as in Lofland's treatment of the encapsulation process. That is, others can, by their behavior, focus one's attention upon the act and hasten or retard closure. Finally, there can be two aspects of the actor per se that are facilitative of closure: knowledge and skills and the subjective availability, based on trait and state factors, of the various possible acts. For example, Clark and Word (1974) found that electrically knowledgeable individuals were more likely to act quickly and safely than were others in their "electrical emergency." In experimental psychology terms, the salience of certain responses, their availability to retrieval and performance, will be higher among those with specific training, even if they have never encountered the particular event before. Subjective availability of an act will differ from person to person as well. Acts that an individual defines as immoral are, for example, not easily available. Albert Schweitzer would not kill even in self-defense and Hindus do not eat beef even when starving. Certain deviant acts, and by analogy certain helping acts, may be unavailable to certain actors on the basis of similar personal predispositions. We feel that certain phobias (about blood, for example) may preclude certain people from intervening. Similarly, personal affinities may increase the likelihood of helping. Huston, Geis, and Wright (1976) claim that their "Angry Samaritans" tended to be aggressive people who had a history of assaultive behavior. Thus when the opportunity to engage in "helping" that involved the possibility of engaging in physical violence arose, they were predisposed to it. We will not yet go into detail on the personality factors that may be involved in "impulsive" helping. We will, instead, summarize what we have just presented and move on in Chapter 8 to a general consideration of the role of individual differences in intervention.

As part of that discussion, we will deal with personality as it relates to impulsive helping.

Summary and Implications for the Arousal:Cost-Reward Model

Our analysis of the "prototypic impulse-generating situation" identified four features: clarity, reality, prior knowledge of (or opportunity to preassess) the victim, and physical orientation of the bystander to the emergency. Our current interpretation of how these features operate to produce the "impulsive" response is as follows:

1. The bystander's attention is initially focused on the victim (e.g., because of a cue such as a cane or because of the nature of the bystander–victim relationship) before the emergency or because the event itself is so compelling (due to loud noises, screams, etc.) that his or her attention is drawn to it.
2. The clarity and reality of the event leads to an immediate, holistic, intuitive appraisal of an iconic, nonverbal sort, in which the essence of the crisis is grasped (Broadbent, 1971, Neisser, 1967, and Berlyne, 1970, all suggest that some sort of nonverbal categorizing of this sort often takes place as a first step in perceptual processing).
3. Simultaneously, and as part of the same process, an emotional response (defense reaction) is generated.[3]

[3] We are again, as in Chapter 6, employing the Leventhal perceptual–motor processing model of emotion (1974, 1980) as the basis for our analysis. To expand somewhat on the very brief explication of it given in that chapter, his model assumes two stages in the "construction" of an emotion: the *perceptual–motor stage*, which "includes the mechanisms which create an experience of emotion" and the *planning–action stage*, in which "both emotional and nonemotional information [are used] for planning and constructing overt action [1980, p. 21]." The theory is very complex. For our purposes, the important features are: (*a*) that perception of physiological arousal *is not necessary* for the initial experience of emotion; and (*b*) that cognitions about the situation and feedback from expressive behavior (facial–motor mechanisms) are combined *out of awareness* to generate the initial experience. Autonomic arousal then follows and can feed back, in combination with perceptions of one's overt responses and the results of them, and amplify or otherwise modify the emotional experience. The fact that arousal is not involved in the initial generation of emotion is the critical feature of the Leventhal model for applicability in the "impulsive" situation, because there is a time lag in "turning on" the autonomic mechanism. The autonomic responses, though, can still be used as indicators that an emotional response has occurred.

The fact that emotional processing occurs out of awareness, during "pre-attentive processing," again makes the model compatible with our understanding of impulsive helping. In fact, Leventhal specifically states that "the eliciting event and expressive reaction must remain in peripheral awareness to be integrated as an emotional experience; focusing separately on these events should disrupt emotional experience [1980, p. 22]." This suggests that bystanders who are attending to their own responses rather than to the victim should be less likely to experience a true emotional response.

4. The first action impulse that is generated is a move towards the victim, and posture facilitating that move, such as already being on one's feet facing the victim, thus could become a factor.
5. Unless stimuli in the focus of attention (e.g., blood on the victim, "live" wires touching the victim) trigger another strong action tendency, or unless someone else intervenes to prevent the bystander from helping, the action will be carried through. Consciousness of acting but not of volition in acting will be subjectively felt.

One can view our "prototype" of the impulse-generating situation as an example of a Weberian "ideal type." According to Weber (1904), an ideal type is

> formed by the one-sided *accentuation* of one or more points of view and by the synthesis of a great many diffuse, discrete, more or less present and occasionally absent *concrete individual* phenomena, which are arranged according to those one-sidedly emphasized viewpoints into a unified *analytical* construct. In its conceptual purity, this mental construct cannot be found empirically anywhere in reality [p. 90].

Adorno's conceptualization of the authoritarian personality, for example, is a collection of characteristics expected to be present in the "ideal" authoritarian—whom one never truly expects to encounter. Thus, our "impulse-generating situation" is also an imaginary entity; no *real* situation can have the extreme level of all the features postulated to define the prototype, but many situations will come close enough to produce an "impulsive" response in most bystanders.

How are non-impulse-generating emergencies different from impulse-generating situations? We suggest—and it will lead to a major revision in the model, as the reader will see in Chapter 10—that the differential impact comes through the attentional process. The critical feature of the *non*-impulse-generating situation is that it allows for a shift in attention away from the victim. We have noted that one way in which this can occur, even in an "ideal-typical" impulse-generating case, is if there are conflict-producing features of the victim per se, as the potential helper approaches. That is, the "impulsive" response can be stopped in midstride if negative cues in the focus of attention are present.

The process leading to the initial generation of the impulse can similarly be prevented much earlier by the absence of one or more ˙of the features enumerated above or, put another way, by the presence of "nonfitting" elements in the situation that trigger some response other than the helping response. We argue that the way this operates is by providing "stall time" (Lofland, 1969) in which either (a) the blockage or dissipation of the defense reaction can occur (e.g., by attending to the self rather than empathizing); or (b) attention can be turned to the costs for helping and/or the personal costs for not helping. For example, lack of "reality" can lead to suspicion, which blocks arousal and causes the bystander to think of the cost of being thought a fool for rushing in. Having no prior knowledge of the victim can block the ability to conjure up an iconic representation of him or her and likely decreases the emotional response. Being seated can lead to enough physical inertia that, by the time one has moved, one's thoughts could also have moved to potential costs for helping, etc.

The implications for the model that follow from this analysis are that we must include the factor of the direction of attention as the mediator between the objective existence of costs and rewards in the situation and their impact on the bystander's behavior.

The Possible Evolutionary Basis for Impulsive Responding

In Chapter 2 we mentioned in passing that we believe that there may be an evolutionary basis for intervention in some types of emergencies. We do not mean that we think all or even most helping in most emergencies is based on "instinct." It is specifically "impulsive" helping as here defined that we believe has such a basis. Our belief is based on two kinds of evidence. First, comparable rapid responding without apparent attention to personal costs occurs widely across other animal species, most obviously among the lowly social insects (Wilson, 1975), but also as shown by the alarm calls of birds and prairie dogs (Barash, 1977; Gramza, 1967), and by the confrontation of predators by dominant male baboons in defense of their troops (Wilson, 1971). Second, there is direct evidence indicating that newborn infants as young as 36 hours of age show more distress in response to the cries of other infants than they do to other sounds of comparable shape and intensity (Sagi & Hoffman, 1976; Simner, 1971). Note that what we are implying here is that it is the defense reaction in response to distress in another individual, perhaps with some associated impulse, that we see as being an innate reaction. This impulse will be stronger in response to the distress of children and of adults categorized as members of the "we-group" (see Wilson, 1975).

If there is such an evolutionary basis for "altruism," why is it that we see so little of it? We are simply suggesting an innate basis for an impulse to intervene, and then only under very specific circumstances. Training out impulse and training in a delay before responding is a feature common to most cultures. If there is, as we propose, an innate tendency to intervene to relieve another's distress, it can still be "trained out" through the learning of impulse control in the same way one "trains out" aggressiveness or gluttony or the free expression of sexuality. The end point of the socialization process as it applies to helping, we believe, is generally the stifling of a natural intervention response without a parallel training for more rational, considered helping, in a pattern similar to the socialization of aggression and sexuality. There is for most of us across most situations a socialized suppression of impulse without an alternative considered and flexible substitute set of responses. For a related discussion, see Hoffman (1977).

Detachment-Involvement

Latané and Darley's (1970) excellent book, *The Unresponsive Bystander: Why Doesn't He Help?*, argues that decent, concerned people may fail to intervene into the problems of others because of inhibitory social factors present during the emergency rather than because they are dispositionally or temporarily apathetic. Our model, too, denies the assumption that people who fail to help during an emergency are necessarily apathetic. Rather, whether or not individuals intervene in an emergency will depend upon how detached or involved they are with the victim's plight. Thus, we would like to introduce the dimension of bystander "detachment versus involvement," which is related to impulsive helping, and which integrates nicely with the arousal:cost–reward model. Although help may be delivered from "detached" bystanders, it is more likely to be forthcoming from "involved" ones, and we believe that the processes underlying the delivery of assistance depends upon the bystander's position on this dimension. Similar to Latané and Darley's orientation, we see the degree of involvement to be not so much related to the bystander's personality, although it may be to some extent, but rather to temporary state factors induced by the immediate circumstances of the emergency. Circumstances of the emergency that relate positively to bystander involvement include the following: the apparent severity and clarity of the emergency, the bystander's physical closeness to the victim, a reduction in the apparent time to act, the bystander's degree of responsibility to intervene as determined by the availability of other capable bystanders, the bystander's degree of felt responsibility as proposed by Schwartz (1977), as well as feelings of closeness, attraction, "we-ness," familiarity, and similarity to the victim.[4]

[4] Schwartz and Gottlieb (1976, 1980) present a similar discussion of detachment.

Specifically, the detachment–involvement dimension represents potential variation in the bystander's emotional perspective analogous to variations in visual perspective that would result from the bystander viewing the same emergency through a zoom lens ranging from 35-mm wide-angle view to perhaps a 300-mm telephoto close-up. The wide-angle, more detached view places the bystander psychologically at a greater distance from the episode than the telephoto close-up. The involved, telephoto close-up focuses the bystander's attention more fully on the victim; the detached, wide-angle perspective reduces the relative salience of the victim. As involvement increases, the bystander experiences a greater magnitude of arousal that more quickly assumes the defense, rather than the orienting, mode. Also, as involvement increases, arousal is more likely to be attributed to the emergency, particularly to the victim's suffering, and also to be subjectively experienced as empathic concern rather than disgust and fear.

Cost–reward factors, too, are affected by the width and clarity of the bystander's attentional field. With increasing involvement, the presence of other bystanders, which would otherwise be influential in reducing costs for not helping, becomes less salient, as do cues warning of potential danger to bystanders who risk intervention. With increased attention to the victim, personal costs (e.g., "I may look foolish.") may become less salient relative to the empathic costs (e.g., "The victim will continue to suffer."). Thus, as involvement increases the victim's needs may become more salient than one's own, increasing the likelihood of intervention. In the extreme case, this should lead to impulsive helping.

Chapter 8

Person Factors in
the Intervention Process

In considering factors related to the individual, as opposed to the situation, the typical first distinction that is made is between trait and state factors. That is, relatively permanent, enduring characteristics of people such as personality, values, needs, and abilities are usually differentiated from transient states such as moods. In this chapter, we will briefly discuss the current status of person variables, of the more enduring type, in social psychological research and theorizing. We will then present the evidence for the operation of such factors in the intervention response, both "impulsive" and "nonimpulsive." In the next chapter, we will review the body of literature on temporary states and helping and discuss their implications for the model.

On Predicting Some of the People Some of the Time:
Trait Factors

Two articles (Bem & Allen, 1974; Mischel, 1973) have influenced the thinking of researchers about the relationship between person variables and situational variables in the prediction of behavior. Lewin suggested not only that behavior is a function of both the person and the environment, but also that the environment is a function of the person and vice versa. Trait approaches that assume that there are "relatively stable, highly consistent attributes that exert widely generalized causal effects on behavior [Mischel, 1973, p. 253]" have, however, held the center stage in research on person variables until very recently. The reason for the tenacity of the trait approach probably lies in some combination of its simplicity, its consonance with common sense conceptualizations of personality, and its relationship to dynamic, Freudian and neo-Freudian theories, which are themselves difficult to disprove. Most social psychologists, less wedded to Freud and generally mistrustful of common sense, have now come to a more complex view of the nature and function of person variables.

There are important implications of the current Person × Situation approach for the understanding of intervention in emergencies. A generalization frequently heard some years ago was that personality variables only relate to helping in nonemergency situations. While this is certainly a possibility, it may be rather too crude a division of situations. Mischel (1973) suggests that the "trait" factors that show the most promise are "cognitive activities and behavior patterns, studied in relation to the specific conditions that evoke, maintain, and modify them and which they, in turn, change [p. 265]." He names five broad groupings: (a) the individual's competencies to construct (generate) diverse behaviors under appropriate conditions; (b) the individual's encoding and categorization of events; (c) expectancies about outcomes; (d) subjective values of such outcomes; and (e) self-regulatory systems and plans.

How might these interact with the nature of help-requiring situations to have led to the generalization cited above? Mischel (1973) suggests the following:

> Psychological "situations" and "treatments" are powerful to the degree that they lead all persons to construe the particular events the same way, induce uniform expectancies regarding the most appropriate response pattern, provide adequate incentives for the performance of that response pattern, and instill the skills necessary for its satisfactory construction and execution. . . . Individual differences can determine behavior in a given situation most strongly when the situation is ambiguously structured . . . so that subjects are uncertain about how to categorize it and have no clear expectations about the behaviors most likely to be appropriate [p. 273].

If one accepts this analysis (which is similar to the analysis of the environmental circumstances under which genetic variability is most likely to be reflected in behavior), the emergency-versus-nonemergency distinction can be seen in different light. It is probably the case that emergencies are typically more compelling than more mundane help-rendering situations.

Thus, we might expect person variables to have less potency in determining bystander response as the situation becomes more emergency-like.

It should be possible, however, to find some relationships between "trait" variables in the individual and helping in emergencies. In particular, by Mischel's analysis we should expect to find these relationships more often in more ambiguous situations; we should probably expect to find them only rarely in "impulse-generating" situations, since we have postulated an extremely strong "pull" in the situation itself. For somewhat less compelling situations, Mischel's five categories may give us a guide for the kinds of trait variables for which to look.

Bem and Allen (1974) have presented an even more "revolutionary" analysis of the nature of cross-situational consistencies than did Mischel. Citing the nearly total lack of empirical support for such consistencies, these authors arrive at the question "Intuitions or research?" stating further, "One of them must be wrong [p. 508]." They then articulate several arguments suggesting that intuitions are wrong and the research is right. However, they continue, "we still believe that intuitions capture reality more faithfully than does the research." Their analysis then proceeds to identify the fallacy underlying the past research on cross-situational consistency as that of using a nomothetic rather than an idiographic approach. They suggest, and the study they present supports their view, that if subjects are given the chance to define the traits that are relevant (as in Kelly's "personal construct" notions), consistencies will appear.

Although Bem and Allen have provided what we believe will be an important framework for future research in cross-situational consistencies in behavior, there is currently very little research in helping behavior that has been done using idiographic assumptions. The exception is the work of Schwartz (1977), in which he has related consistency within a set of moral convictions, and between them and behavioral expectations, to helping responses.

Trait Factors, Emergencies, Crises, and Impulsive Responding

The search for the "generalized helping personality" has been futile. Krebs (1970), in his exhaustive examination of the helping literature, reviewed numerous personality traits and demographic variables and found virtually no consistent results. While there was a tendency for helping to increase with age, there was no consistent difference between the sexes (for either adults or children), and helping was generally unrelated to social approval, authoritarianism, ordinal position in the family, social class, self-esteem, or trustworthiness. Where differences did appear, the results were inconsistent. Gergen, Gergen, and Meter (1972) studied the relationship between numerous personality traits and helping in various situations. They administered a battery of personality tests and later gave subjects five different requests for help. Although a trait sometimes showed a relationship with helping, there were no consistent effects across situations. The impact of person variables seems especially weak in emergency situations. Darley and Latané (1968), for example, found no relationships between intervention in a "seizure" emergency and measures of social desirability, social responsibility, authoritarianism, Machiavellianism, and alienation. Staub (1971) found no relationship between social desirability and helping. Korte (1969) found no effects associated with autonomy, deference, and submissiveness. Also, Yakimovich and Saltz (1971) found no relationship between helping and measures of trustworthiness, independence, and altruism. Past approaches, however, have taken a very empirical approach to the issue of personality effects on helping rather than a theoretical one. We hope that our model can suggest fruitful dimensions in the person as well as in the situation that may facilitate intervention. The basic aspects of the model are arousal, costs for helping, costs for the victim receiving no help, and (now) attention. Person variables that relate to any of these aspects thus seem theoretically promising.

As we have noted, it is almost by definition that trait factors can have no effect in "impulse-generating" situations as we have defined them. However, as we have also noted, the ideal-typical "impulse-generating" situation cannot actually exist. What we see are close approximations to it. Empirically, not every subject responds impulsively even in the situations we have narrowly defined as "pulling" such behavior. The trait factors we would like to identify in this regard, then, are those that will cause some individuals to respond impulsively, without apparent regard for the costs, and others to respond either more calculatively or not at all. The same kinds of trait variables should shift situations, for at least some people, from the nonimpulsive to the impulsive category.

How can Mischel's list of categories of trait variables that show good cross-situational consistencies be of help here? The one that seems to have the most relevance, given our finding that clarity and reality are two of the most critical determinants of "impulsive" responding, is his "encoding and categorizing" classification. Some individuals may simply perceive more clarity than do others in the same situation. A promising variable in this regard is Kagan's MFF Scale, the "Matching Familiar Figures" test (see Kagan, Rosman, Day, Albert, & Phillips, 1964). Individuals scoring high on the MFF both respond very rapidly and make more errors—that is, they do not notice discrepancies in the figures and they do not conduct a thorough scan of the alternatives before they act. Unfortunately, the only test of the relationship of the MFF to helping was done in a highly ambiguous situation (Staub, Erkut, & Jaquette, as described in Staub, 1974). While high MFF scorers stood up more quickly in response to hearing the distress noises from the room next door, they did not help more rapidly. Our prediction would be that in a clearer emergency, scores on the MFF would predict not only more helping but also helping that was relatively unaffected by costs on the part of high scorers.

A more compelling finding comes from a study by Denner (1968). He hypothesized that two person variables, "concern with the real–unreal distinction" and "need for information," would be important determinants of the speed with which bystanders would intervene in a somewhat ambiguous theft. In particular, Denner hypothesized that individuals who were relatively more preoccupied with distinguishing between the real and the unreal would be more reluctant to report a crime than those who were less interested in questioning the reality of their sensations. In addition, he proposed that individuals with a high need for information would be more reluctant to report a crime than those with a low need for information, since they would be more concerned with determining the clarity of their percept. Concern with the real–unreal distinction and need for information were measured in a first session. Subjects high on both measures or low on both measures were invited back for a second session, ostensibly for more work on the tachistoscope task that formed the basis for the need for information measure. During the second session, subjects were sent to wait in a room across from the equipment room. As they opened the door, they saw a young man hurriedly withdraw his hand from a woman's purse. The "thief" looked startled and guilty, and then escaped through another door. The speed with which the subject reported the incident to the experimenter was recorded.

The results indicated a large and significant difference in responding between the "high–high" and the "low–low" groups. Subjects with low need for information and low concern for reality tended to report the theft within 60 seconds. Subjects high on both dimensions typically delayed reporting until the experimenter suggested that they had witnessed something. Most specifically relevant to our interest in impulsive helping, a reanalysis of the raw data indicated that there were eight subjects who responded within 5 seconds, which qualifies as an "impulsive" response by our previous definition. Seven of the eight were in the low–low group. In fact, 41% of the low-need-for-information–low-concern-for-reality group helped "impulsively"; only 6% of the subjects who were high on both needs did so. These data are powerful and highly consistent with our analysis of the parallel situational factors postulated to elicit impulsive helping: clarity and reality. The findings, however, do not speak to the question of the relative impact of costs and rewards in the situation, since the "thief" had fled and presumably could not harm the reporter.[1]

Another obvious possibility with regard to "impulsive" helpers is that they may be highly emotional people with "short fuses." Such tendencies might lead to rapid intervention under emotional circumstances. Huston, Geis, and Wright (1976) offer anecdotal support for this contention in a *Psychology Today* article entitled the "Angry Samaritans." They interviewed approximately half of all those individuals who had received compensatory awards under California's "Good Samaritan Law" up to January of 1976. All of the award recipients had been injured by intervening in a crime in progress. The authors write

> Our impression . . . is that most of our Samaritans are risk-takers, men on familiar and rather amiable terms with violence. . . . The Samaritan's low boiling point was confirmed by their answers to a questionnaire we used, an adaptation of the anger scale developed by psychologist Raymond Novaco . . . . We found that the Samaritans were much more easily provoked than a group of 153 male college students who answered the same questions [p. 64].[2]

Behaviorally, what the majority of the "Good Samaritans" had done was to attack the criminal, not to help the victim directly. The fact that they were all injured is at least suggestive of the lack of impact of obvious costs for intervention. Their high arousal, likely anger in this case, may well have narrowed their attention to their target, who was the criminal, not the victim as we propose usually occurs.

Wilson and his colleagues (Michelini, Wilson, & Messé, 1975; Wilson, 1976) have reported findings that indicate that another person variable, one that does not really fall into one of Mischel's five categories, may also relate to rapid helping and helping that is unresponsive to cost factors in the situation. In the first study (Michelini *et al.*, 1975) it was predicted that "safety-oriented" subjects would help less than "esteem-oriented" subjects in a "dropped objects" problem situation. The "esteem" and "safety" orientations are constructs derived from Maslow's (1970) theoretical need hierarchy and are measured using a sentence completion task (Aronoff, 1970). Esteem-oriented individuals are characterized as achievement-oriented, dominant, and willing to demonstrate their competency in interpersonal situations. In contrast, safety-oriented individuals tend to be anxious, mistrustful, and passive. They often withdraw from social interactions, are dependent on others, and have strong feelings of incompetence. Reykowski (n.d., manuscript B) has elaborated a theory of "self-structure" that in-

---

[1] We would like to thank Bruce Denner for providing us with his data for reanalysis.

[2] Reprinted by permission from *Psychology Today* magazine. Copyright © 1976 by Ziff-Davis Publishing Co.

tegrates well with Wilson's approach. He suggests that under normal conditions behavior is strongly regulated by "dominant cognitive organizations." In Chapter 9 we will go into more detail regarding Reykowski's work and that of other Polish researchers of prosocial behavior, since they have been most interested in temporary states as they affect the salience of self-structures and motives.

Michelini *et al.* selected three groups of male subjects: those in the top 15% on esteem and in the bottom 15% on safety, those in the top 15% on safety and in the bottom 15% on esteem, and those between the 45th and 55th percentiles on both scores. Subjects were brought to a room with two confederates and then, somewhat later, they were confronted with the "dropped objects" crisis; the confederates remained inactive.

The personality variable had the anticipated effect. The percentages of helping in the esteem, mixed, and safety groups were 81%, 46%, and 31%, respectively. More importantly for our purposes here, across the entire group of 16 esteem subjects the mean response time was 5.2 seconds! The middle group, on the other hand, had a mean latency of 13.4 seconds, and the safety-oriented group averaged 15.8 seconds. Thus, in the same situation, one in which both costs for helping and costs for not helping were low, esteem-oriented subjects exhibited more "impulsive" behavior than did safety-oriented and moderate subjects. It seems as though the low costs for not helping (associated with the presence of others and the nonseriousness of the situation) were not attended to by esteem-oriented subjects.

The second study (Wilson, 1976) provides a more explicit test of the relative lack of impact of cost factors on "esteem" subjects as compared to "safety" subjects. Three groups of subjects (esteem-oriented, safety-oriented, and mixed) were selected as in the previous experiment. Both males and females were used in this study. The emergency was, at the same time, slightly less clear but much more arousing. The emergency occurred to someone whom the subject had met (the experimenter), but the victim was part of the experiment and was not visible. These factors make it an ideal situation for some personality types to respond "impulsively" while others do not.

Another manipulated variable allowed for the test of the impact of cost factors on the different categories of subjects. Subjects experienced the emergency either (a) alone; (b) in the presence of two passive bystanders of their own gender; or (c) in the presence of one passive bystander and one who, upon hearing the crash, said, "Oh Jesus, what was that?" and, at between 8 and 13 seconds after the crash, got up to help. Table 8.1 presents the percentages of helpers and the latencies of response among helpers across subject categories and conditions. The effect of the personality factor is clearly seen within both alone and two passive bystander conditions.

Table 8.1

Percentages of Subjects Helping and Mean Latencies to Respond, among Helpers, in the Eighteen Cells of the Wilson (1976) Experiment[a] (White Subjects Only)[b,c]

	Alone		Two passive bystanders		One passive, one helping bystander		
	Percentage helping	Mean latency	Percentage helping	Mean latency	Percentage helping	Mean latency	Percentage helping before bystander
Male subjects							
Need category							
Esteem	100 (11)	12.3 (11)	80 (10)	13.3 (8)	90 (10)	8.7 (9)	67 (9)
Mixed	67 (12)	16.4 (8)	20 (10)	20.4 (2)	100 (10)	11.2 (10)	20 (10)
Safety	70 (10)	17.1 (7)	12.5 (8)	17.0 (1)	75 (12)	14.7 (9)	11 (9)
Female subjects							
Need category							
Esteem	91 (11)	14.3 (10)	60 (10)	12.2 (6)	82 (11)	12.2 (9)	67 (9)
Mixed	64 (11)	15.6 (7)	25 (12)	22.7 (3)	90 (10)	9.6 (9)	33 (9)
Safety	42 (12)	13.6 (5)	20 (10)	20.5 (2)	67 (12)	11.0 (8)	12.5 (8)

[a] From J. P. Wilson, Motivation, modeling, and altruism: A Person × Situation analysis. *Journal of Personality and Social Psychology*, 1976, 34, 1078-1086. Copyright 1976 by the American Psychological Association. Reprinted by permission.

[b] Black subjects have been omitted because of the finding from Gaertner and Dovidio (see Chapter 6) that race is important in emergencies of this type. (There were only four black helpers, two male and two female, all in the esteem group. Although the two females intervened very quickly, the two males intervened more slowly than any other helpers in the entire study. Their data distort the impression otherwise conveyed by the esteem group.)

[c] Ns are given in parentheses. In the "percentage helping" column, the N is the total for the cell on which the percentage is based. In the "mean latency" and "percentage helping before bystander" columns, the N given is the number of

190

Furthermore, the passive bystander condition provides a replication of Michelini *et al.* (1975), with an even larger effect of personality than was obtained before. In particular, esteem-oriented subjects were most helpful.

Looking more closely at the data, male esteem-oriented subjects appeared to respond "impulsively." Across the three conditions, 90% helped, the average latency for helpers was 11.4 seconds, and there were no significant differences among the three bystander conditions. Although the sex difference is not statistically reliable, the emergency seemed to fall just short of being totally compelling for female esteem-oriented subjects. Only 60% of them responded in the presence of two passive bystanders. Our intuitive feeling is that the difference in gender between the victim and the female bystanders was just enough to prevent the nearly total identification that is often required for "impulsive" intervention.[3]

In a somewhat related work, Liebhart (1972) measured "sympathetic orientation" and "disposition to take instrumental action for relief of one's own distress." Explicitly referring to our model of helping in emergencies, he sees these two "trait" variables as reflecting, respectively, the tendency to become aroused in response to another's emergency and the likelihood of choosing to do something about the distress, rather than doing nothing. He therefore predicts that, given exposure to the same emergency situation, individuals high on these two dimensions should be more likely to help and help more rapidly than those low on both or on either one of these dimensions. Liebhart's "sympathetic, instrumental" individuals appear to be similar to Wilson's "esteem-oriented" people in their tendency to be dominant and their willingness to demonstrate competency in interpersonal relationships.

The results did indeed reveal the hypothesized relationship between the trait variables and the speed of response. Bystanders high on both sympathetic orientation and instrumental activity, when contrasted with the other three possible trait combinations, helped significantly more quickly. Whether this effect was due to increased empathy (i.e., arousal) or differential impact of costs cannot be unequivocally determined, although Liebhart suggests that it is mediated by arousal.

In summary, there is empirical evidence suggesting that personal characteristics (traits) can influence helping behavior in emergencies. In particular, some traits may lead some bystanders to respond in an "impulsive" fashion to emergencies or crises to which others respond more calculatively or not at all. These traits may directly affect the relative impacts of costs for helping or costs for not helping, or they may operate indirectly through arousal. That is, a predisposition to respond to an emergency with a particularly high level of arousal should produce an in-

---

[3] We would like to thank John Wilson for providing us with his data for reanalysis.

creased motivation to respond and, through focusing attention on the victim, typically result in a decreased impact of costs for helping. Given the relative paucity of findings, we must emphasize that these interpretations are only suggestive. Denner's measures have been used only once and Wilson's need categories only twice. We feel that further work should be conducted with these promising variables, as well as with other theoretically interesting variables such as MFF, Block's (1971) undercontrol measure, and perhaps tolerance for ambiguity. That is, there are several personal characteristics that should *theoretically* lead to more rapid judgments, faster motor responses, heightened emotionality, and other factors that predispose individuals to impulsive responding. Exploration of these variables would not only reveal their predictive utility but also provide a test of the "ideal–typical" formulation of the nature of impulse-generating situations presented here.

Trait Factors, Crises, Problems, and Nonimpulsive Helping

There appear to be at least two rather general trait factors that have been demonstrated, with various operationalizations, to relate to helping in a diverse set of studies. Interestingly, they fit rather neatly into the cost formulation. First, competence seems to be related to helping in a reasonable number of studies. Second, commitment to moral standards or to personal norms of helpfulness combined with an inability to deny personal responsibility for one's actions seems to be a consistent factor in helping. Competence can be seen as lowering the perceived costs for intervention—general competence through the route of a general expectation for success and specific competence through the route of reduction of effort in the search for actions and alternatives. The moral commitment or personal norms variable, on the other hand, should operate to increase the costs for not helping.

COMPETENCE, SELF-CONFIDENCE, AND HELPING

The research on the relationship between competence and helping comes, as usual, from a range of different situations. Sometimes the investigators measured competence with a scale, sometimes it was assessed from prior behavior or from self-reports of relevant experience, but mainly competence was manipulated, either by telling subjects they are generally capable or that they have relevant specific skills.

The conclusion is general enough that we will not belabor the point at great length. We would like to point out the fact that it appears to be *perceived* competence that is critical, given that both measured and manipulated competence relate to increased helping. Harris and Huang (1973a) suggest three mechanisms through which perceived competence may lead to increased helping: (a) decreased perceived costs for helping; (b) happiness or good mood; or (c) a feeling of "noblesse oblige," that is, an increased sense of responsibility. Good mood can be ruled out as the factor behind the entire set of studies showing competence effects, since it can hardly be involved in those that involve measured competence. Both decreased perceived costs for helping and increased feelings of obligation (increased perceived costs for not helping) would be mechanisms quite consistent with the model being presented in this book.

There are a large number of studies that demonstrate that perceived competence for specific tasks generally facilitates helping behavior. For example, in a series of studies Midlarsky (1971; Midlarsky & Midlarsky, 1973, 1976) has demonstrated that those made to feel more able to handle electric shock are more willing to help others move electrically charged objects. In an "escaped rat" emergency, subjects told that they would find handling rats to be relatively easy were more likely to intervene and intervened faster than did subjects told that they would not be good at it (Schwartz & Ben David, 1976). Harris and Huang (1973a) obtained more volunteers for an aesthetic judgment task among those told they had been very competent on a related task earlier. Clark and Word (1974) found more helping, and more safe, thought-out helping among "electrically experienced" individuals in an electrical malfunction emergency. Form and Nosow (1958) report that helpers in the aftermath of a tornado had both technical knowledge and relevant prior experience. Thus, across a great variety of situations, feelings of competence (often independent of actual competence) consistently facilitated prosocial responding.

General competence, often unrelated to the nature of the helping task, also increases helping behavior. Ashton and Severy (1976) and Kazdin and Bryan (1971) manipulated general perceived competence and found more intervention in an emergency and more volunteering for experiments, respectively. Midlarsky and Midlarsky, in the series of studies cited previously, also manipulated general competence and found that it led to increased helping. In a mildly amusing finding, both Schwartz and Clausen (personal communication) and Piliavin, Piliavin, and Trudell (unpublished, 1974) found more helping, and more rapid helping, among physically larger male subjects in response to emergencies. One could (and we do) interpret this finding as indicative of a generalized feeling of competence to handle situations, especially those involving the need for physical help, among physically stronger people.

We would like also to describe one study in greater detail because it involves an unusual and interesting measure of competence. Firestone,

Lichtman, and Colamosca (1975) brought male undergraduates together in five-person groups and had them work on discussion problems. The group members were rated on a measure of group discussion leadership potential (referred to as LGD) while they were working on this practice problem. In 13 of the groups, there was then an unrigged election for leader; the elected leader was always the person rated most highly by the judges on LGD. This fact, in itself, seems to validate the LGD measure. In another 13 groups, a rigged election was held in which the experimenter reported to the group that the person elected was the individual who, in actuality, had received the lowest LGD rating. In the remaining 13 groups, a randomly selected person was appointed as leader; half of the leaders were above and half below the median on LGD.

Later in the session, an emergency involving an incipient insulin reaction on the part of a group-member–confederate occurred. The person who "took charge" in all 13 of the elected-leader groups was the real leader, the high-LGD man. These groups helped most often (81%) and fastest. In the "rigged"-election and appointed-leader groups, only five of the low-LGD leaders maintained their leadership; in 15 groups they were "over-thrown." As a result, many of the groups did not solve their leadership problem quickly enough to help effectively. When help was received, however, it was always due to the actions of a high-LGD person.

We have described the Firestone *et al.* study in some detail because it illustrates the relevance of situational factors in the operation of even those trait variables, such as competence, disposition to take action, or whatever is involved in LGD, that seem to show some cross-situational promise. The study also demonstrates the importance of attending to social structural variables as well as to situational factors as they are more usually conceptualized. All of the groups had both high- and low-LGD individuals in them, and all groups consisted of five individuals. However, there appeared to be a bystander inhibition effect in the appointed-leader and "rigged"-election groups, but none, or much less, in the real-election groups. This difference can only be due to the effects of role requirements inherent in the structure of the groups in interaction with personal predispositions of the actors.

MORAL STANDARDS, PERSONAL NORMS, AND THE DENIAL OF PERSONAL RESPONSIBILITY

The "normative approach" to helping and altruism was an early and highly influential approach, initiated by Berkowitz (Berkowitz & Daniels, 1963, 1964; Daniels & Berkowitz, 1963; Goranson & Berkowitz, 1966) and continued by Schopler (Schopler & Bateson, 1965; Schopler & Matthews,

1965). The basic premise of this research was that a general "social r_
sibility norm" existed that prescribed that people should help others that
were dependent upon them. As investigators pursued this question, they
found, indeed, that people think they should help others who are dependent upon them, and that others would expect them to do so. Moreover, in
these experiments, subjects would work hard for a dependent other, even
when there was little gain for doing so or even when no one else would ever
know (Berkowitz, 1972).

Serious difficulties with this approach soon became evident. First, it
became clear that in any given situation a multiplicity of norms may exist,
and the action taken can often be consistent with only one of them (Latané
& Darley, 1970). For example, the social responsibility norm would suggest
intervention in a family argument, especially one involving potential
damage to one of the partners. At the same time, there is a strong proscrip-
tion against interfering in others' personal lives. Which norm predicts the
behavior? It is even possible that the norm of social responsibility may be
involved on both sides of such an internal conflict. In a study by Batson,
Cochran, Biederman, Blosser, Ryan, and Vogt (1978), subjects were sent
from one building to another to complete their experimental assignment,
and on their path they encountered an ambiguous emergency—a man
slumped in a doorway, moaning. By varying the apparent dependence of
the experimenter on the data to be provided by the subject, Batson *et al.*
demonstrated that the likelihood of helping the victim was affected by the
responsibility norm as it applied in the subject's relationship to the experimenter. That is, the more dependent the experimenter was on the subject,
the less likely the subject was to stop and help the victim.

A second difficulty with the general normative approach that soon
became apparent was that person factors interacted with the dependency
manipulations that were presumed to make salient the social responsibility
norm. In particular, males often responded to high dependency by providing less rather than more help (Enzle & Harvey, 1979; Schopler &
Matthews, 1965). In other words, the usefulness of the social responsibility
norm as an explanatory construct decreased as both situation and person
factors had to be introduced as modifying variables. Without specifying in
advance which norms will lead to helping by whom in a given situation,
the norm of social responsibility will remain at best a post hoc explanation
for helping.

Schwartz (1977) argues that normative explanations may still be of
value, however. While general social norms may provide us with no better
than vague guides for behavior in concrete situations, the use of *personal*
norms may be valuable in accounting for individual differences in helping
behavior. According to Schwartz, personal norms refer to self-expectations

for behavior in specific situations, and are backed by the anticipation of self-enhancement or deprecation. Personal norms are feelings of obligation to behave in a particular manner in specific situations. They differ from generalized individual dispositions (attitudes, traits, and general norms) in their focus on specific actions, feelings of obligation, and internalized self-expectations concerning appropriate behavior for a given situation. Moreover, different persons are likely to have different personal norms for any particular situation. These individual differences can be measured in advance of behavior. Thus, Schwartz's program of research employs the idiographic techniques advocated by Bem and Allen (1974).

Premeasured personal norms have been used successfully to predict a wide variety of helping behaviors. For example, investigators have found individual differences with behaviors such as volunteering to tutor blind children (Schwartz, 1977), donating blood (Pomazal & Jaccard, 1976; Zuckerman & Reis, 1978), buying lead-free gasoline (Heberlein & Black, 1976), volunteering to be a bone-marrow donor (Schwartz, 1970), pledging to take class notes for students who were mobilized into the army (Rothstein, 1974), and helping peers (Schwartz, 1968).

In Schwartz's model, the relationship between personal norms and behavior in those situations to which the norms apply is moderated by two other variables: awareness of the consequences of one's actions for others (measured by the AC scale) and tendency to deny responsibility for putting one's personal norms into action (measured by the RD scale). These are conceptualized as trait variables or general dispositions and are uncorrelated with the personal norms that are generated in specific situations.

We see Schwartz's conceptualization as quite consistent with our model. Although his motivational construct, a sense of personal normative obligation, differs from ours, it does involve an emotional component. That is, people help because they will feel bad about themselves if they do not act and will feel good about themselves if they do. His AC and RD constructs are, we believe, measures of personal tendencies that affect the costs for the victim receiving no help. Awareness of consequences is related to what we have called "empathy costs." Individuals who are high on awareness of consequences spontaneously attend to possible consequences of their behavior for the welfare of others, while low-AC people need more graphic explanations presented to them. Thus, AC is expected to relate to helping primarily "under low prominence and seriousness of others' need in the stimulus environment [Schwartz, 1977, p. 242]." In a compelling emergency situation, though, AC has been found not to relate to helping (Schwartz & Clausen, 1970).

The RD (responsibility denial) scale relates to a bystander's personal costs for not helping. To the extent that an individual denies personal

responsibility, the perceived negative personal consequences for not helping should be lower. In addition, RD should relate to helping regardless of
the clarity of need. The only circumstances under which it should not affect
helping are those in which (a) responses are "impulsive" in the sense
discussed earlier in the chapter and in Chapter 7 (our interpretation, not
Schwartz's); (b) the structure of the situation is such as to prevent the
possibility of responsibility denial; or (c) the people do not hold positive
personal norms towards helping in the situation. RD should correlate
negatively with helping under all other conditions, since RD scores signify
the strength of the tendency to neutralize personal norms.

The relationship between RD scores and helping is well documented.
Responsibility denial has been significantly related to bystander responses
to a seizure victim (Schwartz & Clausen, 1970), to an experimenter
frightened by an escaped rat (Schwartz & Ben David, 1976), and to moaning and groaning from an adjoining room (Staub, 1974). In nonemergency
situations it has been related to everyday considerateness and helpfulness
(Schwartz, 1968), refraining from littering on a busy street (Heberlein,
1971), volunteering to donate bone marrow (Schwartz, 1970), and pledging
time to raise money for Head Start (Schwartz, 1974). In general, RD was
more strongly associated with helping in nonemergency studies, where the
situation was less compelling and the opportunity to deny responsibility
was not constrained by the conspicuous dependency of a victim upon quick
reactions.

Data collected by Schwartz and Fleishman (1978) illustrate the necessity for personal norms towards helping to be positive for RD to predict
helping. Respondents to a mailed questionnaire had been asked to indicate
their feelings of personal moral obligation to help welfare recipients. A
substantial percentage of respondents had indicated that they felt an obligation *not* to help—a negative norm. Later, volunteering to help make phone
calls for a state-wide campaign to get extra welfare payments for senior
citizens was higher among positive-norm subjects than among negative-
norm subjects. More critically, RD was significantly related to volunteering
among positive-norm people but not among respondents who had expressed negative norms. This finding strengthens the interpretation that RD
is a measure of the tendency to neutralize the impact of norms rather than
some generalized measure of helpfulness in and of itself. A negative norm
requires no neutralization when the request is to engage in the negatively
valued behavior.[4] In terms of our conceptual framework, when personal

---

[4] The fascinating and conclusive test was not done. That would, of course, be to ask
respondents to make calls for a state-wide campaign to reduce welfare payments. Negative-
norm subjects should volunteer more, and RD should predict their response; positive-norm
subjects should volunteer less, and RD should be unrelated to volunteering.

costs for not helping are low (i.e., a negative personal norm), further reduction of the costs for not helping, due to denying responsibility, will have little effect.

Many other studies by Schwartz and his co-workers have found strong moderating effects of both AC and RD on the relationship between measured personal norms and helping. That is, prediction of helping behavior from professed feelings of moral obligation to help in such a situation is good among those high on AC and/or low on RD. With little tendency to think of consequences (low empathy costs, in our conceptual scheme) and with strong tendencies to deny personal responsibility (low personal costs for not helping) the relationship between professed norms and behavior is typically zero. We would like to suggest at this time that both high levels of AC and low levels of RD are related to involvement on the involvement–detachment dimension we introduced in the previous chapter.

There are four other studies of which we are aware that have attempted to assess the relationship between "moral standards" and helping. We will refer to them briefly. First, Horowitz (1976) provided subjects with "feedback" from their responses to Kohlberg moral dilemmas indicating that they were either high or average in moral level (LMD). The statement read to the "highs" emphasized that "a high-LMD person is aware of other people's needs and emotional requirements. This person is concerned with living up to one's own principles [p. 249]." This description is similar to a high-AC, low-RD individual in Schwartz's model. Moderate-level individuals were read a statement stressing their concern with self-respect and honor and being responsible for one's actions. The manipulation of perceived moral level appeared to affect their willingness to volunteer to help a rather desperate Ph.D student under "private" as compared to "public" conditions. That is, when it was not obvious that there could be social sanctions for not helping, the "morality" manipulation had an effect; under highly public conditions, it did not. In another "labeling" study, Swinyard and Ray (1979) had door-to-door interviewers tell half of their respondents that they were "interested in their fellow man." This labeling led to a large increase in expressing the intention to volunteer for Red Cross activities in response to later mailings. In a self-attribution study, Batson, Harris, McCaul, Davis, and Schmidt (1979) induced subjects to attribute an initial helping response to either compassion or compliance by programming a confederate to define her own response to the initial request. Those who had presumably come to see themselves as compassionate volunteered significantly more time in a later unrelated appeal from a community agency.

Finally, Penner, Summers, Brookmire, and Dertke (1976) measured subjects on Rokeach's value instrument and on a "sociopathy" scale. Subjects were placed in what they call a "quasi-laboratory" situation (a campus testing office) and presented with a "lost" dollar, either loose, in an envelope with institutional identification, or in a wallet with personal identification. Rokeach's values "honest" and "a comfortable life" discriminated those who returned the dollar from those who took it; the values "helpful" and "honest" discriminated returners from those who simply ignored the money. The "ownership" and "sociopathy" variables were also significantly related to helping.

In summary, there is evidence that both competence and personal norms and values affect helping responses in a wide range of situations. Competence related to the situation as well as personal norms specific to the situation provide better predictions than do general feelings of competence or more general value orientations. Finally, personal tendencies to think of the consequences of one's actions for others and to accept responsibility moderate the relationship of personal norms to helping behavior.

Two important points should be made here. First, the variables of competence, awareness of consequences, and acceptance of responsibility can all be viewed within the cost–benefit framework, and thus these findings are quite consistent with the model. Second, the importance of viewing the effects of these person factors in relationship to specific situations is clear and reinforces the current attention to Person × Situation effects, rather than to either type of variable in isolation.

GENDER EFFECTS

Within our theoretical framework, the gender of the bystander could affect intervention through arousal and/or cost factors. Although it has been suggested that females may be inherently more sensitive to the distress of others (Hoffman, 1977a; McDougall, 1908), there is only a little empirical evidence demonstrating this difference (Sagi & Hoffman, 1976; Simner, 1971). Instead, the main way in which the gender of the bystander seems to affect helping is through cost–benefit considerations. Differential past experiences, sheer physical size, and sex-related personality differences can probably explain many of the sex differences that have been observed.

Deaux (1976), after reviewing the helping literature, concluded that the general finding that males are more likely to intervene than females may be due to the fact that:

1. Many of the intervention studies have dealt with situations that women may be less adept at handling.
2. The costs and rewards associated with helping may be different for men and women.

3. Since men are more likely to be trained to be initiators, they may be more likely to intervene in any situation in which a direct request is not made.

Actually, Deaux's analysis is easy to subsume under a cost analysis. Having no expertise makes helping more costly. Similarly, physical factors may make helping relatively more costly for females. Also, to the extent that males are trained to be initiators, costs for not helping will be higher for males.

A variety of studies investigating the effects of the gender of the bystander on helping behavior lend support to a cost–benefit analysis. For example, many helping situations offer a unique reward for helping. They can provide a convenient opportunity to initiate interaction with a person of the opposite sex. Indeed, several experimenters have found significant cross-sex helping effects in low-threat, low-cost situations (Bickman, 1974; Dovidio, 1979; Emswiller, Deaux, & Willits, 1971; Hertzog & Hertzog, 1979). A slight increase in threat or costs for helping seems to eliminate this effect, however. No cross-sex helping effects were obtained when Latané and Darley (1970) had experimenters ask pedestrians on the streets of New York for a dime and when Dovidio (1979) had experimenters ask other students for 30 cents (the other studies involved college students on their own campuses). Hertzog and Hertzog (1979) found significantly more cross-sex helping only when the requestor was alone; the presence of a person identified as the requestor's spouse eliminated the effect.

Differential expertise also seems to mediate gender effects in intervention through cost considerations. Several studies have demonstrated differences in the amount of help males and females offer to a motorist in need. Bryan and Test (1967), Pomazal and Clore (1973), and West, Whitney, and Schnedler (1975) all found that males were more likely to stop to help a stranded motorist than were females. Presumably, males have more experience and expertise in auto repair than do women, making the costs for helping relatively lower for males. Other characteristics of the "motorist in distress" situation may also lead to higher costs for helping for females. The need for physical strength and the potential for personal attack would make helping relatively more costly for female bystanders. Given these considerations, it is not surprising that in the subway emergency studies (Piliavin & Piliavin, 1972; Piliavin, Piliavin, & Rodin, 1975; Piliavin, Rodin, & Piliavin, 1969) males were consistently more likely to intervene than were females. Similarly, Borofsky, Stollak, and Messé (1971), in a role-playing situation, demonstrated that males were more likely to intervene than females to break up a "spontaneous" fight between two males or two females (although not when a male was attacking a female). It is particularly surprising, therefore, that Austin (1979) consistently found more intervention to prevent a theft on the part of female bystanders, regardless of the sex of the thief or of the sex of the victim.

Sex-role expectations also appear to exert a powerful influence on prosocial responding. Presumably, performing an out-of-role behavior is more costly than performing an in-role behavior. Consequently, personal costs for helping will typically be higher in situations requiring the benefactor to behave in a manner that is inconsistent with his or her sex role. Part of the sex difference in helping behavior in the "flat tire" studies, in fact, seems to be related to role considerations. In Gaertner and Bickman's (1971) "wrong number" experiment, although the situation was nonthreatening and required no technical expertise, females helped less than males. However, in other situations in which the problem was less traditionally sex-linked (e.g., Baker & Reitz, 1978; Bickman, 1974; Simon, 1971), no sex differences were obtained in response to a phoned request.

Two unpublished studies were designed explicitly to explore sex-role effects in helping situations. Primmer, Jaccard, Cohen, Wasserman, and Hoffing (as cited in Deaux, 1976) had confederates approach shoppers at a local drugstore and ask them to buy either a depilatory or chewing tobacco. As expected, males were more likely to buy the tobacco, while females were more likely to buy the depilatory. In the other study (Dovidio, Campbell, Rigaud, Yankura, Rominger, & Pine, 1978), a confederate asked a subject in a laundromat either to help carry some laundry or to help fold some laundry. Again, a Sex of Subject × Type of Task interaction emerged. Males were more likely to carry the laundry; females more often folded the clothes. Thus, both males and females were less likely to help when assistance was associated with more costly out-of-role behavior.

Sex-role expectations may affect costs for not helping as well as costs for helping. To the extent that males are expected to demonstrate bravery and chivalry and to assume responsibility, personal costs for not helping will be relatively higher for males than for females in many situations. Males, therefore, should be less likely to diffuse responsibility. As we discussed in greater detail in Chapter 6, this seems generally to be the case. For example, Schwartz and Clausen (1970) demonstrated that although female bystanders tended to respond more quickly than males when they were the only witness to an emergency, they helped less often when four other bystanders—some of them males—were present. In a nonemergency study, Latané and Dabbs (1975) demonstrated a similar pattern of results for subjects in groups. In their study, experimenters "accidentally" dropped coins or pencils in front of groups of subjects in elevators in Columbus,

Ohio; Seattle, Washington; and Atlanta, Georgia. The results indicated that males were more likely than females to help, particularly when the experimenter was a female. This effect was most pronounced in Atlanta, where adherence to the traditional male sex role was hypothesized to be strongest.

For females, sex-role expectations may also affect the costs for not helping. Females have been traditionally characterized as nurturant and emotionally supportive, and consequently they may be expected to respond more favorably than males to dependent others. Consistent with this reasoning, Schopler and his colleagues (Schopler, 1967; Schopler & Bateson, 1965; Schopler & Matthews, 1965) found sex differences in helping related to the dependency of the potential recipient. As the dependency of the recipient increased, females helped more and males helped less. Similarly, when Thalhofer (1971) presented subjects with an opportunity to help a mentally disturbed boy, females were more likely to volunteer than males. As noted earlier, Enzle and Harvey (1979) found a positive correlation between the perceived need of another and helping among females and a negative relationship among males, when the need involved emotional support for a depressed person. Thus, an important determinant of gender effects in helping is the nature of the helping context.

In summary, the effects of the gender of the bystander seem most parsimoniously interpreted in terms of cost–benefit considerations. Gender appears to affect both personal costs for helping and personal costs for not helping. Little current evidence suggests sex-related arousal differences, however. Furthermore, gender effects are most clearly understood in a Person × Situation analysis. That is, the type of situation, the type of help required, and the gender of the bystander should all be considered in conjunction. Finally, it is important to realize that gender is an extremely complex person variable. Implicit in sex differences are physiological, anatomical, social, and developmental differences. Thus, it is particularly likely that gender can have multiple effects on helping behavior—simultaneously affecting costs for not helping, costs for helping, and arousal.

Summary and Implications

Our review of the literature on person variables suggests two general conclusions. First, despite the earlier conclusions of researchers, person variables can influence helping behavior. In both emergency and nonemergency situations, several personality traits have been shown to relate in meaningful ways to intervention. Second, the effects of person variables are most clearly understood within a Person × Situation framework. That is, it is the unique interaction of a particular type of personality and a specific kind of situation that predominantly influences helping behavior, as argued by Staub in his two volumes on prosocial behavior (1978, 1979). Furthermore, based on the success of Schwartz's research program concerning personal norms, idiographic techniques appear to provide even greater predictive power.

We feel, in addition, that our model provides a viable framework for organizing past research on personality and helping, and for guiding future investigation. Just as we have used the model to explore situational factors affecting intervention, it may be employed to attempt to identify relevant personality dimensions. Within this theoretical framework, a person variable can be conceptualized as influencing the degree of arousal, the direction of attention, and the relative consideration of costs for helping and costs for not helping. In a relevant situation, a person variable that consolidates the facilitative effects of two or more of these factors would, therefore, be expected to relate especially strongly to helping behavior. For example, Liebhart (1972) found that individuals who were high on "sympathetic orientation" (hypothesized to relate to degree of vicarious arousal) and high on "disposition to take instrumental action for relief of one's own distress" (relating to empathic costs for not helping) helped more quickly in an emergency than bystanders low on one or both of these dimensions.

Finally, in our latest version of the arousal:cost–reward model, the direction of the bystander's attention is also an important factor. As we discussed earlier, a narrow focus of attention, due to high levels of emergency-generated arousal, in which only the costs for not helping are considered, leads to apparently "irrational," impulsive helping. Attention is also important in less compelling problems, if only because the bystander would be more likely to notice that another person is in need. Without awareness of the other's need, empathic and personal costs for not helping would be nonexistent. Obviously then, recognition of another's problem is prerequisite to helping. Also, if attention is important, the extent to which an individual characteristically attends to or monitors the behaviors of others should be related to helping behavior, at least when the costs for helping are low. Moreover, personality traits that are positively related to both attention to others and salience of the costs for not helping should be particularly strongly related to helping.

Many of the traits that have been shown to relate to helping share a common theme. Helpers are generally more "other-oriented" (versus "self-oriented") than nonhelpers on these dimensions. Social responsibility (Berkowitz & Daniels, 1964), extraversion (Cattell & Horowitz, 1952), need for social approval (Crandall, Crandall, & Katkovsky, 1965; Satow, 1975), social interest (Crandall, 1978), and attractiveness as a friend (Friedrichs,

1960) have all been found to be related to helpfulness. Also, Staub (1974) found a relatively strong relationship between helping and a composite index of "prosocial orientation" based on measures of social responsibility, ascription of responsibility, Machiavellianism, moral reasoning, and prosocial values. Thus, although the replicability of each personality measure has not been unequivocally demonstrated, there is a relatively consistent pattern of results in nonemergency situations.

Chapter 9

State Factors and Intervention

The philosopher tells us that we can never step in the same river twice. The psychophysiologist tells us that environmental inputs to the human organism cause little more than "ripples on the sea of autonomic functioning" that is constantly changing. The symbolic interactionist tells us that the self is process, not content, and that every action and every interaction changes the self. It is with this frame of mind that we turn to a consideration of temporary state factors in the bystander as they affect his or her response to the need of another. In particular, we will examine research that relates initial alertness, attention, mental "set," and initial mood states to helping behavior. The findings in this area are complex and often seemingly contradictory. Nevertheless, in this chapter we will attempt to integrate the research findings and to speculate with possible interpretations based on the processes that we have discussed throughout this book. In the second half of this chapter, in particular, we will consider issues that are less directly related to the model in its current form. We have no definitive answers; we make this attempt primarily to organize past research, to suggest future avenues of inquiry, and to explore new directions in which the model may develop.

Prior State, Arousal, and Attention

In Chapter 4 we presented evidence in support of the proposition that arousal created by the observation of another's emergency can affect bystander intervention. In particular, we showed, for bystanders who witness an emergency alone, that a defense reaction (indexed by either heart rate increase or a strong GSR response) is predictive of helping behavior. This is not, however, the only effect of arousal. In Chapter 7 we argued that arousal may limit the focus of attention, resulting in apparent "impulsive" helping. Also, in Chapter 3 we discussed how less intense levels of arousal can facilitate an orienting response. Therefore, temporary states of an organism can affect response to the need of another at several points in the process leading to taking action. Temporary states can affect whether or not environmental stimuli are noticed, how (if at all) they are interpreted, their emotional impact, and the ways that they are used in the decision process regarding action.

A few generalizations from the experimental psychology literature may help to clarify some of the potential effects of temporary states on response to help-requiring situations. First, the activities of perceiving and interpreting events are generally seen as active processes (Broadbent, 1971, 1977; Neisser, 1967). According to Neisser, "seeing, hearing, and remembering are all acts of *construction*, which may make more or less use of stimulus information depending on circumstances [p. 10]." Second, both Broadbent (1977) and Neisser (1967) consider these contruction processes to have two stages. The first stage, referred to by Broadbent as "filtering" and by Neisser as "pre-attentive processing," is fast, holistic, crude, and parallel. The second stage is deliberative, selective, attentive, and sequential. Temporary states could affect processing at either or both of the stages.

At the first, more basic stage of processing, Berlyne (1970) and Broadbent (1971) both suggest that the level of arousal has complex effects on the processing of stimuli. Berlyne suggests that arousal is curvilinearly related to accurate intake of information. As the organism moves from drowsy to alert, more information is taken in. Thus, prior level of arousal can affect whether or not an event is noticed. As arousal increases further, moving into the defense reaction area, narrowing of cue utilization occurs. According to Broadbent, a high level of arousal may cause filtering to be extreme, resulting in evidence being considered almost entirely from one source rather than from any other. We have referred to this effect in our discussion of "impulsive" helping in the previous chapter.

At the second, more deliberative and selective stage of processing, prior states and related expectancy "sets" may affect responsivenes to a stimulus. According to Neisser (1967), processing of an event is often affected by the dimensions of a situation that have been made salient to an individual just prior to the occurrence of the event. Broadbent (1977) adds to this the notion that there are at least two kinds of set: (a) a stimulus set in which the person expects certain things to happen; and (b) a response set in which a person is prepared to do certain things. A stimulus set may affect the likelihood of a bystander defining an event as an emergency; a response set may affect the probability of a person taking a certain type of action in response to an event.

The effects of temporary states on helping behavior, therefore, may be mediated by arousal, attentional, and/or expectancy processes. Prior arousal due to exercise, for example, may be attributed to the emergency and thus increase a bystander's motivation to intervene, as demonstrated in Chapter 4. Less intense prior states of arousal, such as alertness, may facilitate an orienting response and thereby also be related to helping. When an emergency is unclear, requiring considerable interpretation, an attentive bystander may be more likely to define an event as an emergency. With a completely clear, serious, and arousing emergency, however, the effect of prior alertness would likely be minimized by the attention-getting nature of the event itself. Furthermore, regarding the more complex second stage of processing, a prior state that creates a mental set for the individual that either (a) leads to an expectation about the occurrence of an event; or (b) produces a frame of mind that is conducive to the action that will be required once the event occurs, should facilitate bystander responsiveness.

Evidence Regarding the Effect of Alertness on Emotional Response and Intervention

In this section, we will explore some data from the Byeff (1970) and the Piliavin, Piliavin, and Trudell (unpublished, 1974) studies discussed in Chapter 4 in an attempt to discover the nature of the relationship between prior states and the impact of an emergency. In both the Byeff (1970) and the Piliavin, Piliavin, and Trudell (1974) studies, the relationship between subjects' alertness, as indexed by the rate of spontaneous skin responses (SRRs) during the pre-emergency period, and the emotional impact of the event, indexed by the height of the first GSR peak, was examined for alone bystanders. Prior alertness was not a predictor of emotional response to the audio–visual emergency either in the Byeff experiment [r (13) $= -.06$] or in the "fallen woman" episode of the Piliavin, Piliavin, and Trudell investigation [r (33) $= -.12$]. In the audio-only condition of the Byeff study, however, the analysis clearly demonstrated a significant relationship between initial alertness and the emotional impact of the event [r (13) = +.43]. (There was no audio-only condition in the Piliavin, Piliavin, and Trudell study.) It appears, then, that prior state, like trait factors, may operate primarily when ambiguity is present. In this case, those who are paying the most attention in the audio-only condition are most affected emotionally by the event. In the audio–visual condition, however, the emergency is clear and obvious, and so prior level of alertness is not an important factor in subjects' emotional responses.

In a related analysis, both alertness and emotional arousal were entered into a regression equation as predictors of latency to respond. The strength of the arousal–latency relationship, which appears consistently in these studies, was unchanged for audio–visual subjects in both the Byeff [r (13) = −.56] and the Piliavin, Piliavin, and Trudell [r (33) = −.53] investigations. Thus, emotional arousal, under unambiguous emergency conditions, appears to affect bystander responses independent of initial level of attention. For audio-only subjects in the Byeff study, though, both the positive SRR–latency relationship [r (13) = +.41] and the negative arousal–latency relationship [r (13) = −.27] were strengthened (beta = +.64 and −.54, respectively). Therefore, although initial alertness in an ambiguous emergency can indirectly affect responsiveness through facilitating arousal, it can also directly influence subjects' responsiveness. In fact, in this study, alertness inhibited intervention. It was this pattern of findings that first led us to consider the difference between attention (e.g., an orienting response) and emotional arousal (e.g., a defense reaction) in regard to intervention.

Our interpretation of these data, which is, of course, post hoc, is as follows. The audio-only emergency is ambiguous, and correspondingly the response rate is low. To the extent that SRR rate indexes attention paid to external stimuli, we may, with the positive relationship between attention and latency, be picking up the processing that leads many subjects to the conclusion that the ambiguous event is not an emergency. Looking at the regression analysis as a path diagram, one can say that there is one path that goes from paying attention to getting aroused to helping. Presumably, this occurs if the person is attending to the victim's distress cues. There is also, apparently, an independent path that proceeds from paying attention to deciding that it is not an emergency and thus to inaction. Presumably, this path is taken by those who are attending to cues suggesting that the event is not real or at least not serious.

In the remainder of this chapter, we will examine research that relates initial mood states to helping, giving particular emphasis to the related factors of arousal and attention. At the outset, we make special note that:

1. The literature consists almost entirely of studies on helping in non-emergencies.

2. Arousal and attention have not been independently assessed.
3. Investigators emphasize either arousal or attention, but not both processes.
4. The costs for helping and costs for not helping are generally low.
5. Sometimes the findings are complex and contradictory.

Nevertheless, we feel that our model can begin to integrate and systematize the existing, diverse, but not necessarily mutually exclusive theoretical positions.

States, Arousal, and Helping Behavior

TRANSGRESSION, OBSERVED TRANSGRESSION, AND HELPING

Substantial empirical attention has been directed at investigating the effects of an individual's transgression on his or her subsequent willingness to engage in helping behavior. The typical experimental situation in which this relationship has been examined involves inducing an individual to transgress against another individual without initial provocation, and then presenting the transgressor with a subsequent encounter involving either the victim, a witness, or a stranger who makes a direct request for help. In most instances, transgression takes the form of ostensible physical damage to property or physical pain to an innocent other, although a few researchers have induced transgressive behavior such as lying or cheating. In general, the experimental evidence indicates that an individual who has harmed another person is more likely to comply with a subsequent request for help than is an individual who has not harmed another person.

The generality of the transgression-induced helping effect is impressive. The phenomenon occurs when subjects have been induced to transgress by shocking another subject or by providing other unpleasant experiences (Carlsmith & Gross, 1969; Katz, Glass, Lucido, & Farber, 1979, Experiments 1 and 2; Rawlings, 1968, 1970), hindering the experiment (Katz et al., 1979, Experiment 3; Regan, 1971) or damaging experimental apparatus (Brock & Becker, 1966; Wallace & Sadalla, 1966), failing to reciprocate the earning of introductory psychology examination points (Darlington & Macker, 1966), cheating on experimental tasks (Neumann, cited in Berkowitz, 1972; Graf, 1971; McMillen, 1971; Silverman, 1967), upsetting sequenced index cards (Freedman, Wallington, & Bless, 1967, Experiments 2 and 3), dropping slides (Heilman, Hodgson, & Hornstein, 1972) or computer cards (Cialdini, Darby, & Vincent, 1973; Konečni, 1972; Konoske, Staple, & Graf, 1979), lying to the experimenter (Freedman et al., 1967, Experiment 1; Silverman, Rivera, & Tedeschi, 1979, Experiment 2; Wallington, 1973), breaking a camera (Regan, Williams, & Sparling,

1972), or touching objects in a museum or feeding animals at the zoo (Katsev, Edelsack, Steinmetz, Walker, & Wright, 1978).

Similarly, in these studies a wide variety of helping behaviors have been elicited after transgression has been induced. Subjects who have transgressed are more likely to contribute money to a research fund for psychology graduate students (Regan, 1971), to volunteer to distribute questionnaires for a public opinion survey (Freedman et al., 1967, Experiment 3), to pick up dropped items (Katsev et al., 1978; Konečni, 1972), to report accidental harm-doing (Heilman et al., 1972), to volunteer to undergo further experimentation without recompense (Donnerstein, Donnerstein, and Munger, 1975; Freedman et al., 1967, Experiments 1 and 2; Katz et al., 1979, Experiment 3; Silverman, 1967; Silverman et al., 1979; Wallace & Sadalla, 1966), to shock oneself (Rawlings, 1968, 1970; Wallington, 1973); to volunteer to make phone calls to solicit information (Cialdini et al., 1973) or provide organizational support (Carlsmith & Gross, 1969; Noel, 1973); to return a dollar belonging to the experimenter (Graf, 1971); to volunteer to donate blood to a local hospital (Darlington & Macker, 1966), to help an impaired partner with a class assignment (Katz et al., 1979), and to inform the experimenter of candy falling from a grocery bag (Regan et al., 1972). In addition, while most of the foregoing studies found the effect in the laboratory, a few investigators have shown that guilt leads to helping behavior in field settings (Katsev et al., 1978; Konečni, 1972; Regan et al., 1972). In short, the guilt-induced helping phenomenon occurs across a variety of experimental manipulations, types of subsequent requests, and experimental settings.

Transgression-induced helping is also not limited specifically to the person who is harmed. For example, in a study by Regan et al. (1972) a confederate stopped a woman at a shopping center and asked her to take a picture of him with his camera. As the woman took the picture, the camera broke. In the guilt condition the confederate suggested that the subject caused the camera to malfunction, while in the control condition he took great care to communicate to the subject that it was not her fault. Finally, after this incident, the subject encountered another confederate whose grocery bag was ripped. In the control condition 15% of the subjects helped, while in the guilt condition 55% of the subjects intervened. Carlsmith and Gross (1969), in addition, found that subjects are sometimes even more likely to give assistance to a witness of their transgression than to the actual victim of their transgression. One can hypothesize that the costs for helping an observer are less because the subject is less worried about embarrassment or retaliation.

The actual commission of a transgression is not always necessary to increase helping behavior. Additional evidence suggests that merely witnessing another's transgression increases a person's willingness to help others. For example, in a study by Rawlings (1970) subjects were placed in one of three situations: (a) They were led to believe that they were responsible for their partner's receiving electric shocks; or (b) they were aware that their partner was receiving electric shocks but were led to believe that they were not responsible; or (c) they were aware that their partner was not receiving electric shocks. Then, all subjects were given the opportunity to help a third party. The results indicated that both the subjects who believed they were responsible for shocks and those subjects who knew their partner had been shocked helped significantly more than those subjects who were told the partner did not receive any shocks. With only two exceptions (Carlsmith & Gross, 1969; Freedman et al., 1967), additional experiments have demonstrated that witnesses to other people's transgressions help more than do nonwitnesses (Cialdini et al., 1973; Konečni, 1972; Rawlings, 1968; Regan, 1971).

In summary, the results of numerous experiments have been remarkably consistent. Across a wide variety of helping situations, transgressions, and populations, subjects who have transgressed against another person help more than subjects who have not transgressed. This effect occurs even when the beneficiary is not the victim; transgressors become *generally* more helpful toward others. Furthermore, it is not necessary for subjects to be directly involved in the transgression. Observation of a transgression is often sufficient; observers of transgressions are more likely to help than are nonobservers.

TRANSGRESSIONS, AROUSAL, AND HELPING

Cialdini et al. (1973) have proposed a negative relief state model that accounts for the transgressor and observer of transgression effects on helping. According to the negative relief state model, harming another person or observing someone else being harmed produces a negative emotional state (i.e., creates a state of distress). Helping others can be instrumental in alleviating this negative emotional state (Harris, 1977).

Helping others, however, is only one of many mood-enhancing events that can serve to relieve a negative emotional state. Helping can remove the negative emotional state, but so can pleasant experiences like praise or receiving money following a transgression. Thus, according to Cialdini et al. (1973), transgressors and witnesses of transgressions are only more likely to help others if no pleasant experiences occur between the transgression and the helping opportunity. If pleasant experiences follow soon after the transgression, transgressors and witnesses of transgressions should be no more likely to help than nontransgressors, because the former are no longer in a negative emotional state. In support of this theoretical viewpoint, Cialdini *et al.* (1973) found that either causing or witnessing harm increased helping behavior, except among subjects who received a gratifying, pleasant event (e.g., unexpected money or praise) between the occurrence of harm and the opportunity to help.

Additional support for the negative relief state model is provided by three experiments investigating the effect of confession on helping. A common belief in our culture is that confessing sins is good for the soul. By confessing our sins or transgressions we feel better, particularly if we have some assurance of being forgiven. If this is so, persons who confess their wrongdoings should be less helpful than individuals who do not confess, since the negative emotional state of those who have confessed has been ameliorated. Experiments by Carlsmith, Ellsworth, and Whiteside (unpublished, 1969) and Regan (1971) supported this prediction. Also, a field study by Harris, Benson, and Hall (1975) shows less helping by individuals leaving a Catholic church (presumably after confession) than by people entering the same church (presumably going to confession).

It should be noted that, according to the negative relief state model, increased helping should occur after a transgression or an observation of a transgression only if a person actually experiences the emotional state as negative. Therefore, persons who respond in a low-socially-anxious, unemotional way to the needs of others should be less affected in their helping behavior by causing or observing harm to others. This assumption was supported by McPeek and Cialdini (1977). In this study, subjects were selected on the basis of their scores on the social anxiety subscale of Lykken's Activity Preference Questionnaire (Lykken, Tellegen, & Katzenmeyer, 1973). Low scorers on this scale describe themselves as unemotional and behave accordingly. During the experiment low-socially-anxious and moderate-socially-anxious individuals either believed they harmed another person, observed harm to another person, or served as a control group. The results demonstrated that in the direct-transgression and the observation-of-transgression conditions the moderate-socially-anxious subjects were more likely to help than were the low-socially-anxious subjects. These findings, then, indicate that emotional responsiveness to the needs of others is an important mediator of transgression-induced helping behavior.

In summary, the findings associated with the negative relief state model are quite consistent with our model. In fact, they appear to reflect the same basic arousal process that is central to our model. Whether victimization is caused by transgression or by accident, individuals help because helping is instrumental in relieving an unpleasant emotional state. There are, however, two important ways in which our model differs from the model of Cialdini and his associates. First, we believe that transgression will facilitate helping behavior primarily when the residual arousal from the transgression can be attributed to the need of the person later helped. Cialdini *et al.* (1973) imply that misattribution is not necessary. Second, we do not postulate a direct relationship between arousal and the offering of help in all cases. Rather, the likelihood of help is also affected by the perceived costs and rewards in the situation. We would expect the transgression effect to occur primarily under low-cost-for-helping situations. It is thus of particular interest to note that Kenrick, Baumann, and Cialdini (1979) have qualified their model by saying that costs and rewards must be considered before any predictions can be made concerning the effects of transgression-induced moods on helping.

Before we move on, it is important to note that all of the studies on transgression involve negative emotional states that are the result of observing the victimization of another person. In most of these studies, however, moods were not actually assessed. Cunningham, Steinberg, and Greu (1980) and Wallington (1973), though, did find that transgression lowered mood state. However, the process by which transgression facilitates helping is still not entirely clear. Katz *et al.* (1979) found that their harm-doing manipulations led to increases in guilt, bad feelings, and helping, but that the effect of harm-doing on helping was not mediated by affective changes. Silverman *et al.* (1979) found that negative affect after transgression and compliance could be either directly or inversely correlated. Specifically, negative affect and compliance were positively related ($r = +.70$) when an experimenter expressed suspicion that the subject *may* be lying, but negative affect and compliance were inversely related ($r = -.62$) in a condition in which subjects *were* lying but were not confronted. Thus, guilt and negative affect per se are clearly not the entire story.

FEELING GOOD, FEELING BAD, AND HELPING

Mood states have been induced in a wide variety of ways other than transgression. In none of these studies was mood induced by the victimization of another. In general, the experimental paradigms involve exposing individuals to some situation that makes them feel better, worse, or the same (as before the situation). Then the individual is given an opportunity to help another person. For example, Isen (1970) gave suburban school teachers a series of tasks. Subsequently, half were informed that they had done extremely well and the other half were told that they had performed very poorly. Following this experience subjects were given an opportunity to contribute money to an air conditioning fund for the school's library.

The results showed that the subjects who believed they had succeeded on the test donated more to the fund than those subjects who believed they had performed very poorly. Another experiment by Isen (Isen, Horn, & Rosenhan, 1973) again found that successful subjects were more willing than unsuccessful subjects to help a stranger. Thus, these findings suggest that positive and negative moods may affect an individual's response to the needs of others.

The finding that individuals who are in a good mood are more likely to help than individuals who are in a bad mood appears to be very general. This finding has been shown to occur for males and females (Isen, 1970; Isen et al., 1973; Isen & Levin, 1972; Moore, Underwood, & Rosenhan, 1973; Rosenhan, Underwood, & Moore, 1974), for children (Isen et al., 1973; Moore et al., 1973; Rosenhan et al., 1974), for college students (Aderman, 1972; Aderman & Berkowitz, 1970; Berkowitz & Connor, 1966; Isen, 1970; Isen & Levin, 1972), and for adults (Isen, 1970; Isen & Levin, 1972). Furthermore, experimenters have used different ways of inducing good and bad moods: giving subjects bogus feedback on task performances (Berkowitz & Connor, 1966; Isen, 1970; Isen et al., 1973), thanking a person for helping another individual (Aderman & Berkowitz, 1970), having subjects receive unexpected benefits such as cookies or a dime in a phone booth (Isen & Levin, 1972), having subjects read elation statements (Aderman, 1972; Berkowitz, unpublished, 1980), having subjects recall things that made them happy or sad (Moore et al., 1973; Rosenhan et al., 1974) or even using weather as the independent variable (Cunningham, 1979). In addition, numerous types of helping situations have been employed. The number of data pages scored or numbered (Aderman, 1972; Aderman & Berkowitz, 1970; Berkowitz, unpublished, 1980), donations (Isen, 1970; Moore et al., 1973), picking up books and papers (Isen et al., 1973), agreeing to make "polling" phone calls (Benson, 1978), and volunteering to participate in experiments (Isen & Levin, 1972; Aderman, 1972) or be interviewed (Cunningham, 1979). In general, despite variations in subject populations, research settings, ways of inducing good and bad moods, and types of helping situations, it seems clear that individuals who are in a pleasant mood are more likely to help than are individuals who are in an unpleasant mood.

MOODS, AROUSAL, AND HELPING

Before we address the question of why feeling good leads to more helping than does feeling bad, let us briefly discuss an issue that is often overlooked in the literature. On the whole, the effect of positive outcomes is to induce helping and one might expect an analogous effect to occur following negative experiences; helping should be decreased. However, such is not the case. The findings from the studies just reviewed clearly demonstrate that persons in a bad mood (unless it is caused by transgression) generally do not differ from control subjects in willingness or amount of helping. That is, successful subjects are more likely to help than are controls or unsuccessful subjects, with there being no differences between the latter two conditions. Only a few studies have demonstrated that subjects who were in a bad-mood condition differed in the amount of helping from subjects who were in a control condition. Isen *et al.* (1973) found that failure subjects helped more than control subjects. On the other hand, Moore *et al.* (1973) and Weyant (1978) found that happy subjects contributed more than controls, with sad subjects contributing the least.

To say the least, these conflicting results are puzzling. The differences among the results can be partially resolved by looking at additional aspects of the experimental setting other than the bad mood itself that may have contributed to the observed outcomes. One crucial difference among the several failure feedback experiments was the extent to which they allowed the subjects to improve their "image." According to Isen *et al.* (1973) individuals are motivated to present themselves in a better light, particularly after failure experiences. One way of improving one's self-image is to be generous and helpful to others. Thus, this explanation is quite similar to Cialdini *et al.*'s (1973) negative relief state model, as well as our own model.

In addition, according to Isen *et al.* (1973) individuals should be most likely to seek image repair when someone else is aware of their prior failure experience and can observe their helping performance. The implication of this view is clear. The experience of failure leads to helping primarily when an individual has an opportunity to publicly repair his or her reputation. In two experiments using children, Isen *et al.* (1973) found that both failure and success subjects helped more than controls. It was made clear to the children that the experimenter knew of the subject's failure and that the experimenter was involved in a charity drive to which the subjects were asked to contribute. As Isen *et al.* (1973) suggest, donating to a charity drive in which the experimenter was involved might have provided a very good opportunity for image repair. This view seems plausible since when the experimenter was unaware of the subject's prior experiences, failure and control subjects did not differ in helping. In short, the effects of failure on helping depends on the circumstances of the failure and the helping opportunity. In particular, whether the opportunity to help occurs in public or private appears to be an important mediating factor, at least for children. Failure subjects were only more likely than controls to help when they were given a public opportunity to repair their image. It is not surprising, then, that in some instances the failure subjects called it to the experimenter's attention when they did help.

What about the results obtained by Moore *et al.* (1973)? Here, children who were put in a bad mood helped *less* than controls. We think this occurred because those who were put in a bad mood were not given an opportunity that would really allow them to feel better. In this study, to manipulate mood the children were made to "think about bad things." They were then given the opportunity to donate pennies to other children who would not have an opportunity to participate in the experiment and earn money themselves. The circumstances were such that nobody would know whether or not the child had donated. Given the age of the children, it is unlikely that they had internalized a strong self-reward system in relationship to generosity. Furthermore, donations may well be punishing rather than rewarding at young ages, in the absence of strong doses of praise or other social rewards for the behavior. By this interpretation, donating could not serve the purpose of making the depressed children feel better, as it could in the previous studies. Therefore, they donated less.

What we are suggesting here, like Cialdini and Kenrick (1976), is that young children, who are still early in the socialization process, have not learned that helping another person can be self-gratifying or reinforcing and can therefore relieve a negative emotional state. Thus, young children would not use this response to alleviate a negative mood. The available data support this view. Cialdini and Kenrick (1976) demonstrated that for first through third graders, subjects in a negative mood ("reminisce about sad experiences") were slightly *less* helpful than were subjects in a neutral mood ("imagine a book and a chair"). However, for older subjects, tenth through twelfth graders, negative-mood subjects were significantly *more* helpful than neutral-mood subjects. Since the helping opportunity occurred in private ("no one would ever know"), the authors concluded that the younger subjects had not internalized the notion that behaving in a helpful manner can be self-rewarding.

Whereas young children (6–9 years of age) may not have learned that helping, in and of itself, is self-reinforcing, they are sensitive to the value of extrinsic rewards (Bryan & Walbek, 1970; Eisenberg-Berg, 1979; Ugurel-Semin, 1952). That is, young children are aware that social approval will follow a helping act when the act is made in public. To test the hypothesis that primary school children should show an increase in helping as a function of a negative mood state, Kenrick, Baumann, and Cialdini (1979) gave first through third graders either a private (adult absent) or public (adult present) opportunity to help other children after a negative mood induction. In two experiments, they found that negative-mood subjects were only more helpful than neutral-mood subjects in the public condition.

Negative-mood subjects did not differ from neutral-mood subjects in the private condition. These results strongly suggest that primary school subjects are aware that helping has the potential for providing them with social reinforcement and will use a helping response to alleviate a negative emotional state when social rewards have a high probability of occurrence.

The results of the previous two studies along with those obtained by Isen *et al.* (1973) begin to shed some light on why the transgression experiments have consistently led to increases in helping, whereas the experiments on other negative moods have led to mixed results. The data from the former have come from adults who have internalized the reinforcement value of a helping act, and the data from the later have usually come from children who may or may not have internalized the reinforcement value associated with helping others. Until such internalization occurs, children will not see helping, in the absence of extrinsic rewards, as a way of alleviating a negative emotional state.

One can still ask why in a few cases (e.g., Moore *et al.*, 1973) the children in the bad-mood condition donated *less* than the controls, rather than the same amount, as is found in most other research. We are not exactly sure. This discrepancy, though, does suggest that other factors beside negative emotional state, such as attention-related differences (to be discussed in a later section), cost–reward considerations, or other cognitive factors may be operating. For example, a possible partial explanation comes from a study by Weyant (1978). Weyant varied costs for helping and costs for not helping, as well as moods, in an orthogonal design. Overall, subjects in a good mood were more likely to help than were control or bad-mood subjects. However, in the one cell in which the costs for helping were low and the costs for not helping were high, subjects who were in a bad mood were just as likely to help as were the good-mood subjects. Similarly, Benson (1978) found the greatest amount of helping (out of 12 cells in his design) among bad-mood subjects in a low-risk, high-probability-of-social-approval condition. Although the differences were not significant, his results parallel those of Weyant. It may be that, for the children in the two studies in which bad-mood subjects helped less, costs for helping were perceived as high and/or costs for not helping were perceived as low.

An additional point regarding Weyant's and Benson's results needs to be mentioned. The results for the failure subjects cannot be attributed solely to the need for image repair. In all the conditions of Weyant's study, the request for help was made in the presence of the experimenter who was aware of the subject's success or failure. Thus, subjects could repair their image (make themselves feel better) under all cost conditions. Yet, failure subjects were only willing to do so when the request for help involved little effort compared to the benefits. In Benson's (1978) research, the request was made by someone who knew nothing of the subject's poor showing; again, no differences in the potential for image repair were present.

The findings associated with research on the relief of aversive emotional states also appear to have little relevance in explaining the consistent effect of good moods on helping. Even if one extends the current theoretical positions to include avoidance of relatively negative emotional states (e.g., the potential loss of a good mood because of not helping another), supporting evidence is still lacking. Instead, as many researchers currently suggest, explanation of the effect of good moods on helping may primarily involve cognitive influences.

States, Cognition, and Helping Behavior

MOODS, INFORMATION PROCESSING, AND HELPING

The study on moods and cost–reward influences by Weyant (1978), introduced in the previous section, is most relevant to our model. In particular, one might expect that moods could affect a person's perception of the costs and rewards for helping. For example, when we are in a good mood, perhaps we would perceive a helping opportunity as involving less cost and more benefit than when we are in a bad mood. In other words, our assessment of the situation might be influenced by our temporary mood state. Weyant found, however, that *perceived* costs for helping and costs for not helping were unrelated to the mood manipulation. Subjects who were in the good-mood, control, and bad-mood conditions and who were not exposed to the request to help but rather were asked for ratings of perceived costs were equally likely to report that sitting at a desk required less effort than going door-to-door (the costs-for-helping manipulation) and that helping the Cancer Society was more beneficial than soliciting money for Little League uniforms (the costs-for-not-helping manipulation). Apparently, persons perceive the costs and rewards in a given situation similarly regardless of their mood state. It is still possible, of course, that one's mood has a differential effect on one's willingness to pay those costs.

Isen and her colleagues have also investigated the effect of mood states on how individuals process and recall information. In one study, Isen, Clark, and Schwartz (1976) found that individuals who were in a good mood were more likely to think about positive things than were controls. For the former, helping others would then be consistent with their current cognitive state. In a more recent experiment (Isen, Shalker, Clark, & Karp, 1978) the investigators demonstrated that positive outcomes result in general optimism. Subjects who received a gift—a free advertising sample—rated their own possessions (e.g., car, television set) more highly than did subjects who had not received such gifts. From these results, one can conclude that people who are in a good mood are more likely to think about positive things, retrieve from memory positive thoughts, and have a more positive outlook on life than are those who have not recently had a mood-enhancing experience. In addition, they are perhaps more likely to think about the rewards than the costs of helping. A difference in helping would then be consistent, if positive thoughts lead to positive actions.

Unfortunately negative moods were not included in these experiments. Thus we do not know whether subjects who feel bad think about negative things, are more critical of their possessions, or are more pessimistic about life in general. We suspect that this occurs and that helping others would thus be decreased, except under the conditions of extremely easy and quick availability of rewards that could change the mood state with little expenditure of effort.

Consistent with the suggestion that the "feeling good" effect is the result of a cognitive set, studies investigating the duration of the effect (Isen et al., 1976; Schellenberg & Blevins, 1973) have found that "the smile of dame fortune fades" rather rapidly. The Isen et al. (1976) research discovered that the effect of the positive experience (receiving a small free gift) on later helping increased slightly up to 4 or 5 minutes after the gift was received, and then decreased monotonically until, 20 minutes after receipt of the gift, the rate of helping did not differ from that of controls.

What is the evidence that thinking about more positive things leads to more helping? First, there is the Darley and Batson (1973) study in which seminarians were either thinking about the Good Samaritan parable or not when they encountered a person in need of help. More of those pondering the Good Samaritan story helped. There is, however, controversy over whether the result is one on which we can rely. Darley and Batson report the result as nonsignificant; Greenwald (1975), using a different statistical technique, found the result to be statistically significant. There are several other studies (Horowitz, 1976; Jiobu & Knowles, 1974; Paulhus, Shaffer, & Downing, 1977) that show some effect of making altruistic motives, moral decision making, or seasonal (Christmas) generosity salient on increasing the likelihood of helping.

Finally, Hornstein, LaKind, Frankel, and Manne (1975) found that there is an effect of having just heard a newscast reporting good or bad news on likelihood of engaging in cooperative behavior. (For later research in the same vein, see Holloway, Tucker, and Hornstein, 1977, and Veitch, DeWood, and Bosko, 1977.) Their paradigm involves subjects "just happening" to hear a brief report of an outstandingly helpful act or a particularly brutal one. The initial dependent measure these investigators used was cooperation in a zero-sum game. Subjects who had heard the good news were significantly more likely to employ trusting, cooperative strategies. The question the authors then pursued in four more experiments was "Why"? Their interpretation is that the news broadcast momentarily changes the listener's judgments about the likelihood of people in general behaving in positive or negative ways and, thus, leads the subject who has heard the good broadcast to expect cooperative behavior from his or her partner in the game. Later studies in the series have confirmed this interpretation. After hearing good news, subjects think people are more altruistic, honest, clean, decent, upstanding, etc., than do those who have heard bad news. (In this research, control subjects are like "good news" subjects in their judgments of human nature, a somewhat cheering thought.)

In the last two experiments reported in the initial Hornstein *et al.* (1975) article, it was found that the good and bad news broadcasts, contrary to what one might expect, did not affect the mood of the listeners, unless the listeners were specifically instructed to attend to how the broadcast made them feel. The authors point out that in most of the "mood and helping" research, mood per se is never measured. It is merely assumed that it is differences in mood that are creating the effect. They conclude:

> The fact that no significant results were obtained does not necessarily mean that mood is unrelated to helping. Although mood does not seem to be a necessary condition for producing helping, it cannot be dismissed as a potential mediator of one's view about people in general and therefore about helping. Intuition suggests that it is common for good moods to be associated with predispositions to evaluate favorably the social community and bad mood to be associated with the opposite [p. 1046].

The suggestion that is being made here is that if moods have anything to do with the effects that have been found in what is generally referred to as the "moods and helping" literature, it is because moods trigger cognitive processes. This is essentially the conclusion reached by Isen herself, who is the originator and still most involved researcher in the area. The title of her most recent article (Isen *et al.*, 1978) illustrates the way she perceives the process: "Affect, accessibility of material in memory, and behavior: A cognitive loop?"

MOODS, ATTENTION, AND HELPING

Another process by which good and bad moods may operate is through the direction and quality of attention. It has been suggested that good moods direct one's attention outward, while sadness and depression turn one's attention inward. The research that is most consistent with this contention is a set of two experiments reported by McMillen, Sanders, and Solomon (1977). In the first experiment, subjects were given a positive or a negative self-esteem manipulation and then were given an experimental task to do. A white noise generator in the next room was turned on and then increased in intensity on a 12-point equal-interval scale until the subject looked up. A highly significant difference in the intensity of noise required to capture the attention of high and low self-esteem feedback subjects was obtained.

The second experiment tested the hypothesized three-step process linking mood to attention and then to helping. Subjects again received positive or negative feedback from the personality inventory. While the subject was walking to his or her assigned experimental room, an overburdened female confederate needing assistance in opening a door presented the helping opportunity. She either "patted" the side of the large box she was balancing on her knee while wrestling with the door (to attract attention) or did not. Overall helping was not significantly affected by the mood manipulation (although "good mood" subjects helped the most) or by the "patting" manipulation (although "patting" subjects helped more). The only significant effect was that noise made a difference for bad mood subjects. The authors concluded that individuals with lowered self-esteem are unlikely to help because they do not notice the helping opportunity. However, if their attention is directed toward the person in need, they will be at least as likely to help as a person with raised self-esteem.

Two other studies have yielded somewhat more equivocal results. Underwood, Berenson, Berenson, Cheng, Wilson, Kulik, Moore, and Wenzel (1977) asked patrons before and after seeing either sad or neutral movies to donate to the Muscular Dystrophy Association. Although patrons who had just seen the sad movies were less likely to give than any other group, an "attention" manipulation had no effect. The authors conclude, however, that

> there is nevertheless at least one argument which could be made in favor of retaining the hypothesis that attention mediates the mood effects. This argument would maintain that it is not simply lack of attention to the request for a donation which is responsible for the observed effect of negative mood states, but rather a lack of attention to the need for such a donation. Thus sad people may notice that a donation is being requested, but may not donate because they do not really feel that an urgent need for help exists [pp. 57–58].[1]

It is as though the sad person has, by virtue of his or her mood, been directed to attend inwards rather than to attend to the need of others.

The suggested relationship between bad moods, direction of attention, and helping has been further investigated by Thompson, Cowan, and

[1] This excerpt from "Attention, Negative Affect, and Altruism: An Ecological Validation" by Bill Underwood et al. is reprinted from *Personality and Social Psychology Bulletin* Vol. 3, No. 1 (January 1977), pp. 54–58 by permission of the Society for Personality and Social Psychology.

Rosenhan (1980). They also argue that the conflicting data on the effects of negative moods and helping can be resolved, at least in part, by determining the individual's focus of attention. For example, in studies where feeling bad consistently leads to increased helping (transgression literature), the individual's attention is directed toward the misfortunes or mishaps of another person. But, for studies that show no effect or a slight inhibition effect for negative moods on helping (failure, sadness, depression), the individual's attention is focused on himself or herself. Accordingly, the authors proposed that the focus of attention mediates the relationship between negative mood states and helping. Specifically, persons who are in a bad mood will be likely to help when their attention is directed toward the needs of another.

To test this hypothesis, male and female undergraduates' attention was directed either to the worry and anxiety experienced by a dying friend (attention-to-others condition) or to the same emotion that they themselves felt as a consequence of the friend's illness (attention-to-self condition). The control subjects were exposed to an affectively neutral tape, a narrative of a person who was designing a collage. Later, all subjects were given an opportunity to help another experimenter anonymously by answering multiple choice questions.

The results of the study showed that subjects who attended to the feelings of the victim were much more helpful than subjects who attended to their own feelings and were much more helpful than the control subjects (83%, 25%, 25%, respectively). Attention-to-others subjects also spent the most time helping. A check on the mood manipulation indicated that attention-to-self subjects were preoccupied with their own concerns, whereas attention-to-others subjects were concerned about the plight of the victim. These differences in the direction of attention occurred despite the fact that the two groups did not differ on any measures of arousal or sadness. Thus, the authors concluded that negative moods will increase the probability of a helping response when the individual's attention is directed toward the needs of another.

One problem with the results of the Thompson et al. study is that self-focused subjects were not less helpful than controls, as was hypothesized. However, there may have been some problems with the control group. Thompson et al. present evidence that these subjects may have been bored or angered, which led them to depart from the experiment quickly, and not to help. Thus, until a more neutral control group is employed, any conclusions concerning neutral-mood and self-focused, negative-mood conditions is unwarranted. However, the results for other-focused, negative-mood subjects are clear. Individuals who think first about the needs and problems of others are likely to be helpful. The behavior of these subjects resembles the behavior of subjects who are in a good mood or subjects who are experiencing a bad mood due to transgression.

The results of the Thompson *et al.* experiment, though not unequivocal, do provide the clearest evidence to date on the relationship between attention and bad moods. The authors suggest that attention mediates the relationship between bad moods and helping. Berkowitz (unpublished, 1980) has recently demonstrated a similar mediation effect of self-awareness on good moods. In two separate experiments, the effect of reading positive Velten statements on willingness to help others is enhanced by a self-awareness manipulation. Although he interprets his results in terms of an increase in accessibility of positive thoughts and behaviors, other evidence indicates that good moods lead to an increase in attention to the environment (Isen, 1970; Rosenhan *et al.*, 1974) and to increases on a state measure of "social interest" (Crandall, 1978) and that good moods lead to increased helping.

Is it possible, however, for a person to be in a good mood and be virtually unresponsive to external stimuli, and thus be less likely to help? We think it is possible. For example, drugs may create a state of euphoria, but may also focus attention to the self and/or make an outward focus of attention unlikely or impossible. Hence, a helping response would be unlikely. While we realize the speculative nature of this view, we also do not want to underestimate the complexity of the mediating processes underlying moods and helping. Here we would like to reemphasize the point raised at the beginning of the chapter, namely, that prior state can make either stimulus sets or response sets more or less likely. A good mood can make one more attentive to others' needs and requests but can also make one less willing to *do* certain things. Isen and Levin (1972) found that "good mood" subjects were more likely to comply with a request to help another person but were not more willing to harass another. Isen and Simonds (1978) demonstrated that "dime finders" read more positive-mood statements but fewer negative-mood statements, in response to a request, than did controls. Finally, Konoske *et al.* (1979) found that "guilty" subjects agreed to help more than "nonguilty" subjects only when the behavior was really a positive act. They did not comply more when the behavior involved calling up subjects and lying to them.

In summary, evidence is beginning to be accumulated regarding the attentional processes that mediate between having just experienced something pleasant or unpleasant and the subsequent increase or decrease in the likelihood of helping. In general, the evidence indicates that good moods facilitate helping by increasing the individual's attention to the needs of others, whereas bad moods facilitate helping only among persons who are attending to the problems and needs of others.

MOODS AND HELPING: A FINAL NOTE

While we have separately presented evidence indicating how moods affect arousal, information processing, and attention, we do not mean to imply that *one* of these accounts for the mood-helping effect. Rather, there is probably a complex of effects going on simultaneously. We are, in fact, assuming that there are multiple effects of good and bad moods on the person, and that attempts to pin down the effects of them to one process are doomed to failure. By reference to both the research on the relationship of moods to helping that we have just reviewed and to the by now very large literature on depression (e.g., Akiskal & McKinney, 1973; Seligman, 1975), we would like to suggest two clusters of effects that are likely to follow from the induction of good or bad moods. As with the definition of the "impulse-generating situation" presented in the previous chapter, we see these as ideal types. A person in a really good (or bad) mood is likely to be characterized by most of these effects, but not necessarily by an extreme degree of all of them. A positive mood, we suggest, leads, to some degree, to all of the following:

1. An external attentional focus with increased sensitivity to external stimuli
2. A socially outgoing attitude involving the expansion of one's "we-group" to include a wider range of individuals ("I love the whole world today")
3. Salience of positive thoughts and increased availability of positive actions in the response repertoire, both a stimulus set and a response set, in the terminology of Broadbent (1971)
4. Increased energy
5. Feelings of competence, self-efficacy, positive-outcome expectancies?

On the other hand, a negative mood characterized by sadness or depression leads to the following:

1. An internal focus of attention with obsessive thoughts about personal inadequacy
2. Lack of interest in social contacts, misanthropy, a "people are no damn good" orientation, constriction of the "we-group"
3. Salience of negative thoughts, selective availability of actions that could lead easily or quickly to personal regard and/or image repair, unrealistic assessments of great ease or great difficulty of solutions
4. Decreased energy, fatigue, inability to move
5. Feelings of incompetence, negative outcome expectancies?

There is good evidence from the depression literature that these clusters of effects occur together and, with the depressed person, develop into a vicious spiral (e.g., Beck, 1967; Seligman, 1975). The results of the good- and bad-mood studies cited above appear to be at least consistent with such a postulated set of internal effects. We will now explore a few studies that have investigated two of the proposed intervening processes. Note again that we are not suggesting that one of these processes accounts for the effect but rather that there is probably a complex interaction of effects involved.

COGNITIVE OVERLOAD, ATTENTION, AND HELPING

In 1970, Stanley Milgram published an article in *Science* in which he said a large number of things about living in cities, some positive and some negative. The statement with which we must be concerned, however, is his contention that city dwellers, because of the greatly increased cognitive overload with which they must cope, develop a number of devices to protect themselves from stress. These have relevance for the likelihood of helping behavior. He says:

> The principal point of interest for a social psychology of the city is that moral and social involvement with individuals is necessarily restricted. This is a direct and necessary function of excess of input over capacity to process. . . . The ultimate adaptation to an overloaded social environment is to totally disregard the needs, interests, and demands of those whom one does not define as relevant to the satisfaction of personal needs. . . . the time allotment and willingness to become involved with those who have no personal claim on one's time is likely to be less in cities than in towns [p. 1462].[2]

Milgram has clearly stated a hypothesis that the city environment leads to cognitive overload, which leads to certain perceptual adjustments and categorizations of individuals as either relevant or irrelevant to one's life, and that this type of categorization will lead to *less* helping of strangers in cities than in small towns. This hypothesis has been investigated in numerous ways by a large number of investigators, and we will not review all of the research here. The issue we do want to address is the postulated relationship among overload, attention paid and categorization of people, and helping. The reason should be clear; we are interested in this chapter in factors affecting the temporary states of individuals in such a way as to increase or decrease helping. Cognitive overload is potentially one such factor.

There has generally been support for the overall "urban incivility" effect. The following studies have found greater helpfulness among small town dwellers as compared to urban inhabitants: Feinman (unpublished, 1977), Korte and Kerr (1975), Merrens (1973), Milgram (1970), Rushton

[2] Copyright 1970 by the American Association for the Advancement of Science.

(1978), and Takooshian, Haber, and Lucido (1976). However, Schneider and Mockus (1974) and Forbes and Gromoll (1971) failed to find such a difference as did Korte, Ypma, and Toppen (1975) after they had controlled for environmental input level.

Some of the differences between city and small town dwellers can apparently be attributed to a (probably rational) fear of strangers in cities. Studies by Feinman (unpublished, 1977), Lesk and Zippel (1975), Altman, Levine, Nadien, and Villena (see Milgram, 1970), Harris and Meyer (1973), and House and Wolf (1978) suggest that this is a relevant factor. Normative considerations also play a part, as illustrated by the findings of Hackler, Ho, and Urquhart-Ross (1974).

The most interesting factor, if we want to follow up on Milgram's hypothesis, however, is density and its attendant overload. A number of studies have shown an inverse relationship between immediate environmental density and helpfulness. Bickman, Teger, Gabriele, McLaughlin, Berger, and Sunaday (1973) showed that both in Amherst, Massachusetts and in Philadelphia, Pennsylvania, students living in high-rise, high-density dormitories were less likely to return a "lost letter" than were students living in less densely populated housing. The effect was demonstrated on a second measure of helpfulness in the Philadelphia study as well. Kammann, Thomson, and Irwin (1977, Study 2) selected three New Zealand communities matched for population but varying in density. On four measures of helping behavior (the number of people passing a "lost letter" without stopping, the number of "lost letters" returned, archival data on returned lost items, and the number of "good-intentioned" false fire alarms) the least dense town showed the most helping behavior and the most dense town demonstrated the least helping behavior.

Korte *et al.* (1975) similarly controlled for city size in a study in Holland and observed a systematic decrease in helpfulness as a function of "environmental input level," measured as a combination of noise, pedestrian density, traffic, and the number of public buildings. Sherrod and Downs (1974), in a laboratory analog, assigned subjects to overload, overload-with-perceived-control, or no-overload conditions and then exposed them to a helping opportunity. The "no overload" subjects helped the most, and the "overload" subjects helped the least. Finally, in a field experiment in which task complexity and pedestrian density were varied orthogonally, Spacapan and Cohen (1977) found that there were additive effects. Among high-task-complexity–high-density subjects, not one out of ten helped a confederate who was "looking for her contact lens." Eight of the ten subjects in the low-complexity–low-density cell helped.

The explanation of these effects offered by Milgram (1970) is, essentially, that city dwellers, because of overload, simply do not attend to the stimuli in their environment and therefore they do not notice others' need for assistance. Kammann *et al.* (1977) point out, however, that although much of the effect of pedestrian density on helping behavior observed by Krupat and Coury (1975) could be attributed to not noticing the opportunity to be of assistance, failure to notice is not a sufficient explanation for the results of Korte *et al.* (1975)—dropping keys in front of a single pedestrian, asking for a street interview, or for those of Takooshian *et al.* (1976) with a lost child asking for assistance, in which not noticing was unlikely or impossible. A more likely explanation is presented by Spacapan and Cohen (1977), namely that "both exposure to high density and the performance of a high information rate task resulted in a *decreased sensitivity to the needs of another* [p. 6; italics added]." In other words, the stresses produced by living in dense environments probably lead to decreased helping through the route of deadened sensitivities more than through deadened senses.

The only study that has directly manipulated environmental stimulus overload and measured both attention and helping is one by Mathews and Canon (1975). In two studies, one in the lab and one in the field, they manipulated noise level and observed the likelihood of intervention in minor crises. In the laboratory experiment, the helping opportunity was provided by a confederate who dropped "two books, five journals, and miscellaneous papers" directly in front of the subject. It would hardly be possible *not* to notice an event of this sort. As decibel level was increased from 48 (ambient level) to 65 and then to 85, the percentage of subjects helping decreased from 72% to 67% to 37%. The authors interpret their results in terms of Easterbrook's (and other's) suggestion that arousal (presumed to result from stimulus overload) leads to restricted attention in which only salient features of the setting are noticed. This is similar to Milgram's (1970) suggestions discussed above. The authors state:

> One implication of this effect for interpersonal processes is that with noisy environments, individuals may become less aware of relatively subtle cues produced in interpersonal interactions that more clearly define other's meaning, intentions, and behavior. In addition, this approach suggests that the course of ongoing behavior and/or interaction would be less flexible and less likely to change to a new direction, since individuals would be less attentive to events that are not directly related to ongoing activities. This implies that persons may become relatively more single-minded in their actions, and in a situation that involves another in need of assistance, less likely to interrupt present activities to perform helping acts [p. 572].

Of course, as we noted toward the beginning of this chapter, the reverse effect can be contemplated if the need of the individual is in the focus of attention.

In the field study, Mathews and Canon, for reasons inherent in the paragraph just quoted, varied not only noise level but also presence or absence of a cue signalling need for help—a wrist-to-shoulder cast on the confederate who is to have the crisis. The need for help arises when this person, attempting to balance a heavy load of boxes of books, scatters them about 12 feet in front of a suitably selected potential helper. Noise was varied by turning on an unmuffled lawnmower (87 decibels) or leaving it off (ambient level about 50 decibels).

When the book-dropper was not wearing his cast, helping was low regardless of noise level, about 15%. Under high noise, the cast appeared not to be noticed; helping remained at 15%. With ambient noise only, however, helping soared to 80% when the confederate was wearing his cast. We cannot prove that this is the mechanism by which the density effects in the other studies were produced. We cannot even conclusively demonstrate that differences in deployment of attention led to the effect obtained in this study (although Mathews and Canon cite other experimental research showing decreases in attention to peripheral stimuli under high noise levels). The finding, however, is clear and strong and completely consistent with that interpretation.

The reason for this apparent digression into "urban incivility" is to demonstrate again the relevance of the quality and direction of attention for helping behavior. In the previous section on moods, we have tried to argue that good moods operate in part through directing one's attention away from the self toward the possible needs of others (as well as by making "good thoughts" and positive behaviors more salient). Ambient noise levels as well as other unpleasant and demanding aspects of the urban environment can, we suggest, lead to decreased involvement with the needs of others through the same attentional mechanisms. We—literally—are no longer "oriented" to the needs of our fellows in the modern urban environment.

Recent investigations of self-awareness and self-consciousness also suggest the importance of attentional factors in mediating helping behavior. Duval, Duval, and Neely (1979) demonstrated an increase in willingness to help needy groups when self-awareness is increased in conjunction with attention to the problems of the group. In addition, Karylowski (1976; 1977) is conducting a research program in Poland relating internalized values, self-esteem, and objective self-awareness to helping behavior. Derlega (1978) reports, "Karylowski argues that in cases where the presence of a large number of bystanders to an emergency might be expected to produce a diffusion of responsibility, a sense of personal responsibility will be maintained if the person is objectively self-aware [p. 635]." Thus, objectively self-aware individuals would not be expected to exhibit an inhibition effect due to diffusion of responsibility. There are two studies in which self-focus and diffusion effects have been investigated. Wegner and Schaefer (1978), using a Gestalt-based theoretical approach, assumed that one focuses attention on the smaller of two subgroups. Thus, with one helper and more than one victim, self-focus (and helping) should be greatest; with more than one helper and only one victim, self-focus (and helping) should be lowest. Their results for both self-focus and helping were as predicted. On the other hand, Becker-Haven and Lindskold (1978) found, contrary to Karylowski's prediction, that although a deindividuation manipulation (presumably the opposite of a self-awareness manipulation) decreased helping among alone subjects, it increased helping in pairs of bystanders. Additional helping behavior research is currently being conducted on self-awareness in relationship to internalized values (Karylowski) and personal norms (Schwartz, personal communication, 1980). Clearly, the effects of self-focus, accessibility of cognitions, arousal of personal norms and values, attention to others' needs, and helping are complex.

Summary

In this chapter we have examined temporary state factors as they influence a bystander's response to the needs of another person. Even though the findings in this area are complex and often seemingly contradictory, the processes of arousal and attention appear to affect intervention. Preliminary evidence from the Byeff (1970) and the Piliavin, Piliavin, and Trudell (unpublished, 1974) experiments showed that individuals who were paying the most attention prior to an ambiguous emergency were most emotionally affected by the event. We speculated that what the bystander was attending to at the onset of the emergency determined the likelihood of a helping response. We also suggested that negative moods create arousal that the person is motivated to reduce. This arousal is alleviated by helping if the person has learned an internalized self-reward system or perceives external reward, the costs for helping are relatively low, and the person is focusing on the needs and problems of others. The attention factor may also be critically important in accounting for the consistent as well as the discrepant findings in the urban–rural literature on helping behavior. In addition, with good moods, cognitive processes seem to be more important than arousal. Evidence suggests that individuals who are in a good mood are more likely to think about positive things, retrieve from memory more positive thoughts, are more aware of other people, and have a more positive outlook on life than those who have not recently had a good-mood-enhancing experience. Finally, we have found this brief discourse into temporary states both exciting and sometimes frustrating. This is one of the areas of most rapidly changing data and interpretations.

Chapter 10

The Revised Model
and Implications

In this concluding chapter we will review the current arousal:cost–reward model and show how it has developed from the earlier versions. We will also, in the interest of greater clarity, present the revised model pictorially, using both a path diagram and a flow chart. Next, we will attempt to set our model in perspective by relating it to other current social psychological theories. Finally, we will delineate some policy recommendations, derived from the model, that are aimed at increasing the likelihood of bystanders' responding effectively to future emergencies.

Review of the Model

Over several chapters the reader has followed the presentation of the original arousal:cost–reward model and its subsequent modification and expansion. Consistent with our emphasis on process, we have attempted to portray the evolution of the model over the past 10 years in response to the accumulation of new data. The original 1969 version of the model, presented in Chapter 1, was relatively straightforward. There were two basic and independent components: (*a*) arousal; and (*b*) cost–reward considerations. The model proposed that observation of an emergency creates an unpleasant emotional arousal state in the bystander that the bystander can reduce by one of a number of possible responses. The response selected will be a function of the costs and rewards associated with helping or not helping. The arousal:cost–reward model differed from other contemporary theories in that it emphasized both affective and cognitive factors underlying a decision to help. Since it was post hoc in nature, the model was consistent with the empirical findings at that time.

In 1973, Piliavin and Piliavin presented a more formal and elaborate version of the arousal:cost–reward model in an unpublished module, "The Good Samaritan: Why *does* he help?" Essentially, this manuscript explained the model in greater detail than the 1969 version (see Chapter 2) and cited additional supporting evidence. Again, the arousal and cognitive components were basic. The first fundamental proposition was that observation of an emergency arouses a bystander. It was further hypothesized that the degree of arousal is related to (a) perceived severity of the emergency; (b) distance between the bystander and the emergency; (c) the bystander's similarity to and emotional involvement with the victim; and (d) the length of time of the observer's exposure to the emergency, if no intervention occurs.

The review of the research literature on arousal and vicarious arousal, presented in Chapter 3, reveals both supporting evidence for the initial proposition and a need to modify the 1973 version of the model. In particular, the model was quite vague about the very central construct of arousal. We implicitly accepted a unitary, undifferentiated conception of arousal. However, psychophysiologists (e.g., Lacey & Lacey, 1970, 1973; Routtenberg, 1968; Sokolov, 1963) propose that there are two basic arousal systems. One system functions to heighten an organism's sensitivity to novel stimulation, to direct an individual's attention, and to facilitate information assimilation. The other system has a strong autonomic component and is related to emotion. According to Sokolov (1963), the first system is represented by an "orienting response" while the second system is associated with a "defense reaction." Apparently, it is this latter type of arousal system that social psychologists typically associate with the arousal component of emotion and it was this type of arousal that was implicit in the original model. Our most recent version of the model, though, also recognizes the importance of orienting mechanisms.

Is there any evidence that observation of any emergency is arousing to bystanders? As we discussed in Chapter 3, the answer to this seemingly simple and obvious question is complicated by the nature of arousal and the nature of the measurement of arousal. First, as we just mentioned, arousal is not unitary and undifferentiated. Second, several different physiological responses have been measured (e.g., heart rate, skin conductance, palmar sweating, peripheral vasoconstriction) and each may reflect different aspects of arousal. Comparability across studies, therefore, is difficult to obtain. Fortunately, however, a consistent pattern emerges on both indirect measures of arousal such as reaction time (e.g., DiLollo & Berger, 1965; Weiss, Buchanan, Altstatt, & Lombardo, 1971) and direct physiological measures of arousal (Craig & Lowery, 1969; Gaertner & Dovidio, 1977; Krebs, 1975; Lazarus, 1966). Individuals are aroused by the distress of another. This vicarious arousal, generated by witnessing the distress of another, is generally similar to, but less intense than the arousal caused by a more direct threat to self.

It was hypothesized not only that observation of an emergency would be arousing, but also that severity, time, distance, and involvement with the victim would be systematically related to degree of arousal. The evidence, where it exists, is largely supportive of these secondary hypotheses. The findings associated with the effect of severity on bystander arousal are most substantial. For both indirect (e.g., Berger, 1962; DiLollo & Berger, 1965) and direct (e.g., Geer & Jarmecky, 1973; Lazarus, 1966) measures of arousal, situations of greater severity consistently create higher levels of bystander arousal. Similarly, emergencies of greater clarity generate higher levels of arousal (e.g., Byeff, 1970; Sterling, 1977). Where severity concerns the degree of potential injury to a victim, manipulations of clarity (or, conversely, ambiguity) involve variations in the cues (e.g., screams) emitted from an emergency of a given level of severity. There is, in addition, evidence indicating that arousal increases as the length of the observer's exposure to the emergency increases, if no intervention occurs (Gaertner & Dovidio, 1977; Gaertner, Dovidio, & Johnson, 1979a).

Similarity and feelings of closeness with the victim were also proposed to increase bystander arousal in response to the distress of another. Using the extreme example, it is difficult to deny that an emergency occurring to one's own child would be more arousing than the same emergency involving a total stranger. Nevertheless, research demonstrating an effect of closeness with a victim on bystander arousal is surprisingly infrequent. The little evidence that exists, though, supports the hypothesis that closer relationships with the victim increase a bystander's level of arousal (Krebs, 1975; Stotland, 1969). This effect becomes less pronounced, however, in very clear, serious emergencies. For example, for bystanders who witnessed an emergency alone, Gaertner and Dovidio (1977) found no significant difference in the amount of arousal generated by the plight of racially similar (white) or racially dissimilar (black) victims.

Feelings of involvement with a victim may be inhibited or facilitated by situational as well as interpersonal factors. For example, when a bystander witnesses an emergency alone, he or she bears 100% of the responsibility for intervening; when more than one bystander can help, responsibility may be diffused. Thus, an individual believing that others can help may be less emotionally involved with the victim. Consistent with this reasoning, Gaertner and Dovidio (1977) found that bystanders who believed that others were present were less aroused by an emergency than bystanders who believed that they were the only witness. Bystanders who had the opportunity to diffuse responsibility in an emergency involving a racially dissimilar (black) victim showed a particularly low level of arousal. Thus, empirical evidence generally supports the proposed relationship between involvement with the victim and subsequent arousal generated by the victim's distress.

Finally, although physical proximity to a victim theoretically could affect a bystander's level of arousal, either by increasing the clarity or perceived severity of the emergency or by increasing involvement with the victim, there is no published literature relating arousal and distance from the victim. Nevertheless, the empirical evidence relating severity, clarity, and involvement to arousal continues to suggest a direct relationship between proximity and arousal.

The second major proposition presented in the 1973 version of the model states that, in general, the arousal occasioned by the observation of an emergency is unpleasant and the bystander is therefore motivated to reduce it. There is, in fact, substantial indirect evidence as well as more recent, direct evidence supporting this proposition. Much of the research is presented in Chapters 4 and 6. For example, the same factors that are directly related to bystander arousal are also directly related to bystander intervention. The effects of the severity (e.g., Ashton & Severy, 1976; Staub & Baer, 1974) and the clarity (e.g., Clark & Word, 1974; Yakimovich & Saltz, 1971) of an emergency on helping behavior are well documented. Clearer and more severe situations generate higher levels of intervention. Increased proximity to the victim (e.g., Staub & Baer, 1974) also facilitates helping behavior. Finally, several researchers have demonstrated that greater involvement with a victim based on feelings of "we-ness" (e.g., Hornstein, Masor, Sole, & Heilman, 1971), similarity (e.g., Karabenick, Lerner, & Becker, 1973), attraction (e.g., Gross, Wallston, & Piliavin, 1975), and personal responsibility (e.g., Darley & Latané, 1968) produce higher rates of helpfulness.

More directly, studies that have measured both arousal and helping behavior consistently demonstrate a relationship. Greater levels of arousal, measured by self-report (e.g., Gaertner & Dovidio, 1977) or by GSR (e.g., Byeff, 1970; Piliavin, Piliavin, & Trudell, unpublished, 1974) or by heart rate (e.g., Gaertner & Dovidio, 1977; Gaertner, Dovidio, & Johnson, 1979a), are associated with faster rates of intervention. Furthermore, when a bystander is the only witness to an emergency in which there are low costs for intervention, the correlations between physiological arousal and speed of helping typically range from .45 to .77.

Increasingly, evidence is being accumulated that demonstrates that arousal is not merely associated with helping, but that it can, in fact, motivate bystander intervention, as proposed in the original model. Weiss and his colleagues (Weiss, Boyer, Lombardo, & Stich, 1973; Weiss et al., 1971), for example, showed that vicarious arousal can activate instrumental responses that relieve the suffering of victims. Weiss and his colleagues concluded that the findings strongly support the existence of an aversive state being aroused by the suffering of another (due to electric shock), and that this state behaves like other drive states in motivating a person to relieve another's distress. Additional research demonstrates that the attribution of arousal to the other's distress is a critical factor affecting a bystander's motivation to intervene in an emergency. When Gaertner and Dovidio (1977) persuaded subjects to misattribute arousal generated by an emergency to a placebo (described as having side effects associated with autonomic arousal), helping behavior was inhibited. When Sterling (1977) provided an opportunity for prior, irrelevant arousal to be attributed to an unambiguous emergency, bystander intervention was facilitated. These attribution-related effects have also been observed in less emergency-like situations. Harris and Huang (1973b) found that subjects who had the opportunity to attribute arousal to noise described as having arousing side effects were less likely to help a victim with an injured knee. In a less immediate situation, Coke, Batson, and McDavis (1978) found that subjects who were administered a placebo described as having side effects of autonomic arousal volunteered less time for baby-sitting to a student who lost her parents in an accident.

The experiments investigating the effects of attribution of arousal on helping behavior provide strong and consistent support for our proposition that arousal can motivate bystander intervention. Yet, these studies also necessitated a revision of the model. In the early versions of the model, there was little explicit treatment of the subjective experience of arousal. There was only a brief reference in the original model suggesting that arousal could be interpreted as "fear, disgust, sympathy, etc.," but the conditions eliciting different emotions were not considered. The recent investigation by Coke et al. (1978), however, suggests that, depending on the nature of the situation, arousal may be interpreted as quite different emotions. In severe, life-threatening situations, subjects respond with upset and alarm (Gaertner & Dovidio, 1977); in less critical, less intense problem situations, arousal interpreted as empathic concern (e.g., empathic, warm, concerned, softhearted, and compassionate) seems to motivate helping behavior (Coke *et al.*, 1978). Thus, as we have come to consider a broader range of phenomena beyond emergency events, we have also come to consider a broader range of emotional experience—from promotive tension (Hornstein, 1972), on the one hand, to an intense defense reaction, on the other hand. With this broader perspective, we are now able to incorporate these findings, which seem generally consistent with our model, that other researchers have independently obtained. Consideration of this variety of cognitive and physiological experience has also recently led us to adopt the Leventhal (1980) perceptual–motor processing model of emotion as the basis of our analysis. Nevertheless, despite apparent variations in emotional content, the process by which another's need promotes helping seems dynamically similar across a variety of situations. Both in emergency and nonemergency situations, arousal attributed to the distress of another has motivating properties independent of any solely cognitive factors.

The third major proposition of the model presented in 1973 states that the bystander will choose that response to an emergency that will most rapidly and most completely reduce his or her arousal, incurring in the process as few net costs (costs minus rewards) as possible. Chapter 5 deals extensively with this issue. In our most recent version of the model, we have considered two general categories of potential costs and rewards for the bystander: (*a*) those that are contingent upon his or her making a direct helping response; and (*b*) those that would result were the victim to receive no help. The first category, personal costs for helping, involves negative outcomes imposed directly on the benefactor and includes, for example, effort expenditure, physical danger, rewards for other activities forgone, etc. Rewards for helping include feelings of efficacy, admiration from others, fame, awards, etc.

The second general category of costs, namely costs attendant upon the bystander's knowledge that the victim has received no help, conceptually contains two subcategories, although most researchers do not operationally separate the two. There are "personal costs" for not helping, that is, negative outcomes imposed directly on the bystander for failure to intervene. These include self-blame for one's inaction, public censure, etc. The second subcategory, "empathy costs" for the victim receiving no help, depends solely on the knowledge that the victim is continuing to suffer. In particular, these empathy costs involve internalizing the need or suffering of the victim and produce a continued and perhaps increased level of unpleasant arousal.

The results of studies investigating the effects of costs on helping behavior are generally straightforward. As costs for helping increase, due to potential physical harm (e.g., Midlarsky & Midlarsky, 1973), effort and time expended (e.g., Darley & Batson, 1973), money expended or forgone (e.g., Schaps, 1972), violation of existing rules (e.g., Staub, 1970a, 1971, 1974), or stigma (e.g., Piliavin, Piliavin, & Rodin, 1975), helping behavior decreases. Conversely, as the rewards for helping behavior increase (e.g., McGovern, Ditzian, & Taylor, 1975), helping behavior increases. Also, as the costs for the victim receiving no help increase, bystander intervention becomes more likely. For example, manipulations of severity (e.g., Ashton & Severy, 1976) and clarity (Clark & Word, 1974) of the emergency, victim deservingness (e.g., Piliavin, Rodin, & Piliavin, 1969), and focusing of responsibility (e.g., Schwartz & Gottlieb, 1976) or assignment of responsibility (e.g., Tilker, 1970) have all been demonstrated to systematically and predictably affect helping behavior.

The most difficult area for prediction, with respect to cost–reward considerations, is currently that in which both costs for helping and costs for not helping are high. Contrary to our initial expectation, indirect help is not the most typical response under such circumstances. Instead, given a bystander's initial perception of high costs for helping and high costs for the victim receiving no help, it seems that the first most likely response is one of cognitive reinterpretation. Similar to the process that Lazarus (1968) proposed concerning coping with perceived threat, reinterpreting the costs for not helping relieves the bystander's dilemma in a way that effectively reduces a bystander's unpleasant arousal state. Lowering the costs for not helping may be accomplished by redefining the situation as one in which help is unnecessary (e.g., "The situation is not really serious."), diffusing responsibility (e.g., "Someone else will intervene."), or derogating the victim (e.g., "He got what he deserved."). With high costs for helping and lowered costs for not helping, bystanders became less likely to intervene, either directly or indirectly. Only if the nature of the emergency precludes cognitive reinterpretation is it likely that indirect help will occur. Even then, it is critical that the bystander perceives that indirect help is possible. Given the prominent nature of the emergency event in the bystander's attentional focus, it is often likely that the bystander will fail to consider this option unless a mechanism for indirect assistance (e.g., a firebox) is also prominent.

This recent revision involving cognitive reinterpretation contributed to a more general, significant modification of the earlier versions of the model. Specifically, (a) we now explicitly consider cyclical, iterative processing effects; and (b) we more strongly emphasize the notion that arousal and cost–reward considerations are not independent. In particular, if the search to resolve the high–high cost dilemma is satisfied by cognitive reinterpretation, the conclusion reached by the bystander is most likely to be one that not only lowers costs for not helping, but lowers them partially through reduction of unpleasant arousal. For example, bystanders who diffuse responsibility and come to believe that someone will intervene or has intervened will not only reduce their guilt and potential blame for not helping, but will also reduce their arousal, since the emergency is apparently being resolved by another person (e.g., Gaertner & Dovidio, 1977). Thus the model has become more complicated, considering a greater number of interrelationships. Nevertheless, we believe that consideration of multiple, concurrent effects more accurately represents the complexity of the process by which bystanders may intervene in the problems, crises, and emergencies of others.

The fourth fundamental proposition of the 1973 presentation of the model (but absent in the original 1969 version) asserts that there will be certain circumstances that give rise to a rapid, impulsive, "irrational" response. In Chapters 7 and 8 we explored situational and personality factors that facilitate "impulsive" helping. We also speculated about the process underlying impulsive helping. In general, review of the experiments in which impulsive (85% help, with intervention in less than 15 seconds) and nonimpulsive helping occurred revealed several identifying characteristics of impulse-generating situations. One variable appears particularly strongly related to impulsive helping. This is the clarity of the situation, operationally defined as the victim being visible or as someone clearly defining the situation as an emergency. Although we are convinced that severity is also an important factor, we were unable to find a sufficiently clear, observable criterion on which to judge severity across different experiments. Thus we had to omit this variable from our analysis. Two other factors were also related to impulsive helping: (a) reality, defined as the study being done in a field setting or having as its victim a person who is from outside the experiment; and (b) whether bystanders have any prior experience with the victim.

The impulsive behavior of subjects is a rapid, driven, almost reflexive response that appears to be insensitive to potential costs in the situation. Variations in costs for helping (e.g., Clark & Word, 1974) and in personal costs for helping (e.g., Piliavin, Rodin, & Piliavin, 1969) have little impact in impulse-generating situations. The question that remains, however, concerns the process by which this apparent insensitivity to obvious cost factors occurs.

Probably not coincidentally, the same factors that facilitate impulsive helping—clarity, reality, and involvement with the victim—have also been demonstrated to be related to greater levels of bystander arousal. Thus, it is likely that high levels of arousal in impulse-generating situations could interfere with a broad and "rational" consideration of costs. A number of years ago Easterbrook (1959) demonstrated that, in a very basic physiological sense, under high levels of arousal the focus of attention of subjects was narrowed to the fovea. Peripheral stimuli, therefore, were not considered in the determination of subjects' responses. Other researchers (e.g., Broadbent, 1971) have also concluded that organisms in an aroused state devote a higher proportion of time to the intake of information from a dominant source and less from relatively minor ones.

A unique aspect of very clear, serious emergencies is that they are both attention-getting and highly arousing. Thus, the victim's plight becomes the "dominant source" on which bystanders focus. Cost considerations become peripheral and are not attended to. Therefore, the impulsive helping behavior that may appear irrational to an uninvolved observer who considers all the apparent costs and rewards may be a quite "rational" response for a bystander attending primarily to the victim's plight.

Again we have come to consider the interactive effects of arousal and cost–reward considerations on bystander intervention. Just as cost considerations can affect a bystander's state of arousal, as we mentioned earlier, it appears that arousal can influence the impact of costs. Therefore, in our present version of the model we have attempted to explicitly consider the mutual interactive effects of arousal and costs. Also, the role of the "orienting response" and related attentional processes has gained recognition in our current model. Focus of attention is critical in our explanation of impulsive helping; it also becomes important in our consideration, in Chapter 9, of the effects of temporary states of the bystander on helping behavior. For example, although relief of aversive emotional states appears to explain quite well the effect of certain negative experiences such as transgression (e.g., Cialdini, Darby, & Vincent, 1973) on helping, an arousal model of this type seems to have little relevance in explaining the consistent effect of good moods on helping behavior. Instead, in these nonemergency situations, attention-related factors such as expansiveness of attention (e.g., McMillen, Sanders, & Solomon, 1977), sensitivity to the needs of others (e.g., Spacapan & Cohen, 1977), and expectancy and response set (e.g., Isen, Shalker, Clark, & Karp, 1978) seem to be important mediators of the effects of moods on helping.

The original arousal:cost–reward model proposed that emergency helping is a selfish attempt to reduce unpleasant arousal generated by the awareness of another's distress in a manner that maximizes the bystander's own benefits and minimizes accompanying costs. Helping was not conceived to be a purely sympathetically oriented attempt to reduce another's distress. The revised model, while not excluding egoistic intent, also allows for more sympathetic, selfless motives for intervening. To the extent that arousal is interpreted as alarm and concern rather than disgust and upset and the salience of empathic costs for not helping exceed personal cost considerations, the motive for helping has a sympathetic rather than selfish tone. Thus, the needs of another can become one and the same or coordinated with those of the bystander. Nevertheless, there are many instances in which the bystander's motive is more selfish. How marvelous, though, that another's distress could instigate arousal which, even egoistically, impels us to action.

Pictorial Presentations of the Model

For at least some people, a picture is worth a thousand words. You have by now worked your way through many more than a thousand words, aided at times by pictures—or at least graphs. We will now present (in two different pictorial forms) our revised conceptualization of the processes that occur. First, we will use a path analysis format in which we will show what we believe to be the relationships among several categories of variables in the determination of bystander response. Second, we will use a flow chart format in an attempt to present the possible sequences of internal processes and overt responses that bystanders can make. Hopefully, using both presentations will clarify the model more fully than either mode of presentation can do alone.

PATH DIAGRAM FORMAT

In Chapter 1, Figure 1.1 included Figure 10.1 to outline the revised model. In this chapter, we have already explained the changes in the model and the bases for them. One criticism that may be offered is that we consider so many predictor variables and place so much emphasis on process that the model is useless for prediction. There may be some validity to this criticism. However, our attempt has not been primarily to present a predictive model in the usual sense. We have instead attempted to develop a

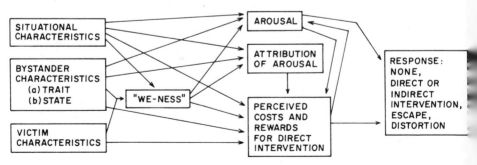

Figure 10.1. The current arousal: cost–reward model.

model that is designed to explain a variety of phenomena, to help researchers understand a complex area of behavior, and to suggest aspects of the phenomenon that have not yet been explored and are not well understood. Certainly prediction is part of this, but it is by no means all of it. Thus, in our presentation of the model we have attempted to organize and to integrate past research, to suggest new ideas, to open new areas of inquiry, and to encourage orderly theoretical development of the area of helping behavior.

One of our basic aims has been to demonstrate the importance of certain factors individually in the determination of intervention responses. We have clearly shown that many situational, personal, and victim characteristics are related to intervention. In addition, we have attempted to show that these factors operate through their impact on two intervening processes: arousal and perceived costs and rewards for direct intervention. In this we have also been successful, although in the process we have rediscovered one of many social psychological truths: mutual influence of intervening processes on each other. In this case, what we have demonstrated is the reciprocal influence of arousal and cost–reward considerations on each other. We have also discovered the intervening variable of perceived "we-ness" as a factor influencing both arousal and cost–reward calculations. Furthermore, we have rediscovered, as have many current researchers in the field of attribution (Abelson, Fiske, Langer, Taylor, etc.), the critical importance of attentional processes in both the speed of response and the nature of the response that is made. Finally, the attribution of the source of arousal is also, under all but the most "impulse-producing" of circumstances, an important factor in what response is made.

Does the increased complexity and the iterative nature of the present model make it impossible to use for predictive purposes, however? We think not. It merely requires that the user (a) attend to more features of the situation, the bystander, and the victim than formerly thought; and (b) be willing to state expectations probabilistically and contingently, depending upon the occurrence or nonoccurrence of certain intervening processes, whose likelihood of occurrence can also be estimated. The overall model as depicted in Figure 10.1, then, may not serve particularly well for predictive purposes because of the highly inclusive, processual nature of the presentation. However, abstraction of certain aspects of the model can readily lead to direct, nonambiguous predictions. For example, in a very simple experiment, clarity of an emergency (for which the subject is the only bystander) can be manipulated. Diagrammatically, the potential effects associated with this manipulation are shown in Figure 10.2. Increased clarity of the emergency should lead to increased arousal. Increased clarity should also

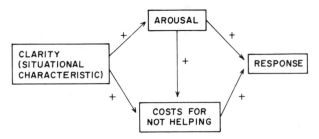

Figure 10.2.   Example of the use of the revised model: The effects of clarity.

increase (both directly and indirectly) the costs for the victim's receiving no help. In the clearer emergency, the bystander would anticipate more guilt, blame, and censure for not intervening. Thus, personal costs for not helping are directly affected. In addition, to the extent that the greater arousal generated by the clearer emergency is experienced by the bystander as unpleasant, empathic costs for the victim's receiving no help would be greater. Clarity, therefore, also indirectly increases the costs for not helping, mediated by the unpleasant emotional state. These processes, taken together, suggest that clarity should have a strong facilitative effect on bystander intervention.

Another example of research that demonstrates how the current model can be applied, one in which more elements are present, is the Gaertner and Dovidio (1977) study involving race of victim (a victim characteristic) and the presence or absence of other witnesses to the emergency (a situational characteristic). As shown in Figure 10.3, being alone with the potential victim is postulated to lead to the perception of "we-ness," regardless of the

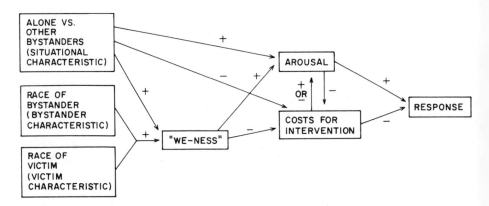

Figure 10.3.   Example of the use of the revised model: The effects of "we-ness."

race of the victim (an illustration of the "situational characteristics to we-ness" path). Being of the same race as the victim (in this case both white) is also postulated to lead to judgments of "we-ness" (an illustration of the "victim characteristics × bystander characteristics to we-ness" path). "We-ness" then leads to increased arousal as well as increased costs for the victim receiving no help. Greater degrees of arousal also can lead to the perception of greater seriousness and therefore to perceived even higher costs for nonintervention (the path from arousal to costs); similarly, perceived high costs for nonintervention can lead to increased arousal through the addition of feelings of moral obligation (Schwartz, 1977) on top of empathic arousal. Not only can the order of obtained outcomes for the conditions of the Gaertner and Dovidio study be predicted with the use of this overall path model, the intervening links can also be tested.

FLOW CHART FORMAT

The previous way of presenting the model allows for the construction of path models involving the variables in an experiment designed to test implications and predictions from the model. What it does not permit is an understanding of the dynamics of the processes that go on as an individual is exposed to and responds to an emergency. The inclusion of the cyclical relationship between arousal and the perceived costs and rewards is the only way we can indicate with a path diagram that these intervening variables can change over the course of the time it takes for the bystander to make a response. The effects of attention shifts, as noted previously, also cannot be adequately indicated in the path model format. Figure 10.4 therefore attempts to present the way a bystander would be expected to sequentially process a situation as a function of variation in the kinds of variables represented in Figure 10.1.

The first step in processing an event that may come to be defined as an emergency is, as with any other change in stimulation, preattentive processing. This crude, holistic categorization is sensitive to only the gross features of situations and roughly sorts them into events not requiring attention (a), events interesting enough to attend to but not requiring immediate action (b), and events requiring an immediate response (c) (see Figure 10.4). Typically, when an event is first identified as requiring attention, an orienting response occurs. As illustrated in section (b) of Figure 10.4, this initial orienting response involves a state of readiness to respond combined with a "wait and see" attitude, increased alertness, and widely deployed attention. Under the normal conditions of some ambiguity and low-to-moderate perceived severity, the bystander will engage both in hypothesis testing regarding the nature of the situation and in decision making involving cost–reward calculations. As section (b) indicates, there are also feedback loops. Feedback from perceptual processing and other cognitive "work" to the emotional system may be either facilitative ($+$) or inhibitory ($-$). What cannot be shown adequately in this or any other

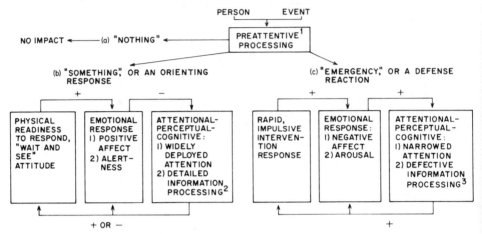

Figure 10.4. Flow chart representation of the revised model.

[1] Preattentive processing is an initial categorizing of the event at a preconscious level. It can be affected by both trait and state factors in the individual (prior set, mood, previous experience, personality) and by factors in the situation, as well as by the "person by situation" interaction. The outcome is a crude three-way categorization as indicated by (a), (b), and (c). Although it clearly does not involve verbal processes, it begins to answer Janis and Mann's (1977) Question 1, "Are the risks serious?" and Question 4, "Is there time to debate the merits . . . ?" Category (a) involves the answer "No" to Question 1. Category (c) involves a "Yes" to 1 and a "No" to 4.

[2] The detailed information processing phase involves shifting attention from the self to the environment, continued sampling of ongoing events for possible new information, and calculation of costs and rewards for all potential courses of action. It is important to point out that the actual situation in crises, problems, and emergencies will not be static; it can deteriorate rapidly or be solved by the intervention of another individual or by the victim's own actions. Note the positive feedback loops to physical readiness and emotion/attention. As time goes by, tension builds so that *some* response is more likely than no response. Where one's attention is located at the time when arousal becomes unpleasant will have important effects on the outcome. Although only one feedback loop is actually drawn, multiple cycles are possible.

[3] It is assumed that the initial preattentive processing or later detailed processing that led the bystander to an "Emergency!" categorization yielded "we-ness" and "serious" judgments (at either a conscious or unconscious level), and that potential costs to the bystander have only been minimally attended to or have been judged to be low. In this parallel defective information processing it is possible but not likely that other information can intrude to stop the process, but only if obvious costs for intervention appear in the focus of attention. Panic, disorganization, etc. may result at this point because of conflict and the very high level of arousal. Otherwise, the indicated positive feedback loops to the intervention response are employed. If this action is perceived as correct, it is continued. The negative feedback loops from action to emotion and perception/cognition are intended to indicate the cessation of arousal.

diagram, however, is the fact that the event itself is also in process. This has two separate implications in our model. The first is that arousal in the bystander continues to build as long as no one does anything. We have attempted to show this with the positive feedback loop from "wait and see" to "emotion" (that is, the longer one waits, other things being equal, the more aroused one becomes) and with the negative feedback loop from "emotion" to "widely deployed attention" (that is, as arousal goes up, the perceptual–cognitive processes become more limited). The second implication of the event continuing to be in progress is that the nature of the incoming information that is the basis of the perceptual–cognitive processing can change at any moment. An experiment by Schwartz and Gottleib (1980, Study 2) is an excellent example of this effect. As the clarity of the emergency underwent an abrupt increase, the rate of helping changed rapidly as well. Given all of these changing conditions, plus the shifting of attention from one aspect of the situation to another, the outcome cannot always be predicted precisely. As time goes by, the likelihood of making some response, however, increases, because of the increasing arousal. Knowing the parameters of the situation overall we can make probability estimates regarding the likelihood of various responses. Were we to know the focus of attention and the level of arousal at any given point in time, we suggest, we could make sharper predictions about both when a response would be made and what that response would be.

Take as an example the collapse of an unknown middle-aged man in front of your house. The man gives no clues as to the reason for his collapse. He does not appear to be unconscious, but he does seem to be having difficulty in getting up again. We hope that the reader will subjectively be experiencing the iterations suggested in Figure 10.4, section (b). Assume that as you continue to watch, he continues to struggle to regain his feet, and nothing else happens. We propose that you will either (1) go out and help him (highest probability); or (2) decide he is a drunken bum and go back to your reading; or (3) call the police (lowest probability). The first reaction will occur with low costs for helping (e.g., if you live in a "nice neighborhood," if you are male, and if the man is well dressed and of your ethnic group, or at least not obviously of some other). The second reaction will occur primarily if there are high perceived personal costs (e.g., the neighborhood is dangerous, you are an elderly female, and the man is large and of dubious background). The last reaction appears unlikely based on the literature on indirect helping, in which it seems that quick solutions such as direct help or derogation are preferred to slow solutions such as calling the police.

Under some circumstances, preattentive processing may identify an event as requiring immediate attention. These situations, discussed in Chapter 7, are characterized by high levels of severity, clarity, perceived reality of the event, and closeness of the bond between the bystander and the victim. The processes hypothesized to occur under these conditions are represented in section (c) of Figure 10.4. The combination of these situational factors seems to trigger an immediate and intense defense reaction and the focus of attention becomes narrowed by the high level of emotionality.

We will use again as our example the sudden collapse of a middle-aged man who is walking down the sidewalk in front of your house. In this case, however, assume that the man is your father, whom you know to have a serious heart condition, and who falls, with no other apparent external cause, clutching his chest. (Your father has also never been known for pulling practical jokes or for having sudden attacks of indigestion.) The situation could not be more clear, severe, or real, nor could rapid action be more needed. Closeness to the victim is also near maximum. Your response is to jump and run out, your attention riveted on your father, your heart pounding. There are also positive feedback loops among most of the elements. For example, rapid, impulsive action leads to increased arousal, through both cognitive and physiological routes. Increased arousal leads to even more narrow attention, focused totally on the needs of the victim (costs for the victim receiving no help) and totally ignoring any personal costs for helping. This focus on your father again increases your arousal and "puts wings on your feet." With this extreme example, it is difficult to see how the cycling could be broken. In fact, it is likely (as suggested by Lofland, 1969) that the process can only be changed by the addition of new information, and this new information must either directly be in the focus of attention or it must be so intrusive (like a very loud gunshot) that it shifts the focus of attention. When such new information does enter in, it is likely to lead to hesitation, reassessment of the situation, and possibly disorganization, because of the high level of arousal.

Relationship to Other Models

We have throughout this book attempted to emphasize the similarities, as well as the dissimilarities, between our model and the models of others. Several theorists working on the same problem should indeed reach some of the same conclusions. For example, both the Latané and Darley (1970) model and the Schwartz (1977) model of helping see the helping act as the final outcome of a decision-making process, as does our model. We have no basic disagreement with conceptualizing the helping act as the outcome of a decision process. Our model, however, has more in common with the general framework for decision making recently presented by Janis and Mann (1977) than it does with the Latané and Darley or Schwartz models.

Janis and Mann make an important distinction between "hot" cognitions (Abelson, 1963) and the "cool," calculated approach to problem solving usually recommended and generally assumed as the model for all kinds of decision making. By "hot" cognitive processes, they mean thinking that is accompanied by emotional arousal. Given our assumption that observation of the crises, problems, and emergencies of others leads to emotional arousal in the observer, the Janis and Mann model, which explicitly builds in the effect of emotion, seems ideally suited to the intervention situation.

In general, the Janis and Mann model of emergency decision making has much in common with our model and other models of bystander intervention (see Figure 10.5). It involves four basic questions a person confronted with a danger or warning asks him or herself:

1. Are the risks serious if I do nothing?
2. Are the risks serious if I do take the most available protective action?
3. Is it realistic to hope to find a better means?
4. Is there sufficient time to search and deliberate?

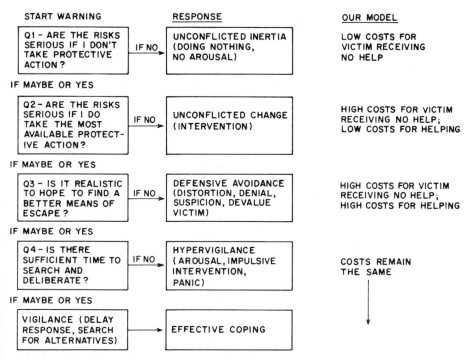

Figure 10.5. Janis and Mann's (1977) model of emergency decision making. [Reprinted with permission of Macmillan Publishing Co., Inc. from *Decision Making* by I. L. Janis & L. Mann. Copyright © 1977 by The Free Press, a Division of Macmillan Publishing Co., Inc.]

Question 1 of Janis and Mann's model is like Latané and Darley's question concerning whether or not the event is defined as an emergency. Question 2 is something like their question about deciding on the degree of personal responsibility, in that personal costs of the most obvious action, intervention, are clearly in the forefront of one's mind when degree of responsibility is being assessed. Finally, Question 3 is similar to Latané and Darley's step involving a decision concerning the specific mode of intervention. Question 4 is new with Janis and Mann.

The Janis and Mann model presents several important insights that are quite consistent with our own approach. First, they assume that in most emergency situations, decisions are not based on purely intellectual deliberation. Instead, the four basic questions in their model are "posed and answered on the basis of a very hasty surmise, sometimes limited to split-second perceptions of what is happening and what might happen [p. 54]." Furthermore, the answers to these questions do not necessarily occur in the sequence shown and some or all of the questions and answers might occur with great rapidity as visual images, rather than in verbal form. This aspect of their model has obvious relevance to our analysis of impulsive helping.

In addition, Janis and Mann hypothesize that simply being faced with a consequential decision leads to stress and arousal. As the individual answers "yes" to each of the first three questions, the arousal mounts. Finally, as he or she answers "no" to the final question, "Is there sufficient time to make a careful search for and evaluation of information and advice?" Janis and Mann argue that the person becomes emotionally excited and makes a quick and incomplete summary of the situation. Consequently, he or she gravitates toward simple-minded decision rules, is unduly influenced by other people, and fails to notice obvious defects in the strategy he or she has selected. Thus, simply the feeling of insufficient time to make a decision can create arousal and consequently affect the nature of the decision process.

The final major contribution of the Janis and Mann approach is related to the above point. Because it is the perception of alternatives and the perception of sufficiency of time that are critical rather than some "objective" reality, person variables are very important for the process and outcome of emergency decisions. "State" variables such as level of arousal at the time of the emergency, trait variables such as self-confidence, past experience, and/or specific training in similar situations all moderate the impact of such highly stressful, high-time-pressure decision situations.

Integration of our model with other models may also be accomplished through a reconceptualization based on a Lewinian notion of "resultant force." Emergency situations (as contrasted with a descending series of crises, problems, and mundane help-requiring situations) are typically characterized by high costs for intervention. It is seldom dangerous to pick up dropped groceries or to donate to the Salvation Army. Intervening in a rape or an armed robbery, on the other hand, involves a high level of personal cost. Thus the forces opposing such intervention are great. In order for a helping act to occur, the force propelling the individual to the act must be stronger than the forces opposing the act. Unpleasant, high arousal associated with the distress of the other (that is, perceived as empathic arousal) is the strongest instigator to intervention (a) because of its immediacy and negative feeling tone; and (b) because the most efficient and immediate way to relieve one's own distress is to alleviate the distress of the other. As the level of arousal decreases, the force leading the individual to "locomote" toward the victim is decreased. Given the same level of costs associated with intervention, then, helping will be less likely as arousal decreases.

On the other hand, with relatively low-cost forms of helping such as returning "lost" letters or contributing money to charity, the strong emotion aroused in a "defense reaction" is not necessary to overcome the forces against taking the action. A relatively mild emotional response, such as Hornstein's postulated "promotive tension," Schwartz's "feelings of moral obligation," or Coke, Batson, and McDavis' "empathic arousal" should be sufficient to energize helping in low-cost situations. It is even possible that other drives or motives, such as physical attraction to the victim or a desire to do something interesting can motivate helping, as long as the costs are low.

Another aspect of Lewinian theory that can help our reconceptualization is that of "life space." In Lewinian theory, the only stimuli that can affect the person's behavior are those that enter his or her phenomenological field. There has always been a problem in Lewinian theory regarding the determination of what indeed will enter the "life space" and become relevant. (Alfred Schutz, 1970, has dealt with this problem in *Reflections on the Problem of Relevance*.) Our research into "impulsive helping" as well as concerns with the effects of attentional focus (both direction of attention and degree of consciousness) on the part of Langer, Nisbett, Taylor, and others appear to provide a solution. It is the salient cues in a situation, those that catch, attract, and hold the attention, that will enter first and with greatest impact into our life space and become relevant for our own conduct. Other things equal, stimuli that are bright, loud, and moving are known to gain our attention. So are those that have personal meaning to us in relationship to values and goals, especially those that have affective power. The bystander's position with regard to the detachment–involvement continuum (see Chapter 7) affects narrowness of attention and arousal, and thus the relative salience of various cost considerations within our model. Finally, persons are more likely to become the focus of our attention than are objects; furthermore, our focus is more likely to be out, toward the world, than in, toward ourselves. "Impulsive" helping can be better understood using this framework. The behavior of the impulsive hero or heroine no longer appears to be "irrational" if one views his or her life space as looking like that depicted in Figure 10.6 rather than that depicted in Figure 10.7. What these figures attempt to show is that, although there may be objective costs in the situation (as shown in Figure 10.7), they have not entered the "hero's" life space (as shown in Figure 10.6). Thus these costs do not deter the action.

From the experimental psychology literature we know that under high arousal, attention span becomes narrowed; in Lewinian terms, fewer factors enter the life space. Furthermore, attention remains outward-focused, preventing the individual from referencing internal stimuli, such as fear, costs attendant upon negative attitudes, other competing commitments, etc. As we have repeatedly stressed, however, under most circumstances the focus of attention is not so narrow; other things do enter the life space. The direction of attention, therefore, becomes particularly important, since initial interpretations and actions tend to be continued in the absence of strong disconfirming evidence (e.g., see Schwartz & Gottleib, 1980). If an impulsive act does not occur, however, we postulate that there will be an immediate shift of focus from the victim to the self in order to reference (a) emotional state; and (b) norms, attitudes, and values, and then there may be a shift back to the "scene" to assess costs of various actions in rela-

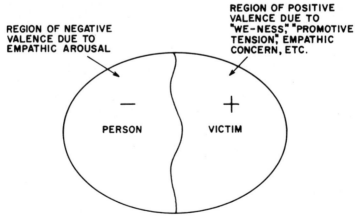

Figure 10.6

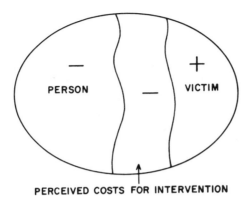

PERCEIVED COSTS FOR INTERVENTION

Figure 10.7

tionship to those internal states. It is at this point that prior state, trait factors, and perceived costs and rewards become relevant.

Several recent programs of research (Bandura, 1977; Scheier & Carver, 1977; Scheier, Carver, & Gibbons, 1979; Scheier, Fenigstein, & Buss, 1974) have begun to delineate the nature of the interactions among arousal, self-focused attention, attributions, and actions. In general, self-focused attention can increase the experienced emotion, once the arousal state has been labeled as due to emotion. The behavior engaged in, then, will be more closely related to the "appropriate" emotion or attitude under self-focused attention than in its absence (Scheier & Carver, 1977).

Furthermore, according to Carver, Blaney, and Scheier (1979), experiencing feedback indicative of increasing arousal, whether due to self-focused attention or other sources, in the course of performing an action can have different effects (a) on people who differ in initial confidence (competence, feelings of self-efficacy); and (b) as a function of the direction of attention. Among confident individuals, experiencing arousal feedback can be expected to lead to increased effort; among less confident subjects, however, arousal feedback can lead to giving up (Carver & Blaney, 1977). The relevance of these ongoing investigations to our revised arousal:cost-reward model is clear. In an emergency situation, the bystander will experience an initial level of arousal, which is a complex function of his or her "arousability" (both chronic and state-related), relationship with the victim, and characteristics of the emergency itself. To the extent that the arousal is initially extremely high, we expect rapid, "impulsive" helping as described in Chapter 7. In situations other than those, the various factors interact and feed back on themselves in complex ways not entirely predictable given our current level of understanding.

Carver *et al.* (1979) present a flow chart (see Figure 10.8) that illustrates one aspect of the process that we would like to see incorporated into our model. The process shown in this figure is one that is applicable to an individual who has already decided to take an action involving some possible negative outcomes and therefore involves arousal—like a bystander to an emergency that involves some personal costs. Self-focus under these circumstances, claim Carver *et al.*, increases the salience of both arousal cues and the goal in relationship to a personal standard. The same might be expected to occur with self-focus in a helping situation; there will be more impact of both personal costs and personal norms under conditions of self-focused attention. Perceived arousal can focus attention on the self as well as providing cues to the severity of the situation and one's own emotional state.

In potential helping situations, however, we are typically dealing with individuals who have not yet committed themselves to a course of action. Thus the perception of arousal can affect not only the action decision but also the judgment of the nature of the situation and therefore the labeling of the arousal. This, further, can focus attention either more intensely on the

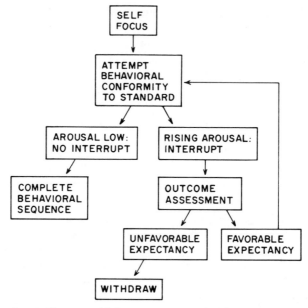

Figure 10.8.   Carver, Blaney, and Scheier's (1979) postulated sequence for self-attention in a fear-provoking behavioral context. [From C. Carver, P. Blaney, & M. Scheier. Focus of attention, chronic expectancy, and responses to a feared stimulus. *Journal of Personality and Social Psychology,* 1979, *37,* 1186–1195. Copyright 1979 by the American Psychological Association. Reprinted by permission.]

self, on the victim, or (when there is one) on a victimizer. To be specific, if the arousal is labeled as fear (as it might well be in witnesses to dangerous emergencies such as muggings, robberies, or major fires), self-focus will be increased and personal costs will be magnified; however, personal norms and competencies should also be referenced. Among persons low in the tendency to deny responsibility (e.g., as measured by Schwartz's, 1977, RD scale) who also have strong helping norms and are high in self-confidence, one would predict an attempt to overcome the fear and to reattribute arousal to empathic distress and, subsequently, intervention attempts. Costs for helping will have been decreased by these coping techniques, while costs for nonintervention will have been accentuated by reference to the personal norms. Among people low in self-confidence and high on RD (regardless of helping norms) arousal labeled as fear should be incapacitating; their response should be withdrawal from the situation or panic.

For any group, arousal initially perceived and labeled as empathic (whether subjectively experienced as unpleasant distress, warm concern, or some mixture of the two) should tend to shift the focus of attention away from the self back to the victim, decreasing the relative impact of costs for intervention (which are doubtless lower at any rate) and increasing the impact of relative severity and victim characteristics. We suspect it should also decrease the impact of the presence of other people. There should still be effects of these factors; they should simply be less pronounced.

Policy Implications of the Model

The problem raised by Latané and Darley (1970) in *The Unresponsive Bystander: Why Doesn't He [sic] Help?* was just that: the high incidence of nonintervention in the momentary emergencies, crises, and problems of others. Without denying that this problem exists and is serious, we have also raised the problems of impulsive helping—when bystanders *do* intervene when they should not. That is, bystanders sometimes intervene "irrationally," without thought to the potential costs for such action. In this section, we will discuss educational programs and other possible changes our society might make to reduce the likelihood of either nonintervention or "irrational" intervention in emergencies and to encourage considered, safe intervention instead.

EDUCATIONAL PROGRAMS

First, and most important, recall that we have assumed that the potential to be aroused by another's crisis is innate, but that socialization changes the labeling of arousal and the form that the response will take. Thus, potential educational programs could cover an extremely large range. We have suggested (in Chapter 6) that strong arousal in response to another's crisis only occurs when a judgment of some sort has been made that the other and I are—at least momentarily—"we." Hornstein makes the same assumption regarding the development of promotive tension. Much literature as well as social science writing has revolved around this deplorable tendency of human societies to divide the world into "us" and "them" for purposes of the sharing of resources, mutual defense, and any other cooperative enterprise. Thus, clearly, one possible educational program suggested by the model could be one that emphasizes the inclusion of all groups into the "we-group." This is clearly unlikely in the forseeable future, but some sort of exposure at an early age to the idea of shared humanity and mutual respect would contribute not only to increased intervention in emergencies but also to more helpfulness and a better quality of life generally.

Along these general lines, we agree with those who argue that societies structure not only the actions of their members but even their perceptions and categorical judgments. We have talked about the "preattentive processing" of situations. In our society, we are trained from an early age to see most of the problems of other people as "none of our business," to close our feelings off from others' experiences. We have only recently "discovered" child abuse, spouse abuse, incest, and other family "traditions" because of the sanctity of the home and respect for others' privacy. This tendency saves all of us a great deal of emotional distress, but it contributes to the bureaucratization of helping in our society and, we believe, to the increasing alienation and self-absorption of which we all are currently being accused. We may need more training as busybodies; respect for privacy prevents empathic arousal and directs one's attention to the costs of intervention, specifically the cost of being thought "intrusive." As it is, we suspect that we filter out—before we ever really "see" them—most of the problems, crises, and even the real emergencies occurring around us. (See, as support for this statement, the rate of premature hang-ups in Gaertner's, 1973, "wrong number" technique research.) Students in classes we have taught that have gone into helping in any detail always report an increased incidence of seeing emergencies. We believe society in general needs to have the salience of strangers' problems increased. This could clearly be taught in the early grades as it has for years been taught to Boy and Girl Scouts.

After one has taught increased attentiveness to others' needs and inclusion of a broader range of people in the "we-group," one needs to work on (a) attribution of responsibility to the self for taking action; and (b) the development of the necessary feelings of competence. Clearly, the educational programming to attain these objectives needs to be coordinated to the developmental level of the children involved. The two components go together. As skills in helping are developed, more responsibility for the welfare of others can be assumed.

Our preferred approach would be based on Bandura's recent discussion of the determinants of self-efficacy (1977). The development of expectations of efficacy—or, simply, beliefs that one can accomplish certain goals—are best fostered by modeled practice, Bandura claims. Programs in school for the training of appropriate interventions could perhaps involve peer problem solving (a la Spivack & Shure, 1974), followed by role playing by all members. The problem solving would emphasize solutions involving prosocial responsibility; the modeling and guided practice would increase self-efficacy. This is how lifesaving, CPR (cardiopulmonary resuscitation), and countless other interpersonal helping skills are taught to adults. Why not try it with children much earlier in pursuit of a helping society?

The apparent preference for the reinterpretation of emergencies as events not requiring personal intervention and/or for the derogation of victims over indirect helping in emergencies involving high costs for helping was discussed in Chapter 5. Educational programs should also include attempts to counter these tendencies by discussions of findings on "diffusion of responsibility" and "derogation of the victim." The availability of indirect responses should be stressed, as well as the maturity and responsibility of those who use them. These efforts must, of course, be supported by increasing the availability and efficacy of such responses (see the "Environmental Modifications" section on page 256).

A final consideration regarding the early teaching of intervention has to do with the "impulsive" helping issue, emotional control, and the problem of "encapsulation." How does one teach attention to the crises of others, inclusion in the ingroup, and taking responsibility to act, without incurring the danger of "fools rushing in?" According to Lofland, encapsulation is most likely with unexpected situations and with individuals who feel threatened and inadequate. For example, Clark and Word's (1974) electrically sophisticated subjects helped rapidly, but with consideration of the realistic costs. Bystanders with little electrical experience, though, intervened in ways that would have caused personal injury. The very training we have just discussed, involving role playing and the development of coping strategies, should be the best defense against panic and either flight or dangerous, irrational intervention. Emotional control goes along with knowing what to do. "Hot" cognitions will become "cool" (see our earlier discussion of Janis & Mann, 1977). What we are suggesting here is a program that will transform the average citizen into a "semiprofessional" helper.

INSTITUTIONAL SUPPORTS FOR "AMATEUR" INTERVENTION

The current availability of CPR training is an example of what we mean by "institutional supports." After a long tradition of discouraging self-help, the medical and therapeutic community, under the pressures of severe personnel shortages and inadequate techniques, have changed their attitudes. It is physically impossible for paid rescue personnel to reliably reach a heart attack victim in under 5 minutes. The critical period for resuscitation is 2 minutes. If the brain goes without oxygen beyond that time, its cells begin to die. The only solution is to train enough of the general population in resuscitation techniques so that the likelihood becomes good that you will have a heart attack near one of them. The training is arduous and one must seek it out, but the population is at least being encouraged to do so and they are responding very positively. (It will be interesting to see on what categories of "others" this training is most frequently used. We suspect that the trainees are largely middle-class individuals with concerns about the health of family members.)

Similarly, programs such as "Widow to Widow" counseling, post-breast-removal self-help groups, and other "it takes one to help one" organizations now have the blessing of the medical and therapeutic community. Many of the problems being grappled with, as with drug addiction, obesity, and alcoholism, were intractable to professional helpers. The encouragement of self-help groups in these areas can be seen in the same light as provision of CPR training; it is a symptom of the realization by professionals that their technology is inadequate. From our point of view, an equally important outcome is the potential increase in "other-orientation" for the individuals doing the helping, a tendency that may generalize and strengthen "we-feelings" in society in general.

Changes in the Good Samaritan laws are just beginning and are another example of what we mean by institutional supports for amateur helping. To the extent that fear of consequences—either of personal injury that cannot be paid for or of being sued for one's altruistic attempts that went awry—can deter intervention, laws can provide a countervailing force. In some states we are now seeing compensation to Good Samaritans, at least those who intervene in crimes. An even stronger institutional support would be laws requiring intervention if no severe danger to the helper was present, such as are on the books in most of Europe. Such laws can provide costs for not helping in situations where the costs for helping are relatively low. In our revised model, that is motivation enough, even in the absence of empathic arousal.

ENVIRONMENTAL MODIFICATIONS

We will leave detailed discussion of these questions to environmental designers. Jacobs (1969), Newman (1972, 1975), and Sommer (1974) have made many suggestions for building safer, more neighborly cities. Many of these suggestions are compatible with the model being presented here. That is, they simultaneously make the likelihood of being exposed to others' crises, and thus the chance for empathic arousal, greater and the difficulties of helping less.

One specific suggestion would be to design housing (in large cities, where the problem of nonintervention seems most acute) in such a way as to make the observation of victimization at as close quarters and as visible as possible (see Newman, 1972, 1975). This close distance should lead to higher arousal in the bystander who observes an incident. It should also lead to more accurate perception of the severity of the problem, which contributes both to arousal and to heightened costs for the victim receiving no help. This design change should also have the long-term effect of neighbors coming to know each other better, leading to greater personal involvement with and perceived "we-group" membership of any victim in the neighborhood. Increasing "we-feelings" will create both higher arousal and higher perceived costs for the victim receiving no help. Many suggestions along these lines have been made by Jane Jacobs in *The Death and Life of Great American Cities* (1969). Such architectural changes are consistent with Lofland's ideas concerning "facilitating places" for the commission of deviant acts.

In regard to "facilitating hardware," to use another Lofland phrase, recall that the low utilization of indirect helping responses has been a surprise in terms of the original model. Clearly, we need to have salient devices for calling for help and these devices must *work*. Phones on which one can call the operator or the police for no charge would be (and are) a start in the right direction. Allowing citizens to report emergencies (especially if they involve criminal victimizations) anonymously is also critical, since it lowers the costs for helping. Increasing the speed and efficiency of police and rescue squads in responding to such calls is, of course, the cornerstone of any such program. If the indirect response, when made, is ineffectual, it will clearly be extinguished rapidly.

Implications for the Victims of Chronic Crisis[1]

At the beginning of this book, we stated that we were restricting our attention to the process of intervention in momentary emergencies, crises, and problems of others. Our reason was that we saw that the nature of the process by which decisions are made to intervene in such crises was different from that of decisions to intervene in nonemergencies. Remember

---

[1] This last section owes a great deal to the thinking of Irving M. Piliavin.

that our definition of an emergency is that of an event that happens suddenly, without warning, and threatens the life or limb of someone if intervention is not immediate. In contrast, there are in any society chronic problems in need of our intervention. The poor, the disadvantaged, the handicapped, the old and indigent are indeed always with us. Many of them are on the edge of disaster all of the time. There is nothing sudden or dramatic about it. We believe our model has something to say about why the continuing desperate situation of these people appears *not* to move us, nor to lead to intervention in their plight. It can also suggest a few ways to increase the likelihood of intervention by the privileged sections of society to improve the lives of these people.

Essentially, most of the privileged are physically and emotionally separated from those who exist in chronic crisis. One cannot be aroused by the distress of others without being exposed to it. Furthermore, the model suggests that it is the rapid change in a person's state, coupled with the need for rapid action if the condition is not to worsen, that leads to the defense reaction that energizes intervention under high cost. A chronic state of deprivation simply does not trigger this kind of response. Furthermore, the perceived costs of attenuating the suffering of all of the disadvantaged in this country (not to mention those around the world) is clearly staggering. Thus the preferred response is likely to be derogation, or "blaming the victim" as Ryan (1971) has so aptly called it, so as to redefine the situation as one of low costs for the victim receiving no help. As the United States Commission on Civil Rights described the problem, specifically in relationship to whites' attitudes toward blacks:

> Many whites, especially those living in suburbs, are almost completely isolated from any direct contacts with life in . . . minority group areas. Hence they fail to perceive the compelling *need* for further remedial action there. Moreover, they do not understand how institutional subordination works. Therefore, these whites think the plight of ghetto dwellers is largely *their own fault*, rather than largely the product of racism expressed by institutions controlled by whites [1970, p. 39].

With regard to all of our disadvantaged groups, this tendency is facilitated by categorizing them as "they" rather than "we" so as to avoid the identification that underlies true empathy.

If this is the case, how can we change the perception of the situation of society's disadvantaged so that it more nearly approximates the circumstances under which emergency intervention seems to occur? There are several policy alternatives, most of which have been both suggested and strongly resisted at other times by other people. For example, if some degree of arousal in the "bystander" (i.e., middle-class, middle-aged, relatively affluent, able-bodied white) is necessary for the problem to be addressed, the first step in a solution is to break down the physical isolation of the majority from the disadvantaged groups. This could involve mixing low- or no-income families with higher-income families, preferably in close proximity such as multilevel-income housing constructed in suburbs. Similarly, "old-age ghettos" such as retirement communities (not really a problem as such since their residents are affluent) and nursing homes should not be tucked away where we cannot see them. More critically, incentives should be given to keep elderly family members at or near their relatives as long as possible. Steps have already been taken by the newly militant handicapped minority to obtain decent housing that allows them to move about the community, for handicapped access to public buildings, and for "mainstreaming" in public schools. Halfway houses for the mentally ill and for ex-convicts and delinquents, again, should not be placed in the "bad" parts of town to hide these people from the rest of us, but should be set in middle-class areas where we can help rather than ignore and derogate them. These attempts can lead both to greater arousal in regard to the distress of the members of all of these groups and to more perception of "we-ness" of us and them.

Another attempt to increase awareness and arousal in response to the plight of the needy could be made through massive media campaigns stressing the personal suffering of clearly blameless individual poor, handicapped, elderly, etc., in prime time. Simultaneously, attempts could be made to combat derogation as the easiest response to the perception of the high cost of helping. In this regard, some public education regarding the "fundamental attribution error" (Jones & Nisbett, 1971; Ross, 1977) would be in order. What is truly needed is a reeducation of the "Protestant-ethic-oriented" middle class to the fact that behavior occurs in an environmental structure, not in a self-determined world, and that there are circumstances under which internal motivations are *not* the major causal factor in the determination of action. A school curriculum emphasizing attributional mechanisms in regard to both victimization and racial and ethnic stereotyping would clearly also be in order.

Finally, since a major problem is the—quite accurately—perceived costs of providing alleviation of the plight of the poor and other disadvantaged groups, the low cost of helping *relative to other responses* should be promulgated through our education and mass media systems. That is, the long-term costs of riots, the costs of individuals who become dependent and criminal through denial of opportunity, and the other effects of ignoring and refusing to alleviate the plight of society's victims should be made explicit. Furthermore, legislation and programs should immediately be developed that, "simultaneously provide benefits for significant parts of the

. . . majority and for deprived or other members of . . . minority groups, so it will be in the immediate self-interest of the former to support programs which aid the latter [United States Commission on Civil Rights, 1970, p. 29]." We are aware that all of the foregoing constitutes a highly idealistic set of suggestions, which would be politically impossible to implement. That fact alone, however, has never been a very good reason for failing to suggest a course of action.

References

Abelson, R. P. Computer simulation of 'hot' cognition. In S. Tomkins & S. Messick (Eds.), *Computer simulation of personality*. New York: John Wiley & Sons, 1963.

Aderman, D. Elation, depression, and helping behavior. *Journal of Personality and Social Psychology*, 1972, *24*, 91–101.

Aderman, D., & Berkowitz, L. Observational set, empathy, and helping. *Journal of Personality and Social Psychology*, 1970, *14*, 141–148.

Akiskal, H. S., & McKinney, W. T., Jr. Depressive disorders: Toward a unified hypothesis. *Science*, 1973, *182*, 20–29.

Alfert, E. Comparison of responses to a vicarious and a direct threat. *Journal of Experimental Research in Personality*, 1966, *1*, 179–186.

Altman, D., Levine, M., Nadien, M., & Villena, J. Unpublished paper, Graduate Center, The City University of New York. Referred to in S. Milgram, The experience of living in cities. *Science*, 1970, *167*, 1461–1468.

Anderson, J. Bystander intervention in an assault. Paper presented at the meeting of the Southeastern Psychological Association, Hollywood, Fla., May 3, 1974.

Aronfreed, J. The socialization of altruistic and sympathetic behavior: Some theoretical and experimental analyses. In J. Macaulay & L. Berkowitz (Eds.), *Altruism and helping behavior*. New York: Academic Press, 1970.

Aronfreed, J., & Paskal, V. The development of sympathetic behavior in children: An experimental test of a two-phase hypothesis. Unpublished manuscript, University of Pennsylvania, 1966.

Aronoff, J. Psychological needs as a determinant in the formation of economic structures: A confirmation. *Human Relations*, 1970, *23*, 123–138.

Ashton, N. L., & Severy, L. J. Arousal and costs in bystander intervention. *Personality and Social Psychology Bulletin*, 1976, *2*, 268–272.

261

Austin, W. Sex differences in bystander intervention in a theft. *Journal of Personality and Social Psychology*, 1979, *37*, 2110–2120.

Baer, R., Goldman, M., & Juhnke, R. Factors affecting prosocial behavior. *Journal of Social Psychology*, 1977, *103*, 209–216.

Baker, L. D., & Reitz, J. Altruism toward the blind: Effects of sex of helper and dependency of victim. *Journal of Social Psychology*, 1978, *104*, 19–28.

Bandura, A. Self-efficacy: Toward a unifying theory of behavioral change. *Psychological Review*, 1977, *84*, 191–215.

Bandura, A., & Rosenthal, T. L. Vicarious classical conditioning as a function of arousal level. *Journal of Personality and Social Psychology*, 1966, *3*, 54–62.

Barash, D. P. *Sociobiology and behavior*. New York: Elsevier Scientific Publishing Co., 1977.

Baron, R. A. Effects of magnitude of model's apparent pain on observer reaction time. *Psychonomic Science*, 1970, *20*, 229–231.(a)

Baron, R. A. Magnitude of model's apparent pain and ability to aid the model as determinants of observer reaction time. *Psychonomic Science*, 1970, *21*, 196–197. (b)

Baron, R. A. Behavioral effects of interpersonal attraction: Compliance with requests from liked and disliked others. *Psychonomic Science*, 1971, *25*, 325–326.

Barton, A. H. *Communities in disaster: A sociological analysis of collective stress situations*. Garden City, N. Y.: Doubleday, 1969.

Batson, C. D., Cochran, P. J., Biederman, M. F., Blosser, J. L., Ryan, M. J., & Vogt, B. Failure to help when in a hurry: Callousness or conflict? *Personality and Social Psychology Bulletin*, 1978, *4*, 97–101.

Batson, C. D., and Coke, J. S. Empathy: A source of altruistic motivation for helping? In J. P. Rushton & R. M. Sorrentino (Eds.), *Altruism and helping behavior*. Hillsdale, N.J.: Erlbaum Associates, in press.

Batson, C. D., Harris, A. C., McCaul, K. D., Davis, M., & Schmidt, T. Compassion or compliance: Alternative dispositional attributions for one's helping behavior. *Social Psychology Quarterly*, 1979, *42*, 405–409.

Batson, C. D., Pate, S., Lawless, H., Sparkman, P., Lambers, S., & Worman, B. Helping under conditions of threat: Increased 'we-feeling' or ensuring reciprocity? *Social Psychology Quarterly*, 1979, *42*, 410–414.

Beck, A. T. *Depression*. New York: Harper & Row, 1967.

Becker-Haven, J. F., & Lindskold, S. Deindividuation manipulations, self-consciousness, and bystander intervention. *Journal of Social Psychology*, 1978, *105*, 113–121.

Bem, D. J., & Allen, A. On predicting some of the people some of the time: The search for cross-situational consistencies in behavior. *Psychological Review*, 1974, *81*, 506–520.

Benjamin, L. S. Statistical treatment of the law of initial values (LIV) in autonomic research: A review and recommendation. *Psychosomatic Medicine*, 1963, *25*, 556–566.

Benson, P. L. Social feedback, self-esteem state, and prosocial behavior. *Representative Research in Social Psychology*, 1978, *9*, 43–56.

Benson, P. L., Karabenick, S. A., & Lerner, R. M. Pretty pleases: The effects of physical attractiveness, race, and sex on receiving help. *Journal of Experimental Social Psychology*, 1976, *12*, 409–415.

Berger, S. M. Conditioning through vicarious instigation. *Psychological Review*, 1962, *69*, 450–466.

Berkowitz, L. Social norms, feelings, and other factors affecting helping behavior and altruism. In L. Berkowitz (Ed.), *Advances in experimental social psychology* (Vol. 6). New York: Academic Press, 1972.

Berkowitz, L. Mood, self-awareness, and helpfulness. Paper presented at the International

Conference on the Development and Maintenance of Prosocial Behavior, Warsaw, Poland, June 29 to July 3, 1980.

Berkowitz, L., & Connor, W. H. Success, failure, and social responsibility. *Journal of Personality and Social Psychology*, 1966, 4, 664–669.

Berkowitz, L., & Daniels, L. R. Responsibility and dependency. *Journal of Abnormal and Social Behavior*, 1963, 66, 429–436.

Berkowitz, L., & Daniels, L. R. Affecting the salience of the social responsibility norm: Effects of past help on the responses to dependency relationships. *Journal of Abnormal and Social Psychology*, 1964, 68, 275–281.

Berkowitz, L., & Friedman, P. Some social class differences in helping behavior. *Journal of Personality and Social Psychology*, 1967, 5, 217–225.

Berkun, M. M., Bialek, H. M., Kern, R. P., & Yagi, K. Experimental studies of psychological stress in man. *Psychological Monographs*, 1962, 76 (15, Whole No. 534), 1–39.

Berlyne, D. E. Attention as a problem in behavior theory. In D. I. Mostofsky (Ed.), *Attention: Contemporary theory and analysis*. New York: Appleton-Century-Crofts, 1970.

Bickman, L. The effect of another bystander's ability to help on bystander intervention in an emergency. *Journal of Experimental Social Psychology*, 1971, 7, 367–379.

Bickman, L. Social influence and diffusion of responsibility in an emergency. *Journal of Experimental Social Psychology*, 1972, 8, 438–445.

Bickman, L. Sex and helping behavior. *Journal of Social Psychology*, 1974, 93, 43–53.

Bickman, L. Attitude toward an authority and the reporting of a crime. *Sociometry*, 1976, 39, 76–82.

Bickman, L., & Kamzan, M. The effect of race and need on helping behavior. *Journal of Social Psychology*, 1973, 89, 73–77.

Bickman, L., & Rosenbaum, D. P. Crime reporting as a function of bystander encouragement, surveillance, and credibility. *Journal of Personality and Social Psychology*, 1977, 35, 577–586.

Bickman, L., Teger, A., Gabriele, T., McLaughlin, C., Berger, M., & Sunaday, E. Dormitory density and helping behavior. *Environment and Behavior*, 1973, 5, 465–490.

Billig, M., & Tajfel, H. Social categorization and similarity in intergroup behavior. *European Journal of Social Psychology*, 1973, 3, 27–52.

Bleda, P. R., Bleda, S. T., Byrne, D., & White, L. A. When a bystander becomes an accomplice: Situational determinants of reaction to dishonesty. *Journal of Experimental Social Psychology*, 1976, 12, 9–25.

Block, J. *Lives through time*. Berkeley, Cal.: Bancroft Books, 1971.

Bloom, L. M., & Clark, R. D., III. The cost–reward model of helping behavior: A nonconfirmation. *Journal of Applied Social Psychology*, 1976, 6, 76–84.

Bonnarigo, P., & Ross, M. The case of the stolen beer. Study reported in B. Latané and J. M. Darley, *The Unresponsive Bystander: Why Doesn't He Help?* New York: Appleton-Century-Crofts, 1970.

Borges, M. A., & Penta, J. M. Effects of third party intercession on bystander intervention. *Journal of Social Psychology*, 1977, 103, 27–32.

Borofsky, G., Stollak, G., & Messé, L. Bystander reactions to physical assault: Sex differences in socially responsible behavior. *Journal of Experimental Social Psychology*, 1971, 7, 313–318.

Brewer, M. B. In-group bias in the minimal intergroup situation: A cognitive–motivational analysis. *Psychological Bulletin*, 1979, 86, 307–324.

Briar, S., & Piliavin, I. Delinquency, situational inducements, and commitment to conformity. *Social Problems*, 1965, 13 (1), 35–45.

Broadbent, D. E. *Decision and stress.* New York: Academic Press, 1971.

Broadbent, D. E. The hidden preattentive processes. *American Psychologist,* 1977, *32,* 109–118.

Brock, T. C., & Becker, L. A. "Debriefing" and susceptibility to subsequent experimental manipulations. *Journal of Experimental Social Psychology,* 1966, *2,* 314–323.

Bryan, J. H. Children's reactions to helpers: Their money isn't where their mouths are. In J. Macaulay & L. Berkowitz (Eds.), *Altruism and helping behavior.* New York: Academic Press, 1970.

Bryan, J. H., & Test, M. J. Models and helping: Naturalistic studies in aiding behavior. *Journal of Personality and Social Psychology,* 1967, *6,* 400–407.

Bryan, J. H., & Walbek, N. The impact of words and deeds concerning altruism upon children. *Child Development,* 1970, *41,* 329–353.

Byeff, P. Helping behavior in audio and audio–video conditions. Senior honors thesis, University of Pennsylvania, 1970.

Byrne, D. *The attraction paradigm.* New York: Academic Press, 1971.

Campbell, D. T. Ethnocentric and other altruistic motives. In D. Levine (Ed.), *Nebraska Symposium on Motivation.* Lincoln: University of Nebraska Press, 1965.

Campbell, D. T. On the genetics of altruism and the counter-hedonic components in human culture. *Journal of Social Issues,* 1972, *28,* 21–38.

Campbell, D. T. On the genetics of altruism and the counterhedonic components in human culture. In L. Wispé (Ed.), *Altruism, sympathy, and helping.* New York: Academic Press, 1978. Pp. 39–58.

Campbell, D. T., & Levine, R. A. *Ethnocentrism.* New York: John Wiley & Sons, 1972.

Carlsmith, J. M., Ellsworth, P., & Whiteside, J. Guilt, confession and compliance. Unpublished manuscript, Stanford University, 1969.

Carlsmith, J. M., & Gross, A. E. Some effects of guilt on compliance. *Journal of Personality and Social Psychology,* 1969, *11,* 232–239.

Carver, C. S., & Blaney, P. H. Perceived arousal, focus of attention, and avoidance behavior. *Journal of Abnormal Psychology,* 1977, *86,* 154–162.

Carver, C. S., Blaney, P. H., & Scheier, M. F. Reassertion and giving up: The interactive role of self-directed attention and outcome expectancy. *Journal of Personality and Social Psychology,* 1979, *37,* 1859–1870.

Cattell, R. B., & Horowitz, J. Z. Objective personality tests investigating the structure of altruism in relation to source traits, A, H, and L. *Journal of Personality,* 1952, *21,* 103–117.

Chaikin, A. L., & Darley, J. M. Victim or perpetrator?: Defensive attribution of responsibility and the need for order and justice. *Journal of Personality and Social Psychology,* 1973, *25,* 268–275.

Cialdini, R. B., Darby, B. L., & Vincent, J. E. Transgression and altruism: A case for hedonism. *Journal of Experimental Social Psychology,* 1973, *9,* 502–516.

Cialdini, R. B., & Kenrick, D. T. Altruism as hedonism: A social development perspective on the relationship of negative mood state and helping. *Journal of Personality and Social Psychology,* 1976, *34,* 907–914.

Clark, R. D., III. Effects of sex and race on helping behavior in a nonreactive setting. *Representative Research in Social Psychology,* 1974, *5,* 1–6.

Clark, R. D., III. On the Piliavin and Piliavin model of helping behavior: Costs are in the eye of the beholder. *Journal of Applied Social Psychology,* 1976, *6,* 322–328.

Clark, R. D., III, & Word, L. E. Why don't bystanders help? Because of ambiguity? *Journal of Personality and Social Psychology,* 1972, *24,* 392–400.

Clark, R. D., III, & Word, L. E. Where is the apathetic bystander? Situational characteristics of the emergency. *Journal of Personality and Social Psychology,* 1974, *29,* 279–287.

Cohen, D. H., & MacDonald, R. L. A selective review of central neural pathways involved in cardio-vascular control. In P. A. Obrist, A. H. Black, J. Brener, & L. V. DiCara (Eds.), *Cardiovascular psychophysiology*. Chicago: Aldine, 1974.

Coke, J. S., Batson, C. D., & McDavis, K. Empathic mediation of helping: A two-stage model. *Journal of Personality and Social Psychology*, 1978, *36*, 752–766.

Collins, B. E. *Social psychology*. Reading, Mass.: Addison-Wesley, 1970.

Cornsweet, D. M. Uses of cues in the visual periphery under conditions of arousal. *Journal of Experimental Psychology*, 1969, *80*, 14–18.

Craig, K. D. Physiological arousal as a function of imagined, vicarious, and direct stress experiences. *Journal of Abnormal Psychology*, 1968, *73*, 513–520.

Craig, K. D., & Lowery, H. J. Heart-rate components of conditioned vicarious autonomic responses. *Journal of Personality and Social Psychology*, 1969, *11*, 381–387.

Craig, K. D., & Weinstein, M. S. Conditioning vicarious affective arousal. *Psychological Reports*, 1965, *17*, 955–963.

Craig, K. D., & Wood, K. Physiological differentiation of direct and vicarious affective arousal. *Canadian Journal of Behavioral Science*, 1969, *1*, 98–105.

Crandall, J. E. Effects of threat and failure on concern for others. *Journal of Research in Personality*, 1978, *12*, 350–360.

Crandall, V. C., Crandall, V. J., & Katkovsky, W. A children's social desirability questionnaire. *Journal of Consulting Psychology*, 1965, *29*, 27–36.

Cunningham, M. R. Weather, mood, and helping behavior: Quasi experiments with the sunshine Samaritan. *Journal of Personality and Social Psychology*, 1979, *37*, 1947–1956.

Cunningham, M. R., Steinberg, J., Greu, R. Wanting to and having to help: Separate motivations for positive mood and guilt-induced helping. *Journal of Personality and Social Psychology*, 1980, *38*, 181–192.

Daniels, L. R., & Berkowitz, L. Liking and response to dependency relationships. *Human Relations*, 1963, *16*, 141–148.

Darley, J. M., & Batson, C. D. From Jerusalem to Jericho: A study of situational and dispositional variables in helping behavior. *Journal of Personality and Social Psychology*, 1973, *27*, 100–108.

Darley, J. M., & Latané, B. Bystander intervention in emergencies: Diffusion of responsibility. *Journal of Personality and Social Psychology*, 1968, *8*, 377–383.

Darley, J. M., Teger, A. I., & Lewis, L. D. Do groups always inhibit individuals' responses to potential emergencies? *Journal of Personality and Social Psychology*, 1973, *26*, 395–399.

Darlington, R. B., & Macker, C. E. Displacement of guilt-produced altruistic behavior. *Journal of Personality and Social Psychology*, 1966, *4*, 442–443.

Deaux, K. *The behavior of women and men*. Monterey, Calif.: Brooks-Cole, 1976.

Denner, B. Did a crime occur? Should I inform anyone? A study of deception. *Journal of Personality*, 1968, *36*, 454–465.

Derlega, V. J. Social psychology in Poland. *Personality and Social Psychology Bulletin*, 1978, *4*, 631–637.

Deutsch, M., & Gerard, H. A study of normative and informational social influence upon individual judgment. *Journal of Abnormal and Social Psychology*, 1955, *51*, 629–636.

DiLollo, V., & Berger, S. M. Effects of apparent pain in others on observer's reaction time. *Journal of Personality and Social Psychology*, 1965, *2*, 573–575.

Dion, K. L. Cohesiveness as a determinant of ingroup–outgroup bias. *Journal of Personality and Social Psychology*, 1973, *28*, 163–171.

Donnerstein, E., Donnerstein, M., & Evans, R. Erotic stimuli and aggression: Facilitation or inhibition? *Journal of Personality and Social Psychology*, 1975, *32*, 237–244.

Donnerstein, E., Donnerstein, M., & Munger, G. Helping behavior as a function of pictorially induced moods. *Journal of Social Psychology,* 1975, *97,* 221–225.

Dovidio, J. F. Costs, anticipated costs, and sex differences in helping. Unpublished manuscript, Colgate University, 1979.

Dovidio, J. F., Campbell, J. C., Rigaud, S., Yankura, J., Rominger, L., & Pine, R. Androgyny, sex-roles, and helping. Unpublished manuscript, Colgate University, 1978.

Dovidio, J. F., & Morris, W. N. Effects of stress and commonality of fate on helping behavior. *Journal of Personality and Social Psychology,* 1975, *31* (1), 145–149.

Dutton, D. G. Reactions of restauranteurs to blacks and whites violating restaurant dress requirements. *Canadian Journal of Behavioral Science,* 1971, *3,* 298–302.

Dutton, D. G. Reverse discrimination: The relationship of amount of perceived discrimination toward a minority group on the behaviour of majority group members. *Canadian Journal of Behavioral Science,* 1973, *5,* 34–45.

Dutton, D. G., & Lake, R. A. Threat of own prejudice and reverse discrimination in interracial situations. *Journal of Personality and Social Psychology,* 1973, *28,* 94–100.

Dutton, D. G., & Lennox, V. L. Effect of prior "token" compliance on subsequent interracial behavior. *Journal of Personality and Social Psychology,* 1974, *29,* 65–71.

Duval, S., Duval, V. H., & Neely, R. Self-focus, felt responsibility, and helping behavior. *Journal of Personality and Social Psychology,* 1979, *37,* 1769–1778.

Duval, S., & Wicklund, R. A. *A theory of objective self-awareness.* New York: Academic Press, 1972.

Easterbrook, J. A. The effect of emotion on cue utilization and the organization of behavior. *Psychological Review,* 1959, *66,* 183–201.

Edelberg, R. Electrical properties of the skin. In C. C. Brown (Ed.), *Methods in psychophysiology.* Baltimore: Williams & Wilkins, 1967.

Ehlert, J., Ehlert, N., & Merrens, M. The influence of ideological affiliation on helping behavior. *Journal of Social Psychology,* 1973, *89,* 315–316.

Eisenberg-Berg, N. The relationship of preschoolers' reasoning about prosocial moral conflicts to prosocial behavior. *Child Development,* 1979, *50,* 356–363.

Emswiller, T., Deaux, K., & Willits, J. E. Similarity, sex, and requests for small favors. *Journal of Applied Social Psychology,* 1971, *1,* 284–291.

Enzle, M. E., & Harvey, M. D. Effects of a third-party requestor's surveillance and recipient awareness of request on helping. *Personality and Social Psychology Bulletin,* 1977, *3,* 421–424.

Enzle, M. E., & Harvey, M. D. Recipient mood states and helping behavior. *Journal of Experimental Social Psychology,* 1979, *15,* 170–182.

Epstein, Y. M., & Hornstein, H. A. Penalty and interpersonal attraction as factors influencing the decision to help another person. *Journal of Experimental Social Psychology,* 1969, *5,* 272–282.

Eysenck, M. V. *Human memory: Theory, research, and individual differences.* Oxford: Pergamon Press, 1977.

Farra, J. D., Zinser, O., & Bailey, R. C. Effects of I-E of donor and race and locus of cause of failure of recipient on helping behavior. *Journal of Social Psychology,* 1978, *106,* 73–81.

Feinman, S. Effects of city size, sex and appearance of stranger, and sex of subject on altruism. Unpublished study, 1977.

Feldman, R. H. L., & Rezmovic, V. A field study on the relationship of environmental factors to helping behavior. *Journal of Social Psychology,* 1979, *108,* 283–284.

Field, M. Power and dependency: Legitimation of dependency conditions. *Journal of Social Psychology,* 1974, *92,* 31–37.

Firestone, I. J., Lichtman, C. M., & Colamosca, J. V. Leader effectiveness and leadership conferral as determinants of helping in a medical emergency. *Journal of Personality and Social Psychology*, 1975, *31* (2), 343–348.

Forbes, G. B., & Gromoll, H. F. The lost-letter technique as a measure of social variables: Some exploratory findings. *Social Forces*, 1971, *50*, 113–115.

Form, W. H., & Nosow, S. *Community in disaster*. New York: Harper, 1958.

Franklin, B. J. Victim characteristics and helping behavior in a rural southern setting. *Journal of Social Psychology*, 1974, *93*, 93–100.

Freedman, J. C., Wallington, S. A., & Bless, E. Compliance without pressure: The effect of guilt. *Journal of Personality and Social Psychology*, 1967, *7*, 117–124.

Friedrichs, R. W. Alter versus ego: An exploratory assessment of altruism. *American Sociological Review*, 1960, *25*, 496–508.

Gaertner, S. L. Helping behavior and racial discrimination among liberals and conservatives. *Journal of Personality and Social Psychology*, 1973, *25*, 335–341.

Gaertner, S. L. The role of racial attitudes in helping behavior. *Journal of Social Psychology*, 1975, *97*, 95–101.

Gaertner, S. L. Nonreactive measures in racial attitudes research: A focus on "liberals." In P. A. Katz (Ed.), *Towards the elimination of racism*. New York: Pergamon Press, 1976.

Gaertner, S. L., & Bickman, L. Effects of race on the elicitation of helping behavior: The wrong number technique. *Journal of Personality and Social Psychology*, 1971, *20*, 218–222.

Gaertner, S. L., & Dovidio, J. F. The subtlety of white racism, arousal, and helping behavior. *Journal of Personality and Social Psychology*, 1977, *35*, 691–707.

Gaertner, S. L., Dovidio, J. F., & Johnson, G. Race of victim, non-responsive bystanders, and helping behavior. Paper presented at the 87th Annual Convention of the American Psychological Association, New York, 1979. (a)

Gaertner, S. L., Dovidio, J. F., & Johnson, G. The subtlety of white racism: The effects of the race of prevailing authority, opportunity for diffusion of responsibility, and race of victim on helping behavior. Unpublished data, University of Delaware, 1979. (b)

Geer, J. H., & Jarmecky, L. The effect of being responsible for reducing another's pain on subjects' response and arousal. *Journal of Personality and Social Psychology*, 1973, *26*, 232–237.

Gelles, R. J. *The violent home: A study of physical aggression between husbands and wives*. Beverly Hills: Sage, 1972.

Gergen, K., Ellsworth, P., Maslach, C., & Seipel, M. Obligation, donor resources, and reactions to aid in three cultures. *Journal of Personality and Social Psychology*, 1975, *31*, 390–400.

Gergen, K. J., Gergen, M. M., & Meter, K. Individual orientations to prosocial behavior. *Journal of Social Issues*, 1972, *8*, 105–130.

Goffman, E. *Stigma: Notes on the management of spoiled identity*. Englewood Cliffs, N. J.: Prentice-Hall, 1963.

Goodstadt, M. S. Helping and refusal to help: A test of balance and reactance theories. *Journal of Experimental Social Psychology*, 1971, *7* (6), 610–622.

Goranson, R., & Berkowitz, L. Reciprocity and responsibility reactions to prior help. *Journal of Personality and Social Psychology*, 1966, *3*, 227–232.

Gottlieb, J., & Carver, C. S. Anticipation of future interaction and the bystander effect. *Journal of Experimental Social Psychology*, 1980, *16*, 253–260.

Gouldner, A. The norm of reciprocity: A preliminary statement. *American Sociological Review*, 1960, *25*, 161–178.

Graf, R. G. Induced self-esteem as a determinant of behavior. *Journal of Social Psychology*, 1971, *85*, 213–217.

Graf, R. G., & Riddell, J. C. Helping behavior as a function of interpersonal perception. *Journal of Social Psychology*, 1972, *86*, 227–231.

Graham, F. K., & Clifton, R. K. Heart-rate change as a component of the orienting response. *Psychological Bulletin*, 1966, *65*, 305–320.

Gramza, A. F. Responses of brooding nighthawks to a disturbance stimulus. *Auk*, 1967, *84* (1), 72–86.

Greenwald, A. Does the Good Samaritan parable increase helping? A comment on Darley and Batson's no effect conclusion. *Journal of Personality and Social Psychology*, 1975, *32*, 578–583.

Gross, A. E., Wallston, B. S., & Piliavin, I. M. Beneficiary attractiveness and cost as determinants of responses to routine requests for help. *Sociometry*, 1975, *38*, 131–140.

Gruder, C. L., & Cook, T. D. Sex, dependency, and helping. *Journal of Personality and Social Psychology*, 1971, *19*, 290–294.

Hackler, J. C., Ho, K. Y., & Urquhart-Ross, C. The willingness to intervene: Differing community characteristics. *Social Problems*, 1974, *21*, 328–344.

Haner, C. F., & Whitney, E. R. Empathic conditioning and its relation to anxiety level. *American Psychologist*, 1960, *15*, 493. (Abstract)

Harris, M. B. Effects of altruism on mood. *Journal of Social Psychology*, 1977, *102*, 197–208.

Harris, M. B., & Baudin, H. The language of altruism: The effects of language, dress, and ethnic group. *Journal of Social Psychology*, 1973, *91*, 37–41.

Harris, M. B., Benson, S. M., & Hall, C. L. The effects of confession on altruism. *Journal of Social Psychology*, 1975, *96*, 187–192.

Harris, M. B., & Huang, L. C. Competence and helping. *Journal of Social Psychology*, 1973, *89*, 203–210. (a)

Harris, M. B., & Huang, L. C. Helping and the attribution process. *Journal of Social Psychology*, 1973, *90*, 291–297. (b)

Harris, M. B., & Meyer, F. W. Dependency, threat, and helping. *Journal of Social Psychology*, 1973, *90*, 239–242.

Hatfield, E., Walster, G. W., & Piliavin, J. A. Equity theory and helping relationships. In L. Wispé (Ed.), *Altruism, sympathy, and helping: Psychological and sociological principles.* New York: Academic Press, 1978.

Heberlein, T. A. Moral norms, threatened sanctions and littering behavior. Unpublished doctoral dissertation, University of Wisconsin, 1971.

Heberlein, T. A. H. Conservation information, the energy crisis and electricity consumption in an apartment complex. *Energy Systems and Policy*, 1975, *1* (2), 105–117.

Heberlein, T. A., & Black, J. S. Attitudinal specificity and the prediction of behavior in a field setting. *Journal of Personality and Social Psychology*, 1976, *33*, 474–479.

Heilman, M. E., Hodgson, S. A., & Hornstein, H. A. Effects of magnitude and rectifiability of harm and information value on the reporting of accidental harm-doing. *Journal of Personality and Social Psychology*, 1972, *23*, 211–218.

Hertzog, R. L., & Hertzog, D. J. Ingratiation as a mediating factor in intersex helping behavior. *Journal of Social Psychology*, 1979, *108*, 281–282.

Hockey, G. R. J. Signal probability and spacial location as possible basis for increased selectivity in noise. *Quarterly Journal of Experimental Psychology*, 1970, *22*, 37–42.

Hockey, G. R. J. Changes in information-selection patterns in multisource monitoring as a function of induced arousal shifts. *Journal of Experimental Psychology*, 1973, *101*, 35–42.

Hodgson, S. A., Hornstein, H. A., & LaKind, E. Socially mediated Ziegarnik effects as a function of sentiment, valence, and desire for goal attainment. *Journal of Experimental Social Psychology*, 1972, *8*, 446–456.

Hoffman, M. L. Empathy, role taking, guilt, and development of altruistic motives. In T. Lickona (Ed.), *Moral development and behavior.* New York: Holt, Rinehart & Winston, 1976.

Hoffman, M. L. Sex differences in empathy and related behaviors. *Psychological Bulletin,* 1977, *84,* 712–720. (a)

Hoffman, M. L. A three component model of empathy. Paper presented at the meeting of the Society for Research in Child Development, New Orleans, La., 1977. (b)

Holloway, S., Tucker, L., & Hornstein, H. A. The effects of social and nonsocial information on interpersonal behavior of males: The news makes news. *Journal of Personality and Social Psychology,* 1977, *35,* 514–522.

Hornstein, H. A. Promotive tension: The basis of prosocial behavior from a Lewinian perspective. *Journal of Social Issues,* 1972, *28,* 191–218.

Hornstein, H. A. *Cruelty and kindness: A new look at aggression and altruism.* Englewood Cliffs, N. J.: Prentice-Hall, 1976.

Hornstein, H. A. Promotive tension and prosocial behavior: A Lewinian analysis. In L. Wispé (Ed.), *Altruism, sympathy, and helping: Psychological and sociological principles.* New York: Academic Press, 1978.

Hornstein, H. A., LaKind, E., Frankel, G., & Manne, S. Effects of knowledge about remote social events on prosocial behavior, social conception, and mood. *Journal of Personality and Social Psychology,* 1975, *32,* 1038–1046.

Hornstein, H. A., Masor, H. N., Sole, K., & Heilman, M. Effects of sentiment and completion of a helping act on observer helping: A case for socially mediated Ziegarnik effects. *Journal of Personality and Social Psychology,* 1971, *17,* 107–112.

Horowitz, I. A. The effect of group norms on bystander intervention. *Journal of Social Psychology,* 1971, *83,* 265–273.

Horowitz, I. A. Effects of experimentally manipulated levels of moral development and potential helper's identifiability on volunteering to help. *Journal of Psychology,* 1976, *44,* 243–259.

House, J. S., & Wolf, S. Effects of urban residence on interpersonal trust and helping behavior. *Journal of Personality and Social Psychology,* 1978, *36,* 1029–1043.

Howard, W., & Crano, W. D. Effects of sex, conversation, location, and size of the observer group on bystander intervention in a high risk situation. *Sociometry,* 1974, *37,* 491–507.

Huston, T. L., Geis, G., & Wright, R. The angry Samaritans. *Psychology Today,* June, 1976, 61–64; 85.

Isen, A. M. Success, failure, attention, and reaction to others: The warm glow of success. *Journal of Personality and Social Psychology,* 1970, *15,* 294–301.

Isen, A. M., Clark, M., & Schwartz, M. Duration of the effect of good mood on helping: "Footprints on the sands of time." *Journal of Personality and Social Psychology,* 1976, *34,* 385–393.

Isen, A. M., Horn, N., & Rosenhan, D. L. Effects of success and failure on children's generosity. *Journal of Personality and Social Psychology,* 1973, *27,* 239–247.

Isen, A. M., & Levin, P. F. Effect of feeling good on helping: Cookies and kindness. *Journal of Personality and Social Psychology,* 1972, *21,* 384–388.

Isen, A. M., Shalker, T. E., Clark, M., & Karp, L. Affect, accessibility of material in memory, and behavior: A cognitive loop? *Journal of Personality and Social Psychology,* 1978, *36,* 1–12.

Isen, A. M., & Simonds, S. F. The effect of feeling good on a helping task that is incompatible with good mood. *Social Psychology,* 1978, *41,* 346–349.

Jacobs, J. *The death and life of great American cities.* New York: Random House, 1969.

Janis, I. L., & Mann, L. *Decision making.* New York: The Free Press, 1977.

Jiobu, R. M., & Knowles, E. S. Norm strength and alms-giving: An observational study. *Journal of Social Psychology,* 1974, *94,* 205–211.

Johnson, G., Gaertner, S. L., & Dovidio, J. F. *The subtlety of white racism: Differential susceptibility to conformity pressures to remain inactive during an emergency involving a black or white victim.* Technical Report to the Office of Naval Research, Organizational Effectiveness Research Program. Contract Number N00014–76–C–0062. 1978.

Johnson, R. W., & Dickinson, J. Class differences in derogation of an innocent victim. Unpublished manuscript, St. Francis Xavier University, 1971.

Jones, E. E., & Nisbett, R. E. The actor and the observer: Divergent perceptions of the causes of behavior. In E. E. Jones et al. (Eds.), *Attribution: Perceiving the causes of behavior.* Morristown, N. J.: General Learning Press, 1971.

Kagan, J., Rosman, B., Day, D., Albert, J., & Phillips, W. Information processing in the child: Significance of analytic and reflective attitudes. *Psychological Monographs,* 1964, *78* (1, Whole No. 578).

Kammann, R., Thomson, R., & Irwin, R. Unhelpful behavior in the street: City size or immediate pedestrian density? Paper presented at the 85th Annual American Psychological Association Convention, San Francisco, August, 1977.

Karabenick, S. A., Lerner, R. M., & Beecher, M. D. Relation of political affiliation to helping behavior on election day, November 7, 1972. *Journal of Social Psychology,* 1973, *91,* 223–227.

Karylowski, J. Self-esteem, similarity, liking, and helping. *Personality and Social Psychology Bulletin,* 1976, *2,* 71–74.

Karylowski, J. Explaining altruistic behavior: A review. *Polish Psychological Bulletin,* 1977, *8,* 27–34.

Katkin, E. S. The relationship between a measure of transitory anxiety and spontaneous autonomic activity. *Journal of Abnormal Psychology,* 1966, *71,* 142–146.

Katsev, R., Edelsack, L., Steinmeltz, G., Walker, T., & Wright, R. The effect of reprimanding transgressions on subsequent helping behavior: Two field experiments. *Personality and Social Psychology Bulletin,* 1978, *4,* 326–329.

Katz, I. Experimental studies of Negro-white relationships. In L. Berkowitz (Ed.), *Advances in experimental social psychology* (Vol. 5). New York: Academic Press, 1970.

Katz, I., Cohen, S., & Glass, D. Some determinants of cross-racial helping behavior. *Journal of Personality and Social Psychology,* 1975, *32,* 964–970.

Katz, I., Farber, J., Glass, D. C., Lucido, D., & Emswiller, T. When courtesy offends: Effects of positive and negative behavior by the physically disabled on altruism and anger in normals. *Journal of Personality,* 1978, *46,* 506–518.

Katz, I., Glass, D. C., & Cohen, S. Ambivalence, guilt, and the scapegoating of minority group victims. *Journal of Experimental Social Psychology,* 1973, *9,* 423–436.

Katz, I., Glass, D. C., Lucido, D., & Farber, J. Harm-doing and victim's racial or orthopedic stigma as determinants of helping behavior. *Journal of Personality,* 1979, *47,* 340–364.

Kazdin, A. E., & Bryan, J. H. Competence and volunteering. *Journal of Experimental Social Psychology,* 1971, *7,* 87–97.

Kenrick, D. T., Baumann, D. J., & Cialdini, R. B. A step in the socialization of altruism as hedonism: Effects of negative mood on children's generosity under public and private conditions. *Journal of Personality and Social Psychology,* 1979, *37,* 756–768.

Kessler, K. F. Cited in Kropotkin (p. 19), as "a lecture 'On the law of mutual aid.'" Delivered at a Russian Congress of Naturalists, Jan., 1880.

Kobasigawa, A. Observation of failure in another person as a determinant of amplitude and speed of a simple motor response. *Journal of Personality and Social Psychology*, 1965, *1*, 626–630.

Konečni, V. J. Some effects of guilt on compliance: A field replication. *Journal of Personality and Social Psychology*, 1972, *23*, 30–32.

Konečni, V. J., & Ebbesen, E. B. Effects of the presence of children on adults' helping behavior and compliance: Two field studies. *Journal of Social Psychology*, 1975, *97*, 181–193.

Konoske, P., Staple, S., & Graf, R. G. Compliant reactions to guilt: Self-esteem or self-punishment. *Journal of Social Psychology*, 1979, *108*, 207–211.

Korte, C. Groups effects on help-giving in an emergency. *Proceedings of the 77th Annual Convention of the American Psychological Association*, 1969, *4*, 383–384.

Korte, C., & Kerr, N. Response to altruistic opportunities in urban and nonurban settings. *Journal of Social Psychology*, 1975, *95*, 183–184.

Korte, C., Ypma, I., & Toppen, A. Helpfulness in Dutch society as a function of urbanization and environmental input level. *Journal of Personality and Social Psychology*, 1975, *32*, 996–1003.

Kovel, J. *White racism: A psychohistory*. New York: Baron, 1969.

Krebs, D. L. Altruism—an examination of the concept and a review of the literature. *Psychological Bulletin*, 1970, *73*, 258–302.

Krebs, D. Empathy and altruism. *Journal of Personality and Social Psychology*, 1975, *32*, 1134–1146.

Kropotkin, P. *Mutual aid*. London: Allen Lane, Penguin Press, 1972 (1902, 1914).

Krupat, E., & Coury, M. The lost letter technique and helping: An urban–nonurban comparison. Paper presented at the 83rd Annual Convention of the American Psychological Association, Chicago, September, 1975.

Kuhn, T. S. *The structure of scientific revolutions*. (2nd Ed.). Chicago: University of Chicago Press, 1970.

Lacey, J. I. Somatic response patterning and stress. In M. H. Appley & R. Trumbull (Eds.), *Psychological stress: Issues in research*. New York: Appleton-Century-Crofts, 1967.

Lacey, J. I., & Lacey, B. C. Some autonomic–central nervous system interrelationships. In P. Black (Ed.), *Physiological correlates of emotion*. New York: Academic Press, 1970.

Lacey, J. I., & Lacey, B. C. Experimental association and dissociation of phasic bradycardia and vertex-negative waves: A psychophysiological study of attention and response-intention. In W. C. McCallem & J. R. Knott (Eds.), *Event-related slow potentials in the brain*. New York: Elsevier, 1973.

Lang, P. J. The application of psychophysiological methods to the study of psychotherapy and behavior modification. In A. E. Bergin & S. L. Garfield (Eds.), *Handbook of psychotherapy and behavior change*. New York: John Wiley & Sons, 1971.

Langer, E. J., & Abelson, R. P. The semantics of asking a favor: How to succeed in getting help without really dying. *Journal of Personality and Social Psychology*, 1972, *24*, 26–32.

Lanzetta, J. T. Group behavior under stress. *Human Relations*, 1955, *8*, 29–52.

Latané, B., & Dabbs, J. M., Jr., Sex, group size and helping in three cities. *Sociometry*, 1975, *38*, 180–194.

Latané, B., & Darley, J. M. *The unresponsive bystander: Why doesn't he help?* New York: Appleton-Century-Crofts, 1970.

Latané, B., & Darley, J. M. *Help in a crisis: Bystander response to an emergency*. Morristown, N.J.: General Learning Press, 1976.

Latané, B., & Elman, D. The hand in the till. Study reported in B. Latané and J. M. Darley, *The unresponsive bystander: Why doesn't he help?* New York: Appleton-Century-Crofts, 1970.

Latané, B., & Rodin, J. A lady in distress: Inhibiting effects of friends and strangers on by-stander intervention. *Journal of Experimental Social Psychology*, 1969, 5, 189–202.

Lazarus, R. S. *Psychological stress and the coping process*. New York: McGraw-Hill Book Co., 1966.

Lazarus, R. S. Emotions and adaptation: Conceptual and empirical relations. In W. J. Arnold (Ed.), *Nebraska Symposium on Motivation* (Vol. 16). Lincoln: University of Nebraska, Press, 1968.

Lazarus, R. S., Opton, E. M., Jr., Nomikos, M. S., & Rankin, N. O. The principle of short-circuiting of threat: Further evidence. *Journal of Personality*, 1965, 33, 622–635.

Lazarus, R. S., Speisman, J. C., Mordkoff, A. M., & Davison, L. A. A laboratory study of psychological stress produced by a motion picture film. *Psychological Monographs*, 1962, 76 (34, Whole No. 553), 1–31.

Lerner, M. J. Desire for justice and reactions to victims. In J. Macaulay & L. Berkowitz (Eds.), *Altruism and helping behavior*. New York: Academic Press, 1970.

Lerner, M. J. Justice, guilt, and veridical perception. *Journal of Personality and Social Psychology*, 1971, 20, 127–135.

Lerner, M. J. Social psychology of justice and interpersonal attraction. In T. Huston (Ed.), *Perspectives on interpersonal attraction*. New York: Academic Press, 1974.

Lerner, R. M., & Frank, P. Relation of race and sex to supermarket helping behavior. *Journal of Social Psychology*, 1974, 94, 201–203.

Lerner, M. J., & Simmons, C. H. Observers' reactions to the "innocent victim." *Journal of Personality and Social Psychology*, 1966, 4, 203–210.

Lesk, S., & Zippel, B. Dependency, threat, and helping in a large city. *Journal of Social Psychology*, 1975, 95, 185–186.

Leventhal, H. Emotions: A basic problem for social psychology. In C. Nemeth (Ed.), *Social psychology*. Chicago: Rand-McNally, 1974.

Leventhal, H. Towards a theory of affect. In L. Berkowitz (Ed.), *Advances in experimental social psychology* (Vol. 13). New York: Academic Press, 1980.

Liebhart, E. H. Empathy and emergency helping: The effects of personality, self-concern, and acquaintance. *Journal of Experimental Social Psychology*, 1972, 8, 404–411.

Lincoln, H., & Levinger, G. Observer's evaluations of the victim and the attacker in an aggressive incident. *Journal of Personality and Social Psychology*, 1972, 22, 202–210.

Lindskold, S., Forte, R. A., Haake, C. S., & Schmidt, E. K. The effects of directness of face-to-face requests and sex of solicitor on street corner donations. *Journal of Social Psychology*, 1977, 101, 45–51.

Lofland, J. *Deviance and identity*. Englewood Cliffs, N. J.: Prentice-Hall, 1969.

Lykken, D. T., Tellegen, A., & Katzenmeyer, C. *Manual for the Activity Preference Questionnaire*. University of Minnesota, 1973 (mimeo).

Lynch, J. G., Jr., & Cohen, J. L. The use of subjective expected utility theory as an aid to understanding variables that influence helping behavior. *Journal of Personality and Social Psychology*, 1978, 36, 1138–1151.

Lynn, R. *Attention, arousal, and the orientation reaction*. Oxford: Pergamon Press, 1966.

Macaulay, J. R. A shill for charity. In J. Macaulay and L. Berkowitz (Eds.), *Altruism and helping behavior*. New York: Academic Press, 1970.

Macaulay, J. R. Familiarity, attraction and charity. *Journal of Social Psychology*, 1975, 95, 27–37.

MacDonald, A. P., Jr. Derogation of a victim: Justice or guilt? Unpublished manuscript, West Virginia University, 1971.

Mandler, G., Mandler, J. M., Kremen, I., & Sholiton, R. D. The response to threat: Relations among verbal and physiological indices. *Psychological Monographs*, 1961, 75 (9, Whole No. 513), 1–19.

Marshall, G. D., & Zimbardo, P. G. Affective consequences of inadequately explained physiological arousal. *Journal of Personality and Social Psychology, 1979, 37,* 970–988.

Martin, D. *Battered wives.* New York: Pocket Books, 1977.

Maslach, C. Negative emotional biasing of unexplained arousal. *Journal of Personality and Social Psychology, 1979, 37,* 953–969.

Maslow, A. H. *Motivation and personality.* New York: Harper & Row, 1970.

Mathews, K. E., & Canon, L. K. Environmental noise level as a determinant of helping behavior. *Journal of Personality and Social Psychology, 1975, 32,* 571–577.

McDougall, W. *An introduction to social psychology* (5th ed.). Boston: John W. Luce & Co., 1913. (Originally published 1908.)

McGovern, L. P. Dispositional social anxiety and helping behavior under three conditions of threat. *Journal of Personality, 1976, 44,* 84–97.

McGovern, L. P., Ditzian, J. L., & Taylor, S. P. Sex and perceptions of dependency in a helping situation. *Bulletin of the Psychonomic Society, 1975, 5,* 336–338.

McMillen, D. L. Transgression, self-image, and compliant behavior. *Journal of Personality and Social Psychology, 1971, 20,* 176–179.

McMillen, D. L., Sanders, D. Y., & Solomon, G. S. Self-esteem, attentiveness, and helping behavior. *Personality and Social Psychology Bulletin, 1977, 3,* 257–261.

McNemar, Q. *Psychological statistics* (2nd ed.). New York: John Wiley & Sons, 1955.

McPeek, R., & Cialdini, R. Social anxiety, emotion and helping. *Motivation and Emotion, 1977, 1,* 225–233.

Merrens, M. R. Nonemergency helping behavior in various sized communities. *Journal of Social Psychology, 1973, 90,* 327–328.

Michelini, R. L., Wilson, J. P., & Messé, L. A. The influence of psychological needs on helping behavior. *Journal of Psychology, 1975, 91,* 253–258.

Midlarsky, E. Helping under stress: The effects of competence, dependency, visibility, and fatalism. *Journal of Personality, 1971, 39,* 132–149.

Midlarsky, E., & Midlarsky, M. Some determinants of aiding under experimentally induced stress. *Journal of Personality, 1973, 41,* 305–327.

Midlarsky, M., & Midlarsky, E. Status inconsistency, aggressive attitude, and helping behavior. *Journal of Personality, 1976, 44,* 371–391.

Milgram, S. The experience of living in cities. *Science, 1970, 167,* 1461–1468.

Mischel, W. Toward a cognitive social learning reconceptualization of personality. *Psychology Review, 1973, 80,* 252–283.

Moore, B. S., Underwood, B., & Rosenhan, D. L. Affect and altruism. *Developmental Psychology, 1973, 8,* 99–104.

Moriarty, T. Crime, commitment, and the responsive bystander: Two field experiments. *Journal of Personality and Social Psychology, 1975, 31,* 370–376.

Mulder, M., & Stemerding, A. Threat, attraction to group, and need for strong leadership: A laboratory experiment in a natural setting. *Human Relations, 1963, 16,* 317–334.

Myrdal, G. *An American dilemma.* New York: Harper, 1944.

Neisser, U. *Cognitive psychology.* New York: Appleton-Century-Crofts, 1967.

Nemeth, C. Effects of free versus constrained behavior on attraction between people. *Journal of Personality and Social Psychology, 1970, 15* (4), 302–311.

Neumann, S. Unpublished data cited in Berkowitz, L., Social norms, feelings, and other factors affecting helping and altruism. In L. Berkowitz (Ed.), *Advances in experimental social psychology* (Vol. 6). New York: Academic Press, 1972. P. 84.

Newman, O. *Defensible space.* New York: MacMillan, 1972.

Newman, O. *Design guidelines for creating defensible space.* Washington, D. C.: National Institute of Law Enforcement and Criminal Justice, 1975.

Nisbett, R. E., & Schachter, S. Cognitive manipulation of pain. *Journal of Experimental Social Psychology*, 1966, *2*, 227–236.

Noel, R. C. Transgression-compliance: A failure to confirm. *Journal of Personality and Social Psychology*, 1973, *27*, 151–153.

Pandey, J., & Griffitt, W. Attraction and helping. *Bulletin of the Psychonomic Society*, 1974, *3*, 123–124.

Pandey, J., & Griffitt, W. Benefactor's sex and nurturance need, recipient's dependency, and the effect of number of potential helpers on helping behavior. *Journal of Personality*, 1977, *45*, 79–99.

Paulhus, D. L., Shaffer, D. R., & Downing, L. L. Effects of making blood donor motives salient upon donor retention: A field experiment. *Personality and Social Psychology Bulletin*, 1977, *3*, 99–102.

Pavlos, A. J. Effects of Machiavellianism, reward-cost outcomes, and modeling on altruistic behavior in a crisis. Paper presented at the Southern Society for Philosophy and Psychology, University of Georgia, Athens, Georgia, 1971, April.

Penner, L. A., Dertke, M. C., & Achenbach, C. J. The "flash" system: A field study of altruism. *Journal of Applied Social Psychology*, 1973, *3*, 362–370.

Penner, L. A., Summers, L. S., Brookmire, D. A., & Dertke, M. C. The lost dollar: Situational and personality determinants of a pro- and anti-social behavior. *Journal of Personality*, 1976, *44*, 274–293.

Piliavin, I. M., Hardyck, J. A., & Vadum, A. Reactions to a victim in a just or non-just world. Paper read at the Society of Experimental Social Psychology meeting, Bethesda, Md., August, 1967.

Piliavin, I. M., Hardyck, J. A., & Vadum, A. Constraining effects of personal costs on the transgressions of juveniles. *Journal of Personality and Social Psychology*, 1968, *10* (3), 227–231.

Piliavin, I. M., Piliavin, J. A., & Broll, L. The effect of similarity, severity, and costs for helping on prevention of harm to another. Unpublished study, University of Wisconsin, 1974.

Piliavin, I. M., Piliavin, J. A., & Rodin, S. Costs, diffusion, and the stigmatized victim. *Journal of Personality and Social Psychology*, 1975, *32*, 429–438.

Piliavin, I. M., Rodin, J., & Piliavin, J. Good Samaritanism: An underground phenomenon? *Journal of Personality and Social Psychology*, 1969, *13*, 289–299.

Piliavin, I. M., Vadum, A., & Hardyck, J. A. Delinquency, personal costs, and parental treatment. *Journal of Criminal Law, Criminology, and Police Science*, 1969, *60* (2), 165–172.

Piliavin, J. A., & Piliavin, I. M. The effects of blood on reactions to a victim. *Journal of Personality and Social Psychology*, 1972, *23*, 253–261.

Piliavin, J. A., & Piliavin, I. M. The Good Samaritan: Why *does* he help? Unpublished module, University of Wisconsin, 1973.

Piliavin, J. A., Piliavin, I. M., & Broll, L. Time of arrival at an emergency and likelihood of helping. *Personality and Social Psychology Bulletin*, 1976, *2*, 273–276.

Piliavin, J. A., Piliavin, I. M., & Krutsch, P. Arousal from movies and helping in emergencies. Unpublished data, University of Wisconsin, 1973.

Piliavin, J. A., Piliavin, I. M., & Trudell, B. Incidental arousal, helping, and diffusion of responsibility. Unpublished data, University of Wisconsin, 1974.

Pomazal, R. S., & Clore, G. L. Helping on the highway: The effects of dependency and sex. *Journal of Applied Social Psychology*, 1973, *3*, 160–164.

Pomazal, R. S., & Jaccard, J. J. An informational approach to altruistic behavior. *Journal of Personality and Social Psychology*, 1976, *33*, 317–327.

Primmer, C., Jaccard, J., Cohen, J. L., Wasserman, J., & Hoffing, A. The influence of the sex-appropriateness of a task on helping behavior in the laboratory and the field. Unpublished manuscript, University of Illinois, 1974.

Rabbie, J. M., & Horwitz, M. Arousal of ingroup–outgroup bias by a chance win or loss. *Journal of Personality and Social Psychology,* 1969, *13,* 269–277.

Ratcliffe, J. M. *The good Samaritan and the law.* Garden City, N. Y.: Anchor Books, 1966.

Rawlings, E. I. Witnessing harm to another: A reassessment of the role of guilt in altruistic behavior. *Journal of Personality and Social Psychology,* 1968, *10,* 377–380.

Rawlings, E. I. Reactive guilt and anticipatory guilt in altruistic behavior. In R. Macaulay & L. Berkowitz (Eds.), *Altruism and helping behavior.* New York: Academic Press, 1970, 163–177.

Raymond, B. J., & Unger, R. K. "The apparel oft proclaims the man": Cooperation with deviant and conventional youths. *Journal of Social Psychology,* 1972, *87,* 75–82.

Regan, D. T. Effects of a favor and liking on compliance. *Journal of Experimental Social Psychology,* 1971, *7,* 627–639.

Regan, D. T., Williams, M., & Sparling, S. Voluntary expiation of guilt: A field experiment. *Journal of Personality and Social Psychology,* 1972, *24,* 42–45.

Regan, J. Guilt, perceived injustice, and altruistic behavior. *Journal of Personality and Social Psychology,* 1971, *18,* 124–132.

Reykowski, J. Cognitive development and prosocial behavior. *Polish Psychological Bulletin,* 1977, *8,* 35–43.

Reykowski, J. Egocentric and prosocial orientations. Undated manuscript A, University of Warsaw.

Reykowski, J. Position of self-structure in a cognitive system and prosocial orientation. Undated manuscript B, University of Warsaw.

Rosenhan, D. L., Underwood, B., & Moore, B. Affect moderates self-gratification and altruism. *Journal of Personality and Social Psychology,* 1974, *30,* 546–552.

Ross, A. S. Effect of increased responsibility on bystander intervention: The presence of children. *Journal of Personality and Social Psychology,* 1971, *19,* 306–310.

Ross, A. S., & Braband, J. Effect of increased responsibility on bystander intervention: II. The cue value of a blind person. *Journal of Personality and Social Psychology,* 1973, *25,* 254–258.

Ross, L. The intuitive psychologist and his shortcomings: Distortions in the attribution process. In L. Berkowitz (Ed.), *Advances in experimental social psychology* (Vol. 10). New York: Academic Press, 1977.

Rothstein, H. R. Attitudes and behavior: The effects of perceived payoffs and facilitating intrapersonal conditions. Unpublished master's thesis. Hebrew University, Jerusalem, 1974.

Routtenberg, A. The two-arousal hypothesis: Reticular formation and limbic system. *Psychological Review,* 1968, *75,* 51–79.

Rushton, J. P. Urban density and altruism: Helping strangers in a Canadian city, suburb, and small town. *Psychological Reports,* 1978, *43,* 987–990.

Ryan, W. *Blaming the victim.* New York: Random House, 1971.

Sagi, A., & Hoffman, M. Empathic distress in the newborn. *Developmental Psychology,* 1976, *12,* 175–176.

Samerotte, G. C., & Harris, M. B. Some factors influencing helping: The effects of a handicap, responsibility, and requesting help. *Journal of Social Psychology,* 1976, *98,* 39–45.

Satow, K. L. Social approval and helping. *Journal of Experimental Social Psychology,* 1975, *11,* 501–509.

Schachter, S. The interaction of cognitive and physiological determinants of emotional state. In L. Berkowitz (Ed.), *Advances in experimental social psychology* (Vol. 1). New York: Academic Press, 1964.

Schachter, S. *Emotion, obesity, and crime.* New York: Academic Press, 1971.

Schachter, S., & Singer, J. E. Cognitive, social, and physiological determinants of emotional state. *Psychological Review,* 1962, *69,* 379–399.

Schaps, E. Cost, dependency, and helping. *Journal of Personality and Social Psychology,* 1972, *21,* 74–78.

Scheier, M. F., & Carver, C. S. Self-focused attention and the experience of emotion: Attention, repulsion, elation, and depression. *Journal of Personality and Social Psychology,* 1977, *35,* 625–636.

Scheier, M. F., Carver, C. S., & Gibbons, F. X. Self-directed attention, awareness of bodily states, and suggestibility. *Journal of Personality and Social Psychology,* 1979, *37,* 1576–1588.

Scheier, M. F., Fenigstein, A., & Buss, A. H. Self-awareness and physical aggression. *Journal of Experimental Social Psychology,* 1974, *10,* 264–273.

Schellenberg, J. A., & Blevins, G. A. Feeling good and helping: How quickly does the smile of Dame Fortune fade? *Psychological Reports,* 1973, *33,* 72–74.

Schneider, F. W., & Mockus, Z. Failure to find a rural–urban difference in incidence of altruistic behavior. *Psychological Reports,* 1974, *35,* 294.

Schopler, J. An investigation of sex differences on the influence of dependence. *Sociometry,* 1967, *30,* 50–63.

Schopler, J., & Bateson, N. The power of dependence. *Journal of Personality and Social Psychology,* 1965, *2,* 247–254.

Schopler, J., & Matthews, M. The influence of perceived causal locus of partner's dependence on the use of interpersonal power. *Journal of Personality and Social Psychology,* 1965, *2,* 609–612.

Schutz, A. *Reflections on the problem of relevance.* New Haven, Conn.: Yale University Press, 1970.

Schwartz, S. H. Words, deeds, and the perception of consequences and responsibility in action situations. *Journal of Personality and Social Psychology,* 1968, *10,* 243–250.

Schwartz, S. Elicitation of moral obligation and self-sacrificing behavior: An experimental study of volunteering to be a bone marrow donor. *Journal of Personality and Social Psychology,* 1970, *15,* 283–293.

Schwartz, S. H. Awareness of interpersonal consequences, responsibility, denial, and volunteering. *Journal of Personality and Social Psychology,* 1974, *30,* 57–63.

Schwartz, S. H. Normative influences on altruism. In L. Berkowitz (Ed.), *Advances in experimental social psychology* (Vol. 10). New York: Academic Press, 1977.

Schwartz, S. H., & Ben David, T. Responsibility and helping in an emergency: Effects of blame, ability, and denial of responsibility. *Sociometry,* 1976, *39,* 406–415.

Schwartz, S. H., & Clausen, G. T. Responsibility, norms, and helping in an emergency. *Journal of Personality and Social Psychology,* 1970, *16,* 299–310.

Schwartz, S. H., & Fleishman, J. Personal norms, legitimacy, and helping. *Social Psychology Quarterly,* 1978, *41,* 306–315.

Schwartz, S. H., & Gottlieb, A. Bystander reactions to a violent theft: Crime in Jerusalem. *Journal of Personality and Social Psychology,* 1976, *34,* 1188–1199.

Schwartz, S. H., & Gottlieb, A. Bystander anonymity and reactions to emergencies. *Journal of Personality and Social Psychology,* 1980, *39,* 418–430.

Seligman, M. E. D. *Helplessness: On depression, development, and death.* San Francisco, Calif.: W. H. Freeman, 1975.

Shaffer, D. R., Rogel, M., & Hendrick, C. Intervention in the library: The effect of increased responsibility on bystanders' willingness to prevent a theft. *Journal of Applied Social Psychology,* 1975, *5,* 303–319.

Sherif, M. *The psychology of social norms.* New York: Harper and Brothers, 1936.

Sherif, M., Harvey, O. J., White, B. J., Hood, W. R., & Sherif, C. W. *Intergroup conflict and cooperation: The robbers' cave experiment.* Norman, Okla.: University Book Exchange, 1961.

Sherrod, D. R., & Downs, R. Environmental determinants of altruism: The effects of stimulus overload and perceived control on helping. *Journal of Experimental Social Psychology,* 1974, *10,* 468–479.

Shotland, R. L., & Huston, T. L. Emergencies: What are they and do they influence bystanders to intervene? *Journal of Personality and Social Psychology,* 1979, *37,* 1822–1834.

Shotland, R. L., & Straw, M. K. Bystander response to an assault: When a man attacks a woman. *Journal of Personality and Social Psychology,* 1976, *34,* 990–999.

Silverman, I. Hedonistic considerations concerning altruistic behavior. Paper presented at meeting of the Southeastern Psychological Association, Hollywood, Fla., May 2–4, 1974.

Silverman, L. J., Rivera, A. N., & Tedeschi, J. T. Transgression–compliance: Guilt, negative affect, or impression management? *Journal of Social Psychology,* 1979, *108,* 57–62.

Silverman, L. W. Incidence of guilt reactions in children. *Journal of Personality and Social Psychology,* 1967, *7,* 338–340.

Simner, M. Newborn's response to the cry of another infant. *Developmental Psychology,* 1971, *5,* 136–150.

Simon, W. E. Helping behavior in the absence of visual contact as a function of sex of person asking for help and sex of person being asked for help. *Psychological Reports,* 1971, *28,* 609–610.

Simons, C. W., & Piliavin, J. A. The effect of deception on reactions to a victim. *Journal of Personality and Social Psychology,* 1972, *21,* 56–60.

Smith, R. E., Smythe, L., & Lien, D. Inhibition of helping behavior by a similar or dissimilar nonreactive fellow bystander. *Journal of Personality and Social Psychology,* 1972, *23,* 414–419.

Smith, R. E., Vanderbilt, K., & Callen, M. B. Social comparison and bystander intervention in emergencies. *Journal of Applied Social Psychology,* 1973, *3,* 186–196.

Snyder, M. L., Kleck, R. E., Strenta, R. E., & Mentzer, S. J. Avoidance of the handicapped: An attributional ambiguity analysis. *Journal of Personality and Social Psychology,* 1979, *37,* 2297–2306.

Sokolov, E. N. *Perception and the conditioned reflex.* Oxford: Pergamon Press, 1963.

Sole, K., Marton, J., & Hornstein, H. A. Opinion similarity and helping: Three field experiments investigating the bases of promotive tension. *Journal of Experimental Social Psychology,* 1975, *11,* 1–13.

Solomon, L. Z., Solomon, H., & Stone, R. Helping as a function of number of bystanders and ambiguity of emergency. *Personality and Social Psychology Bulletin,* 1978, *4,* 318–321.

Sommer, R. *Tight spaces: Hard architecture and how to humanize it.* Englewood Cliffs, N.J.: Prentice-Hall, 1974.

Spacapan, S., & Cohen, S. Density, task load and helping: Interpreting the aftereffects of stress. Paper presented at the annual meeting of the American Psychological Association, San Francisco, 1977.

Spivack, G., & Shure, N. B. *Social adjustment of young children: A cognitive approach to solving real life problems.* San Francisco: Jossey-Bass, 1974.

Staub, E. A child in distress: The effects of focusing responsibility on children on their attempts to help. *Developmental Psychology,* 1970, *2,* 152–154. (a)

Staub, E. A child in distress: The influence of age and number of witnesses on children's attempts to help. *Journal of Personality and Social Psychology,* 1970, *4,* 130–140. (b)

Staub, E. Helping a person in distress: The influence of implicit and explicit "rules" of conduct on children and adults. *Journal of Personality and Social Psychology*, 1971, *17*, 137–144.

Staub, E. Helping a distressed person: Social, personality, and stimulus determinants. In L. Berkowitz (Ed.), *Advances in experimental social psychology* (Vol. 7). New York: Academic Press, 1974.

Staub, E. *Positive social behavior and morality*. Vol. 1: *Social and personal influences*, 1978. Vol. 2: *Socialization and development*, 1979. New York: Academic Press.

Staub, E., & Baer, R. S. Stimulus characteristics of a sufferer and difficulty of escape as determinants of helping. *Journal of Personality and Social Psychology*, 1974, *30*, 279–284.

Stein, D. D., Hardyck, J. A., & Smith, M. B. Race *and* belief: An open and shut case. *Journal of Personality and Social Psychology*, 1965, *1*, 281–289.

Sterling, B. The effects of anger, ambiguity, and arousal on helping behavior (Doctoral dissertation, University of Delaware, 1977). *Dissertation Abstracts International*, 1977, *38* (4), 1962.

Stern, J. A., Winokur, J., Graham, D. T., & Graham, F. K. Alterations in physiological measures during experimentally induced attitudes. *Journal of Psychosomatic Research*, 1961, *5*, 73–82.

Stokols, D., & Schopler, J. Reactions to victims under conditions of situational detachment: The effects of responsibility, severity, and expected future interaction. *Journal of Personality and Social Psychology*, 1973, *25*, 199–209.

Stotland, E. A theory and experiments in empathy. Paper presented at the meeting of the American Psychological Association, New York, September, 1966.

Stotland, E. Exploratory investigations of empathy. In L. Berkowitz (Ed.), *Advances in experimental social psychology* (Vol. 4). New York: Academic Press, 1969, 271–314.

Stotland, E., Mathews, K. E., Sherman, S. E., Hansson, R. O., & Richardson, B. Z. *Empathy, fantasy, and helping*. Beverly Hills: Sage, 1978.

Stotland, E., Sherman, S. E., & Shaver, K. G. *Empathy and birth order: Some experimental explorations*. Lincoln: University of Nebraska Press, 1971.

Strong, P. *Biophysical measurements*. Seaverton, Oreg.: Tektronix, 1970.

Swinyard, W. R., & Ray, M. L. Effects of praise and small requests on receptivity to direct-mail appeals. *Journal of Social Psychology*, 1979, *108*, 177–184.

Takooshian, H., Haber, S., Lucido, D. J. Helping responses to a lost child in city and town. Paper presented at the meeting of the American Psychological Association, Washington, D. C., 1976.

Thalhofer, N. N. Responsibility, reparation, and self-protection as reasons for three types of helping. *Journal of Personality and Social Psychology*, 1971, *19*, 144–151.

Thayer, S. Lend me your ears: Racial and sexual factors in helping the deaf. *Journal of Personality and Social Psychology*, 1973, *28* (1), 8–11.

Thomas, W. I., & Thomas, D. S. *The child in America*. New York: Knopf, 1928.

Thompson, W. C., Cowan, C. L., & Rosenhan, D. L. Focus of attention mediates the impact of negative affect on altruism. *Journal of Personality and Social Psychology*, 1980, *38*, 291–300.

Tilker, H. A. Socially responsible behavior as a function of observer responsibility and victim feedback. *Journal of Personality and Social Psychology*, 1970, *14*, 95–100.

Tomes, H. The adaptation, acquisition, and extinction of empathically mediated emotional responses (Doctoral dissertation, Pennsylvania State University, 1963). *Dissertation Abstracts*, 1964, *24* (8), 3442–3443.

Trivers, R. L. The evolution of reciprocal altruism. *Quarterly Review of Biology*, 1971, *46*, 35–37.

Ugurel-Semin, R. Moral behavior and moral judgment of children. *Journal of Abnormal and Social Psychology*, 1952, *47*, 463–474.

Underwood, B., Berenson, J. F., Berenson, R. J., Cheng, K. K., Wilson, D., Kulik, J., Moore, B. S., & Wenzel, G. Attention, negative affect, and altruism: An ecological validation. *Personality and Social Psychology Bulletin*, 1977, *3*, 54–58.

Ungar, S. The effects of effort and stigma on helping. *Journal of Social Psychology*, 1979, *107*, 23–28.

United States Commission on Civil Rights. *Racism in America and how to combat it.* Washington, D.C.: U.S. Government Printing Office, 1970.

Veitch, R., DeWood, R., & Bosko, K. Radio news broadcasts: Their effect on interpersonal helping. *Sociometry*, 1977, *40*, 383–386.

Von Bertalanffy, L. General systems theory. *Main Currents in Modern Thought*, 1955, *71*, 75–84.

Wagner, C., & Wheeler, L. Model, need and cost effects in helping behavior. *Journal of Personality and Social Psychology*, 1969, *12*, 111–116.

Wallace, J., & Sadalla, E. Behavioral consequences of transgressions: I. The effects of social recognition. *Journal of Experimental Research in Personality*, 1966, *1*, 187–194.

Wallington, S. A. Consequences of transgression: Self-punishment and depression. *Journal of Personality and Social Psychology*, 1973, *28*, 1–7.

Walster, E., & Piliavin, J. A. Equity and the innocent bystander. *Journal of Social Issues*, 1972, *28*, 165–189.

Walster, E., Walster, G. W., & Berscheid, E. *Equity: Theory and research.* Boston: Allyn & Bacon, 1978.

Weber, M. *The methodology of the social sciences.* Glencoe, Ill.: The Free Press, 1949. (Originally published 1904).

Wegner, D. M., & Crano, W. D. Racial factors in helping behavior: An unobtrusive field experiment. *Journal of Personality and Social Psychology*, 1975, *32* (5), 901–905.

Wegner, D. M., & Schaefer, D. The concentration of responsibility: An objective self-awareness analysis of group size effects in helping situations. *Journal of Personality and Social Psychology*, 1978, *36*, 147–155.

Weiss, R. F., Boyer, J. L., Lombardo, J. P., & Stich, M. H. Altruistic drive and altruistic reinforcement. *Journal of Personality and Social Psychology*, 1973, *25*, 390–400.

Weiss, R. F., Buchanan, W., Altstatt, L., & Lombardo, J. P. Altruism is rewarding. *Science*, 1971, *171*, 1262–1263.

West, S. G., & Brown, T. J. Physical attractiveness, the severity of the emergency and helping: A field experiment and interpersonal simulation. *Journal of Experimental Social Psychology*, 1975, *11*, 531–538.

West, S. G., Whitney, G., & Schnedler, R. Helping a motorist in distress: The effects of sex, race, and neighborhood. *Journal of Personality and Social Psychology*, 1975, *31*, 691–698.

Weyant, J. M. Effects of mood states, costs, and benefits on helping. *Journal of Personality and Social Psychology*, 1978, *36*, 1169–1176.

Wilson, D. W., & Kahn, A. Rewards, costs, and sex differences in helping behavior. *Psychological Reports*, 1975, *36*, 31–34.

Wilson, E. O. *The insect societies.* Cambridge: Harvard University Press, 1971.

Wilson, E. O. *Sociobiology: The new synthesis.* Cambridge, Mass.: The Belknap Press of Harvard University Press, 1975.

Wilson, J. P. Motivation, modeling and altruism: A person × situation analysis. *Journal of Personality and Social Psychology*, 1976, *34*, 1078–1086.

Wispé, L. G., & Freshley, H. B. Race, sex and sympathetic helping behavior: The broken bag caper. *Journal of Personality and Social Psychology*, 1971, *17* (1), 59–65.

Wolfgang, M. *Patterns in criminal homicide.* Philadelphia: University of Pennsylvania Press, 1958.

Worchel, S., Andreoli, V. A., & Folger, R. Intergroup cooperation and intergroup attraction: The effect of previous interaction and outcome of combined effort. *Journal of Experimental Social Psychology*, 1977, *13*, 131–140.

Yakimovich, D., & Saltz, E. Helping behavior: The cry for help. *Psychonomic Science*, 1971, *23*, 390–400.

Zillman, D., Katcher, A. H., & Milavsky, B. Excitation transfer from physical exercise to subsequent aggressive behavior. *Journal of Experimental Social Psychology*, 1972, *8*, 247–259.

Zuckerman, M., & Reis, H. T. Comparison of three models for predicting altruistic behavior. *Journal of Personality and Social Psychology*, 1978, *36*, 498–510.

Author Index

Numbers in italics refer to the pages on which the complete references are listed.

Subject Index

289